DESIGNING YOUR BUSINESS

DESIGNING YOUR BUSINESS

Professional Practices for Interior Designers

SECOND EDITION

GORDON T. KENDALL

HEIDI PAINCHAUD

Fairchild Books
An imprint of Bloomsbury Publishing Inc

BLOOMSBURY
NEW YORK · LONDON · OXFORD · NEW DELHI · SYDNEY

Fairchild Books
An imprint of Bloomsbury Publishing Inc

1385 Broadway	50 Bedford Square
New York	London
NY 10018	WC1B 3DP
USA	UK

www.bloomsbury.com

**FAIRCHILD BOOKS, BLOOMSBURY and the Diana logo
are trademarks of Bloomsbury Publishing Plc**

This edition published 2016

First edition published 2005

© Bloomsbury Publishing Inc, 2016

All rights reserved. No part of this publication may be reproduced or transmitted in any form or by any means, electronic or mechanical, including photocopying, recording, or any information storage or retrieval system, without prior permission in writing from the publishers.

No responsibility for loss caused to any individual or organization acting on or refraining from action as a result of the material in this publication can be accepted by Bloomsbury Publishing Inc or the author.

Library of Congress Cataloging-in-Publication Data
Names: Kendall, Gordon T., author. | Painchaud, Heidi, author.
Title: Designing your business : professional practices for interior
designers / Gordon T. Kendall, Heidi Painchaud.
Description: Second edition. | New York : Fairchild Books, 2016.
Identifiers: LCCN 2015038431 | ISBN 9781501313950 (paperback)
Subjects: LCSH: Interior decoration—Practice. | Small business—Planning. |
BISAC: ARCHITECTURE / Interior Design / General. | ARCHITECTURE / Professional Practice.
Classification: LCC NK2116 .K46 2016 | DDC 747–dc23
LC record available at http://lccn.loc.gov/2015038431

| ISBN: | PB: | 978-1-5013-1395-0 |
| | ePDF: | 978-1-5013-1396-7 |

Typeset by Lachina
Printed and bound in the United States of America

CONTENTS

Extended Contents vii
Preface to the Second Edition xii
Acknowledgments xv

PART 1
YOU AND YOUR WORK 1

Chapter 1 Introduction to Professional Practices 3
Chapter 2 Becoming a Professional 25
Chapter 3 Working Ethically 41

PART 2
YOU AND YOUR BUSINESS 61

Chapter 4 Understanding Law and Your Business 63
Chapter 5 Planning Your Business Finances 89
Chapter 6 Managing Your Business 109
Chapter 7 Marketing and Promoting Your Business 127

PART 3
YOU AND YOUR CLIENTS 145

Chapter 8 Defining Your Services 147
Chapter 9 Charging Clients for Your Services 161
Chapter 10 Managing Your Client's Project 181
Chapter 11 Defining the Client Relationship 201

PART 4
YOU AND YOUR RESOURCES 217

Chapter 12 Working with Vendors 219
Chapter 13 Working with Service Providers 239

PART 5
YOU AND YOUR CAREER 253

Chapter 14 Beginning Your Work Life 255
Chapter 15 Planning Your Career 275

Glossary 291
Credits 297
Index 299

EXTENDED CONTENTS

Preface to the Second Edition xii
Acknowledgments xv

PART 1
YOU AND YOUR WORK 1

Chapter 1 Introduction to Professional Practices 3
Introduction to Interior Design Professional Practices 3
The Context for Professional Practice Skills in Interior Design 4
Characteristics of the Interior Design Profession 5
  Interior Design as a Recognized Profession 5
  Interior Design as an Entrepreneurial Profession 5
Toward a Working Definition of Interior Design Professional Practices 6
  Objectives of Other Professions 6
  Objectives Related to Work in a Service Profession 7
  Additional Distinctions to Consider 7
Developing a Formal, Skills-Based Definition for Professional Practices 7
Previewing Core Skills Defining Professional Practices 8
  Advancing the Profession and Your Career 10
Decision Making in Professional Practice 11
Consequences of Business Decision Making 12
Developing Further Your Professional Practice Skills 12
Procedures and Processes for Managing Interior Design Projects 13
  Box 1.1 Interior Design Project Scheme 14
Troubleshooting Strategies in Professional Practice 16
Applying Professional Practice Skills 19
Notes from the Field 22
Practical Activity 22
Review Questions 23

Chapter 2 Becoming a Professional 25
Introduction to Becoming a Professional 25
An Overview of Interior Design's History 26
  Interior Design's Early Origins 27
  The Impact of the Industrial Revolution on Interior Design's Development 27
  Increased Urbanization and Interest in Interior Design 28
  Expanding Roles for Women in Society 28
  Economic and Other Considerations Affecting the Rise of Interior Design 29
  The Rise of Professional Interior Design Organizations 30
  Changes in Perspectives and Names 30
  Development of Interior Design Professional Organizations 31
Interior Design Education 32
CIDA Accredited Programs 32
National Council for Interior Design Qualification and the NCIDQ Exam 33
Licensing and Registration of Interior Designers 35
Preparing Yourself for the Future 36
Preparing the Interior Design Profession for the Future 37
Notes from the Field 38
Practical Activity 39
Review Questions 39

Chapter 3 Working Ethically 41
Introduction to Working Ethically 41
Perspectives on Ethics 42
A Definition and Understanding of Ethics 43
The Business Context of Ethics 45
    Ethics, Management, and Human Resources 45
    Ethics and the Use of Company Resources 45
    Ethics and Stakeholder Confidence 46
    Managing Real and Apparent Conflicts of Interest 46
Interpretation of Codes of Ethics 48
Enforcement of Ethical Codes 49
A Place for Ethics in the Practice of Interior Design 50
Codes of Ethics and Mission Statements 51
Box 3.1 ASID Code of Ethics and Professional Conduct 52
Practical Examples of the ASID Code of Ethics 54
Notes from the Field 58
Practical Activity 59
Review Questions 59

PART 2
YOU AND YOUR BUSINESS 61

Chapter 4 Understanding Law and Your Business 63
Introduction to Law and Your Business 64
A Legal Definition of the Profession and Work of Interior Designers 64
Part One: Laws Related to the Interior Design Profession and Businesses in General 64
    Task One: Engage in the Authorized Practice of Interior Design 65
    Task Two: Participate in a Legally Recognized Business 68
    Task Three: Recognize Federal Laws Related to General Business Activities 72
Part Two: Laws Related to the Work of Interior Designers 73
Notes from the Field 73
    Task Four: Work on Behalf of Clients 74
    Task Five: Enter into Legally Enforceable Agreements with Others 76
    Task Six: Purchase Products for Resale to Clients 78
    Task Seven: Plan Accessible Spaces for Safe and Lawful Use 79
    Task Eight: Specifying Appropriate Fixtures, Furnishings, and Equipment for Use 80

What Is the Best Way to Protect Yourself as an Interior Designer? 84
    Importance of "Admissibility" of Written Records 84
    Knowing the Right Questions to Ask 85
How Can Designers Keep Up with Legal Changes? 86
Notes from the Field 86
Practical Activity 87
Review Questions 87

Chapter 5 Planning Your Business Finances 89
Introduction to Planning Your Business Finances 89
Objective #1: Financial Administration 90
Objective #2: Financial Measurement 90
Objective #3: Financial Evaluation 91
More Details about Chapter Objectives 92
    How Are Finances Administered? 92
    How Are Business Finances Measured? 93
    What Questions about Business Finance Does the Evaluation Process Answer? 94
Problem-Solving Strategies for Financial Planning 96
Sources of Funding for Your Interior Design Business 96
    Public Sources of Business Funding 98
    Private Sources of Business Funding 101
Accountants in Your Interior Design Practice 104
    The Role of Accountants 104
    Questions to Ask Accountants about an Interior Design Business 105
Notes from the Field 106
Practical Activity 106
Review Questions 107

Chapter 6 Managing Your Business 109
Introduction to Management of Interior Design Businesses 109
Management Functions 111
Personnel Management 113
The Organization Chart 114
Structure of Interior Design Businesses 114
The Task of Communicating Information and Evaluating Workers 115
Factors Influencing Management Decisions 116
Influence of Employment Laws 118

Internal Factors in Business Development 119
  Developmental Stages of a Business 119
  Services Offered by a Business 121
Management Policies and Procedures 122
Project Team Management 123
Is Management in Your Future? 123
Notes from the Field 124
Practical Activity 124
Review Questions 125

Chapter 7 Marketing and Promoting Your Business 127

Introduction to Marketing and Promoting Your Business 127
Marketing and Promotion for Interior Designers and Their Business 128
Basics of Interior Design Marketing 128
  Marketing Analysis 129
  Marketing Plans and Budgets 129
  Market Segmentation and Niche Marketing 131
Competition for Interior Design Services 133
Promotional Methods 134
  Advertising and Sales Promotion 135
  Brokerage Services 136
  Selling 137
  Publicity 139
Multichannel Marketing for Interior Designers 140
What Interior Designers Need to Know about "Tech" Marketing 141
Brand Building for Designers and Their Businesses 142
Notes from the Field 143
Practical Activity 144
Review Questions 144

PART 3
YOU AND YOUR CLIENTS 145

Chapter 8 Defining Your Services 147

Introduction to Defining Your Services 147
A Context for Scope-of-Service Analysis 148
Evaluation of Client Needs 149
Elements of the Scope-of-Services Analysis 150
The Designer's Duties 151
Procedures and Processes for Defining Your Scope of Services 152
  Evaluation of a Project and What It Will Entail 152

Type and Size of Project under Consideration 153
  Methods of Gathering and Assessing Project Information 154
Problem-Solving Strategies Related to Scope-of-Service Analysis 156
Notes from the Field 158
Practical Activity 158
Review Questions 159

Chapter 9 Charging Clients for Your Services 161

Introduction to Charging Clients for Your Services 161
A Strategy for Charging for Your Services 162
The Financial Need of Your Business 163
  How Businesses Calculate Revenue 163
  How Businesses Calculate Expenses 164
Ways to Charge for Your Services 167
Rate-Based Methods 169
  Fixed Fee 169
  Hourly Rate 170
Sale of Merchandise-Based Methods 171
  Retail Method 171
  Cost Plus Percentage Markup 172
  Discounting of Percentage Off Retail 173
  Percentage of Merchandise and Product Services 173
Combination Methods 173
  Cost Plus Percentage Markup with Fixed Fee 173
  Cost Plus Percentage Markup with Hourly Fee 173
Other Methods 174
  Square-Foot Method 174
  Value-Based Method 174
A Project's Potential for Profit 175
A Strategy for Charging and Collecting for Your Services 176
Accounts Receivable, Credit, and Interest 176
Billing and Collection Procedures 177
Hypothetical Billing Scenarios 177
Notes from the Field 178
Practical Activity 178
Review Questions 179

Chapter 10 Managing Your Client's Project 181

Introduction to Managing Interior Design Projects 182
Initial Perspectives on Interior Design Project Management 182

Professionalism and Project Management   182
Profitability and Project Management   183
Design Intent and Project Management   183

Phases of Interior Design Projects and Their Management   183

The Role of the Project Manager in Interior Design Projects   184

The Functions of Project Documents   185

Programming Phase of Interior Design Projects   186
Associated Tasks of the Programming Phase   186
Documents Related to the Programming Phase   188

The Schematic Design Phase of Interior Design Projects   190
Associated Tasks of the Schematic Design Phase   190
Documents Related to the Schematic Design Phase   190

The Design Development Phase of Interior Design Projects   191
Associated Tasks of the Design Development Phase   191
Documents Related to the Design Development Phase   191

The Contract Document Phase of Interior Design Projects   193
Associated Tasks and Documents Related to the Contract Document Phase   193

The Contract Administration Phase of Interior Design Projects   194
Associated Tasks of the Contract Administration Phase of Interior Design Projects   195

Factors to Consider When Managing Interior Design Projects   196
Residential Interior Design Concerns   197
Factors Related to Residential Interior Designers   197

Notes from the Field   198
Practical Activity   199
Review Questions   199

Chapter 11   Defining the Client Relationship   201

Introduction to the Designer-Client Relationship   201

Contracts and the Client Relationship   202
Forms of Interior Design Contracts   202

Box 11.1   Letter of Agreement for Interior Design Services   202
General Contract Requirements   203
Specific Requirements for Interior Design Contracts   204
Other Interior Design Contract Provisions   205

Contracts: Presentation and Negotiation   206
Residential Interior Design Contracts   207
Contracts and the Contract Interior Design RFP Process   207

Practical Realities of Contracts and Interior Design   210
Must There Even Be a Contract?   210
Is a "Perfect" Client Contract Possible?   210
What Tips Are There for Working with Contracts and Clients?   210
What Tips Are There for Working with Contracts and Legal Advisers?   211

Notes from the Field   212
Practical Activity   213
Review Questions   213
Box 11.2   Sample "Standard Form Agreement"   214

PART 4
YOU AND YOUR RESOURCES   217

Chapter 12   Working with Vendors   219

Introduction to Working with Vendors   219

Availability of Vendors and Project Merchandise   220

Notes from the Field   221

Vendor's Pricing and Other Policies   223
List Price and Manufacturers' Suggested Retail Price   223
Designers' Markups and Vendors' Discounts   223

General Tax Issues Related to Merchandise Sales   224

Product Delivery Issues in Interior Design   225
Forwarding, Storage, and Installation Issues   226
Terms and Conditions of Sale   226

Anticipation and Resolution of Potential Problems   226
Issues with Vendors   226

Box 12.1   Terms and Conditions of Sale Outline   227
Client Issues Related to Vendors and Merchandise   230

Perspective on the Vendor/Client/Designer Relationship   234

Notes from the Field   236
Practical Activity   236
Review Questions   237

Chapter 13 Working with Service Providers 239

Introduction to Working with Service Providers 239

Identification and Location of Service Providers 240

    General Contractors 240

    Craftspeople 240

    Independent Contractors 241

    Identification of Service Providers 241

    Evaluation of Service Providers 242

    Referrals, Recommendations, and Bids 243

Work Strategies for Service Providers: Residential Interior Design 243

Work Strategies for Service Providers: The Competitive Bidding Process 244

Troubleshooting Problems Related to Work with Service Providers 248

Notes from the Field 251

Practical Activity 251

Review Questions 252

PART 5
YOU AND YOUR CAREER 253

Chapter 14 Beginning Your Work Life 255

Introduction to Beginning Your Work Life 255

The Résumé and Cover Letter 256

    Developing Your Résumé's Content 256

    Selecting a Format for Your Résumé 259

    Completing a Cover Letter 259

Box 14.1 Cover Letter Worksheet 260

    Getting Your Résumé—and You—Known 261

Your Portfolio 262

Internship Participation 263

    Reasons to Participate in Internships 263

    Reasons Organizations Sponsor Internships 264

    Student Considerations about Internships 265

    Internship Documentation and Activities 265

Preparation for an Employment Interview 266

    What to Expect during an Interview 266

Box 14.2 Internship Timesheet 267

    Interview Formats 268

    Questions an Employer May Ask You 269

    Questions to Ask an Employer 270

    Key Interview Issues 271

Notes from the Field 272

Practical Activity 273

Review Questions 273

Chapter 15 Planning Your Career 275

Introduction to Planning Your Career 275

Career Evaluation: Identifying Your Interests and Focusing on Your First Career Choices 276

Interior Design Career Options 277

    Residential Interior Design 278

    Commercial or Contract Interior Design 279

    Retail and Wholesale Interior Design Professionals 281

    Retail Sales Associates 281

    Vendor and Showroom Representatives 282

    Academic Institutions 283

    Other Interior Design-Related Careers to Consider 284

The Merits and Challenges of Different Work Situations 284

Box 15.1 Careers List 285

Emerging Issues and Areas of Practice 286

The Glocal Phenomenon 287

Notes from the Field 288

Practical Activity 288

Review Questions 289

Glossary 291

Credits 297

Index 299

PREFACE TO THE SECOND EDITION

A decade ago, the first edition of *Designing Your Business* appeared. Many embraced its accessible approach to the complex, multidimensional topic of professional practices for interior designers. Based on those responses, it is with pleasure we bring you the second edition. "We" because the most remarkable change in this edition are the contributions of co-author Heidi Painchaud, co-founder and principal, IN Studio, Toronto, Ontario, Canada.

The first edition called out for a strong visual presence, an approach that melded its traditional textbook format with an interior designer's image portfolio. Thanks to Heidi's untiring efforts, this second edition is packed with effective, inspirational visuals. These certainly enhance and reinforce text topics while adding to the readers' own visual knowledge. Ultimately, they impart authority to the study of professional practices. Professional practice skills *were* part of the process required to bring about the environments represented. Skills you can learn, beginning with this text!

Heidi has held numerous creative and management roles in interior design. Throughout the text, you will find her Mentor Memos and Notes from the Field. The experiences and insights contained in both mirror her accomplishments and apprise you of typical situations you can expect to encounter in your own work. Importantly, these excerpts can serve as a beginning point for addressing similar issues should they arise in your own interior design practice.

The numerous subjects encompassed in the study of professional practices make for numerous pages of explanations with examples. To assist you as you make your way through these topics, this new edition has been edited substantially. Greater clarity and readability have been achieved. In some instances, entire chapters were rewritten or reorganized, whereas only sentences and paragraphs were modified in others. Overall, text materials are less cumbersome for you to access, recall, and, ultimately, use.

As with the original, this text is organized in five parts, each intended to provide information that will help you make sound decisions about working with clients and others as well as about the operation of interior design businesses.

TEXT ORGANIZATION

Welcome to the world of professional practices! Concepts making up this broadly encompassing discipline include those related to interior design industry accreditation, ethics, business principles, law, marketing, and career development among others, as you will discover here:

Part 1: You and Your Work The text opens with a full-scale introduction to professional practices and explores several professional practices concepts. It then discusses the development of interior design as a profession and explores the importance of ethical practices in interior design.

Part 2: You and Your Business It has been said a career in interior design is a career in business. This part takes that observation to heart and considers the four basic business components—law, finance, management, marketing—required to operate or to participate in an interior design business.

Part 3: You and Your Clients Meaningful, responsive interior design work depends on designers' abilities to develop and maintain strong client relationships. This part explores how you might handle this responsibility when it comes to defining and charging for your professional services and managing clients' projects.

Part 4: You and Your Resources Interior designers rely on a host of other professionals, trade sources, and service providers among them to realize their designs. This part of the text explores how to access such suppliers of merchandise and services and develop strong working relationships with them.

Part 5: You and Your Career Careers are, truly, works in progress. From building your first résumé to interviewing for a job, plus planning for long-term practice, this part begins your fact-finding process to acquire and build skills necessary to develop Project You.

TEXT AND CHAPTER FEATURES

This text of *Designing Your Business: Professional Practices for Interior Designers* is much more reader-friendly than its predecessor. Reference and glossary elements have been moved to the back of the text to aid your easier understanding of each chapter's concepts and terms. With fewer interruptions, you should be better able to enjoy their following features:

Mentor Memos These features begin each chapter and occur regularly throughout the text. Hear the voice of an accomplished interior design professional comment on the topics discussed, their importance, how they apply in actual practice, and provide perspectives about how to interpret their meanings and applications.

Learning Objectives After reading each chapter, you should be able to accomplish the list of goals set out at its outset to help you get the most from the text's materials and discussions.

Chapter Introductory Paragraph Focus is important as you begin any new undertaking, including new studies. Each chapter, therefore, begins with a paragraph directing your attention to topics that will follow. Of note as well are **highlighted words** found in all chapters. These are key terms related to chapter topics.

Notes from the Field How might chapter concepts arise in the usual course of interior designers' work? Hear from designers, experienced in both design and management, as they share their sometimes hard-won knowledge of how they learned to incorporate chapter subjects into meaningful business practices.

Practical Activities This section proposes a short project, based on issues identified in the preceding Notes from the Field section or otherwise related to chapter content. To get you and others thinking and talking about real-world applications of professional practice skills, these activities are intended to generate class discussion while you are studying the chapter.

Chapter Review Questions How best to know you have grasped chapter subjects than with a series of review questions? Based on the learning objectives, these queries are included at the end of each chapter to ensure you have identified and understood what the text chapters are all about.

Whether your goal is to have your own studio or to combine design work with management at a large firm, lead a team of others, educate future designers, or perhaps segue way your career into product development, you will daily call upon topics this text addresses.

As you develop and grow in your career, remember many clients will expect of you, in the words of American designer Billy Baldwin (1903–1984), "the same kind of different." That is, that you are always the "same" competent business professional no matter the situation, but also that you have your own, "different" creative point of view. This text is intended to help you develop into such a multifaceted interior design professional.

ACKNOWLEDGMENTS

Writing has been likened to a journey, one where its destination is not clear at the outset. That description would certainly apply to my experience with *Designing Your Business: Professional Practices for Interior Designers*. Along the path this project has taken, I have had the great fortune to meet and work with incredible, accomplished interior design and publishing professionals. Each, in their way, has shared his or her experiences and expertise to shape the current edition. As a result, I have developed as a writer in ways I could not have imagined when I first signed on to the original project in 2002.

Heidi Painchaud joined this journey as co-author in 2014 and took this project in an exciting new direction. The profession of interior design is visual in aspect, thoroughly process-oriented in practice, and business driven in reality. Heidi's development of this edition's art program and real-life contributions brought those elements and many more to life in this text. I deeply appreciate her willingness to reinvigorate the original text concept and make this current edition even more reflective of the dynamic nature of the profession. As well, appreciation and thanks are due her clients for their gracious permission to reproduce many of the images contained in this edition. Quite simply, this edition would not exist without Heidi's involvement.

The editors at Fairchild Books, now Bloomsbury, have long championed *Designing Your Business*, and it has been a pleasure to work with them for over a decade. I appreciate the time Priscilla McGeehon, Publisher, Joe Miranda, Development Manager (and part of the first edition team), and Edie Weinberg, Art Development Editor, took early on to focus this edition and shape its contents with Heidi and me. It was also a pleasure to work again with Noah Schwartzberg, Acquisitions Editor, as he guided this project from draft manuscript to completed text.

My friends in Austin and Dallas, Texas, as well as in New York and New Jersey, remained ever curious about the project, and I thank them for their interest and encouragement. Of course, my husband Michael Regier was right alongside them with much appreciated assistance. My mother-in-law, Virginia Regier, an award-winning journalist and former newspaper editor, regrettably, no longer shares this journey with me. However, she, and her unwavering support for this project and belief in me, will not be forgotten.

The following interior design educators, selected by the publisher, provided valuable feedback in their reviews of the text: Amy Crumpton, Mississippi State University; Bhakti Sharma, Buffalo State University; Stacy Sawyer, Endicott College; and Stephen Anderson, Portsmouth University, UK.

To the instructors and students using this book, I would like to acknowledge the importance your contributions in the form of thoughtful comments and suggestions can make to future editions. This input will allow *Designing Your Business* to progress on its journey and remain a relevant, useful information source.

Gordon Kendall

What a journey. As a practicing interior designer, putting pen to paper in collaboration with Gordon Kendall on this book has been both fulfilling and rewarding. I thank you Gordon for your guidance and for extending me the opportunity to be a part of this exciting endeavor. For my partner in both life and design, Guy Painchaud, I am grateful for your patience and wisdom during this epic and wonderful process. And, for my beautiful daughter Roene, your words of encouragement and laughter fueled my day, and every effort of this book.

A sincere thank you to the countless clients that generously provided use of their projects' images. We are so grateful for your contribution. And lastly, to my fearless Partners at IN Studio, your tireless assistance and knowledge were simply outstanding every step of the way. I am proud and honored to work with you every day. Thank you for being the outstanding team that you are. I have grown and learned as much as I have shared, thank you to those who choose to go on the journey of becoming a great interior designer.

Heidi Painchaud

YOU AND YOUR WORK PART 1

"You have to start somewhere!" Undoubtedly you have heard that before when you started something new. Your course in professional and business practices is new and probably quite different from other interior design subjects you may have studied. What then, might be a logical way to start this unfamiliar, new topic? This part begins your study by exploring the "basics" of practicing interior design, general fields of specialization, and ethical considerations.

Chapter 1. Introduction to Professional Practices: Provides a sense of context and purpose for your work in overview fashion.

Chapter 2. Becoming a Professional: Addresses what it means to be a professional and areas of interior design that appear poised now to offer future opportunities to practitioners.

Chapter 3. Working Ethically: Seeks to reach a practical understanding of the meaning, application, interpretation, and enforcement of professional standards of ethics in the practice of interior design.

CHAPTER 1
INTRODUCTION TO PROFESSIONAL PRACTICES

MENTOR MEMO
Soon you will know, that you don't know . . . what you don't know.

After reading this chapter, you will be able to

- Identify various disciplines from which interior designer professional practices derive;
- Define the term professional practices as it applies to interior design;
- Articulate reasons study of professional practices is important for interior designers;
- Distinguish characteristics of professionals and entrepreneurs, and note how they may be alike;
- Describe components of a SWOT analysis, even explain circumstances when designers might use them;
- Explain the process used by interior designers to organize and manage projects;
- Name ways by which professional practice decisions may be monitored and controlled;
- Explain how you may further develop and enhance professional practice skills.

INTRODUCTION TO INTERIOR DESIGN PROFESSIONAL PRACTICES

What does the day-to-day practice of interior design involve? How will clients and trade professionals describe their experiences working with you? Can you explain the work you do and the value you add to those who may have only an idealized, "as seen on TV" impression of designers and their work? The answer to these and many other

---

Interior designers impact users' interactions with physical spaces they conceive and realize.

questions will reflect how well you understand and apply the concepts introduced here and expanded on throughout this text. In this chapter, you will gain a first impression of what comprises the organizational and business concepts—the professional practices, that is—of interior designers.

With so many subjects to cover, you may wonder where this discovery process will begin. To provide that context, this chapter identifies several objectives for you to consider. These include classifying the professional practice of interior design within the business world; identifying disciplines from which components of interior design professional practices derive; describing processes interior designers may implement to make informed professional decisions; and, lastly, introducing systematic procedures by which interior design projects are planned and managed.

THE CONTEXT FOR PROFESSIONAL PRACTICE SKILLS IN INTERIOR DESIGN

Interior designers now play a critical role in advising clients about much more than surface decoration details. Designers work to realize both residential and commercial projects in physical environments made increasingly more complicated by technology, regulation, and a growing awareness of the value design can add to physical spaces. To continue, designers need to know about those complex constraints and how to work best within their parameters to complete a client's projects. Furthermore, designers must be willing and able to continue learning long after their formal education is completed. Particularly, designers need to be aware of how best to work with sophisticated clients and a wide variety of equally sophisticated consultants and trade resources. To do so, designers must have enough knowledge to establish credibility and engender trust in their business dealings.

Also, think practically about the uniquely interpersonal, one-on-one nature of interior design work. Throughout your study of interior design, you have come to realize how much sensitive information you must learn about your clients to mesh their functional goals for the project with your proposed design concept. In addition to knowing how to handle sensitive and personal information, shouldn't you also have sufficient business knowledge to be entrusted with the large sums of money typically required to complete interior design projects? Your study of professional practices aims to make tasks such as these manageable as you carry out your work.

You probably realize by now you cannot function as an interior designer without assistance. After all, you are not an architect, carpenter, painter, general contractor, or any of a host of others on whom you will come to rely in your practice. You are, however, the link, sometimes the only link, between these professionals and your clients. As the interior designer "of record" on a project, you have prescribed responsibilities to clients and to various others to make working relationships as efficient, as beneficial, and as ethically imbued as possible. You might also note that other programs of professional study, such as those for architects, attorneys, accountants, and physicians, also include required courses of a similar nature. It seems logical for interior design professionals to be offered such a course as well.

Another reason to devote special consideration to this topic is professional practices-based questions are included on exams used by a growing number of accrediting agencies to license interior design professionals within their jurisdictions. This text is not intended as a study guide for such exams, but it does serve as an introduction to the material included on those exams. Perhaps, however, the most obvious reason for studying professional practices is the pride in accomplishment for a job well done and the satisfaction of having clients describe you and your work as "professional."

CHARACTERISTICS OF THE INTERIOR DESIGN PROFESSION

How would you classify the practice of interior design in relation to other occupations? Which trends in the business community would be particularly applicable to interior designers?

Interior Design as a Recognized Profession

Sociologists, who study interactions among groups of people, have noted a marked increase since World War II in the numbers of occupations now considered professions, or work requiring specialized education, experience, usually with some form of authoritative credentialing and oversight. This trend has affected the practice of interior design. Previous generations of consumers largely considered the occupation to fall in the domain of decorators, or populated by "imaginative, magnetic amateurs high on the social scale."

Contrast that view with the rigorous education now required to obtain credentials as an interior designer. This extensive, specialized education together with the sophisticated management skills required, among other characteristics, indicate interior design is, indeed, a profession. The current definition of interior design, as promulgated by the National Council for Interior Design Qualifications (NCIDQ) underscores this:

> Interior design is a multifaceted profession in which creative and technical solutions are applied with a structure to achieve a built interior environment. These solutions are functional, enhance the quality of life and culture of the occupants and are aesthetically attractive. Designs are created in response to and coordinated with the building shell and acknowledge the physical location and social context of the project. Designs must adhere to code and regulatory requirements and encourage the principles of environmental sustainability. The interior design process follows a systematic and coordinated methodology, including research, analysis and integration of knowledge into the creative process, whereby the needs and resources of the client are satisfied to produce an interior space that fulfills the project goals. (NCIDQ, 2012)

Previously some argued the trend toward professional status for interior designers was not yet complete, noting that "to date, interior design has not been adequately acknowledged as a profession that requires a distinct set of core competencies that extend well beyond simple decoration; nor has the broad social and economic impact of the profession been recognized." However, as the recent NCIDQ definition of interior design indicates, such concerns are ever more being addressed by the profession.

Interior Design as an Entrepreneurial Profession

In addition to their acknowledgment as professionals, many interior designers may also be considered entrepreneurs, who are distinguished by a willingness to take business-related risks, such as assuming responsibility for business ownership and pursuing new opportunities. Entrepreneurship is a hallmark of most practicing interior designers whether they work for themselves or are formally employed by others. A solo designer operating a home-based studio is a good example of a designer pursuing an entrepreneurial venture. So, too, would be an interior designer who is a shareholder (partial owner) in a large architecture/interior design firm. Both practitioners, to varying degrees, have assumed business ownership risks, and both rely on obtaining new clients or capitalizing on new opportunities to earn their income and advance their professional interests.

Although employees generally do not, by definition, assume risks of business operations, choosing to work instead in a salary-based position under the direction and supervision of others, there is a trend toward entrepreneurial thinking among them. These employees identify and, with their employer's consent, individually pursue new opportunities on behalf of their companies. In this way, even an interior designer employed by someone else has become a new breed of business entrepreneur.

TOWARD A WORKING DEFINITION OF INTERIOR DESIGN PROFESSIONAL PRACTICES

With this understanding of the environment in which interior design functions, is it possible to arrive at a working definition of the all-encompassing term professional practices that you may conveniently use in your study? In this text, professional practice skills include an understanding of the subjects and processes necessary for the competent and profitable completion of services rendered by an interior designer to a client.

You must have a sound, basic knowledge of certain subjects to begin your work. For interior design students, these subjects include aspects of business such as accounting, commercial law, finance, and marketing; each is a separate discipline with its own core of concepts and terminology necessary for the successful conduct of any business. Your knowledge of these fields will grow as you proceed in your work. Right now, however, as daunting as the prospect of learning "all that stuff" may seem, there are ways—interesting ways—to introduce you to the application of these subjects in your work. The components of the working definition include the objectives of other professions with which interior designers will work, the aspects of working in a service profession, and others.

Objectives of Other Professions

This book is organized so that the objectives an accountant, lawyer, marketer, salesperson, or other professional might seek on behalf of an interior designer are listed first. The application of these aspects of business to interior designers and their practice follows. For example, many interior designers sell products to clients in the course of their business. Objectives related to that sales activity include evaluating records of the purchase and sale of those items (accounting); drafting effective agreements for the sale of goods (law); and assessing client satisfaction with the goods (marketing). This approach enables you to appreciate the relevance of business topics because they are directly applied to the very tasks you will undertake as an interior designer. Interior designers can and should also develop processes that enable them to operate efficiently; this means maintaining accurate financial records and drafting useful, up-to-date written business forms. Knowing how to apply these business-related skills in your work and how to implement related processes are two important components of the definition of professional practices for interior designers.

All businesses, including interior design firms, must be organized and run with the objective of earning more in revenue than is needed for the operation of the business. As a result, you must complete every project you undertake profitably. It is only partially true that "it takes money to make money." It is more accurate to say that it takes a professional's knowledge to know when agreeing to a project will cost the designer more in time and resources than the client could ever be expected to pay. Gauging accurately the potential for profit (or financial headache) is part of the ability to thoroughly assess the requirements that will be placed on you, the designer, to complete a project.

Objectives Related to Work in a Service Profession

Interior design is a service profession. Unlike the making and selling of tangible products, or goods, you will become a professional whose stock in trade is the specialized knowledge and expertise you bring to design projects. Accordingly, engaging in professional services practices means understanding the unique challenges involved when working with clients who may have different ideas about what knowledge and expertise they want to buy. For this reason, one of the most important professional practices designers can develop is the ability to define the scope of services they will perform for any client on any particular project. Defining a set of services offered in this way and making the client aware of what those services will be are central to the work of an interior designer and to a definition of the designer's professional practices.

Additional Distinctions to Consider

The study of professional practices does not address or evaluate the creative and technical aspects of an interior designer's work. Instead, this discussion of professional practices considers the idea of competent completion as accomplishing design tasks in a rational, accurate, profitable, and ethical manner. For example, a completed project may be entirely acceptable to a client but will need to be modified or even entirely redone because the designer submitted faulty specifications that did not comply with applicable building codes. Other examples of questionable practices occur when a designer fails to adhere to budget guidelines or orders products without client consent. Understanding the interplay of the variety of rules, laws, and expectations that apply to each project is an important measure of a designer's professional competency.

DEVELOPING A FORMAL, SKILLS-BASED DEFINITION FOR PROFESSIONAL PRACTICES

Putting all these pieces together, this text has identified the following as skills necessary to enhance a designer's professional practice abilities and, as such, has established a formal definition of the subject:

1. Understanding the context for interior design within the business community
2. Understanding ways in which businesses, including those focused on interior design, are organized and why
3. Knowing the ethical obligations and implications of interior design work
4. Having a working knowledge of basic business law and its application to interior design

5. Knowing the basics of business finance and how it applies to the practice of interior design
6. Understanding basic principles of management and how they relate to interior design businesses
7. Realizing the importance of marketing and promotion activities for interior designers
8. Providing quality professional services to your clients by first defining your services
9. Knowing how to use a description of your services to determine an effective way to charge clients for the work you do
10. Implementing effective project management techniques and processes
11. Using contracts incorporating elements that define your relationship with the client
12. Working with vendors
13. Working with contractors and other service providers
14. Becoming and maintaining your status as an interior design professional
15. Planning a meaningful and rewarding career

PREVIEWING CORE SKILLS DEFINING PROFESSIONAL PRACTICES

Many people differentiate businesses only by the products or services they offer. In fact, the ways in which commercial ventures are formed vary greatly according to the financial and other objectives their founders wish to achieve. Besides making money, what other business objectives might businesspeople, interior designers included, formulate? To get yourself thinking about these objectives, consider that you and a friend wish to open an interior design practice together. In what ways might you organize that business to establish a clear understanding between you and your friend about how the business is to be run and what responsibilities each of you has?

The various methods of business formation are described in laws that address these concerns of ownership and responsibility not only between operators of a venture but also between them and outsiders, such as creditors, those to whom the business owes money. Considerations about which business formation to utilize are, or should be, the first commercially oriented decisions made regarding any new business; they comprise a professional practice skill set required of interior designers.

Ethics, especially in the highly competitive world of business, are both elusive to define and, if in recent reports the media are to be believed, equally elusive to apply. No text or course can teach anyone to be ethical. Ethics must personally be understood as a necessary component of one's working life and practiced accordingly. What can be explored are the ways in which ethical challenges appear in the practice of interior design and how practitioners may recognize and resolve them. The study of ethics, no matter how brief, and suggestions for resolving ethical concerns highlight an important fact: failure to work within ethical bounds may result in serious consequences, even preventing a designer from working as an accredited professional.

Your professional practices course may offer you your only exposure to general business topics during your study of interior design. An entrepreneurial interior designer wishing to become involved in business ownership will first be called upon to comply with laws regarding the ways in which businesses are organized. In fact, laws and the legal system control virtually every aspect of modern business, and some knowledge of their application is a practical requirement. Savvy businesspeople, however, do not need to know as many details of business law as an attorney. They do need to know enough to operate their business within the requirements of the law, and, equally important, they need to learn to recognize legal problems to prevent their occurrence. Interior designers routinely enter into agreements, purchase and resell products, and work as their clients' agent as they execute projects. Awareness of general business law principles is therefore a professional practice skill required of interior designers. A competent businessperson needs to also know the limits of his or her knowledge of business law and recognize when to seek the advice of a professional.

The study of finance may seem daunting or uninteresting to innovative young design professionals who intend to make their mark creatively. Nevertheless, most viable businesses rely on gathering correct financial information and interpreting it to make decisions. Not all financial information is used for the same purposes, however; some of it is gathered and interpreted with the aim of disclosure to others outside the business. For example, financial accounting practices include interpreting the monetary activities of a business for the purpose of tax reporting. Other information is gathered and used to make decisions about the way in which the business is operated. Managerial accounting interprets financial data primarily for the internal use of the company to make decisions about such issues as how best to attain profitability. Pricing goods and services offered to consumers are examples of managerial accounting concerns. These financial professional-practice skills are necessary for interior designers who want to be both creative and profitable.

Management skills are important if you work in a design firm and, especially, if you own a firm. General management skills are certainly important professional practice skills, but in the practice of interior design employment policies should be considered less in terms of large-scale corporate, standardized applications and more as an integral part of the creative vision for the design firm. Developing and implementing management policies in this context may help to ensure a shared vision of the business among employees and management.

Marketing and related forms of promotional activities, such as personal selling, are necessary professional practice skills. After all, how will potential clients even know of your existence without some planned effort on your part to make them aware of you and the services you offer? Unique to the marketing function is the close relationship marketing can have with the creative vision of the designer or the design firm: Through marketing you may define a unique business niche distinguishing you and your work from other designers. When you use marketing techniques to create such an identity, it can cost you both time and money. Marketing requires the careful allocation of these resources so that other business goals are not jeopardized.

The 1998 "Analysis of the Interior Design Profession" concluded, among other things that "the skills that competent interior designers demonstrate include the ability to . . . manage contracts, money, data, people, and projects." Central to the management of "people and projects," which encompasses the majority of an interior designer's professional practice skills, is the scope-of-services analysis that an interior designer must perform before taking on any project. Quite simply, before a project is started, it must be detailed in writing. Thoroughly describing the many tasks required for project completion is one facet of this professional practice skill; another facet is describing these steps to clients who are unfamiliar with interior design processes and terminology.

Determining what to charge your clients for the work you perform is linked to that definition of services. The profitability or insolvency of a designer or design venture results from how well informed that decision is. In this respect, understanding when and how various methods of charging clients are applicable is a critical professional practices skill. Both defining the scope of services you will perform for a client and detailing the method, or methods, by which you will be monetarily compensated for carrying out those services involves the understanding and careful use of written agreements. Many of these agreements exist in the form of prepared, fill-in-the-blank documents. Using these forms correctly is one of the processes inherent in professional practices.

As a professional interior designer, you will wear many hats and serve clients in many different capacities, not the least of which will be your function as an agent. Understanding how this agency relationship affects the handling of your client's money and project are related professional practice skills. The buying and selling of goods is a business function designers undertake as a routine part of their work. Understanding the set of laws related to agreements involving the sale of goods is a professional practice skill; its mastery will help to ensure that products destined for use in a project arrive as specified and in a timely manner. Again, laws and rules related to buying and selling goods require not only a thorough understanding of how they relate to your business but also an ability to explain to clients and relevant trade sources how they apply and affect the delivery of goods.

Advancing the Profession and Your Career

You are in the process of becoming a professional, a member of an occupational group with a long, colorful history and expansive possibilities for future growth. Understanding that history as well as reasons for advancing the professional status of designers and

SWOT analysis is one way interior designers make decisions related to their businesses.

the practice of interior design is an important professional practice skill. Perhaps the strongest way to grow the professional status of interior designers is through advocacy or advancing their interests through political processes. Knowledge of the story of interior design and an awareness of the industry's agendas are different than business skills, but they are equally important.

Finally, professional practices skills are also personal in nature. You have already expended considerable effort, time, and resources in the pursuit of your design education. Does it surprise you to know that you may have to devote large amounts of time to keeping abreast of relevant changes in the profession and future career opportunities for yourself? Learning does not stop after leaving school. Career development is therefore a personal professional practice skill, which is necessary to develop plans for a successful, fulfilling future. As you can see, the professional and entrepreneurial nature of interior design work requires a great many business and personal career development skills. How might you learn to make effective decisions about professional practice matters using the information you know and will come to learn?

DECISION MAKING IN PROFESSIONAL PRACTICE

At the very heart of learning about professional practices is learning how to make decisions. Suppose, for example, an interior designer with a thriving practice wishes to develop and market new products. That is, to be sure, a professional practice decision of great consequence. How might the designer determine whether to pursue such interests? This chapter has identified specific areas of knowledge that play a part in professional decision making, but more than knowledge of these topics alone is necessary to make informed professional decisions.

One method of business decision making used to assess a problem or issue is known as a **SWOT analysis**. SWOT is an acronym that stands for strengths, weaknesses, opportunities, and threats. Businesspeople first determine the objective or outcome to be accomplished and then employ the SWOT evaluative approach to reach a conclusion. For example, the designer might state as a business objective the development, manufacture, and introduction into the market by a certain date of a new line of furniture bearing his or her name. A SWOT analysis might first reveal issues internal to the designer's business in the form of the firm's strengths as they relate to the objective. For example, the designer might note as strengths the facts that he or she enjoys tremendous name recognition in the community and has previously won awards for product design. However, related weaknesses might also be discovered, such as the fact that the designer is less well-known outside of the community as well as the great expenses associated with developing new products. By applying the SWOT analysis, the designer might ascertain an opportunity and thus a demand for the proposed new products since they would be unlike others currently available. Yet, they face a clear threat since they might easily be cheaply copied once introduced.

This brief summary shows how a SWOT analysis is applied. Most businesspeople are familiar with it and employ it in some form when making their decisions. It remains, however, the businessperson's task to accurately assess the actual situation surrounding the proposed business objective, and he or she must rely on a realistic and honest determination as to whether the facts really do support a desired outcome or are merely hopeful justifications for action. More thorough methods of business analyses are introduced and explored in later chapters. The Strategic Planning Project at the end of each chapter, for example, asks you to perform a personal SWOT analysis as you brainstorm about your ideal interior design venture.

CONSEQUENCES OF BUSINESS DECISION MAKING

You now have some sense of the scope of information that influences professional practice decisions. Ask yourself next about those decisions. As you know, consequences result from any decision. The business and professional decisions an interior designer makes are no exception. The consequences of some erroneous decisions may result in merely minor inconveniences, whereas other errors may result in substantial financial loss or even physical injury. The entrepreneurial designer wishing to develop new products could just as easily enjoy very beneficial results from a decision or he or she may not be so fortunate. The next stage in considering the role of professional practice-based decisions in a designer's working life is to understand how and by whom those practices are controlled and what consequences they may impose.

Perhaps the most obvious controls placed on decisions are those imposed by laws. Civil and criminal laws provide what are referred to as *remedies* to either aggrieved private individuals, by way of civil law, or to governmental units seeking enforcement of criminal statutes. These remedies are one way in which professional practices are enforced and, in general, are usually available to those who seek accountability for an interior designer's actions.

Voluntary associations also play an active role in the enforcement of professional practices of interior designers. Organizations such as the **American Society of Interior Designers (ASID)** and many others promulgate rules relating to professional practices and ethics. These professional organizations are a potent source of supervision and enforcement of professional practices among their members, since they make available grievance or complaint procedures to those who feel that a designer's actions were in some way harmful to them. These groups also provide for reprimands and membership revocations as ways of enforcing professional practices.

DEVELOPING FURTHER YOUR PROFESSIONAL PRACTICE SKILLS

Innovation, new ideas and concepts, and new things are probably some characteristics of the practice of interior design that attracted you to the profession in the first place. Although you may not eagerly await or seek out new business publications with the same gusto as a new furniture catalog, there is also much innovation and excitement in the practices side of the profession. New business technologies help to ensure that clients are correctly charged and billed, and new laws are passed that directly affect how designers will interact with clients and the built environment. Examples of new developments in professional practices occur daily and are almost endless. You must keep abreast of these new ideas, but, more importantly, you must also be willing to adopt them in your work. *Hidebound* should apply only to the furniture you specify, not to you!

How might you respond to these new ideas? First, you should simply accept change as a fact of business life. Although that may seem obvious, think how easy it is to fall into a routine. Although it may feel comfortable and familiar, it may also make you appear *dated*, or out of touch, in the estimation of potential clients. Keeping up with changes in your industry and picking up professional practice tips from other designers through formal continuing education seminars and meetings is one way of staying up to date; it is required of designers with licenses and professional group affiliations. Informal networking can also help. Reading business publications on a frequent basis is another way to keep up with issues related to professional practices, as is asking advice of professionals such as attorneys and accountants. Listening to your clients and understanding how best your business and professional practices can meet their needs is another way to be responsive to the need for change. Currently, a number of books address the need to keep abreast of change and accept its challenges. As one of these authors has expressed, "If you do not change, you become extinct."

PROCEDURES AND PROCESSES FOR MANAGING INTERIOR DESIGN PROJECTS

"The interior design process follows a systematic and coordinated methodology" (definition of interior design, NCIDQ). Interior design does not just happen. It comes about through planning and organization, skills you will begin to acquire in this chapter. Have you thought about how your projects will proceed from conversations with clients to actual completion? Although you are creative and likely have a thorough knowledge of decorative styles and products, as well as building codes and standards, do you also know what formal steps designers take to turn such knowledge into completed, usable installations? Because project management tasks will encompass a large part of your work, this chapter's final objective is to introduce the commonly accepted sequence in which interior design work is carried out. This method is inherent in the definition of interior design provided by the NCIDQ and cited here for your reference. Furthermore, its terminology is used in discussions throughout this book. Project management issues are fundamental to many of the problems you will address in your studies of professional practices and as a working interior designer.

This "systematic and coordinated methodology" is detailed and lengthy since it comprises many separate sets of interrelated procedures. The focus of this chapter's discussion, however, is to acquaint you with the terminology and sequence of constituent phases in the project management process and to provide a basic description for each phase. In fact, the names of phases in the process become so familiar among professionals that they sometimes employ only phase names as a shortcut to denote the kinds of tasks on which they are working. Interior design clients, however, may not be as familiar with either the process or its related terminology. Finally, this section focuses on the beginning stage in a designer's association with a prospective client. A stage so early, in fact, that a formal project may not really be said to have begun. What should occur as both designer and prospective client come to know one another and discuss what lies ahead? Understanding the role of this phase and its application in the simulation will enable you, as a young interior designer, to form a useful strategy for handling project details from the outset.

> **BOX 1.1**
>
> ## INTERIOR DESIGN PROJECT SCHEME
>
> **Programming Phase**
> Associated Tasks
> - Consult/review initial project requirements
> - Document project requirements
> - Prepare project budget/schedule
> - Determine physical/budgetary feasibility
> - Provide written program of requirements
>
> **Schematic Design Phase**
> Associated Tasks
> - Prepare preliminary functional diagrams
> - Review alternative approaches to project
> - Prepare space allocations/utilizations
> - Prepare design concept studies
> - Submit preliminary cost estimates
>
> **Design Development Phase**
> Associated Tasks
> - Prepare documents to fix/describe final project
> - Complete documents with final appearance/function
> - Recommend colors/materials/finishes as necessary
> - Prepare presentation boards, related materials
> - Advise on cost-of-work adjustments
>
> **Contract Documents Phase**
> Associated Tasks
> - Prepare final working drawings/specs
> - Advise on further cost adjustments
> - Obtain necessary approvals/permits
> - Qualify vendors/suppliers/contractors
> - Assist client in assessing bids for project
> - Assist in preparing/awarding furniture, fixtures, and equipment (FF&E) bids
>
> **Contract Administration Phase**
> Associated Tasks
> - Assist with final bids
> - Job-site management
> - Procure furniture/furnishings with orders
> - Maintain project management records
> - Visit job site periodically for correct completion
> - Supervise installation
> - Assist in determining substantial completions payments/releases
> - Prepare postoccupancy evaluations/adjustments

How do you think the formal stages of managing an interior design project might be described? Interior design professionals have commonly identified five unique phases through which projects advance: programming, schematic design, design development, contract documents, and contract administration. In your later practice, you may find these phases may be less demarcated and in actuality may blend into each other. The circumstances of some projects may also result in their developing according to slightly different sequences. As your own expertise develops, your way of sequencing project management tasks may vary. That said, however, learning the names of these phases and the order in which they appear should give you a better understanding of how the sequencing of interior design tasks defines the work to be done:

1. **Programming Phase** Once designer and client have entered into an agreement to work together, this phase begins. It can be thought of as the stage in which project information is obtained and assessed by the designer. During programming, designer and client consult with one another about project goals through interpersonal communication, as in residential work; or designers conduct interviews with those affected by or required to function in the completed space, as occurs in nonresidential interior design work. Designers of both residential and nonresidential projects may inventory and evaluate items for possible use in the new installation. Client preferences are noted extensively throughout this stage, and designers frequently provide feedback concerning their feasibility. A designer will research possible project constraints by considering applicable building codes or other standards that may apply. For example, a designer must understand what design solutions will be required to make public spaces compliant with laws such as the Americans with Disabilities Act (ADA).

2. **Schematic Design Phase** After the designer obtains project information from the client and any relevant consultants, that knowledge is translated into the project design concept during the schematic design phase. This phase is the stage in which the designer prepares the first round of design, budget, and schedule considerations for client review. The designer prepares preliminary space and adjacency plans and selects project merchandise; he or she also prepares a preliminary budget and work schedule for the project. The next project phase usually begins after the client reviews and approves these efforts.

3. **Design Development Phase** In this phase, the designer and client finalize details such as space configurations, merchandise selections, and other specifications needed for the project. Notice the incremental way projects develop through the use of this methodology. Gradually, designers learn project requirements from the clients and their own expertise about project requirements. Then they research and present alternatives for client consideration, refine and finalize those initial results, and move on to the next phase of the project.

4. **Contract Documents Phase** After decisions about the project have been finalized, it is the designer's task to prepare documents ordering merchandise; to file for permits required for construction and installation of the finished project; and to request, obtain, and review bids from contractors. At the outset of the contract documents phase, the designer's tasks assume an administrative and supervisory nature. The extent of the designer's supervision of the project can become more apparent in the final stage of interior design project management.

5. **Contract Administration Phase** After the client has approved final selections and chosen construction contractors, the final phase of project management may begin.

During this stage, designers may perform tasks such as tendering purchase orders to vendors and, where permitted, supervising work progress. This may be thought of as the installation phase of the project, although projects are by no means completed after installation has occurred. The contract administration phase usually concludes after all corrections and adjustments have been made and all outstanding payments for goods and services have been issued.

There are a great many more details and issues to consider during each phase of interior design project management. This overview should highlight for you an important component of your work: As an interior designer you will likely provide an extensive range of services to your clients. What do you think is an important service interior designers should perform both for prospective clients and for themselves as they make early contact?

TROUBLESHOOTING STRATEGIES IN PROFESSIONAL PRACTICE

At first meetings with prospective clients, gaining and responding to useful information will be necessary for all involved. Interior design is exciting to both designer and patron—so much so that it is easy for important project issues to be ignored or simply glossed over. Later, both designer and client may regret not having engaged in more meaningful dialogue before becoming immersed in a project. It is therefore important for designers to listen and then assess implications of what potential clients ask them to accomplish. **Active listening** may be defined as identifying and evaluating the implications of what is said by another. By actively listening, designers perform a great service for these prospects and for themselves. Through dialogue with the client, coupled with their own knowledge and insight, designers come to know how (or even if) they should be involved in a project.

Active listening is an important component of the practice of interior design. Some prospective clients may be new to the interior design process and may honestly not be aware of the time involved to complete even a small residential project. As a result, they may want a completed installation within a few months when it reasonably should take much more time. Nonresidential clients may want the designer to achieve the best results with an unrealistically small budget. In short, potential clients may not know what is required of a designer. By actively listening, and thus considering the implications of what clients want to be accomplished, designers can better serve their clients by educating them about what is *really* required. Active listening benefits designers as well. By considering what they will have to do in carrying out a project, designers educate themselves about the client and determine whether they will be able to successfully complete the client's project. Active listening requires practical experience as well as knowledge of professional practices. It also requires a designer to know how to ask meaningful questions of the client, even at the first meeting. Certainly experience can teach designers what important questions to ask. As you begin to learn about the interior design process, what are some questions to ask prospective and actual clients that will engage your active listening skills to better serve both them and yourself?

First, acknowledge your excitement about meeting a prospective client and the possibility of gaining a new—perhaps your very first—project. Reaching this stage has involved a great deal of work on your part. As you will learn in later chapters that deal with marketing and promotional activities, designers face a crowded marketplace for their services: Consumers have a large number of interior designers from which to choose. That you were able to interest a prospect in you and your work, not to mention your services, is an accomplishment.

What are some questions you should ask prospective clients? According to the American Society of Interior Designers website (https://www.asid.org), consumers who are interested in retaining the services of an interior designer tell prospective clients to expect a designer to ask the following questions. What inferences would a young designer make in beginning to actively listen to responses to the following questions?

1. *For whom is the space being designed?* It may seem obvious, but the implications of responses to this question may surprise you! Residential clients may simply say "for us" and offer no further elaboration. By considering the people for whom a project is ultimately intended, designers may assess whether they have the know-how to produce an appropriate space. Imagine if "us" meant a young couple, active in sports, or if "us" meant a baby boomer couple approaching retirement age: Each couple would present different physical situations or challenges that a designer should recognize from just knowing the intended users of the space. With this information, designers should be able to address their clients' needs in their recommendations. Nonresidential projects may have many individual users; in those cases, the designer must step back a minute and consider the project itself. Who might likely inhabit or frequent such an establishment? What might they expect of a place of business they patronize, and, more importantly, what requirements are mandated for such a space? Designers focused primarily on residential space might want to assess whether they have the knowledge and experience to produce that kind of nonresidential space. By knowing who intends to use the space, designers who actively listen can discover the physical needs of the space as well as the personalities of those involved in the project.

2. *What activities will take place there?* Needless to say, a living room and a child's playroom have different design requirements, as would a restaurant in comparison to a large office space. What would an interior designer who actively listens conclude from responses to this question? Theoretically, understanding these implications gets to the core of what interior design is all about. To be more specific, however, think for a moment about all the details you have learned about specifying textiles and architectural finishes. Details about carpet grades and the abrasion resistance of surface textures (to give just a few examples) relate to their end use, that is, to their abilities to withstand activities to which they will be subjected. Responses to questions about activities that will take place in the project space should quickly bring to mind these issues. In addition, they should evoke your familiarity with the relevant design details, so that you know as soon as possible whether you can make the appropriate choices or need to research some more.

   The implications of this question can pose further challenges for designers. Clients may intend to use a space for one purpose but make demands inconsistent with that use. This can happen, for example, when clients express a desire for light-colored carpeting in residential or nonresidential projects subject to heavy foot traffic. Even when correctly specifying the appropriate grade of carpet for installation, a designer should know and explain the main implication of using light-colored floor coverings in such situations: It may be difficult to keep the carpet looking clean. Using their education, project knowledge, and, as in this example, common sense, designers can explain to clients how the intended uses of a project space inform decisions that the designer makes.

3. *How long do you plan to occupy the space?* It may seem strange to ask this question; however, in doing so, a designer should not think only in chronological terms. "Moving-up" residential clients interested in occupying a home only until they can afford a better one—perhaps for a few years at most—may not want to allocate a large budget for a design project. Other clients may feel that they have truly "come home" and, accordingly, wish to spend more on a designer's services. From the responses to this question, designers can determine how attached the client is to the project and, by implication, the client's flexibility about items such as budget and product quality. Clients indifferent to the amount of time they intend to stay in a residence may have less interest in spending more than was budgeted for upgraded products or high-quality workmanship. Again, it is the designer's task to listen to what is said, to make appropriate deductions from that information, and to suggest solutions and point out potential problems.

   Nonresidential work is frequently installed in leased space for a predetermined time. A client may tell the designer that the space is available for use for only a certain number of years. Again, gaining a sense of the duration of use is important but so is the designer's awareness that a client tied to a lease of any appreciable length of time should be educated about the need for a budget permitting the appropriate product and workmanship specifications.

4. *What is your time frame?* Clients, especially those new to the interior design process, may not have a realistic idea about how long it takes for a project to come together. To them, a designer's work may seem to require very little time. It is critically important that you hear more than a designated time frame when seeking a response to this question. Instead, a designer who actively listens should understand whether the client has a reasonable, realistic understanding of how long a project will take to complete. Here, experience becomes useful when gauging a project's time frame. You will come to know approximately how long it takes to complete similar installations based on past projects. You can also learn to estimate time frames by consulting with other designers about their projects and the time it took to complete them. Remember that no matter how excited you may be about taking on a project, you must first listen to clients' expectations about project completion dates and then inform them about how plausible their proposed time frames are for their projects.

5. *What is your budget?* Interior designers have been known to walk away from a proposed project after hearing the response to this question. Those designers are undoubtedly familiar with lawsuits that have arisen when designers have agreed to complete a project with a budget inadequate to accommodate the amount or quality of work necessary. When actively listening, a designer should hear more than a dollar amount or even a range of dollars. As in the time-frame inquiry, the designer should hear whether the client has a reasonable understanding of the many expenses interior design projects incur. Experienced designers therefore will not take on work budgeted for less than an amount the designer believes is plausible. Whether you adopt this approach, you should listen very carefully to the client's suggested budget and then educate the client about the plausibility of completing the project (or any project) given those financial constraints. No matter how much you may want to do a project or work with a particular client, failing to ask beforehand for budget

information or to inform the client about difficulties imposed by an inadequate budget sets the stage for serious problems later on.

6. *Are you relocating or remodeling?* The response to this question may give the designer some idea of how committed the client is to the project. Clients who want to fix up a residence for subsequent resale likely do not wish to spend a large amount of money on items or work they believe will not dramatically enhance sale proceeds. However, a full-scale remodeling of a residence in which the client wishes to remain may mean a larger budget with which to work.

7. *What image do you want to project?* The response to this question may help you determine whether you and a potential client share the same creative and aesthetic vision for the project. It may also help you to determine whether, if chosen for the project, you could work with the client to create a final product that both achieves the client's goals and serves as a useful addition to your own portfolio. As an interior designer, you likely have preferences for particular styles and objects as well as the final impression you would like your work to convey. Clients who indicate that they do not want the same results may be better assisted by another designer.

8. *What is the approximate square footage to be designed (for commercial projects)?* Many nonresidential projects are budgeted according to the amount of square footage involved. Although details of that practice will be explained in later chapters, it is important for you to know now that responses to this question give contract interior designers or design firms an early idea of the budget for a proposed project. As noted, it is important that designers learn to listen for the implications found in the answer to even the most straightforward questions. This section has sought to make you aware of the need to do more than simply hear—rather, to understand through use of critical listening skills what services you will be required to perform in your work.

APPLYING PROFESSIONAL PRACTICE SKILLS

The work of any professional includes knowing how to resolve problems. Often, young professionals find this to be an especially difficult task because they lack experience in recognizing situations that may be problematic. This section of each chapter is devoted to exploring how you, as a young interior designer, may recognize how particular problems may develop in your practice. With the ability to recognize troublesome situations comes the ability to apply your knowledge of professional practices to resolve them.

This chapter has provided an overview of the many nondesign-related disciplines that interior designers must call upon as practitioners. Although application of many of these skills may seem obvious, are you aware of how subtle professional practice issues may arise in your day-to-day work? Just knowing terms and concepts abstractly will be of little benefit to you otherwise. Experience, also known as hard knocks, will teach you over time where professional practice skills should have been better applied, but there must be a way to help you now to understand the professional practice skills that apply in various aspects of your work.

Even though there may never be a typical interior design job, any more than there is a typical interior designer, all designers take similar steps to complete projects and conduct business operations. There may be exceptional examples, of course, requiring additional or unusual tasks, but carrying out even the most outlandish residential or technically advanced commercial project requires following the same pattern of identifiable steps from project to project. Is there a simple way to begin the process of learning which professional practice skills relate to particular aspects of your work?

You are undoubtedly familiar with templates of the kind found somewhere on your drafting board. You use them to consistently produce the same results such as a circle of a particular size. The following overview of the sequential processes a designer completes during a project is similar to that template. In this text, the tasks designers routinely perform are illustrated by the practice issues that appear rather consistently. Comments on the practice issue are designed to help you recall that issue for later use in chapter projects and to set the stage for further text discussion. After reading each step, can you foresee what concerns might apply?

1. **The designer is introduced to a potential client and discusses ideas for a project.**
   Practice Issue to Recognize: Professional networking
   Networking—making personal contacts and then following up with the contacts later—is one way designers obtain new clients. So, too, are referrals from existing clients, other designers, and professional organizations. Making the most effective use of even casual meetings can help you build rapport with prospective clients. Learning about their interests and recording them for future reference is one professional practice process that may help you turn these prospects into full-fledged clients. Prospective clients are also getting to know you at this time.

2. **The designer responds to formal written request to present concept proposals for a contract project.**
   Practice Issue to Recognize: Marketing
   Nonresidential interior design work is characterized by formal processes and interactions with many different people. Detailed written proposals for interior design work are usually prepared for review and comparison with other proposals. These proposals are as much marketing devices as the glossy ads and personal contacts acquired through social networking.

3. **The designer learns confidential, sensitive information while gathering project information from a client. That information could greatly benefit the designer if he or she uses it for personal advantage.**
   Practice Issue to Recognize: Ethics
   Whether to act on information learned from a client or about a client should call to mind the issue of ethical conduct. Most professions impose some standards of ethical obligations on their practitioners. Interior design does as well through ethical codes adopted by governmental entities charged with supervising the profession and by voluntary groups such as the American Society of Interior Designers.

4. **The designer and the client sign an agreement to work together.**
   Practice Issue to Recognize: Law
   The presence of agreements of any kind should signal to you that law relating to contracts is the issue for you to consider. Contracts are agreements that are legally enforceable through court actions in the event that one of the parties does not fulfill the promised obligations.

5. **The designer meets with the client and presents the final project proposal.**
   Practice Issue to Recognize: Project management skills
   Project should signal to you the issue of project management, particularly an aspect of it referred to as the scope-of-service analysis. Before beginning a project, the scope of services a designer is to perform must be detailed in writing. This

detailed list usually is prepared as a result of negotiations between the designer and client. A major concern is to draft the scope of services in such a way that both the designer and the client know what is expected.

6. **The designer meets with the staff to review office budget and to interview candidates for the new office receptionist position.**
   Practice Issue to Recognize: Business accounting and management
   Profitability is the business goal sought in any occupation. Correctly maintaining records of financial transactions, income, and expenses for later interpretation is a practices-related process important for those businesses, such as interior design, that require the expenditure of fairly substantial sums to operate. Management decisions in business must be made with the idea of not only maintaining profitability but also being sensitive to employment laws.

7. **The designer and the client discuss the project budget and project schedule.**
   Practice Issue to Recognize: Project management
   Project management issues are concerned with making efficient allocations of available resources. A key practice issue for interior designers is to determine whether these allocations have been accomplished in a way that satisfies the client's expectations for the project as well as the designer's goal of earning a reasonable profit.

8. **The designer and the client discuss ways in which the designer will be paid for services.**
   Practice Issue to Recognize: Charging methods and billing practices
   There are many different methods for determining a design fee. The key issue is whether the method agreed upon by the designer and the client adequately considers the nature of the work the designer will perform. Will the designer be required to purchase large quantities of merchandise for the project or devote a large amount of time to some aspect of the project? Different tasks make different demands on the designer. Careful preparation of the scope-of-services analysis will help the designer determine the most appropriate charging method.

9. **The designer specifies and pays for custom-designed furniture in trade showroom.**
   Practice Issue to Recognize: Law and working with trade sources
   Here the designer has entered into an agreement with the trade source. Agreements should call to mind issues related to contracts and contract law. With respect to transactions involving the sale of goods, however, a particular set of laws takes precedent. These laws are based on what is called the Uniform Commercial Code and have been adopted by almost all states. When faced with practice issues related to the sale of goods, you must first consider whether these specialized forms of contract law apply. In addition to laws relating to the sale of goods, vendor relationships also affect interior design work. A designer's previous history of payment as well as individual showroom policies related to purchasing are all issues to consider when obtaining project merchandise from trade sources.

10. **The designer considers leaving present work situation and going solo.**
    Practice Issue to Recognize: Career development
    The time arrives when a designer perceives the need to seek out a new career direction. That may mean operating a solo or small group practice. Information about the operation of small businesses and related concerns is necessary to balance career aspirations with practical concerns such as earning a living.

This overview of the application of professional practices is, of course, just that: a general outline of what are, even for seasoned designers, complex tasks and decisions. Of course, there are exceptions, and many practice issues will likely require assistance from other professionals such as lawyers and accountants. However, as you are presented with steps or objectives throughout the text, think about what key professional practices issues are raised for you to resolve. In so doing, you will learn how and why professional practice skills apply to the work that you do.

> **NOTES FROM THE FIELD**
>
> The employer's point of view on entering the interior design field is a great subject to discuss. In today's interior design programs, many good schools incorporate internships and work exchange programs, which will be discussed in the chapters ahead. If these opportunities have presented themselves in your academic career, be sure to take advantage. What's important to note, is your first day of work in your job is the beginning of yet another learning experience and should be viewed as the continuation of your education: "you don't know . . . what you don't know" or so my first employer reminded me daily. Being professional, diligent, and creative are a given. Remembering that you are spending other people's hard-earned money, with your solutions, can't be underestimated. Remaining positive, despite many do-overs or hours spent correcting red lines on your paper, could make the difference between going forward in your career and not advancing within your firm or practice.
>
> Consider these words of wisdom. Your first few days in a new job will be a wild experience of new faces, technology, and tasks. Take it all in. We often advise new hires to listen first and ask questions second and more questions third. Your senior advisor will understand that all of this is new and will take the time to explain your tasks fully; if you don't get a complete explanation, ask again. If you are joining a larger practice, seek out assistance with intermediate staff, they will remember what you are going through and help you out with the small housekeeping, prioritizing efforts and the valuable time of principals and partners.
>
> I have two important pieces of advice for new hires: first (the small point), be thorough. Attend to the details, write down everything, and check your work before handing it to your advisor for proofing. Nothing will frustrate your employer more than marking up something up twice. The design process needs to uncover the fine points not always obvious on a plan, and getting bogged down with poorly executed documents will not allow the design process to unfold as it should. Second (the big point), the interior design profession is entirely about places . . . for people, created by people. This means your entire professional career will be spent taking the time to understand the needs of your clients and following through the process to execute on those big ideas. Your professionalism will put your clients at ease, and they will trust you with the risky ideas that are the foundation of groundbreaking interior designs, that have never been built before. This is the ultimate reward. Do have patience; you will get there! As mentioned earlier, soon you will "know . . . what you don't know."

Practical Activity

Although you have much to discover, as the preceding Notes from the Field indicates, there is much you do know right now. You know, for example, what you are interested in, the kind of work you would like to do. Research existing interior design firms in your area, or where you would like to work. Take time to find three to five firms that are engaged in the kind of work that interests you. As well, look for those that seem to have vision similar to your own. Describe in a paragraph how and why you believe you might be a "good fit" for each of the interior design firms you selected.

Review Questions

1. Define the term *professional practices* and indicate how and why it applies to interior designers.

2. Identify the various disciplines from which interior designer professional practices derive.

3. Explain the process used by interior designers to organize and manage projects.

4. Articulate the reasons the study of professional practices is important for interior designers.

5. Distinguish characteristics of *professionals* and *entrepreneurs*, and note how they may be alike.

6. Describe components of SWOT analyses, and explain circumstances when designers might use them.

7. Name ways in which professional practice decisions may be monitored and controlled.

8. Explain how you may further develop and enhance professional practice skills.

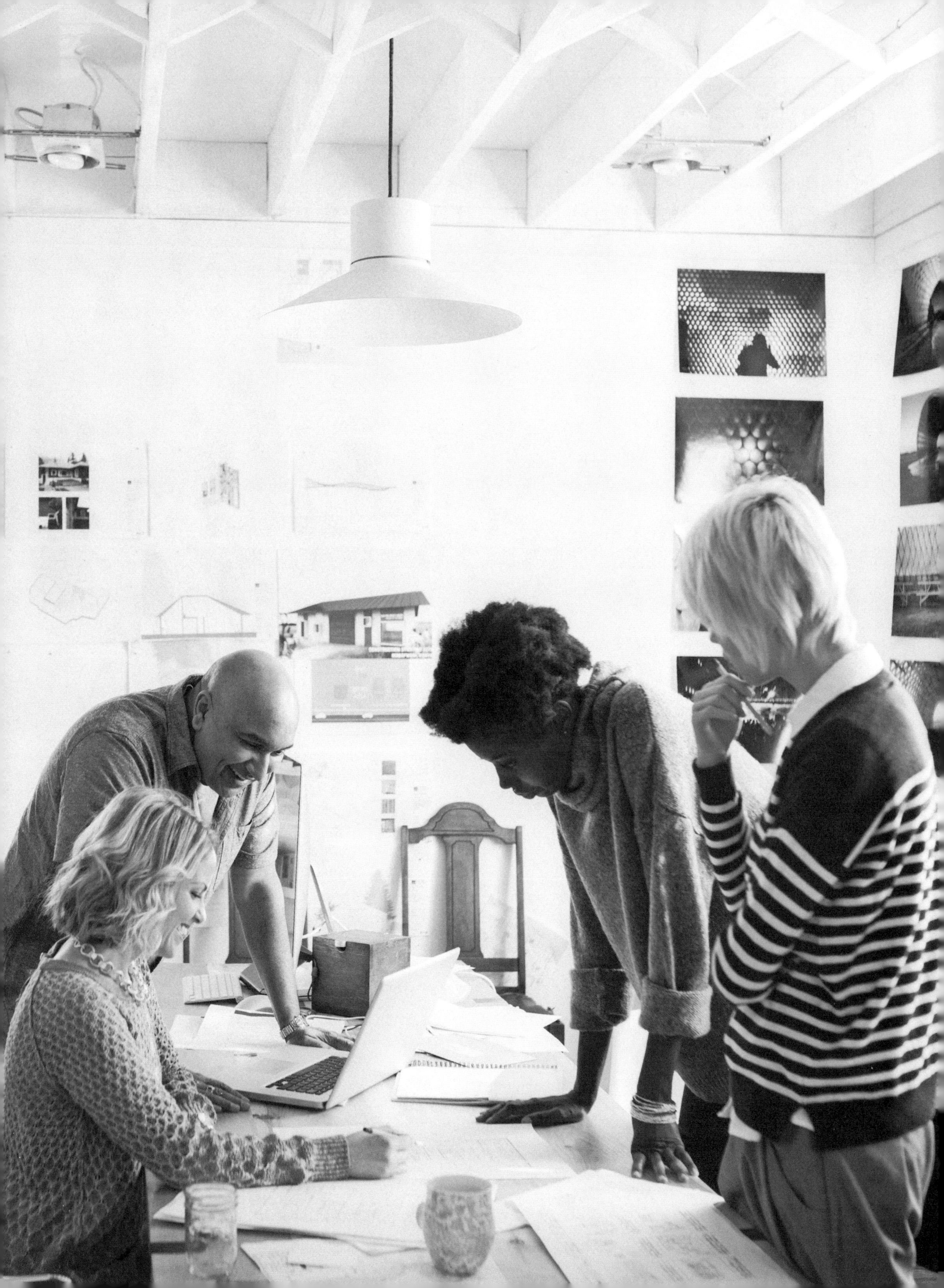

CHAPTER 2
BECOMING A PROFESSIONAL

MENTOR MEMO

You have just spent 4+ years achieving your design degree. (Congratulations!) You have a wealth of new words and a new language that is entirely unique to your profession. At the first meeting, you must remember—you and your client are speaking different languages. Know your clients comfort for understanding your language. This is a particularly valuable message—one that you should understand on your very first day as a professional.

After completing this chapter, you will be able to

- Describe elements that contributed to the rise of interior design as a profession;
- Explain the ways in which the individual U.S. and Canadian provinces control the practice of interior design;
- Define advocacy and how may it be applied to influence the future of interior design;
- Distinguish between practice and title acts as they pertain to interior design;
- Note several reasons that designers should engage in early project documentation practices, and how they may do so.

INTRODUCTION TO BECOMING A PROFESSIONAL

The previous chapter established a context for defining the professional practices of interior designers by identifying disciplines influencing the discipline. It also provided an overview of the distinct phases in which designers classify tasks required to complete projects, thus introducing you to the systematic procedures by which designers impart a sense of context to their activities. This chapter discusses factors that contributed to the development of the interior design profession. It then examines various educational and

---

Interior design has transitioned from the pastime of socially connected amateurs to a profession of educated, experienced practitioners.

accreditation pathways that now provide entry into the profession. As well, it explores basic ways current practitioners may influence the profession's evolution. This information will enable you to form your own working strategies and set you on your way to becoming the professional you aspire to be.

The Mentor Memos and Notes from the Field found in this chapter stress the team-building skills now necessary for interior designers to carry out their work; not only do most modern practitioners need to understand the requirements of their jobs, but they must also know how to communicate that to clients and other stakeholders. As you read these sections, begin thinking about the other professionals interior designers will need to call upon and the kinds of skills they—and the designer—will need if they are to work together.

MENTOR MEMO

Unless clients have been through this process before, they would not know what SD, DD, CD, and CA. For reference this is Schematic Design, Design Development, Construction Documentation, and Construction Administration, the core steps to delivering a project. Your first meeting needs to include a clear description, in layman's terms, of what you will do and how you will do it. Ask the question "has anyone on the client team, been through a project like this before? Are you comfortable reading a floor plan?" Recently, in a meeting with a client, I could tell the client was not comfortable reading the plans when he asked me, first, "How big is this room compared to what I have now?" followed by, "How big is this room, compared to the room I am sitting in?" (I had asked the client privately if he could read plans, and he communicated that he was okay with the plan review but was perhaps too embarrassed to share his lack of comfort with this exercise.) If this does happen—and it will—move to 3D immediately in order to move the project along. Never embarrass the client by calling attention to this shift. If necessary, add scale information such as desks, beds, or filing cabinets to the plans to provide an immediate sense of measure. Get those scale concerns off the paper; tape them on the floor or go move to mock-ups to reduce the fear and increase the understanding of what lies ahead. Local jurisdictions will dictate how far into the CD (Construction Documentation) process you can endeavor. Often an LDI (local drawing institute) will take control of drawing the work you create. Ideally, there will be a peer review process so that your team can oversee the work to ensure design intent. In my experience, given those elements alone, there are less production staff and more design talent on those teams. Often large firms will use production support in developing countries to offset the cost of their design talent closer to home. In either scenario, and no matter where in the world you are working, the structure of your team is governed by the final product.

AN OVERVIEW OF INTERIOR DESIGN'S HISTORY

What is historical context for the interior design profession? Its development as a formal vocation involves a highly colorful account of the creative triumphs and travails of individuals described as "imaginative, magnetic amateurs high on the social scale." Whereas anecdotes about the introduction around 1900 of Elsie de Wolfe's "revitalize[ed]" interiors, devoid of Victorian "jumble," as one commentator described, are interesting and perhaps inspiring, it is important to consider the surrounding social factors that influenced the origins of the profession in the first place and that, arguably, still affect it to this day. Certainly, an era in which indoor plumbing and telephones were obscure rarities can seem much removed from the realities of today. However, certain factors common to society then and now continue to shape the interior design profession and bode strongly for influencing its future.

Interior Design's Early Origins

The arrangement of articles and the use of ornamentation, either symbolic or decorative, in personal dwellings are practices that are centuries old, as is the interior organization of structures intended to accommodate large-scale public use. Early examples of these practices seem far removed from today's highly sophisticated practices; however, think for a moment about what made possible the prehistoric rendering of animals on cave walls in France and England as well as the building of ancient Greek and Roman structures. Did these examples of early design come about for much the same reasons that modern interior designers specify wall coverings that meet fire safety standards and plan commercial spaces that will foster the productivity, safety, and overall welfare of those who work in them?

As people become more knowledgeable about the world around them and learn how to apply that knowledge to enhance their interactions with that world, they may be said to have learned how to apply technology. Early examples of technology—which for centuries comprised mostly hand tools powered by manual labor—and of its application include the early cave drawings made of primitive, colored clays and the hewn ancient structures erected entirely by hand. From those earliest times until about the last 150 years, the technology used in building and furnishing physical structures was constrained in an important respect so as to prevent its wide-scale application.

During this period, the individual architects and craftspeople who are remembered today had learned to refine available technology and, in combination with an equally refined aesthetic sense, to produce items and structures still valued for their sophistication. A good example of these skills is found in the decorative products and structures produced in Western Europe during the eighteenth century. Versailles, the royal court of Louis XIV, is an epitome of available technology and skilled labor; and the objects found in the Sun King's court had been the provenance of royalty and of the extremely wealthy for as long. As advanced as the technology was for the time, it still required painstaking manual labor to animate it and give shape to its beautiful forms. It would take gigantic advances to make the products of technology readily available to a larger population and thus transform the once exclusive into the readily attainable.

The Impact of the Industrial Revolution on Interior Design's Development

Sociologists—or those who study human society and social interactions—credit the Industrial Revolution and the process of industrialization with transforming societies of the nineteenth and early twentieth centuries from cultures that depend on agriculture and handmade products to cultures that are based on manufacturing and related industries. The technological advances of mass production, in which items could be produced quickly and in large amounts, brought about a society in which something like the interior design profession could develop. No longer did one or a few artisans produce a single product in its entirety. Instead, a large labor force could be trained to carry out individual tasks that together would produce many examples of an item and often made with greater uniformity and precision than those made by their artisan predecessors.

The making of textile products was one domain of manufacturing where the effects of technology were earliest felt. Cloth became neither time-consuming to personally produce nor expensive to purchase after the complex elements of its production were influenced by advances in spinning, dyeing, and weaving technology. In its ability to manufacture items that previously cost a great deal of time and labor to produce, such as furniture and household goods, the technological advances of the Industrial Revolution may be considered as providing the material context for the development of the interior design profession. The effects of technology, however, were even farther reaching, for with the greater use of technology appeared other factors that contributed to the development of interior design.

Increased Urbanization and Interest in Interior Design

With the industrialization that took place between 1760 and 1850 arose a phenomenon sociologists refer to as urbanization, which occurred when increasing numbers of people began to live in cities rather than in rural areas. This trend to move away from rural life was a response to the effects of industrialization, as more and better-paying jobs became available in factories situated in or near the cities. Perhaps most relevant for the interior design profession was the increase in the number of people who became city-dwelling consumers instead of the rural-based producers they had once been. Urbanization and in particular technology-based industrialization are considered to have set in motion the origins of enterprises such as the modern-day fashion industry. With respect to the development of interior design, however, an additional factor was needed to provide a platform from which its practice as a profession could spring.

The rapid and wide-sweeping changes occurring in society through the effects of industrialization and urbanization also brought about new perceptions of the roles of men and women in that expansive society. In the United States, many of these changes in perception were borne out by action. Typically, in Victorian America, especially among its middle class, women were expected to manage the family home and assume responsibility for it. Toward the end of the nineteenth century, their growing dissatisfaction with limits on their ability to participate in society other than through opportunities afforded by home, family, and church life gave women an impetus to find new outlets for their interests and talents.

Expanding Roles for Women in Society

What such outlets might be for women remained problematic. By the late 1800s, most historical sources acknowledged women were becoming interested in earning money and assuming greater independence in society. Yet, most aspects of daily life remained bound by social constraints. Nevertheless, one such way women might pursue their goals deemed acceptable by society involved the furnishing and embellishment of homes.

An early advocate for the development of "interior decoration," as it was known, was Candice Wheeler (1827–1923), who was responsible for establishing, in 1877, the

New York Society of Decorative Art, an organization intended to serve as an educational resource for women and as a marketplace for their handicrafts. Wheeler was also responsible around 1883 for the founding of Associated Artists, a multifaceted firm responsible for services now recognized as interior design as well as the design of decorative products. Wheeler was also an early writer on the topic of interior design, publishing articles about the suitability of interior decoration as a career for women around 1895 as well as a book on decorating principles in 1903.

The novelist Edith Wharton is credited with being influential in focusing attention on interior decoration with the publication, in 1897, of *The Decoration of Houses* with the New York architect Ogden Codman, Jr. Around 1904, there was sufficient interest in the subject of decorating to warrant offering classes in the subject at the New York School of Applied and Fine Arts (now known as Parson's School of Design). Thus, the technology of the Industrial Revolution, the demographic effects of urbanization, and the interest among women for greater participation in society coalesced in the early twentieth century to give rise to what is now the profession of interior design.

These forces next needed a catalyst in the form of a charismatic personality to bring them together. Elsie de Wolfe (1865–1950) is traditionally regarded as the "first" interior decorator, with her seminal project, in 1905, of New York's Colony Club, which is considered the first to be carried out by someone other than an architect or antique dealer. She is also held to be responsible for authoring the first how-to book on interior decoration, *The House in Good Taste*, published in 1913 and, like Wharton's earlier book, still influential and widely available today.

Economic and Other Considerations Affecting the Rise of Interior Design

This survey of early developments in the interior design profession has emphasized the importance of a variety of social factors. Economic and social welfare considerations also influenced the development of interior design as a professional occupation. For example, publication in 1903 of *The Jungle* by Upton Sinclair prompted outrage at the working conditions and sanitation practices then prevalent in the American meatpacking industry. This outcry was instrumental in the establishment of the federal agencies responsible for protecting workers and the public against the kinds of horrific conditions Sinclair depicted.

The issues of worker and workplace safety again came to the public's attention in 1911 in response to the Triangle Shirtwaist Factory fire in New York City, in which more than 100 young women perished. It would take some time before issues of consumer protection and worker safety would come to the attention of interior design professionals; nevertheless, these early events set in motion laws and practices that greatly affected interior designers and their practices.

After World War I, America entered a time of economic and social expansion. Women had gained the right to vote, and the United States enjoyed a period of prosperity. Even though much of that prosperity would later prove to have rested on dubious business and investment practices—mostly those of a speculative nature—the affluence it generated permitted new design practitioners to flourish with many fewer constraints than those faced by their predecessors. One notable practitioner was Dorothy Draper (1889–1969), who is credited with being among the first to concentrate her design practice on commercial interiors. The affluence of the times contributed to interior design in other ways. With greater discretionary income, household consumers began to seek information about how they might better enjoy their homes. For that information, they increasingly looked to department stores and magazines. Examples of good taste, of the modern style, were often themes of store displays or magazine features, which provided an early means of instruction that laypeople could adapt on their own.

The Rise of Professional Interior Design Organizations

These sources continued to whet the appetites of consumers for the items they portrayed and for the services of designers. In the late 1920s, design practitioners were becoming increasingly interested in their status as professionals and seeking more formal ways of organizing. To that end, there was a rise of "decorator clubs" in various locations throughout the United States. Clearly, there was an interest among consumers for interior design-related goods and services, thanks to factors such as magazines and department stores, even the lavish movie theaters and motion picture productions of the time. Equally clear was an interest among practitioners to be considered design professionals. The economic events of the next decade would provide an impetus for that recognition.

The economic depression that began in 1929 persisted in many parts of the country throughout the next decade. Its devastating effects on consumers and on life in general during that period have been well chronicled. Perhaps less obvious is their inspiration for founding the modern interior design profession. In 1931, at a time considered by some to be the nadir of the Great Depression, businesses providing many different kinds of goods, including furniture, were faced with the prospect of going out of business. As part of a national trade show to promote American-made furniture, held in 1931 in Grand Rapids, Michigan, a conference was planned to give voice to those practitioners seeking to establish an organization that would represent their interests as design professionals. From that conference came the founding of the American Institute of Interior Decorators, which in 1936 became the American Institute of Decorators (AID). These early beginnings set the stage for the later development of the interior design profession. It would take the advent of new technologies and manufacturing techniques, as well as economic change, for the modern interior design profession to emerge as the force it has become.

The post-World War II era—from 1945 through much of the 1950s—was, for the most part, another era of economic expansion in the United States. Many forms of technology developed during the 1940s that were soon adapted to consumer use, with both residential and commercial applications. Urbanization was still a potent force in society; only now workers, including former members of the military services, were drawn to cities to participate in educational activities and to work in offices. Magazines, stores, and television (a new medium) also stimulated the desire for new items for the home and workplace. "Going to work" was a recognized and accepted fact of life for millions, and the state of the workplace became an important concern for design practitioners.

Changes in Perspectives and Names

By the mid-twentieth century, whether a design practitioner should be referred to as a *designer* rather than a *decorator* had been an issue for decades. As the demands of technology as well as the building, health, and safety codes of the 1950s and 1960s required greater expertise to apply, the work of practitioners who were educated and experienced in resolving these issues seemed less like the activities of the "magnetic" and "imaginative" practitioners of earlier. During these times, design practitioners began to embrace new behavioral and psychological research and to incorporate it into their work. Furniture placement and surface embellishment used to comply with standards of good taste (or conspicuous consumption) seemed far removed from the contributions of greater safety and functionality that social research added. Thus, the distinction between the designer, trained in building and safety codes as well as psychology, and the decorator, concerned with furniture arrangement and the use of surface finishes and effects, became better understood and appreciated.

Development of Interior Design Professional Organizations

Since 1936, AID had served the interests of the design community; however, in 1957 some of its members formed a separate group referred to as the National Society for Interior Designers. In 1975 the two merged to form what is now known as the American Society of Interior Designers (ASID). The 1950s saw the first attempt, in 1951, at statewide regulation of the interior design profession in California. Although not successful at that time, it was the first of such attempts. Not until 1982 did the first state, Alabama, adopt such regulation.

The 1960s saw many changes in the professional development of interior design. Education was increasingly seen as important, and in 1963, the Foundation for Interior Design Education and Research (**FIDER**) was founded, assuming responsibility for reviewing and accrediting interior design educational programs. Although initially responsible for accrediting both undergraduate and graduate programs, it now focuses

Educated, experienced interior designers know how important it is to correctly specify project items.

on the former. In 2006, FIDER became known as the Council for Interior Design Accreditation (**CIDA**). It remains the foremost organization responsible for accrediting interior design education programs in U.S. and Canadian universities and colleges.

The 1970s marked the advent, specifically in 1974, of the National Council for Interior Design Qualification (**NCIDQ**). Among other tasks, it is responsible for the preparation and administration of a qualifying examination now used as the basic method of determining minimum competencies in interior design skills and knowledge. The 1970s also saw a greater interest in the issue of consumer safety and its regulation. An awareness of the importance of safety, both in the workplace and in products available to consumers, was a social trend of the early 1900s. This early trend gained momentum during the 1970s, reflected in court decisions and jury awards for damages in increasingly large amounts. The issue of legal liability, or fault, is still a concern of interior designers and other professionals. Subsequent chapters will discuss ways in which interior designers can structure their business activities to reflect these concerns.

INTERIOR DESIGN EDUCATION

From its early beginnings in response to industrialization and urbanization, the practice of interior design has developed by reflecting and responding to social concerns. This historical and cultural overview of the interior design profession provides a context for understanding the emergence of the profession's current system of education and accreditation.

Essentially, courses of interior design study may be classified as degreed or certificate programs. Graduation from a four-year educational institution with a bachelor's degree in interior design is a clear-cut example of a degreed course of study. There are also two- and three-year programs found principally at local community colleges and specialized art and design schools. Programs offered at these institutions usually award associate degrees in interior design upon successful completion. Certificate programs, however, offer instruction in various interior design subjects, but with little emphasis on other educational material.

CIDA ACCREDITED PROGRAMS

After deciding which program is most appealing and appropriate for career goals, students choosing degreed plans should next assess whether a chosen program has received accreditation from CIDA. From 1970 to 2005, CIDA, then known as FIDER, as noted earlier, sought "[to lead] the interior design profession to excellence by setting standards and accrediting academic programs." CIDA "sets standards for postsecondary interior design education, evaluates college and university interior design programs (and) publishes a list of accredited programs that meet the standards."

Institutions seeking CIDA accreditation voluntarily submit their interior design curriculum, or course of study, for extensive review by organization auditors. Central to CIDAs determination of professional-level accreditation is whether the institution's program offers at least 30 semester credit hours of instruction in disciplines other than interior design—for example, liberal arts, humanities, social science, or science. CIDA leaves requirements for specific courses and course sequencing to the discretion of the individual institution.

Currently, CIDA offers no accreditation other than *professional level*. Four-year bachelor's degree programs that meet CIDA standards are accorded this designation, as are those two- and three-year programs that meet the instructional standard of 30 hours in other disciplines. Many interior design programs are available that do not offer CIDA professional-level accreditation, or have pending accreditation. What are the benefits associated with choosing a CIDA-accredited program?

As a result of its own research and the involvement of interior design educators and professional associations, CIDA derived what it styles as a common body of knowledge required for the professional practice of interior design. According to the CIDA website, this lengthy skill set includes, among other topics, the importance of understanding "the application of laws, building codes, regulations and standards that affect design solutions in order to protect the health, safety and welfare of the public." It also includes knowledge of "the methods and practices of the business of interior design; and an appreciation of a code of ethics." Requiring professional practices classes of all its member institutions is one example of CIDA's efforts to ensure uniformity of instruction in all CIDA-accredited interior design programs. By undertaking study in such a program, students are assured that the education they receive is in accordance with recognized and authoritative standards within the interior design profession. The public is assured students from CIDA-accredited programs are "responsible, well-informed skilled professionals who make beautiful, safe, and comfortable spaces that also respect the earth and its resources."

NATIONAL COUNCIL FOR INTERIOR DESIGN QUALIFICATION AND THE NCIDQ EXAM

As you approach the end of your formal interior design studies, you will undoubtedly come across another acronym: NCIDQ. The National Council for Interior Design Qualification is an organization responsible for promulgating that definition and other industry-related standards, the most important concerning individual professional certification. The mission of NCIDQ is to "aid and assist the general public by establishing and administering an examination to determine which practitioners of interior design shall be certified as competent to practice in the field of interior design" (NCIDQ 2003). Further activities include maintaining a list of individuals who successfully completed the exam and assisting in the reciprocity process by which an interior design practitioner educated and experienced in one state may practice in another without losing professional status.

NCIDQ is gatekeeper to many industry organizations since successfully passing the NCIDQ exam is

> a prerequisite for professional registration in those American states and Canadian provinces that have enacted licensing or certification statutes to protect the health, safety and welfare of the public. The NCIDQ examination must also be passed by every interior designer applying for professional membership. Passage of this important exam is also a prerequisite for *professional* entry into other organizations such as ASID and the IIDA among others. Ultimately, the council seeks the acceptance of the NCIDQ examination as a universal standard by which to measure the competence of interior designers to practice as professionals.

NCIDQ is a not-for-profit organization incorporated in 1974 and located in Washington, D.C. Its incorporation documents provide that only state and provincial regulatory agencies, not individual interior design practitioners, may be members of the council, as is also true of other interior design professional associations. Nonetheless, individuals usually apply directly to the council's administration first to determine exam preparedness and then for exam admission. Texas is a notable exception to this procedure, since exam candidates first apply to the Board of Architectural Examiners—the agency responsible for supervising interior design registration in that state—to determine their eligibility for exams. One research task you should undertake is to learn whether you must first apply to an agency in your state of preference or directly to NCIDQ prior to taking the exam.

The minimum educational requirement for exam eligibility is two years of academic instruction. You will note that NCIDQ does not require that study to take place at a CIDA-accredited, or any other kind of, educational institution. However, the NCIDQ has different eligibility requirements for those holding degrees from non-CIDA-accredited institutions and for those who have degrees from schools that are CIDA-accredited. States that have enacted registration laws for interior designers already require, or will soon require, applicants to have completed their course of study in CIDA-accredited programs. You should check if there are CIDA requirements in the registration or licensing rules of any state where you are interested in establishing your practice.

In evaluating educational achievement, NCIDQ requires the two-year minimum course of study to include at least 40 semester credits or 60 quarter credits of interior design-related course work. Remember, this is the baseline educational standard for exam eligibility. Three-, four-, and five-year educational achievement may also be considered. Educational programs are evaluated on the basis of whether the course of study comprises 60 semester credits (or 90 quarter credits) for three years; 120 semester credits, of which 60 or more must be interior design-related (or 180 quarter credits, with 90 or more being interior design-related) for four years; and 150 semester credits, with 90 or more hours related to interior design (or 225 quarter credits, with 135 or more interior design-related) for five years of study.

Even though these standards of evaluation permit exam eligibility without regard to a particular course of study, they do pinpoint the number of educational hours devoted to interior design that must be successfully credited for exam eligibility. Students enrolled in college or university interior design programs will likely meet the educational requirements simply by completing their studies leading to associate and bachelor degrees. Interior designers working in the field who have not undertaken a formal course of instruction may not be eligible to sit for the NCIDQ exam since they cannot fulfill the two-year minimum educational requirement. As a result, these practitioners may not be eligible for professional-level membership in organizations such as ASID.

Education is one criterion for NCIDQ exam eligibility. Work experience is another. NCIDQ has also set forth full-time work requirements in detail. Quite simply, remember the number *six* and you will have in mind the combined education and work experience required for exam eligibility. With two years of education, for example, NCIDQ requires at least four years of full-time work experience; with three and four years of education, the full-time work requirement is three and two years, respectively. To be considered full-time work experience, it should comprise not less than 35 hours a week of interior design-related work activity. The council recommends, but does not require, work to be supervised by an NCIDQ-certified interior designer, a licensed architect, or an interior designer recognized by a state or provincial regulatory board. NCIDQ requires course transcripts and letters of recommendation to complete the application for exam eligibility.

Twice a year, usually in March and October, candidates found eligible by NCIDQ are seated for the two-day-long examination. Passing this exam is the last requirement—after confirmation of education and full-time work experience—for NCIDQ certification. The council estimates that, over the course of its administration, approximately 13,000 candidates, or 75 percent of those attempting the exam, have successfully completed all sections of the exam on either their first or successive attempts. The council does permit retesting of sections unsuccessfully attempted and, unless a state rule provides to the contrary, imposes no time limit for passing all sections of the exam.

The exam is comprised of three sections. The first section, "Principles and Practices of Interior Design," contains 150 multiple-choice questions usually related to codes, building systems, construction standards, and contract administration, to be answered in 3½ hours. The second section of the exam "Contract Development and Administration," contains 125 multiple-choice questions related to design application, project coordination, and professional practice, for completion in 3 hours. The first two sections are conducted on the first day of exam administration. The council offers for purchase an examination guide that includes sample questions taken from all sections of the exam.

The final section of the exam is the practicum, a design-scenario portion in which candidates are asked to present a solution to a design problem. This section is presented on the second day of the exam and is administered in two parts over a total of 7 hours. It asks examinees to respond to a design scenario in which they have to address space planning, lighting design, egress, life safety, restrooms, systems integration concerns, and design millwork. In addition to the examination guide containing one sample practicum, NCIDQ also makes available for purchase additional design scenarios with critiqued solutions.

Approximately fourteen weeks after taking the NCIDQ exam, candidates receive their results in the mail. After they have passed this exam, successful candidates may present their names and credentials (along with a fee) for formal registration to the appropriate regulatory agency in their state. Those agencies then request verification from NCIDQ that successful candidates have received certification from that organization. The council subsequently maintains records of candidates on file.

Interior designers, depending on their career interests may receive even further certification from such organizations as the Green Building Certification Institute (GBCI), which offers recognition for expertise in sustainable design with its LEED, or Leadership in Energy and Environmental Design Professional Accreditation (LEED AP, LEED Green Associate). Other specialized certifications include those for lighting—LC, or Lighting Certified—by the National Council on Qualifications for the Lighting Professions (NCQLP) as well as for kitchens and baths by the National Kitchen and Bath Association (NKBA).

LICENSING AND REGISTRATION OF INTERIOR DESIGNERS

There are twenty-seven U.S. jurisdictions, as of 2013 with laws permitting accomplished individuals to use the title interior designer in their professional undertakings after registration. Eight Canadian provinces, as of the same date, similarly have passed laws allowing for postregistration use of the interior designer title. Of particular interest are the laws relating to interior design in the states of Alabama, Florida, Louisiana, and Nevada, and Washington, D.C. and Puerto Rico. These jurisdictions have passed very detailed laws, referred to as *practice laws*, defining the tasks practitioners may or may not perform. Furthermore, laws in these jurisdictions provide for the voiding of contracts entered into by unlicensed practitioners as well as the levying of penalties. These laws are comparable to laws regulating other professionals, such as attorneys, accountants, and physicians.

Sixteen of the remaining states have passed what are referred to as *title laws*, which do not require formal licensing as do states with practice laws. Under title acts, individual practitioners do not have to obtain licenses to engage in interior design activities. Title acts also do not constrain individuals from providing interior design services. As the name suggests, these kinds of laws regulate who may hold themselves out as being registered interior designers unless they have met minimum standards of education, experience, and examination set by that state. As of the date of this text, title act states include Arkansas, Connecticut, Georgia, Illinois, Kentucky, Maine, Maryland, Minnesota, Missouri, New Jersey, New Mexico, New York, Tennessee, Texas, Virginia, and Wisconsin.

Two states, California and Colorado, have slightly different laws, referred to as *self-certification* and *permitting*, respectively. The self-certification model for interior designers followed by California acknowledges that California has established an independent certifying board that is not run by the state. That body permits the use of NCIDQ exam results for certification and requires an additional examination of candidates on knowledge of state codes. Colorado's permitting statute states that interior designers who have met education, experience, and examination standards set by the state are permitted to prepare interior design documents for filing and obtaining building permits.

PREPARING YOURSELF FOR THE FUTURE

Do you believe that your learning is finished when your formal education is complete? In fact, interior design professionals are always learning. Interior design is always changing, in both a professional direction and the concepts it adapts. This section focuses on ways to solve common problems that may arise after you leave school and as you develop professionally. Accordingly, it addresses three basic tasks interior designers should consider to keep abreast of changes in the interior design profession:

1. Consider taking the NCIDQ exam even if your jurisdiction does not require it. The exam promulgated and administered by the NCIDQ has become the accepted norm for entry into the profession. Even if the aspect of interior design in which you plan to or actually do practice does not require it, one day it may.

2. Consider receiving ancillary certifications such as a general contractor license. Some states such as California make clear the division between interior design work and

construction supervision work (which many clients assume designers provide as part of their services) by requiring a general contractor license.
3. Keep current with education trends and proposed legislation affecting designers. Keep current with issues and proposed changes that affect you as a businessperson and an interior designer. By doing so, you will be aware of current developments affecting your industry—and your professional and financial livelihood. The history and practice of interior design is fascinating to observe and study. The challenge today for students and practitioners alike is finding ways to contribute to the continued development of interior design as a recognized, value-adding profession.

PREPARING THE INTERIOR DESIGN PROFESSION FOR THE FUTURE

So far, this chapter has emphasized issues affecting the past and present of interior design. What about the future of the profession? What can you do to further its progress as well as your own? To be sure, membership in such organizations as the American Society for Interior Design would be one way for you to keep abreast of the course the profession is taking.

According to information provided by ASID, the organization has a membership of 34,500 and "establishes a common identity for professionals and businesses in the field of interior design." The association notes that it has 48 chapters throughout the United States and more than 450 international members. As you will recall from the historical overview presented earlier in this chapter, ASID was formed in 1975 through the combination of two earlier interior design organizations, the American Institute of Decorators and the National Society of Interior Designers.

Membership in professional organizations is one way you may shape the future course of interior design. What might be other ways? Advocacy is defined as the process of supporting a cause, a belief, or a particular course of action. The various laws related to the interior design profession came about as a result of advocacy actions. These actions involved providing information, research, and proposed legislation that state lawmakers could use to propose new licensing laws. What might be other issues affecting the interior design profession, causes for which you could advocate?

The United States and Canada have adopted legislation affecting who can...and cannot...legally engage in the practice of interior design. How about other countries? Some have no regulation and oversite. Shouldn't the public in those areas be afforded the same protection as in the United States and Canada? Perhaps calling upon the standardized interior design accreditation on a global scale intrigues you to call for action through your advocacy efforts?

It is practitioners who have studied and applied their knowledge to the built environment of interior spaces. Yet, for their expertise, there is a roadblock for any project: the requirement that licensed architects "sign off" on their work before permits can be granted. Do you think that is fair to designers? How might you go about changing that current reality? Again, does this intrigue or anger you enough to advocate for change?

NOTES FROM THE FIELD

Building a team is an exercise in reverse engineering, starting with the end result and working your way to the beginning. Team assembly is based on task, talent, and the scope you are being asked to service. Assembly of your team is an entirely different exercise in North America when compared to other global markets. The local North American perspective is an excellent place to start, using internal and external teams as examples.

Internal Teams Let's talk through an example. You have secured a new job with a technology company that has offices in multiple cities. You have already been successful answering the RFP (request for proposal), and you have quoted a general fee. I always recommend including language in your proposal response that allows you to revisit the fee in the event the scope and scale of the project shift during programming. Look for tips on this in upcoming chapters. What do the programming, fee, and scope have to do with building a team? Pretty much everything.

Ideally in order to quote your fees, assuming it was either a lump sum bid or cost per square foot (or meter), you completed a work plan. There are examples of work plans in upcoming chapters, but, for this discussion, know that it is a tool that allows you to calculate labor to complete the work at full-burdened rates. Knowing what the client's expectations are is essential. That will determine WHO is your labor and how much they can be compensated to complete the work. Internal team labor will depend on your talent pool available in your practice. Making these decisions is a huge part of what managers actually do. Marrying the right talent to both the client and the needed tasks is an art form.

A typical commercial interior design team for a 20,000 square foot tenant improvement might include one senior designer, one FF&E specialist, and one production leader. If it's a residential project, you are adding a procurement element. If it's a hospitality project, the furniture can be a much larger component of the project (often 40+ percent) in which case your team will need to accommodate those skills and requirements. Healthcare involves medical planners and hospital equipment specialists, just to name a few of many specialized team members. Every project you take on will need team assembly. The types of projects you choose to take on should reflect the talent you have on staff. If you choose to take on a project that does not have the right staff or team, you are introducing liability not just for your client but for yourself.

Scenarios to consider: If your client does not speak English well, you will need a staff member who can translate in the room during meeting and provide written meeting notes that your client can understand. Or, your client may not be able to read plans. In which case, you will need to staff the project for more 3D analysis and axonometric planning. The extra team members can be a cost premium at the outset but often pays off at the end of the day. Perhaps there are questionable code concerns in the layout that you might want to call a third-party expert to be a part of your team. Every person you add to the team adds labor costs. Your fee must be designed to accommodate all the professionals needed to do the work efficiently and effectively. Given the soft cost labor typically does not exceed 10 percent in a typical corporate environment, but that 10 percent is in control of the remainder of the project's budget so it is in the best interest of your and your client to choose your teams wisely.

Once your team's organizational chart is established you will need a BOD, or basis of design, summary that outlines the projects goals and measures for success. A strong PM (project manager) should put this process in place immediately.

External Teams If you are placing or moving a wall, adding or removing a ceiling, placing or relocating an electrical outlet, or changing anything that is more than just color, you will have an extended team. As stated earlier, choosing your internal team is critical to the success of the work, but choosing your external team is equally thoughtful.

Practical Activity

Using the preceding Notes from the Field as a guide, imagine a small-scale project for which you are responsible. Perhaps it is a residential space such a living room. It could be, on the other hand, a public space such as an individual office. Describe the teams you will need to work with and the skills they should have if you are going to successfully complete this project.

Review Questions

1. What factors gave rise to interior design as a profession?

2. Who were early advocates for interior design as a profession and what were their contributions?

3. What are practice and title acts and how do they differ?

4. Describe the differences between degreed and certificate interior design programs.

5. Identify steps in the interior design accreditation process, particularly those that apply to your education and experience.

6. What role has the National Council for Interior Design Qualification (NCIDQ) played in developing the interior design profession?

7. What are some of the requirements related to education and experience that must be met in order to be eligible to sit for the NCDIQ accreditation exam?

8. What are some of the specialty certifications interior designers may obtain?

9. What is advocacy, and how might it benefit the interior design profession and you?

10. What are some professional organizations related to interior design, and how might they help both students and practitioners?

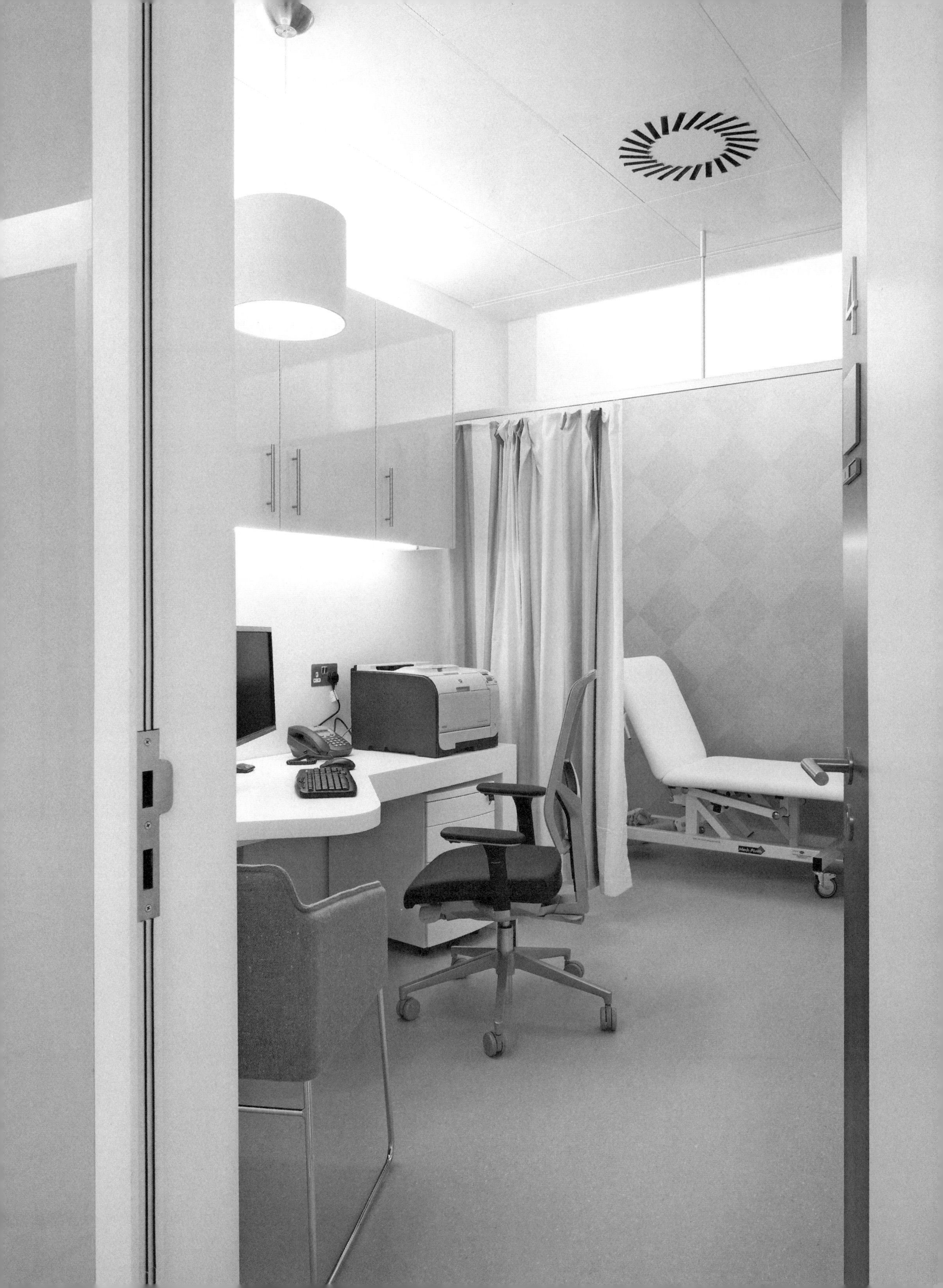

CHAPTER 3
WORKING ETHICALLY

MENTOR MEMO

It is unfortunate that a chapter needs to be dedicated to the subject of working ethically, but unfortunately there are far too many situations in our business that fall outside these professional boundaries. As a working professional with twenty-five years of experience, I have seen many a situation that discredits our industry, and I can assure you that you will need to make choices in your own career as to what is right . . . and what is wrong.

After reading this chapter, you will be able to

- **Provide a general definition of ethics and relate it to the practice of interior design;**
- **Identify notable philosophers who shaped modern understandings of ethics;**
- **Explain four areas of business practices where ethical issues are likely to arise;**
- **Give examples of unethical behavior that can occur in interior design;**
- **Define what constitutes proprietary information;**
- **Explain ethical issues related to kickbacks and similar practices;**
- **Distinguish between the use of** *may* **and** *should* **in ethical codes.**

INTRODUCTION TO WORKING ETHICALLY

This chapter brings a more introspective approach to your study of the professional practices of interior design. Publicity surrounding corporate misdeeds has only emphasized the importance of ethical principles and behavior in business dealings. As you read this chapter, think of the many incidents of unethical business practices reported in the media. If ethics are so important, why do these problems arise? What business practices are likely to lead to ethical controversies? What motivates businesspeople to act unethically? What are "ethics," anyway? This chapter identifies and examines ethics

Would it be ethical for an interior designer to put his or her profitability above client and health needs in environment such as this?

and ethical behavior to reach a practical understanding of what they mean and how they can be applied in the practice of interior design. What ethical considerations do you need to bring to your work to inform your business decisions? This chapter will help you determine that for yourself.

PERSPECTIVES ON ETHICS

Ethical behavior is increasingly expected of businesspeople, especially those presenting themselves as professionals. Many groups responsible for regulating occupations, including those overseeing the practice of interior design, impose ethical standards on practitioner conduct by adopting *ethical codes*. These ethical codes are examples of professional practice standards. The state licensing and registration boards overseeing the practice of interior design in certain states, along with **ASID** and the International Interior Design Association, or **IIDA**, are examples of state and industry groups that place ethical obligations on their members. The ethical requirements are detailed in writing, and members of these professional organizations agree to abide by them as a condition of membership and to obtain and keep licenses or registration/certification.

Despite these rules, ethics remain an elusive concept to explain, much less apply. Definitions of ethics may be written and the conduct of businesspeople analyzed to determine what constitutes ethical behavior; much discussion may focus on ways to *learn* ethics. Yet, despite these efforts, can ethical concepts really be taught and applied consistently in business situations? In many cases, ethically sensitive decisions go contrary to an organization's goal of gaining competitive advantage over other companies in their pursuit of customers and greater profitability. Competition of this kind is one of the hallmarks of a free-enterprise system in which businesses vie with each other to gain customers or clients, a process that may result in benefits for consumers. For example, competition may bring to consumers a greater selection of goods and services at more favorable prices. However, competition may result in harmful business practices in cases where business decision makers pursue greater profits rather than the welfare of those involved with the company. Examples in which the actions of individuals in large corporations have financially injured others through questionable business practices are still very much in the news and the subject of media coverage. Do these large-scale debacles—or scandals, as they have been termed—have any significance for the practice of interior design?

The repercussions of these large-scale occurrences of unethical business conduct are not as isolated as they might seem, and they have affected virtually every profession. A belief in the perceived lack of ethics in business is widespread enough that of 1,100 U.S. college students, not yet in the business community, surveyed in 2002 by Students in Free Enterprise (SIFE), 84 percent responded that the United States currently faces a "business-ethics crisis." Furthermore, many professions are undertaking a thorough self-examination of the role of ethics in their industries as a result of incidents such as those involving Enron and Global Crossing, to mention two prominent examples. Why might professionals—especially those in industries not involved in any scandal—be willing to undergo such self-imposed scrutiny?

You have already learned about the characteristics defining professions. Sociologists have identified additional features, including the autonomy professional workers enjoy. Professionals often make their own decisions, sometimes based on information available only to them. In exchange for these freedoms, workers in professions, at least implicitly, agree to govern themselves as a way of protecting others with whom they interact. This self-governance manifests itself in the creation of codes of ethics or other rule of professional conduct that all members of that profession voluntarily agree to follow. Failure to follow these guidelines usually results in loss of professional status.

Interior designers are no different in these respects from most other professionals. Most of the organizations regulating the interior design profession have adopted a code of ethics for their members to follow. Those who are found to have violated these rules lose their acknowledged status as interior design professionals. With the increasing interest and emphasis on the application of ethics in business practices, interior design practitioners can expect greater scrutiny from their supervising bodies, from clients, and from members of the general public. How might your own business practices as an interior designer look when viewed under such scrutiny? This chapter cannot teach ethics. Nothing can do that. However, this chapter can explain what the codes attempt to accomplish. How you address these concerns indicates how you will define yourself as an interior design professional. Solving the problem of the real and perceived lack of ethics in business simply begins with you.

A DEFINITION AND UNDERSTANDING OF ETHICS

What exactly are ethics? Many dictionary definitions of the term describe it as "a set of moral principles or values." However, this general statement may create more questions than answers for those seeking a definition of the term or an understanding of what it means to behave ethically. Because the concepts of *moral principles* and *values* have so many connotations, philosophers have explored the contours of ethics for centuries. In their writings, they have usually concentrated on considering the factors that determine whether the actions of individuals are *ethical, moral, good,* or *bad*. In ancient Greece, for example, the philosopher Plato (427–347 B.C.) initiated inquiries of this nature by exploring value-related concepts such as justice and its meanings in *The Republic*. Over time, the study of ethics by philosophers developed along several distinct lines. One of the most influential has been termed *utilitarianism*, a school of thought that stresses goal actions performed to maximize happiness—what was known as the common good—for the greatest number of people while minimizing the harm to that group. Nineteenth-century philosophers Jeremy Bentham (1748–1832) and John Stuart Mill (1806–1873) are considered the seminal proponents of utilitarian thought. Contrary to this belief was the view espoused by philosophers such as Immanuel Kant (1724–1804). Referred to as the deontological or nonconsequentialist approach, this school of thought held that ethical conduct was based on duty, what was known as the *moral imperative* and carried out under the guidance of a highly rational set of rules. Kant particularly stressed the idea that ethical conduct involved a sense of what he termed *respect* toward others. Kant argued that this concept of respect was more important in promoting ethical behavior than Bentham's idea of satisfying the common good. This respect, he further reasoned, should govern an individual's conduct toward others. Other people were to be treated not as the means by

Interior design clients increasingly rely on ethically attuned practitioners to ensure stakeholder satisfaction.

which individuals could achieve their own goals but as ends in themselves who are worthy of respect.

Vestiges of these philosophers' thoughts have provided theoretical bases for drafting many modern laws and codes of ethics. In particular, you will note that codes of ethics like those produced by ASID and other interior design-related governing bodies speak in terms of *responsibilities* owed to others in the same vein as Kant's philosophy. These responsibilities impose a duty on those who agree to follow the codes. They also provide rules to guide design practitioners to protect groups that are defined by proponents of utilitarianism. The ASID Code of Ethics and Professional Conduct defines those to whom a responsibility is owed as being "the public, clients, other interior designers and colleagues, the employer (where the designer works as an employee)," and, finally, "the profession." Although ethics may be a difficult subject to fully define, various governing bodies regulating the interior design profession can and have set basic standards of ethical conduct expected of practitioners and further defines those to whom ethical duties are owed.

THE BUSINESS CONTEXT OF ETHICS

How and when do questions of ethics arise in the operation of business? What specific situations arising in an interior designer's daily working life call for application of ethical concepts? Recent writers in general business ethics have detailed four aspects of working life in which ethical problems can arise. As a businessperson, a practicing interior designer will have to deal with these issues. They include

1. Making business decisions related to human resources;
2. Using company resources;
3. Maintaining stakeholder confidence in the company and its practices; and
4. Managing real and apparent conflicts of interest.

Ethics, Management, and Human Resources

Management and human resources have been identified as domains that require ethical evaluation and decision making. The hiring, advancing, and terminating of employees are common examples in the business world of such human resource issues. You may already be familiar with the negative implications of these issues in those instances where actions taken by individuals on behalf of companies exclude the contributions of others based on their race, gender, ethnic origin, or religious beliefs. These types of discriminatory decisions are unethical and also proscribed—that is, made illegal—by state and federal laws.

This area of concern has been expanded in recent years by increasing interest in the status of workers who produce goods for consumption. This human resource issue involves workers who are compelled against their will, and with little or no compensation, to produce items frequently intended for export to be used in other countries. Knowledge of the conditions surrounding the working environment of laborers who produce goods may be particularly lacking or sketchy where items are manufactured in foreign countries. However, even when actual knowledge of harmful working practices and conditions is lacking, should an ethically conscious interior designer be responsible for inquiring of their trade sources about such issues? Section 2.6 of the ASID code of ethics reads: "Members shall not assist or abet *improper* or illegal *conduct of anyone* in connection with a project" [emphasis added]. Does this section of the code address the matter? What issues should trigger ethical inquiries regarding the status of workers on the part of the designer?

Ethics and the Use of Company Resources

Business decisions involving the use of company resources also call for businesspeople to make ethical evaluations. Theft by employees is one situation in which unethical decision making results in the misallocation of company assets. However, this context may also examine whether business decision makers seek to prevent or ignore the actual or perceived occurrence of what is referred to as *conflicts of interest*, or undisclosed form of favoritism.

Decisions that reflect conflicts of interest usually do not or only superficially consider the merits of the candidates under consideration. Examples of such conflicts of interest may be quite familiar to you from media reports. **Kickback** schemes—in which monies are paid after receiving some form of favorable treatment—or outright **bribes**—in which direct payments are made to ensure favors—are clear conflicts of interest that are ethically and legally prohibited. Other examples of conflicts of interest include actions such as awarding contracts for work on the basis of personal relationships or paying undisclosed commissions or fees to encourage patronage of a business. Imagine a trade showroom offering designers financial incentives to place large orders, particularly when those incentives are not disclosed to that designer's clients—and you get an idea of an overt form of this type of conflict. Should designers accept such arrangements, they would have personal and financial reasons to specify products at odds with their clients' interest in obtaining the most appropriate goods for their projects.

Ethics and Stakeholder Confidence

Many businesses have strict policies to prevent the occurrence of overt forms of conflicting business practices. For example, they may require and enforce competitive bidding for work among contractors. These policies have another purpose as well. Companies and individuals running businesses of any size rely on the goodwill generated by their operation to attract customers and employees as well as other tradespeople. The appearance of a conflict of interest can hamper good feelings about patronizing, working for, or doing business with a company. Whether a conflict of interest actually exists, ethical decision making seeks to prevent its actual and perceived occurrence.

Managing Real and Apparent Conflicts of Interest

Conflicts of interest may also take more subtle forms. Imagine all the information you will come to know about a client and a client's business as an interior designer. But using the knowledge you gain on the job for purposes other than completing your client's project raises issues of conflicts of interest. Essentially, your own interest in using the information you learned on the job may interfere with the ownership or proprietary—that is, property—rights of those individuals or businesses from which you obtained this knowledge. This issue is usually termed misuse of **proprietary information.** Businesses control more than just their physical property; they control the know-how necessary to produce the goods or services with which the business is identified. Think of the expertise required to produce complex computer software programs. Knowledge of this kind is an example of that company's proprietary information. But how can something as intangible as knowledge be misused?

It is not uncommon for a designer to work on multiple projects at once. To work on, say, two or more residences or commercial projects at a time, and perhaps even in the same location, probably would not cause a conflict of interest. Yet, as a practical matter, how easy do you think it might be to inadvertently use or disclose knowledge about one client to another? Not only can misuse of proprietary information give you an unfair advantage over others who do not have this information, but it may also give your clients an unfair advantage over their competitors.

Misuse of proprietary information may also occur in cases where interior designers take information they obtained while employed with another designer or design firm and act on that information after they leave. Marketing, billing, client, and trade source knowledge are types of information that would give competing firms a business advantage over the firm a designer is leaving. To prevent the use of such information, the policy of many companies is to require departing workers to agree in writing not to disclose this critical business information. Again, as a practical matter, how easy might it be to use or disseminate such information?

Customer confidence is another area that calls for ethical evaluation and decision making. Inducing customers to purchase goods or services based on a company's claims that are later found to be false or misleading is one clear example of unethical—and illegal—conduct directly related to customer confidence. More complicated examples of ethical misconduct include the business practices of companies—especially large corporations—in which stockholders and employees are victimized by elaborate financial schemes that deprive them of monetary or other benefits. Unethical actions also include business decisions that are found to adversely affect the environment through excessive pollution. Questionable labor practices in which workers are exploited by company actions are yet another example.

MENTOR MEMO

Allow me to start by first telling you the end of my story. Accepting any gift, small or large, from vendors in exchange for preferential treatment in a bid situation, is not acceptable. This is that story. I was ten years into my professional career and had just been made partner, at my firm.

It was something I had worked diligently for; I was proud in the moment. Over a lunch with a furniture vendor, who had become a good friend, I shared the news, and we shared a toast. As we often did over our industry lunches, we talked about the current furniture pieces we liked, who was up to what in the design world, and what new products were coming to market and when. She asked me, "What is your absolute favorite piece of furniture made today?" It was a quick answer, given I had coveted one chair my entire career, but alas I did not have the salary to afford one . . . sigh. I took this conversation as a simple chat with a friend and nothing more.

Six weeks later, as I came home from the office, I spied a giant package in the driveway with the name of the company that made the chair I coveted stamped on the side of the box. Stopping dead in my tracks, I gasped. Had this come from my friend? Was this a gift? Did my friend and vendor know, this was not okay? Could I accept such a gift given it was from a friend . . . who is also a vendor? The answer to all of these questions is, no.

At the time this gift arrived, the same furniture company was midstream in a bid response to a large project, being managed by my team. When I asked my friend and colleague about the package, she said it was a celebration of my new role as partner. I am sure you can see the obvious conflict of interest in play. This was not the first occasion to have this happen, and it would not be the last in my professional career. In this case, leaving the package unopened, I called my colleague and advised her to pick up the package the next day. We discussed how this would be considered a conflict of interest, and would compromise her company's position on the bid and my integrity in the eyes of the client. Kickbacks or favors are unfortunately common, but they can and will ruin your career and reputation as a professional should you choose to turn a blind eye.

The most important rules of the road in understanding the ethics of business can be found in your local and national associations' standards of professional behavior. Fully read and digest them. Second and specific to a project, when you are working with established clients, they likely have detailed procurement policies and contracts in place that will govern how communication takes place between vendors and contractors that are bidding for a project. For example, there may be an opportunity to ask questions during the bid window, and all questions will be summarized to those submitting to allow for an equal playing field. Ethics cannot be taught; however, both activities and perception of professional practice is essential.

Day-to-day business practices call for the application of ethics to complex and competing goals. Businesspeople need not work unprofitably, but they should not work irresponsibly. By applying ethical guidelines, they can balance both of these concerns. Many times an ethical decision may not be as profitable as an unethical decision. However, there are costs—both financial and professional—for failing to operate according to ethical guidelines in business. The consequences of unethical decision making affect those who are directly involved. But they also create negative perceptions that have repercussions throughout particular industries and, if substantial enough, throughout the larger business world.

INTERPRETATION OF CODES OF ETHICS

Nuances affect interpretation, whether you are specifying color choices for a design or closely reading the language of ethical codes. As you read different codes of ethics, your understanding of their meaning will be enhanced if you can make some important distinctions based on their language. What, for example, are the differences in meaning between *shall* and *may* in state codes of ethics and the ASID code of ethics and professional conduct? How can you read these codes for greater understanding?

Most codes employ the term *shall* or, alternatively, *shall not* in their statements. Use of the term *shall* is generally interpreted as imposing an affirmative obligation upon another to act in a certain way or to perform a specific task. Likewise, *shall not* is generally construed as imposing an affirmative obligation *not* to act in a certain way. Terms such as *must* also carry the same meaning as *shall*.

The meanings of these terms differ from the common understanding of the term *may*, as you are probably aware. Whereas language using the term *shall* imposes requirements, *may* simply permits action of some sort. Provisions in the ASID code allow a member designer to "offer professional services to a client for any form of legal compensation" and to render second opinions to clients and serve as an expert witness in dispute-resolution proceedings; since the provision does not require a designer to fulfill these duties, a designer may decline to engage in these activities: Design services are not mandatory.

Finally, one provision of the ASID code states that "members *should* respect the confidentiality of sensitive information obtained in the course of their professional activities." Use of this term imparts a more subtle meaning to that provision and bears further explanation. Were the term *may* substituted for *should*, the provision would read as permissive in nature. With such language in place, a professional member could be free to disclose to whomever any sensitive client information without fear of censure. Surely, a client is entitled to more protection than that.

Alternatively, were the term *shall* employed, the designer would be required to *always* respect confidential information, even if it so means incurring some penalty. To put this provision into context, you should be aware that communications between clients and professionals such as clergy, lawyers, and physicians are considered privileged in legal actions and not subject to disclosure except in very few instances. Interior designers enjoy no such form of privileged communication with their clients. In other words, revelation of information a designer learns from a client may be compelled by a court of law. A designer obligated by code language to prevent such disclosure would likely subject the designer to legal contempt penalties. As a result, a designer *should* keep confidential information confidential, *unless* a court of law requires otherwise. Should clients tell you something confidentially, it might be a good idea to remind them of this constraint.

Understanding code language is important with regard to membership in professional organizations. It is also relevant to understanding the rules of professional conduct that many states have in place regarding the formal practice of interior design. Membership in professional organizations such as ASID is optional. Designers may join such groups if they wish. Should designers want to obtain formal certification or registered status in a particular state, then they must comply with the provisions that jurisdiction has enacted. Many of those provisions include codes of conduct using language very similar to that found in the codes discussed here. Understanding how to interpret that subtle use of language is therefore a *must* for the designer.

ENFORCEMENT OF ETHICAL CODES

Considering the importance of ethics in the conduct of business, how are ethical provisions enforced? Are penalties incurred for failure to comply with these requirements? As you might imagine, a professional found to have violated ethical provisions may face fairly severe penalties. However, recall the concept of proprietary information. An interior designer who has obtained state certification or is a member of a professional design group possesses something similar to proprietary information. In this case, a designer is said to have a proprietary interest in the license, certification, or trade-group affiliation. In other words, designers' memberships in these groups are their "property." Because of this interest, a state license, certification, or organizational membership cannot be taken away from the designer simply on the basis of a complaint. To assess the merit of the complaint and protect the practitioner's proprietary interests, important procedural steps are taken by the appropriate authority. These steps make up the process by which ethical codes are enforced.

Enforcement of ethical codes begins with determining whether the practitioner against whom an action is brought is a member of a professional board. The first issue involves the membership status of the designer against whom the complaint is brought. In order to invoke the enforcement powers of either a state board responsible for supervising the interior design profession or an industry group such as ASID, the designer must hold a license or certification from that state or be a member of the industry group. Lacking these qualifications, the only recourse against a designer to satisfy an ethical complaint would be through formal civil law proceedings such as a civil lawsuit.

Another threshold issue concerns the status of bringing a client ethics charge against a designer. This person or group of people is usually referred to in administrative, nonlegal actions as the **complainant** or complainants. This party must show what is referred to as **standing**. This requirement is usually met by the person proving he or she was harmed or suffered damage in some form from actions caused by the plaintiff. In all likelihood, it would only be persons so injured who would bring such claims either before a state board or a trade group. However, reread the ASID code. Little is said about exactly who may bring a complaint, and the same is true of many state codes. Usually, the regulatory body that oversees the ethics hearing makes a formal determination on whether this requirement has been satisfied.

After these initial concerns have been addressed, a formal written statement defining the problem is made by the complainant. This document is made available for the designer's response and sets out in detail the circumstances giving rise to the complainant's concerns. A designer's response to the original complaint may satisfactorily resolve the matter for the complainant. If not, the matter continues with the complaint being forwarded to an ethics committee for review. If that committee determines that an ethics code has been violated, the process continues with a formal review by a committee of the state board or a national trade group formed to render decisions on these and related complaints. These types of committees are usually referred to as **judicial committees**, although they are not courts of law.

The judicial committee holds a formal hearing in which both the designer and the person bringing the action have an opportunity to present their respective versions of the issue. Because resolution of the matter could result in the deprivation of a designer's proprietary right to practice or use a professional affiliation, lawyers representing both sides may be present at these formal hearings. After the presentation of evidence through the form of oral testimony and written documents, the disciplinary committee then makes a final determination on the controversy by determining whether an ethics violation occurred and, if so, the degree of punitive, or punishing, action that might be indicated. If the judicial committee does not find an ethical violation, they may simply dismiss the complainant's action altogether. However, if an ethical violation is found, it may result in censure of the designer and even revocation of state certification and group membership. The names of designers against whom such penalties are invoked are published in disciplinary action sections of state professional journals and in industry periodicals such as ASID's magazine, *ICON*.

A PLACE FOR ETHICS IN THE PRACTICE OF INTERIOR DESIGN

The challenge now is to find a way to incorporate ethics as standard operating procedure into your practice. Fundamentally, of course, business decision makers need to believe in the importance of ethics and their application. No set of rules or codes can effectively instill beliefs that are not shared among decision makers. The need to recognize standards of ethics within an organization is primary. But what if no such need is perceived or is ignored in favor of the aggressive pursuit of profits? Increasingly, the actions of all sorts of professionals are scrutinized and challenged by consumers and industry-specific trade groups. To ignore ethical constraints can thus become a liability affecting an organization's future and the professional status of those involved in it.

MENTOR MEMO

What if I am asked to work for free? Putting aside the fact that designers make their living by charging for their services, you might be surprised how often we are asked to provide services at no cost. The request can be an innocent lack of understanding by a client, which is often the case, or a structured no-fee request in parts of the world where the governing regulatory design body does not prevent these questions or requests being asked. It is important to know your rights, your insurance regulations, and the laws that prevail.

CODES OF ETHICS AND MISSION STATEMENTS

In light of the growing concern about ethical business practices, many organizations seek to integrate these concepts by implementing and enforcing their own ethical codes. These codes can guide the actions of those involved in the operation of the enterprise by clearly establishing what ethical standards the organization has agreed to pursue and maintain. Many business plans include values statements, or **mission statements**, which offer similar insight into the ethical fiber of an organization. As you might suspect after reviewing the ASID code of ethics, codes may be substantially more detailed. However, both codes and mission or values statements emerge from a unified effort throughout an organization to promulgate ethical standards. Input from organizational stakeholders, such as employees and leaders, concerning the goals and content of such codes set in motion the process of integrating ethics into the organization. These early efforts are then usually refined into preliminary codes and then finalized before adoption. Once the codes are implemented, formal review procedures have been put in place to evaluate questionable conduct and make corrective recommendations.

Process aside, what do such codes contain? Business writers usually note that these codes should reflect the company's *values, traditions, and unwritten rules*. As a practical matter, draft versions of such codes should also be checked for industry and legal compliance before final company-wide adoption. Imagine, for example, a large interior design firm—whose principles and employees were subject to the ASID code of ethics—that chose to adopt ethical standards condoning actions not permitted by the ASID code or actions of an illegal nature. In such a case, how effective or even persuasive would the company code really be? As you contemplate this chapter's first project, ask yourself to define the ethical principles that guide you and that you believe should be incorporated into your business code of ethics. Even small businesses can adopt procedures similar to those used by large organizations to instill ethical values into daily practice.

BOX 3.1

ASID CODE OF ETHICS AND PROFESSIONAL CONDUCT

- Preamble
- Responsibility to the Public
- Responsibility to the Client
- Responsibility to Other Interior Designers and Colleagues
- Responsibility to the Profession
- Responsibility to the Employer
- Enforcement

1.0 Preamble

Members of the American Society of Interior Designers are required to conduct their professional practice in a manner that will inspire the respect of clients, suppliers of goods and services to the profession, and fellow professional designers, as well as the general public. It is the individual responsibility of every member of the Society to uphold this Code and the Bylaws of the Society.

2.0 Responsibility to the Public

2.1 Members shall comply with all existing laws, regulations and codes governing business procedures and the practice of interior design as established by the state or other jurisdiction in which they practice.

2.2 Members shall not seal or sign drawings, specifications, or other interior design documents except where the member or the member's firm has prepared, supervised or professionally reviewed and approved such documents, as allowed by relevant state law.

2.3 Members shall at all times consider the health, safety and welfare of the public in spaces they design. Members agree, whenever possible, to notify property managers, landlords, and/or public officials of conditions within a built environment that endanger the health, safety and/or welfare of occupants.

2.4 Members shall not engage in any form of false or misleading advertising or promotional activities and shall not imply through advertising or other means that staff members or employees of their firm are qualified interior designers unless such be the fact.

2.5 Members shall neither offer, nor make any payments or gifts to any public official, nor take any other action, with the intent of unduly influencing the official's judgment in connection with an existing or prospective project in which the members are interested.

2.6 Members shall not assist or abet improper or illegal conduct of anyone in connection with a project.

3.0 Responsibility to the Client

3.1 Members' contracts with a client shall clearly set forth the scope and nature of the project involved, the services to be performed and the method of compensation for those services.

3.2 Members may offer professional services to a client for any form of legal compensation.

3.3 Members shall not undertake any professional responsibility unless they are, by training and experience, competent to adequately perform the work required.

3.4 Members shall fully disclose to a client all compensation which the Member shall receive in connection with the project and shall not accept any form of undisclosed compensation from any person or firm with whom the member deals in connection with the project.

3.5 Members shall not divulge any confidential information about the client or the client's project, or utilize photographs or specifications of the project, without the express permission of the client, with an exception for those specifications or drawings over which the designer retains proprietary rights.

3.6 Members shall be candid and truthful in all their professional communications.

3.7 Members shall act with fiscal responsibility in the best interest of their clients and shall maintain sound business relationships with suppliers, industry and trades.

4.0 Responsibility to Other Interior Designers and Colleagues

4.1 Members shall not interfere with the performance of another interior designer's contractual or professional relationship with a client.

4.2 Members shall not initiate, or participate in, any discussion or activity which might result in an unjust injury to another interior designer's reputation or business relationships.

4.3 Members may, when requested and it does not present a conflict of interest, render a second opinion to a client, or serve as an expert witness in a judicial or arbitration proceeding.

4.4 Members shall not endorse the application for ASID membership and/or certification, registration or licensing of an individual known to be unqualified with respect to education, training, experience or character, nor shall a Member knowingly misrepresent the experience, professional expertise or moral character of that individual.

4.5 Members shall only take credit for work that has actually been created by that Member or the Member's firm, and under the Member's supervision.

4.6 Members shall respect the confidentiality of sensitive information obtained in the course of their professional activities.

5.0 Responsibility to the Profession

5.1 Members agree to maintain standards of professional and personal conduct that will reflect in a responsible manner on the Society and the profession.

5.2 Members shall seek to continually upgrade their professional knowledge and competency with respect to the interior design profession.

5.3 Members agree, whenever possible, to encourage and contribute to the sharing of knowledge and information between interior designers and other allied professional disciplines, industry and the public.

6.0 Responsibility to the Employer

6.1 Members leaving an employer's service shall not take drawings, designs, photographs, data, reports, notes, client lists, or other materials relating to work performed in the employer's service except with permission of the employer.

> 6.2 A member shall not unreasonably withhold permission from departing employees to take copies of material relating to their work while an employee of the member's firm, which are not proprietary and confidential in nature.
> 6.3 Members shall not divulge any confidential information obtained during the course of their employment about the client or the client's project or utilize photographs or specifications of the project, without the express permission of both client and employer.
>
> **7.0 Enforcement**
> 7.1 The Society shall follow standard procedures for the enforcement of this Code as approved by the Society's Board of Directors.
> 7.2 Members having a reasonable belief, based upon substantial information, that another member has acted in violation of this Code, shall report such information in accordance with accepted procedures.
> 7.3 Any deviation from this Code, or any action taken by a Member which is detrimental to the Society and the profession as a whole shall be deemed unprofessional conduct subject to discipline by the Society's Board of Directors.
>
> *Adapted from* https://www.asid.org/content/asid-code-ethics-professional-conduct

PRACTICAL EXAMPLES OF THE ASID CODE OF ETHICS

How well do you believe you understand ethical principles? Refer to the ASID code of ethics to help you find out. Each of the following ministudies profiles a specific action on the part of an interior designer that may violate the ASID code. After reading the facts of these occurrences, determine first what, if any, prohibited action occurred; then locate and name the relevant section of the ethical code you believe was violated. Assume that all designers are professional members of the group and therefore subject to the provisions of the code.

1. **Jonathan S**. This interior designer frequently selected paintings and other works of art for use in his projects from an art gallery in the city where he was located. The gallery owner would take the designer out for expensive meals several times a year to express her gratitude. One of the designer's clients, having observed the two having lunch, now seeks your opinion as to whether these free meals might be grounds for an ethics complaint against the designer. "Of course, he's going to choose objects from that particular dealer after all that schmoozing!" the client has told you.

2. **Audrey W**. This interior designer received a remarkable commission to fully plan and furnish the multifloor office space occupied by a prestigious law firm in downtown Chicago. To make the already substantial budget go even further, the designer ordered low-quality, cheaply plated brass desk lamps that somewhat resembled the custom-made solid brass models shown in the project presentation. "No one, and I mean no one, can tell the difference just by looking at them. By doing this, we now have more money in the budget for something else. This is

supposed to be a high-class project after all!" she told her team. Soon after final installation of the project, one of these lamps shorted out, igniting its shade and setting fire to the contents of an office, causing extensive damage. The law firm seeks your opinion about what ethical grounds it might have to pursue disciplinary action against the designer.

3. **Sidney B**. As a prominent interior designer in the Hancock Park section of Los Angeles, California, this designer usually has several large-scale residential projects under way at the same time. He frequently spends money given to him by one client toward completing another client's project. None of the designer's clients are aware of this practice, although they do complain about the length of time products take to arrive. They also do not understand why the designer can never answer their questions about the status of orders. "My method of paying for items and billing clients usually just works itself out. I wait for money to come in from clients, then figure out which projects need attention at the time," he has been heard to say to them. Nonetheless, one of his clients, tired of waiting for a rug that never arrived, asks your opinion about the conduct of this designer.

4. **Laura G**. Tired of the constant phone calls from clients asking about the status of their projects, this designer instituted call blocking on her telephone line. The client has not been able to reach the designer for several weeks either by phone or mail. The designer's home phone number was not listed with directory assistance. "I'll call her back when I know more myself," the designer has told her assistant. The client has asked your opinion about the designer's ethics based on these actions.

5. **Gail S**. Having purchased two étagères with her clients' funds, the designer determined that using both pieces would crowd usable floor space in the clients' den. So she retained one set of shelves for use in her own home. The clients were aware that the designer had ordered two of these items, but they were not aware that the designer had taken the other one for her own use. "Oh, the clients always understand these little things. After all, we are such good friends; besides it's part of my fee to take a piece now and then," the designer said to one of her staff. After the clients received the final bill and noticed the discrepancy, they have asked you whether the actions of this designer are "all right."

6. **Henry F**. This designer competed with another designer to obtain the same lucrative project. Unfortunately for Henry F., the other designer was selected. At a party, Henry F. told the clients who did not give him the job that he was "surprised" they chose the other designer. "I'd make sure you check every bill he sends you," he continued. "After all, you know he went broke last year and has to pay off all his debts somehow." It is true that Henry F.'s rival did file for bankruptcy protection, although not many people were aware of it. The client mentioned this conversation to Henry F.'s rival, but chose to ignore the comments. The rival interior designer asks you to comment on the ethics of Henry F.'s actions.

7. **Diane D**. This noted authority on commercial interior-space planning was shocked to learn that a contract project she was "sure" she would get was awarded to a design team she felt had little experience with offices. "You should have seen their last project," she told the client who hadn't offered her the job. "It was a disaster! Doors banging into each other, incorrect furniture and textile choices for a working environment. If I were you, I'd rethink your decision. Those guys don't know what they are talking about!" To prove her point, the designer showed

photographs of the other team's work. "Do you really want your office to look that that?" she asked. The client ultimately decided not to work with the original choice, then chose to hire this designer based on her representations. The team that was originally selected now asks you to consider whether the actions of Diane D. violated any ethical codes.

8. **George K**. This experienced contract interior designer, over the course of his twenty-year career, had dealings with most of the contractors in the city where he worked. The designer knew that one contractor in particular was in the habit of *skimming*, or taking a portion of the client's money from project funds for personal use. The designer chose to do nothing. "No one will know," he said. No one, in fact, ever learned whether the designer ever knew about the contractor's actions. Are there any ethical grounds for a complaint against the designer?

    What if in exchange for receiving a "cut" of the client's money that had been skimmed by the contractor, this designer would frequently modify client billing records to "clarify" billing discrepancies. "No one will know," he said. An accountant for one of the designer's clients did, however, discover the designer's actions. The client now wants to know whether there are any ethical grounds for filing a complaint against the designer.

9. **Roy G**. Because this designer's drafting and rendering skills are mediocre, he would frequently hire college architecture or interior design students with superior skills to execute work for him. He would then affix his own name and seal and present this work to clients as his own and use this work for his own projects. Unfortunately, in one such drawing, a student failed to include several important plumbing details that were not incorporated into the finished project. Correcting these deficiencies resulted in delay of the project installation. The plumbing contractor pointed out the omission to the client, who then asked the designer for an explanation. The designer could not give an adequate answer since he had barely looked at the finished drawing some time ago. The client asks you whether there might be any grounds for an ethical complaint against the designer.

10. **Angela W**. This residential interior designer did not think she had enough time to write out in elaborate detail all the tasks she had been hired to perform for a client, so she wrote only "living-room interior design consultation and realization" in the letter of agreement describing her scope of services for the project. The client understood the scope of services to mean that the designer was being paid to work on both the home's living room and entry area, since the two were not physically separated and were visually interrelated as well. The designer insisted that she was hired to work only on the living room interior design, and she refused to do any work related to the home's entry area unless the client paid her an additional fee. "After all," she told the client, "the living room is all that I agreed to do." The client has come to you to determine what, if any, ethical grounds might exist for filing a complaint against this designer.

    This same residential interior designer did not think she had time to specify in detail all the expenses related to the project, and so she did not include in the project budget sales tax estimates for the goods she ordered. Since the designer had not told the client she would have to charge sales tax in accordance with state law, and the client was not aware that sales taxes were imposed in this situation, the client was surprised to receive an additional invoice from the designer for many thousands of dollars in sales tax that the designer claimed was owed. The client refused to pay the sales tax. Angela refused to deliver the furniture to the client. The furniture then languished in a warehouse where it was damaged and rendered useless. The client asks you to determine if there are ethical grounds for filing a complaint against this designer.

11. **John G**. As a fully accredited interior designer and owner of The Antique Hutch, this designer frequently runs advertisements in which he describes the salespeople in his shop as experienced "interior designers." None of his sales staff received formal design training. A customer of the shop engaged the services of a sales clerk, believing him to be a designer and was dissatisfied with the outcome of the project. In your opinion, based on your knowledge of the ASID code of ethics, is there any justification for the client to file an ethics complaint? If so, should the client file the complaint against John G. or the sales clerk?

12. **Ann L**. Although recently out of school and having completed few design projects of any kind, this designer nonetheless accepted a commission to complete the interior of a 10,000-square-foot mansion. Although the designer felt swamped and was at times unsure of her ability to handle the project, it was completed. "How do you ever learn to handle a project and client relationships without just diving right in," the designer tells you. The clients, however, were unhappy that the project took as long to complete as it did and that it cost more than they initially had thought it would. They accepted the final results, but they have asked you to look into whether they might have grounds to file an ethics-based complaint against the designer.

    This designer also accepted a commission to complete the interior of her client's private jet plane. Neither the designer nor the client ever discussed her qualifications for undertaking such a project. The clients loved her design concept and considered that alone as their reason to hire her. The designer spent a great deal of time attempting to learn the many rules and regulations related to aircraft interior design. The finished jet, however, did not receive authorization from the appropriate authorities to fly until after her numerous mistakes were corrected. The clients were upset with the designer for the delays and considerable additional expenses caused by the many denials of authorization. They have asked you to look into whether they might have grounds to file an ethics-based complaint against the designer.

13. **Michael L**. This much sought-after Boston, Massachusetts, interior designer was commissioned to complete the interiors of a 25-room luxury hotel and restaurant in Provincetown, Massachusetts. The project involved both renovation work to an old house and a newly constructed addition for the restaurant. The clients, affluent Bostonians, were away on a trip when this designer made an executive decision and ordered all new, custom-milled windows for installation. Originally, he had specified only refurbishment of the original windows; but in the midst of the project, the contractor pointed out the window glazing was "just a mess" and would cost almost as much to fix as to replace. The new windows cost many thousands of dollars more than was originally budgeted for all the windows in the new facility. "I only do quality work. After all, I have my reputation on the line with every project," the designer told the clients when they returned. The clients have asked you to advise them on the ethics of this designer's actions.

14. **Christopher Q**. This designer sought to leave the prestigious firm with which he had been associated for nearly ten years. The design director of that firm refused

to allow the designer to take any drawings or renderings from the premises on the day his resignation letter was received. "They all belong to the firm, not to you," he was told by the director. This designer has come to you for an evaluation of the situation and for advice about the ethical grounds on which the firm could make such a decision.

15. **Adrian H.** This designer and his team were responsible for the execution of the interiors of the corporate headquarters of a large financial firm. The company president told the designer many details about his and other directors' questionable business practices. The designer swore to keep these details to himself. At the president's legal trial related to these practices, the designer was called to testify about what he knew about the alleged misconduct. The designer

---

NOTES FROM THE FIELD

My team received a request for proposal (RFP) for a large, multinational tech headquarters. The RFP was a very clear request for approach, methodology, résumés of the team members, organizational chart of both our team and our consultants, and a detailed fee outline for all parties. A very exciting opportunity and we were thrilled to participate.

This particular opportunity was approximately 200,000 RSF (rentable square feet) a good size project, anywhere in the world. Our submission was not to exceed 150 pages, and we had 3 weeks to prepare our submission in a bound format. We asked the project manager how many firms were being considered, to which they advised us ten firms were in competition for the work. The playing field of firms was made up of the world's best design practices, so being considered in this field was a privilege. That said, there are no points for second place when choosing a design firm in a competitive arena.

Four weeks after the submission date, we were informed that our team made the short list, and we were requested to come in for an interview. (Yippee!) We would have 1 hour to present to the client and the management team, why we were the best team for the job. These steps are considered typical in the process of selecting a firm; therefore, we had no cause for alarm just yet.

The interview went well! Our team all prepared diligently, and the team members practiced and rehearsed their roles; we were ready to answer any questions posed during the interview...with the exception of one. After our pitch, the PM called to inform our team, that it was down to us and one other firm. And, the only way for the client to get a true feel for how we would tackle a project challenge, was in a head-to-head design competition with the other firm,

with the expectation that we would come in and present our solutions to the client, ten days after the problem was posted. When we asked the question, was this a paid competition, the answer was, no. We were devastated. Why? The rules of our professional practice did not allow for us to perform noncompensated work. We would have had to withdraw from our most important opportunity of the year. So what did we do?

Our first step was to inform the PM that we could not accommodate this request and to explain why. It turns out that the PM was not aware that working without compensation was against our governing laws of licensed professional practice. Our next step was to ask whether the client would consider a paid competition, with a very modest stipend to cover basic costs and allow for us to complete the competition without compromising our professional position. The answer was, yes, with enthusiasm and apologies for the unknowing mistake. What did we learn? This was not only a good client but a great client, wanting to make things right and be transparent in the process.

Upon completion of the competition, we were awarded the work. Our hard work had paid off. The client learned instantly that our veracity and integrity when dealing with the craft of design was not to be compromised. Our peers that were not successful in landing the client, thanked our team for having the courage to ask, and their marketing costs were no longer lost. We knew if the client declined the request, we would lose our opportunity; however, if the client had declined the request for payment, our fees would have been at risk from the first day of the project, which is not where you want a project to start.

refused to testify, claiming that to do so would violate the designer's obligation of client confidentiality. Were the designer's actions ethically proper? Are there any limits imposed on confidentiality rules?

The study of ethics and concern about ethical violations have developed over many centuries, but the topics remain very much a contemporary matter. With this chapter's introduction, you have gained some understanding of the nature of ethical concepts and how they emerge in daily business. You also are aware that ethics are enforced not only by voluntary professional organizations, but also by the professional licensing and accreditation boards of those states that oversee the profession. Both groups as well as the general public will expect designers to practice according to ethical guidelines. And in the course of your work, you will frequently be called upon to make ethically based decisions.

Practical Activity

This chapter has been about ethics. It has indicated that mission statements can be much less formal than the codes by which groups make known their positions. How about individuals? Why couldn't individuals draft personal mission statements? Consider what you know about ethics and such statements after reviewing this chapter. Draft your own ethics-based mission statement, and explain how you intend to put its provisions into practice.

Review Questions

1. Define the role ethics play in business decision-making processes.

2. What incentives do professions have to enforce ethical goals among practitioners?

3. Name several influential writers on ethics. What are their contributions to modern ethical codes and rules?

4. In which areas of business does ethical decision making occur?

5. How does goodwill relate to the perceptions consumers have about businesses?

6. What is proprietary information, as distinguished from proprietary interests?

7. Explain the differences in meaning between *shall* and *may* as the terms are used in ethical codes.

8. What is a privileged communication as understood by the legal community? Does it apply to interior designers and their clients?

9. What does the concept of standing entail, and how does it relate to a complainant in an ethical-code dispute?

10. What are some penalties imposed for failure to adhere to codes of ethics and professional standards of conduct? How does the disciplinary process relate to enforcement of ethical codes and rules among interior designers. What actions may be brought against a designer who is not a member of a professional trade group?

YOU AND YOUR BUSINESS

PART 2

This part explores four domains of business knowledge relevant to the practice of interior design. These include an overview of the legal issues with which an interior designer should be familiar; managerial and financial accounting practices pertaining to the operation of an interior design business; design-office management; and the challenges involved in marketing interior design services:

Chapter 4. Understanding Law and Your Business: Identifies the steps you will take in the process of completing a design project and then defines the important legal issues related to those tasks of which you should be aware.

Chapter 5. Planning Your Business Finances: Defines financial objectives that are important for interior designers to consider as well as the financial concepts underlying those objectives.

Chapter 6. Managing Your Business: Discusses specific management objectives important to interior designers whether they own and manage their own design businesses or are employed by others.

Chapter 7. Promoting Your Work: Enables you to combine promotional or marketing skills with your own creative point of view.

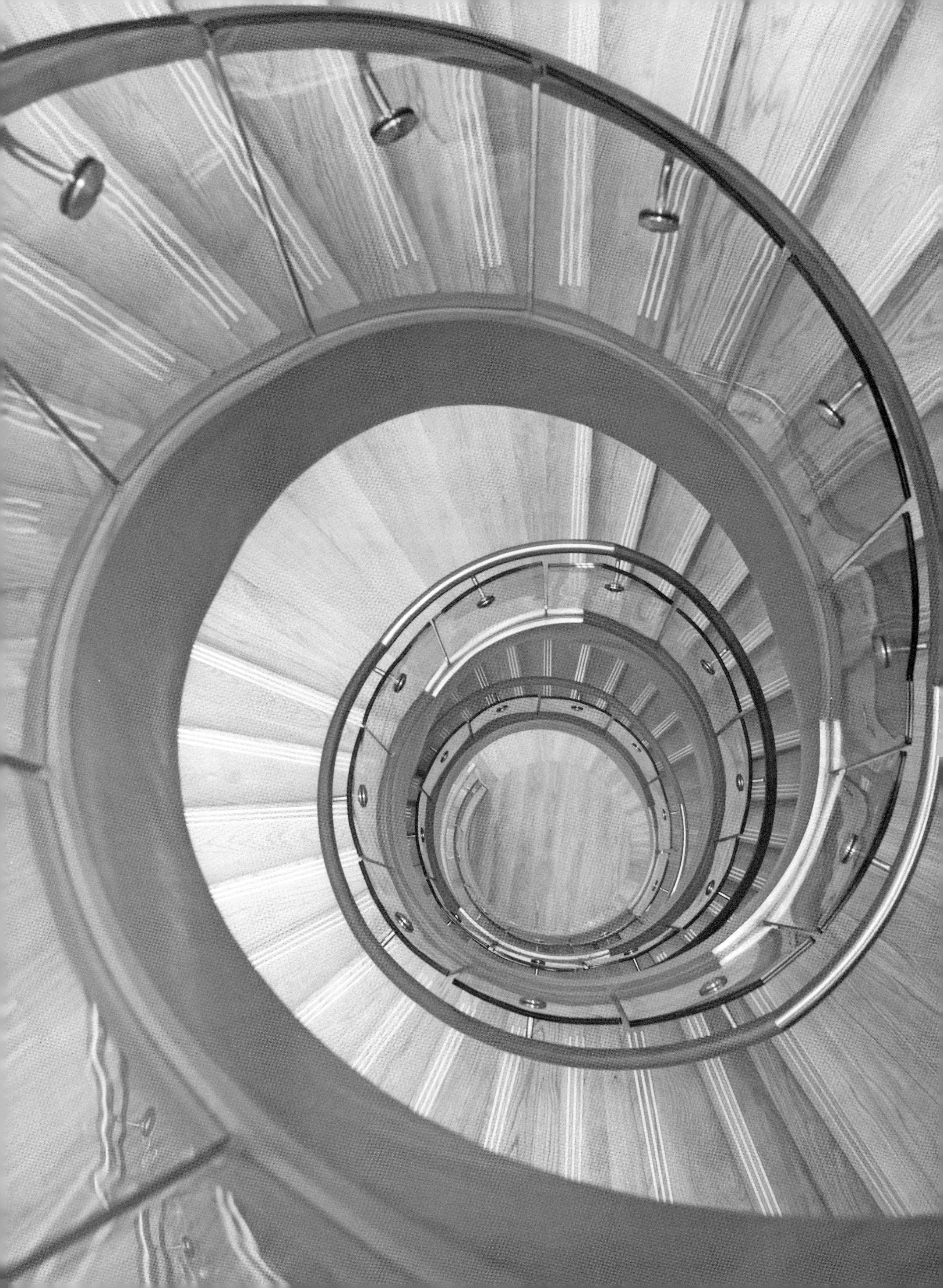

CHAPTER 4
UNDERSTANDING LAW AND YOUR BUSINESS

MENTOR MEMO

I am an interior designer, educated and licensed to practice at that craft. I am not a lawyer. I am not a doctor or a dentist; don't do surgery on the side or fix my own teeth. We would not venture into these fields unless we were educated to practice in them, and the same is true of those who practice law. But as stated, it's important to understand when you need to hire an outside professional to provide guidance and direction relative to the legal aspects of professional practice and the liabilities that lie within it. Knowing your limitations and parameters to practice within are critical. Having a team to support you when a situation presents itself that you cannot navigate (much like a doctor) is the same. Many working interior design professional has been caught in unknown legal territory. What happens if a client asks me to purchase a product and I receive the wrong product? What happens if one of the product I specify fails, and a person is injured? What do I do if a competitor calls to discuss industry fee benchmarking? Do I take the call? This chapter will give you the legal perspective on these very typical hurdles.

After reading this chapter, you will be able to

- **Understand the legal environment in which interior designers and their businesses operate;**
- **Recognize ways interior design businesses may be legally organized and operated;**
- **Describe several objectives of those starting businesses, including interior design businesses, and how laws impact those actions;**
- **Explain the agency relationship interior designers have with clients;**
- **Recognize the importance of contracts, elements required to form them, and how they impact the professional work of interior designers.**
- **Analyze and organize a process for personally understanding the legal environment of interior design businesses.**

A step-by-step approach to understanding the legal environment of interior design can make it seem less complex.

INTRODUCTION TO LAW AND YOUR BUSINESS

This chapter is important to you because it introduces legal concepts fundamental to both interior design as a profession and as a business. It further illustrates these topics with concise, useful definitions and uses examples from the actual day-to-day work of designers. To focus your study, this chapter contains two major sections. Part One describes legal issues related to the interior design profession at large and to businesses generally. Part Two focuses on legal issues arising from interior designers' actual, day-to-day work. The task-based approach used here is intended to assist those beginning their design practices identify and learn how and why legal concepts affect their professional endeavors and the businesses related to them.

A LEGAL DEFINITION OF THE PROFESSION AND WORK OF INTERIOR DESIGNERS

You have spent a great deal of time and effort learning intricacies of interior design and its practices. Step back, figuratively, from that necessary, but highly detailed perspective. Think about what designers "do." Using such a broad point of view, it is then possible to delineate basic tasks related to the practice of interior design and operation of businesses related to them. These include

Part One: Laws Related to the Interior Design Profession and Businesses in General
  Task One: Engage in the authorized practice of interior design;
  Task Two: Participate in a legally recognized business;
  Task Three: Recognize basic legal concepts related to general business activities.

Part Two: Laws Related to the Work of Interior Designers
  Task Four: Work on behalf of clients;
  Task Five: Enter into legally enforceable agreements with others;
  Task Six: Purchase products for resale to clients;
  Task Seven: Plan accessible spaces for safe and lawful use;
  Task Eight: Specify appropriate fixtures, furniture, and equipment for use.

Descriptions of legal concepts found in this chapter follow this task list. As you grow in your practice and as the profession evolves, keep them in mind. They can serve as a starting point—"Now, how will this task that I perform as a designer be legally affected?"—for structuring your own growing knowledge of legal issues affecting interior design.

PART ONE: LAWS RELATED TO THE INTERIOR DESIGN PROFESSION AND BUSINESSES IN GENERAL

Practicing interior designers and other businesspeople recognize the basic laws pertaining to their professions. As you might suspect, any list of legal subjects that might apply under such circumstances could potentially be endless. What follows, therefore, might best be thought template descriptions of general legal concepts to begin your own recognition process.

Most legal terms, concepts, and requirements may be referenced through Internet use no matter time or place.

Task One: Engage in the Authorized Practice of Interior Design

At present, twenty-four states have promulgated laws related to interior design. Previous discussion in this text focused mostly on legal requirements for entry into the profession. Those laws, however, also define the kinds of activities in which interior designers may and may not engage. Such descriptions of interior design activities are ways in which laws prescribe the professional limits within which interior designers must work. The remaining states, which have no laws specifically related to the practice of interior design, do, however, have laws related to the practice of architecture and can also prescribe qualifications for those who supervise construction projects. Whether a specific state has considered the professional activities of interior designers or, instead, defined the practice of architecture and construction supervision, states have imposed some form of legally prescribed limit on the practice of interior design. What are some of these limits, and why should a designer be aware of them?

Origins of Laws Related to the Practice of Interior Design

To begin, many of the state laws related to interior design track the definition of interior design promulgated by NCIDQ by including in their definitions the organization's stated intent of "protecting the health, safety, and welfare of the public." Furthermore, the interior design laws of several states, such as Arkansas and Illinois, note, as does NCIDQ, that an interior designer is one who is "qualified by education, experience, and examination." Many of these laws then specify those activities in which an interior designer may engage, again in language drawn from the NCIDQ model. For example, the laws of Connecticut specifically mention that interior designers perform "services relative to interior spaces, including: programming (and) design analysis." Other state laws—Michigan's, for example—note that interior design includes specifying "finishes, systems, furniture, furnishings, fixtures, equipment." For purposes of this discussion, it is important to focus on the legal language that establishes limits on the activities of designers.

Prohibition against the Practice of Architecture and Engineering

Paramount among these legal constraints is the prohibition against interior designers engaging in the practice of architecture by making specifications concerning load-bearing interior construction systems and components. One state, Louisiana, clarifies the activities specifically excluded from interior design in that state as follows:

> Interior design specifically excludes the design or the responsibility for architectural and engineering work except for specification of fixtures and their location within interior spaces. Interior design also specifically excludes construction of structural, mechanical, plumbing, heating, air-conditioning, ventilation, electrical or vertical transportation systems, fire rated vertical shafts in multistory structures, fire-related protection of structural elements, smoke evacuation, and compartmentalization, emergency sprinkler systems, and emergency alarm systems.

Many state laws even prohibit interior designers from working on other details. Some states, notably California, also allow designers to prepare only plans of a nonseismic nature, essentially prohibiting designers from specifying engineering-related work. Other states, such as Florida, specifically prohibit interior designers from engaging in engineering work. After you have identified a state or jurisdiction where you wish to practice, your next step is to determine whether any specific prohibitions exist regarding the practice of interior design and to understand those limits.

This knowledge is important to you because designers who practice outside legal limits can incur severe penalties such as possible incarceration or loss of license to practice, as would be the case in states such as New York, Illinois, and California. In addition, designers can incur financial loss in the form of penalties. Courts of law also do not permit interior designers to receive any financial compensation from a client when they were not legally permitted to do the work that they performed. In short, failure to understand the scope of permissible professional activities can seriously endanger a designer's career.

Interior design practitioners are gaining increasing stature as professionals. Many states now formally recognize the interior design profession and its practitioners through licensing and certification processes. Greater industry recognition by state governments will undoubtedly come to mean greater accountability to consumers for the actions of interior designers as well as greater educational supervision from state-controlled accreditation agencies. Whether your area of specialization is residential or commercial interior design, your clients will look to you to be up to date on laws that affect your industry. A greater understanding of laws related to the interior design profession undoubtedly will be required as a result of this expansion.

Other Legally Imposed Prohibitions on the Practice of Interior Design

Should a designer—who probably knows the project better than anyone else—supervise the very projects he or she conceives? Some states, such as California, permit only those licensed in that state as general contractors to supervise or inspect the progress of construction. Interior designers in such cases must also be licensed general contractors to engage in project supervision and related activities.

Designers can avoid this issue by requiring their clients to engage the services of a general contractor, but doing so requires that designers know beforehand whether they are legally permitted to supervise project construction. Many clients are not aware of such provisions, and designers who also do not know the laws risk loss of compensation and imposition of legal penalties. Performing prohibited activities may invite legal sanctions against the designer by state regulatory agencies as well as civil law actions brought by the designer's clients. Knowing how relevant laws define the tasks that constitute an interior designer's professional activities is a necessity.

Laws and the Globalization of Interior Design

The practice of interior design grows globally every day. Designers now source products from more distant countries. They also seek out clients across the world to develop new markets for their services. Through foreign-based contacts, designers give and take client referrals, forming their own worldwide professional network. Even this text came about through the collaboration of a Canadian designer and a U.S.-based author. International business practices and legal concepts involved in these and many other global enterprises are highly detailed and subject to constant change. What basic "take aways" should you have about these complex subjects, to understand their importance in your work and to take part in opportunities afforded by globalization of the interior design profession?

Think about what you will do as an interior designer. You may be called upon to work on a project sited in another country. How, for example, will you be able to complete installation of it? Likely, you, or your firm, will require the services of an expediter, contractor, local liaison, or other service provider there. International business is a shorthand term for cross-border practices and procedures intended to facilitate commerce. What business practices are followed in the project-site country? How do those differ from those in your country? Researching different commercial customs and interpersonal business etiquette and even gaining language facility can be essential for working with necessary local contacts. Enhancing international business skills such as these can also distinguish designers from other design practitioners.

Turning to your day-to-day work, consider how many of items you specify like textiles and case goods come from other countries. Consider further how many times you will have to inform clients of their ever-increasing costs and delays. Have you ever wondered why such items grow more expensive and time-consuming to obtain? Federal laws impose tariffs, or taxes, on many of these kinds of items. They also impose quotas, specific numerical limits on them. These add to the item's cost and length of time it takes to obtain that item. Another factor is customs regulations. Protecting consumers from foreign-made products that could be potentially dangerous or illegal and from ever-increasing international security concerns fall under the purview of U.S. customs regulations. Designers should have a general understanding of trade treaties, or agreements affecting commerce that are entered into by the president of the United States with the leaders of other countries, which often pertain to tariffs and quotas placed on the goods they specify. This area of law is heavily politicized and, as a result, changes frequently. As if the practice of interior design were not exciting enough, increased globalization of its scope and practices—and effects of so many laws on that trend— certainly makes it more so!

Task Two: Participate in a Legally Recognized Business

How many times have you heard references made to "corporations," "partnerships," or other forms of businesses? Who, or what, decides what kind of business will be established and how it will be organized and run? It is entrepreneurs, those who assume the (many) risks of starting and running businesses who make such decisions. These could be one person, or any number who engage in a professional and/or commercial venture. There are also many reasons why they might chose to open businesses, why they might wish to work alone, or with others. Perhaps one person wants to "go his own way" after working in a large firm. Maybe several people share a creative vision for the kinds of projects on which they wish to work. Economic necessity may bring others together.

Whatever the number of participants, or reasons they have for joining, entrepreneurs often have several objectives—besides being successful—that they seek for their businesses. These goals include

1. Keeping the business form simple and easy to understand;
2. Conserving time and money when starting and operating businesses;
3. Ensuring flexibility in starting, ending, or adding members to the business;
4. Protecting the assets (money and property) of those involved in the business;
5. Limiting the legal responsibilities of those involved in the business;
6. Minimizing the effects of taxes on both themselves and the business;
7. Preserving the business over long periods of time.

Keeping It Simple: Sole Proprietorships and Partnerships

Imagine you were ready to go out on your own, to own and operate a design studio doing what you—and only you—wanted to do professionally. As an individual entrepreneur, you, as others like you, often operate as a **sole proprietorship**. They may do so because of the *advantages* that the sole proprietorship offers.

1. They are easy to start and manage.
2. Sole proprietors keep all the profits that remain after paying expenses and taxes.
3. Sole proprietors report those profits as personal earnings. Accordingly, they are taxed only once at the individual sole proprietor's effective tax rate. Deductions for business expenses can, therefore, lower the taxes the sole proprietor pays.

On the other hand, with these advantages come some fairly serious *drawbacks* to sole proprietorships.

1. Sole proprietors are personally liable for the full amount of any and all debts, taxes, and legal judgments brought against or accruing to the business. Insurance payments add to the expenses sole proprietors incur;
2. Sole proprietors are self-employed, a status requiring them to file specific income tax forms detailing their business's finances. Thus, the sole proprietor needs to keep accurate financial records while attending to the business. Self-employed individuals are also required to pay self-employment taxes and are not eligible for unemployment benefits.
3. Sole proprietors must multitask well. Not only must they know how to attract new business while carrying out existing work, but they also must maintain operational

Just you and your abilities will be responsible for your success as a sole proprietor.

aspects of the business, which include paying income taxes quarterly and maintaining financial records and their office facilities—all at the same time.
4. Because the sole proprietor *is* the business, it usually ends with the death of the sole proprietor unless he or she is able to convey it to another person or business entity before death, a goal that may not be realistically possible.

You and a friend think it might be economically advantageous to work together, to operate a design studio with, perhaps, a connected retail store. How might you do so in as simple a way as possible? Two or more individuals who prefer a type of business similar to a proprietorship usually consider forming a **general partnership**. This form has some of the same *benefits* as sole proprietorships.

1. General partnerships are fairly simple ventures to start. Although written agreements between the partners are prudent, they are not required.
2. Provided all the general partners agree, management and control of the business can be easily accomplished. The success of general partnerships relies on how well members agree regarding business decisions and on their mutual trust of one

CHAPTER 4 UNDERSTANDING LAW AND YOUR BUSINESS • 69

another. Profits earned by partnerships are taxed at the individual tax rates of the general partners.

There are *disadvantages* to general partnerships.

1. General partners are personally liable for the full amount of any and all debts, taxes, and legal judgments brought against or accruing to the partnership. Even if one partner were not responsible for or involved in the activity causing the debt, expense, or injury, he or she would still be legally and financially responsible for it.
2. Should the assets of the partnership be insufficient to satisfy partnership obligations, those who seek financial satisfaction may look to the partners' personal assets.

General partnerships dissolve, or cease to exist, at the death or incapacity of one of the members. This could create problems if that partner's assets are closely tied to the business.

Assessing Merits of Other Partnership Forms

Interior design businesses are expensive, to begin, to operate, and to keep up to date. In short, everything related to them requires money. Through contacts such as former clients, you may know someone interested in investing in an interior design business with you at the creative helm. However, this benefactor does not wish to be in a "full" partnership with you. How might you both work together under such circumstance?

Establishing some kinds of businesses may be likened to designing complex interior spaces.

Limited partnerships enable entrepreneurs to obtain financial backing from others without forming a general partnership. These backers are usually referred to as **limited partners**, whereas the entrepreneur is usually called the **general partner**. Unlike a general partnership, limited partners may contribute funds to the business without making management decisions. A limited partner is allowed to share in profits earned by the limited partnership and has responsibility for the partnership's obligations only for the amount of money the limited partner has contributed to the business. Limited partners do not, therefore, have the virtually unlimited exposure to risk that they would in a general partnership. Such an arrangement is advantageous for the limited partner, but the general partner, or partners, are each liable for partnership obligations as if they were in a regular general partnership—that is, unlimited personal exposure for all obligations of the partnership!

Perhaps the time will come when you want to expand your practice to include more than interior design services, but products as well. What business form might enable you to do that and why? Many entrepreneurs form **joint ventures**. These come about when two or more individuals or businesses enter into binding agreements under the terms of which these members consent to share financial and other obligations necessary to complete their undertakings. After accomplishing their objectives, or after they agree, the joint venture ends.

This form of doing business offers opportunities to bring about projects that might not otherwise be possible. Imagine, for example, that you wanted to start a line of home accessories but did not have the substantial funding or extensive manufacturing contacts necessary to do so. A joint venture arrangement with an individual, or company, with both might be appropriate. This form of business is complicated and usually requires expert advice regarding the correct structure and tax consequences.

Protecting the Business and Minimizing Risks: The Corporate Business Form

You know the "big name" design firms and perhaps are familiar with how they operate. Likely, you have noticed such large firms do not seem at all like the kinds of businesses described so far. What form of business are they? Most are corporations. Even though these are often perceived as only being large businesses, corporations may also be as small and familiar as the local dry-cleaning establishment you patronize. A corporation's defining characteristic is not its size but rather its separation from those involved in its operation. In other words, a **corporation** is a legal being or entity in its own right, a business entirely separate from those organizing and running it. You will recall founders of sole proprietorships and partnerships are one and the same; when one owner dies, the business ceases to exist. The same is not true for corporations. After they are established and given that they are run correctly, corporations may continue after their founders' deaths. Thus, corporations are said to have potentially perpetual life.

The corporate form of business organization requires the greatest allocation of time, money, and specialized expertise to originate. Those who wish to use the corporate form to organize business ventures must first prepare and then file a document called the **articles of incorporation**. Usually, the assistance of an attorney is required in order to prepare this and other documents related to corporations. Once completed and duly signed by officers/directors of the new corporation, the articles are filed for review with a state governmental officer charged with overseeing corporations.

Organizers are attracted to the corporate form because it allows them to limit their personal financial responsibility for the business. This means those who start corporations and those who are stockholders are generally not responsible for paying money to run the corporation or to satisfy legal claims; they are responsible for paying only the amount of money they have invested in the corporation. Failure to properly form (and legally run) corporations risks jeopardizing the very benefits making that business form attractive. For their investments, stockholders—also called shareholders—receive dividend income, or a portion of the corporation's profits, based on the percentage of the corporation they own. At interior design firms operated as corporations, annual distributions of financial dividends to shareholders/principles are much anticipated events!

Blending Advantages of Partnerships and Corporations

A business organized as a **limited liability company (LLC)** is, essentially, a blend of partnerships and corporations. This means that organizers are able to protect their personal assets from claims (as with corporations) and engage in fewer organizational and operational formalities (as would be the case in partnerships). Many small interior design firms operate in this business form for those reasons.

Task Three: Recognize Federal Laws Related to General Business Activities

The few U.S. federal laws set out here are but a sampling of the vast numbers of laws and legal concepts related to business activities. To be sure, these laws may seem far removed from the practice of interior design. However, their applicability is widespread among all businesses. Moreover, they are important to interior designers because the laws can affect how designers work with other designers and determine prices of goods they sell to clients. These laws include the Sherman Antitrust Act and the Robison-Patman Act.

The **Sherman Antitrust Act of 1890** sought to curb monopolies. These occur when large companies exercise their considerable economic power over smaller, less powerful ones, in order to prevent them from beginning, or remaining in business. Large companies usually attempted to do so through agreements among themselves that restrained the abilities of others to "trade," or operate. In the past, larger companies were able to control prices to make competition from others unprofitable. Suppose two or more interior design companies agreed among themselves to operate only in certain geographic locations. In particular, these entities agreed not to operate in areas where any other parties to that same agreement operated. The reason behind this agreement was that they did not want to compete with each other for customers. With less competition from other businesses, those companies already established in a given area could reap enormous economic benefits.

Another example of how this act applies to interior design concerns price fixing. At the time of the original act, many manufacturers required merchants to sell goods they made only at prices set by the maker, a practice known as *price fixing*. The Sherman Antitrust Act prohibited this practice. As a result, manufacturers may now only suggest retail prices at which their goods may be sold; interior designers, acting as merchants when they sell goods to clients, may ignore manufacturers' prices.

Think about this: What if a group of designers began talking among themselves about the fees and commissions they charged their respective clients and, specifically, how there should be a standard, set percentage, or at least a minimum dollar amount, clients in that area should be charged for interior design services. Might such discussions give rise to a Sherman Antitrust Act complaint? Real estate professionals and auction houses (both of which compete among themselves for business and charge variable rates of commission) continue to grapple with this Sherman Antitrust Act concern.

Another federal law based on the Sherman Antitrust Act is the **Robinson-Patman Act**, passed in 1936. Of importance to interior designers is a provision of that act that prohibits price discrimination among merchants. Simply put, a merchant, such as a manufacturer, must charge another merchant, such as a store or even an individual interior designer selling goods to the public, the same price for a specific item that they charge any other merchant for that same product. A manufacturer, in other words, cannot favor merchants and charge beneficial prices to one that would result in less-favored merchants being disadvantaged.

Creativity is your stock in trade, but so, too, is your professionalism. Even though only lawyers have the ability to keep up with the latest federal legal developments affecting businesses, design practitioners should be at the very least aware of general legal topics such as these in order to provide competent design services for their clients. Doing so not only enhances designers' professional abilities but further enables them to assist legal advisers should a controversy develop.

PART TWO: LAWS RELATED TO THE WORK OF INTERIOR DESIGNERS

Are you curious about how laws relate to the work of designers? Consider the following recap of an actual project and the legal issues that arose. Look closely at what the designer and team did to solve problems. This will introduce you to the extent to which laws and legal concepts can and will relate to you as an interior designer.

NOTES FROM THE FIELD

One of my clients hired me to complete the design of its new headquarters. In its early days, everyone was excited; the project was over 100,000 square feet, with a great budget to design within. The building in which my client signed the lease was already under construction with four of the seven floors already poured. The base building contractor was not the interior contractor, and we knew going into the project that there would be multiple trades working in tandem on site—not unusual when the schedule is compressed. Our team of designers and engineers, worked around the clock to get the design done and the drawings in for the building permit. The permit would be ready in 21 days, and during this wait window, the contractor intended to preorder materials and start the submittal process—basic studs and drywall—so that we could hit the ground running when the permit was ready.

The client was concerned because the time necessary to wait for a permit would undermine the scheduled move in. As a team, we had communicated with the client explaining how the contractor intended to expedite the schedule; there was a plan in place. The client, however, felt differently and directed the contractor to begin work on site without a permit. This fact alone is worth note: however, that is not the entire story. This building was brand new and was not yet enclosed. The floors and steel well under way, but the curtain wall (windows) were not installed, and the rainy season was upon us. Neither the client nor the contractor informed us, the design team, that work had begun. We learned of this at the kickoff meeting, walking into a partially finished office interior, complete with walls and carpet but otherwise open to the elements. I was younger in my career when this occurred, and I did not understand all aspects of the liability, but I did know that rainwater, carpet, and exposed drywall are not a happy combination.

Immediately, I informed my supervisor, and one of our licensed architects was sent to site to photograph the conditions. Second, we informed the client in writing that the products that were subject to the elements were now at risk. Any mold or dampness absorbed into the walls could undermine the products performance. The firm's legal advisers reviewed the letter and were copied on all correspondence. The client accepted responsibility, acknowledged the risks, but proceeded anyway.

One Year Later
Black started to appear at the corners of the walls, and the flooring adhesives had failed due to moisture. Unfortunately, the client felt the design team had failed to produce good specifications to prevent this from happening. A defensive response, that is not uncommon in our industry, therefore you must document along the way. In this case, and, after a lengthy and expensive forensic evaluation, a third party determined the design team was not at fault, and the failure of the product was due to exposure to the elements and moisture on the job site. Suffice it to say, the cost to evaluate the conditions, defend our position, and document the process was not something planned for, but it was required. The client's costs (which where their costs) to temporarily relocate, replace all products and, again, renovate were staggering.

There is no question that the entire situation was avoidable. What is of note is the importance of documentation at the time the situation occurred in preparation for the future. In this case, there was a very unhappy ending; however, had the practice not been legally prepared to address at the time of incident, the insurance and costs to our practice would have been devastating. Without question, every opportunity to warn the client of the risks they were taking on was documented, and that documentation was in writing. Clients will sometimes take matters into their own hands, but the appropriate reaction should always be documented.

What happened next in this case? Everyone involved (especially the contractor) learned a valuable lesson, and the entire design team and engineers made the decision to assist the client, address the problem, at cost (meaning reduced fees). This client was gracious and welcomed our assistance and guidance for *every* decision going forward.

Task Four: Work on Behalf of Clients

It seems obvious to state that interior designers work for clients. But how might that relationship be formally defined in legal terms, and what importance does such a definition hold for you? Designers become **agents**, or those who owe duties or obligations to others, of their clients when they agree to perform interior design services and related activities. Such services often include those with which you are familiar, like rendering professional services or purchasing merchandise. Clients, under agency laws, are considered **principals**, or those to whom duties or obligations are owed. The agency relationship may begin when both enter into written contracts for designers' services. It may also begin less formally when the designer begins work without formal written agreements. No matter how an agency relationship comes about, legal duties exist governing the relationship of the parties to each other. Agents (designers) are traditionally considered to owe their principal (clients) such duties as

1. Using reasonable diligence and skills in the performance of their activities;
2. Working obediently for the principals and their interests;
3. Informing the principal of all matters related to the agency relationship;
4. Expressing loyalty to the principals and their interests.

Interior designers are creative professionals and agents of their clients able to anticipate and resolve issues related to space and its use.

Similarly, principals (clients) have been found to owe their agents (designers) duties like

1. Providing reasonable compensation for the services of the agent;
2. Repaying expenditures the agent incurred during the course of the agency relationship;
3. Indemnifying, or providing financial compensation, to anyone injured as a result of the agent's action while the agent acted within the scope of the agency relationship.

In the event that a court of law finds one party to have failed to satisfy its respective duty or duties to the other, the court may award the injured party monetary damages. In the usual course of business, agency relationships arise from and are detailed in enforceable written agreements or contracts.

MENTOR MEMO

Here are some insights from a practitioner. First, always limit your risks and reverse engineer your process, assuming something can and will go wrong. For example, what do I do if a product arrives on site that is not correct? Your process should be designed in such a way that you sign off on a sample submittal. Be clear; ask the manufacturer how big and specific the submittal will need to be (i.e., an actual cut from the bolt of fabric ordered); and if you have multiple orders, request a cutting from every bolt to ensure dye lot consistency. If you have specified a lot of product, fly there so that you can see it and physically sign for it to ensure it's not switched. Protect your client's investment. You must be clear in your specifications, to adhere to the manufacturer's recommended installation, application, and environmental concerns when installing any product.

Task Five: Enter into Legally Enforceable Agreements with Others

Given all the complexities of any interior design project, how do designers define their agency relationship with clients? For that matter, how do they define their working relationship with vendors, service providers and others? Something more than an "understanding" seems necessary. Designers, like other businesspeople, use contracts, legally enforceable agreements that form the backbone of most professional and commercial relationships. This discussion of the basic tenants of contracts is intended to set the stage for subsequent discussions in this text related to agreements between designers and clients and designers and other professionals.

At the onset, they should be distinguished from "contract documents," which are referred to by architects, interior designers, and contractors. Contract documents are *all* the many individual pieces of design projects, such as drawings, plans, specification sheets, and schematic representations; they are a compilation of drawings, notes, invoices, and the like. Note that businesspeople frequently use the term "the contract document" to mean the actual written agreement.

What Makes a Contract a Contract?

You will note contracts are described not as just agreements but as enforceable ones. This means courts of law can impose penalties against one of the parties involved should they not do—or in legal terms, "perform"—as they indicated they would. Before, however, discussing performance and penalties, what makes an agreement a legally enforceable contract?

Contracts are determined to exist when courts find the following elements present: all the parties to it have legal capacity, that is they are of sufficient legal age and mental abilities, the contract is for a legal purpose, an offer by one party to perform (or not perform) not a specified activity, an acceptance of that offer by another party, and the exchange of consideration between the parties. An **offer** is said to exist when courts determine there was an indicated intent on the part of the parties to enter into a binding agreement. Examples of offers might include a designer offering to complete a project for a client or a vendor volunteering to sell a piece of furniture to the designer for a specified price. **Acceptance** of an offer may be found when the parties have agreed to each and every term of it, with no additional or different change or condition.

The requirement of **consideration** is not exactly what you might think. Consideration here means a "bargained for" exchange between the parties. For example, after a designer receives a fee, consideration is said to have passed, the agreement bargained for, and, assuming the parties are legally able to enter into contractual relationships, a contract for the interior designer's services exists.

There are two distinctions to make about contracts. A **unilateral contract** occurs when an offer is accepted through the actions of the other. The performance of the requested act serves as an acceptance of the offer. Alternatively, a **bilateral contract** is said to result where one party makes a promise (usually when a designer promises to complete a project), and, as a result of that first promise, another party promises to do (or not to do) something, as the client agrees to pay the designer for completing the project. Most contracts for interior design services are bilateral in nature.

Do Contracts Have to Be in Writing and Signed to Be Valid?

Are contracts required to be in writing to be enforceable? The answer is an unequivocal maybe! For transactions involving many real estate activities, for the sale of goods over $500, for certain offers such as those to pay someone else's debts or to marry someone, or for agreements "not to be performed within one year of (their) making," writing is universally required. On the other hand, oral agreements may be enforceable agreements if contract terms can be established in court through other facts. What does this mean? Consider a statement made by a designer—heard by witnesses—in which the designer offered services to work on an individual's entire 10,000-square-foot house for only $10,000. Such might be enforceable against the designer if the person to whom that offer was made accepted it.

A question related to the writing requirement is whether a contract needs to be signed in order to be valid. From early times to present, courts have generally held that a signature is required for a contract to be valid. Suppose you begin your interior design work without having your clients sign a contract indicating their agreement for you to do so. In such cases, you may face a lengthy and expensive court battle to receive any design fees you might have earned, should any client fail to recognize the existence of that agreement and refuse to pay your fees.

What Happens When Something Goes Wrong with a Contract?

A valid contract had been formed; yet performance either did not occur or was materially different from what was agreed upon. In other words, someone, or some event caused a **breach of contract**. This means the contract terms, as agreed upon by the parties, were not met in some way. The party who did not receive what they bargained for usually seeks contract damages. These may take two forms: financial compensation for the economic losses the nonbreaching party suffered or court-ordered completion of the performance. An order of specific performance in which the party that breaches the contract is compelled to carry out the actions initially agreed upon is rarely imposed in the case of contracts for services, which would characterize contracts for interior design work. Awards of specific performance are rare and are usually applied in such instances as when real property is involved. Usually, monetary damages are awarded in instances involving services. If monetary damages are the legally preferred method of remedying contract breaches, how are they determined?

Monetary damages may compensate the injured party for the actual amount of financial loss. These are known as actual damages. On the other hand, the court, if sufficiently shocked at the actions of the breaching party, may impose punitive damages, an amount additional to actual damages and sufficiently large enough to set an example for others to not act as the breaching party did. Other forms of economic damages exist as well, notably **nominal damages**, in which a court makes a token, relatively small award to the injured party, usually in cases where any form of compensatory damages would be speculative or conjectural.

This overview of contracts sets the stage for other discussions related to agreements for the sale of goods (see below) and for those related to working with vendors and service providers in subsequent chapters.

Task Six: Purchase Products for Resale to Clients

Many designers purchase products, such as furniture and textiles, from trade sources such as manufacturers and other vendors. When they do, they employ contracts. In these instances, however, such agreements are mostly governed by a different set of laws than those related to their agreements with clients. The latter are controlled by *case law*, or legal understandings that have come about over time, as reflected in court holdings. However, when the sale of goods or merchandise is involved, provisions of Section 2 of the Uniform Commercial Code (UCC) will usually apply. All states, except Louisiana, have merchandise sales laws based on the UCC.

The goal of UCC laws is to facilitate commercial transactions, to make, in this example, the sale of goods easier between sophisticated, professional buyers and sellers. Most of the provisions of the UCC follow the same legal principles as the case law governing other matters. Several provisions of the UCC are important for interior designers, especially those who purchase goods from vendors.

1. Under the terms of the Uniform Commercial Code, contracts for the sale of goods over the amount of $500 must be in writing to be enforced (UCC 2-201 (1));
2. A common problem confronting designers concerns the actual receipt of goods for which the designer contracted. In many instances, the merchandise received is not the merchandise ordered. For example, one type of fabric received is not of the type ordered by the interior designer; perhaps the one received is of a different quality or has different characteristics. Such goods are considered under the code to be *nonconforming* with what was ordered. What should a designer do in such a case? The code provides buyers with a specific right to inspect goods that are delivered before accepting or rejecting them (UCC 2-513). Furthermore, in the event those goods are found to not be in compliance with what was agreed upon, the buyer may then reject all or any part of the nonconforming order received (UCC 2-601). To avoid having to pay for any nonconforming items, the designer must then notify the seller of the nonconformity and of their rejection of them.

Task Seven: Plan Accessible Spaces for Safe and Lawful Use

What should interior designers understand about the law related to planning accessible spaces for safe, lawful use? Two important considerations are the **Americans with Disabilities Act (ADA)**, which applies nationwide, and local fire and safety codes.

Interior Designers and the Americans with Disabilities Act

In 1992 Congress enacted the Americans with Disabilities Act. This legislation sought, among other goals, to make public and some private buildings more accessible to all individuals regardless of their physical abilities. In other words, it sought to create barrier-free public environments that were as accessible to handicapped individuals as to the nonhandicapped. Title III of the act sets forth building or retrofitting requirements for those areas it describes as "places of public accommodation." This section of the act includes new construction requirements for public places built after its effective date and also includes what the act terms requirements for "readily achievable" modifications to preexisting places of public accommodation. This legislation has particular application to nonresidential interior designers, since the ADA does not apply in all but a few nonresidential spaces. Private residences, for example, are excluded from the purview of the law, as are those "commercial facilities" that although nonresidential in nature, are not open for access to the general public.

Provisions of the ADA are enforced by the U.S. Department of Justice; however, state and municipal governments throughout the United States have adopted the ADA regulations in their own codes or have made the ADA applicable through local passage of enabling laws. In general, an individual claiming a Title III violation must first file a complaint with the U.S. Department of Justice, which will then initiate an investigation and, if appropriate, attempt to negotiate an agreement with those against whom the complaint is brought. Should attempts to reach a settled agreement fail, then suit may be brought in federal court by the Department of Justice on behalf of the claimant to compel compliance with provisions of the law. As a practical matter, every effort should be made to comply with the provisions of the ADA, even in those instances where an exception might exist. In some instances, individual business owners have claimed that ADA-required modifications to their existing facilities are too costly and thus not—in the language of the ADA—"economically feasible." Even without suing establishments in federal court for their failure to comply with the ADA, there have been instances where disabled customers have protested outside places such as restaurants and bars to raise the public's awareness of the problem and to seek the owners' compliance.

Interior Designers and Building and Fire-Safety Codes

Municipalities pass various codes related to the safe occupancy of structures within their jurisdiction that should be of interest to interior designers. These codes are usually classified as building and fire-safety codes. Compliance with these codes is necessary in order to obtain a final certificate of occupancy or other authorization that the structure complies with code. Failure to conform to these codes carries with it penalties from heavy fines to closing the premises for public use. Professional competency requires designers to know and understand relevant building and fire-safety codes. They must also be aware of the legal consequences for failing to correctly apply their provisions.

The challenge for the interior designer is to keep abreast of changes in the requirements imposed by these local rules. Each city or town has its own codes describing the types of construction techniques and materials that may be used. Currently, local building codes may be based on any of several sets of codes that have been used throughout the United States. Existing codes are drawn from three sets of building codes: Uniform Building Code; Standard Building Code; and the Basic/National Building Code. Recently, the International Building Code (IBC) has been promulgated with an eye toward achieving building-code uniformity. At present, this new model of code has not been adopted. Code manuals may be fairly easy to obtain from building sources and online. These codes apply to structures within the jurisdictional purview of the relevant municipality. For that reason, an interior designer's library should contain up-to-date codes that apply to the locations of their ongoing projects.

Task Eight: Specifying Appropriate Fixtures, Furnishings, and Equipment for Use

Designers research and choose products for projects. What legal responsibilities do designers have to clients, even to the general public, regarding items they specify? Put another way, what laws might apply if designers' choices damage property or injure others?

Tort Law and the Standard of Care in Interior Design

Designers, as with all professionals, are considered to have a legal duty to clients. That means working as any other reasonable and prudent interior designer would work. This duty is furthermore referred to by law experts as designers' standard of care. The area of civil jurisprudence governing duties owed by professionals to others and their standard of care is referred to as **tort law**. How might tort law apply to designers? Suppose a practitioner disregarded basic principles of interior design and product safety such as those you have learned. The project that resulted was determined to be unusable for the client's needs, not in reasonable conformity to any objective standard prevailing among interior designers in that area, and even caused obvious injury. Tort laws provide remedies, known as damages when practitioners are found to have acted negligently. From this description, you can see negligence-related tort laws cover actions where a duty, or duties, owed to others was breached, that is, not met. Moreover, such failure was the direct proximate cause of an obvious or foreseeable injury to property or persons. Monetary damages are usually awarded to satisfy those who successfully bring negligence claims.

Implications of Tort Law and the Work of Interior Designers

Negligence does not arise merely because a client does not like a designer's final work product. The project at completion may not be what the client expected, or hoped for, in which case the client and designer should attempt to find an acceptable resolution through additional negotiation. Standards of taste and beauty vary from person to person and thus are not easily defined even by a court of law. Rather, what courts usually consider in tort law would be whether the work actually carried out by the designer was done in a manner consistent with interior design industry standards as evidenced by the work standards of other designers in that area. Although the finished project, completed strictly in compliance with specifications, might be unacceptable to the particular taste of the client, that same project might not have been produced in a negligent manner if it was found to have been completed according to the professional standards prevailing among other interior designers in the community. For example, were the specifications appropriate for that type of project? Did the designer adequately inform the clients of any risks associated with those specifications, including issues about their installation? Communication between designer and client is necessary to facilitate a project's successful completion. In the modern world of business, that communication now includes written documentation of virtually every aspect of a project, whether there is good news or bad news to report. A history of careful communication should be of assistance in documenting that the interior designer conformed to the necessary standard of care.

Defenses to Claims of Negligence

"Venetian" plaster wall finishes, glossy tile floor treatments, wrought-iron light fixtures incorporating open-flame, lit candles are several popular interior design details that many practitioners select. Even though such specifications might work well in low-traffic, residential environments, how might they fare in public spaces? What if a client insisted—as one actually did—on installation of these features, say, to make an al fresco, Tuscan-themed public dining area seem like a private Mediterranean villa? Later, faced with cracked, crumbling walls, patrons with broken ankles and legs, and safety citations from the local fire marshal, the client makes a legal claim against the designer. Question: was the designer negligent to include them, even when demanded by the client? Any determination as to outcome would depend on what actually happened as the designer and the client carried out the project. Did, for example, the designer attempt to educate and inform the client (in writing) of risks involved with such delicate, inappropriate specifications? In other words, did the client assume the risk these features might incur, even going so far as to consent to them with full knowledge? Negligence claims may be defended against by those to whom they are brought with findings of assumption of the risk. If so, those bringing negligence claims, **plaintiffs**, would be denied compensation from the party against whom the claim was brought, defendants.

Another defense to a claim that a designer acted negligently arises when defendants can prove that the plaintiffs were in some way negligent in their actions as well. This defense is known as **contributory negligence**. Assume an interior designer was sued for negligence because the plaintiff asserted the designer's actions resulted in the delay of a project's completion and that such delays were the cause of damage to the client. For example, the client paid more to complete the project because of the designer's actions. To prevail on a contributory negligence defense, an interior designer would have to show that the clients themselves acted in some way that was negligent. Some examples of such negligence might be failure on the part of the client to review and approve work in a timely manner or make payment for that work to keep the project going. Most states have adopted **comparative fault** laws, which apportion percentages of fault as a means of calculating damages. Under these laws, the percentage of fault of each side would be determined, and damages, if any, would be awarded based on that determination.

In an effort to discourage negligence claims before they are brought, many businesspeople attempt to limit possible liability for perceived negligence by making oral or written statements claiming they take no, or only very limited, responsibility for their actions. Signs posted in parking garages stating that the garage owner is not responsible for damage to cars parked in that garage is a common example. Attempts to limit the liability of professionals, however, may take many sophisticated forms, such as written clauses to that effect in contracts. In general, attempts to limit possible damages accruing from the actions of a professional found to be negligent are not viewed favorably by courts, and the use of disclaimers and limits on liability may ultimately prove futile. Professionals are often seen as having better bargaining positions than their clients because of their education and experience and, thus, are more likely to offer agreements that are more favorable to themselves.

Product Liability and Deceptive Trade Practice Laws

In addition to negligence, other types of civil tort laws arose with the idea of protecting the public. These more specific consumer protection laws came about within the last several decades through the passage of specific codes—groups of related laws—affecting those who make or sell merchandise or other consumer goods. Most states now have some form of consumer protection law designed to protect the general public by defining what standards must be followed when making or selling certain types of products or when making certain representations in the course of conducting business. A design professional should be aware of two of these laws, known in general as product liability and deceptive trade practice laws.

Product liability laws protect consumers from those items that are deemed, according to the language in most statutes, to be defectively designed, manufactured, or marketed. Defectively designed products are considered to be inherently dangerous. Although these products may well perform the task for which they were intended, some characteristic of the defective product makes it dangerous to use. Manufacturing defects occur when the item is made, whereas defects in marketing are considered to have occurred when the consumer is provided with improper instructions and warnings.

Product liability refers to the liability for damage of any party involved from the chain of manufacture to final selling of a product. Possible affected parties in this liability scheme include the maker of components used in the product, the entity assembling the product, and the wholesaler and store selling the product to the consumer. Interior designers, since they function as wholesalers selling the product as part of their services, would likely be included in a product liability action. If you break product liability laws, it is considered to be a *strict liability* offense; finding a product to be defective triggers liability on the part of an individual or a company selling these products. As part of their product knowledge, designers should be aware of current legal news and technical information relating to the products they specify for use. The use of particular products should be avoided if any court, even one in a different jurisdiction, has determined under product liability law that a particular product is dangerous.

Implications for Designers

Licensing and product development can be one way in which a local interior designer may branch out to attract a wide, possibly international, audience. However, designers who take an active role in the creation and development of products should be aware that they and any manufacturer who employs them to design these items—or that designers themselves employ to produce them—may be liable for injuries sustained by a consumer, even if that consumer misuses the product in some way. There is no effective way to completely design and produce a product that will never be linked to an injury. Rather, designers should make every effort to ensure that the products they specify are in accordance with the standards prevalent for all such products used in the industry.

Designers' product knowledge should include awareness of the latest legal and technical developments in order to know which products to avoid. Furthermore, any contract between a manufacturer and designer should include language describing as completely as possible how the parties will defend themselves against any such lawsuit, knowing that both parties would likely be called as defendants in a product liability action. Interior designers who might be involved in product development should consult an attorney specifically about how their jurisdiction's product liability laws could be invoked.

Deceptive Trade Practices Laws

Is the item specified for use in a project an authentic, swing-arm Hansen lamp, or a "Hansen-style" one? Do textiles selected have the flammability characteristics designers claim they have? Representations designers make, either orally or in writing, about a particular object or item they specify may be the deciding factor in the clients' decisions to authorize an item's purchase or use. In the case of antiques, rare decorative objects, and works of art, the representations made about an object may be as alluring as an item itself. Preventing false or misleading statements made by any seller of goods is the intent behind **deceptive trade practices** legislation. Many states have adopted some form of these laws, which encompass a wide variety of business practices. In essence, these laws seek to prohibit the dissemination of statements that are found to be false concerning such matters as the quality or other characteristics of consumer goods offered or sold, false representations concerning the quality of a competitor's goods, or false reasons for sale prices. The determination that a businessperson has engaged in deceptive trade practices carries with it in many states large monetary damage penalties.

Common sense might conclude that there should be some liability on the part of a designer who intends to deceive clients by making false statements. However, what should happen in cases where a designer unwittingly passes on a source's representations of goods that later are proven by the client to have been false? Most designers, as a practice, specify items based on the representations of their sources. The designer in such a case may have clearly made a false statement without the intent to deceive. Many states now have in place statutes listing a set of proscribed representations, including representations that claim a product has certain qualities or characteristics it, in fact, does not have. In some instances, the designer's reliance on the source's representation may limit the designer's liability if such reliance was found to have been reasonable according to that jurisdiction's law. For example, the court may find it to have been reasonable for a designer to have relied on the written statements provided by the vendor, such as certificates of authenticity. This might occur when the designer had no reason to question the veracity of the representation made by the vendor that the designer then passed on. Designers should aim to work with vendors who have a reputation for making honest, well-founded representations; however, there is no guarantee for preventing claims of this nature.

Puffing, or making grandiose statements about goods to sell them, is a long-standing practice; it is not legally proscribed. However, enticing language can become misleading and result in false, prohibited representation. The interplay of puffing and deceptive trade practices is illustrated in the following example. Suppose a designer claims: "This is the most luxurious and comfortable Baker sofa ever made!" The item was later found to be stuffed with hard-packed sawdust and made by an unknown company. The terms *luxurious* and *comfortable* may reflect the designer's personal opinion as to the sofa's characteristics, used to "puff" the sofa. However, the fact the sofa was not made by the stated company could give rise to a claim of a deceptive trade practice against the designer, especially if priced as if it were made by that company.

WHAT IS THE BEST WAY TO PROTECT YOURSELF AS AN INTERIOR DESIGNER?

What might be the one—very simple—thing to do to protect yourself as a designer, and as a businessperson, from potential legal issues? Is it enough, for example, to tell clients there is or could be a problem? As the following Mentor Memo illustrates, informing clients of issues is a good start, one expected of you as a professional. Going further, however, there is something more to do: document, document, document!

MENTOR MEMO

Whether or not your practice has in-house counsel or a trusted adviser on speed dial, it's absolutely critical to document your process and your product. Your product is your creative end result, but your process is the road that gets you there. Every meeting should have a structured agenda, informing the client of your intentions for the meeting. And every meeting should have meeting minutes to document the decisions that were made and the client's direction. A good habit is to send minutes within 24 hours of every meeting while the information is fresh and to advise the client that if no response is received to the minutes, they will be considered accepted for content. What you are trying to avoid is a he said-she said situation in the future, in the event anything goes wrong.

Importance of "Admissibility" of Written Records

Suppose a legal issue does arise in your practice, making its way to trial proceedings. Your (former) client proclaims in open court that they do not recall your mentioning, much less advising what to do about, some potential problem that, unfortunately, became a real one. When it is your turn to respond, what will you do? Armed with your written, dated minutes of the meetings in which you noted the matter *was* discussed and which you *did* advise of the likelihood of problems, you state your position and have your "silent witness"—your own notes—backing you up.

These documents are then determined by the court to be "admissible"; they are found to be records kept in the usual course of business. You records are now part of the proceedings. They may even be determined to be the "best evidence" of what actually happened! Again with the legalese, your records could be found to have "high probative value," certainly higher than the client's memory and oral testimony. It is a very good position for you to be in!

Your take away from this should be that protection of you, your professionalism, and your business begins by keeping regular, written documentation of every phone call, meeting, and interchange in which business matters with clients, contractors, and anyone else connected with a project are discussed. Is documentation too much work? Yes, it may be, but your own, written, truthful records, regularly kept as part of business practices, become your spokesperson. They are your witnesses in the event of controversies as to what happened. So powerful are written records that their presence and detail have been known to prevent issues from spiralling into formal proceedings.

During the course of their education and experience, attorneys—like interior designers—develop areas of specialized knowledge. When you consider engaging an attorney, the assistance of an attorney who understands construction and design-build issues and other concerns related to interior design work will likely serve your purpose better than someone who is unfamiliar with these topics. Be sure to do research and ask other designers to refer you to attorneys who have worked successfully with interior designers and their businesses.

Knowing the Right Questions to Ask

Documentation is a critical skill. So, too, is knowing the right questions to ask of legal experts. What might those be? The following can give you a better idea of how to interact effectively with them:

- What are the legal limits on the activities in which an interior designer can engage in this state?
- How is the business for which I work organized—sole proprietorship or corporation—and how does that affect employees?
- What do the provisions of the firm's standard form design contract mean?
- How can the firm for which I work help employees when legal issues arise in the course of work?
- Who owns the design documents I prepare—the firm or me?

Be aware that the assistance of a legal professional should strongly be considered when opening your own interior design business. In that event, an attorney can answer a great many questions, including the following:

- What are the legal limits on activities in which an interior designer can engage in this state?
- Which form of business organization is best under the circumstances for my business as planned?
- What kinds of documentation are necessary to establish the indicated business entity, and what has to be done to keep those documents up to date?

- What provisions should my firm's contract for design services contain, and why?
- What are ways to limit exposure to lawsuits for me and my firm, and are insurance policies enough?

These are only a few of the questions to ask an attorney when you are starting a new business. Accountants and attorneys are professionals who can assist you with your business needs. Will you need others to assist you in completing project installations? Later you will learn troubleshooting strategies that you can use in assembling a team of construction and design-trade resources to assist you in executing those installations.

HOW CAN DESIGNERS KEEP UP WITH LEGAL CHANGES?

It is essential to keep abreast of legal developments arising from and affecting business practices. This can be done fairly easily by regularly reading local newspapers and most major business periodicals, such as *The Wall Street Journal*, or by checking various Internet news sites, such as CNN or others that carry legal news and analyses of current business events and practices. Industry-specific resources—such as ASID publications—also routinely provide updates about legal developments affecting design professionals.

NOTES FROM THE FIELD

After years and years of practice, you learn to recognize good clients and difficult clients, even before they become difficult. You will read in upcoming chapters stories of how to work with difficult clients and how to earn their trust and gain their confidence. A masterful designer will do this effortlessly, and the client will become a repeat client for years to come, but sometimes that simply won't happen.

In this story, our design team was struggling to get a client to commit to decisions and move to the next step. As creative people, if a client does not like your ideas, it's natural to be disappointed, but as professionals, you must leave the room with enough specifics to provide a new solution that they will like. If you don't, the design process will never end! This client was on its fifth design meeting. It was a small project that should have been wrapped up in a few weeks. Common reactions from this client were "I just don't know" or "I am not sure." Items that were documented as approved, the client was prone to changing his mind, at a moment's notice. As our team started what would be the final presentation, I said to the client "Would you mind if I recorded the meeting, it's important we have a record of your needs to ensure our final solutions are correct and spot on." The client responded, "Yes I do mind."

The design team was blindsided by this response. When we inquired as to the reasoning, we were informed, "We reserve the right to change our minds." Within our contract, we had clearly outlined the number of options and revisions they would be receiving, to which we were grossly over. Knowing this troublesome client would not take accountability for decisions in any way, we politely completed the work at a financial loss and made the decision not to work with that client in the future. Our team and this client were simply not a match.

Practical Activity

Law surrounds all professions and professionals. Locate an article about a legal matter of the kind explored in this chapter that relates to an interior designer or the design-build, architecture industry. Summarize it, and explain its relevance.

Review Questions

After completing this chapter, you should be able to answer the questions that follow. Include your responses in the professional practices portfolio you have created.

1. Describe some of the limitations imposed on interior designers by various laws that seek to regulate their practices.

2. What are the ways in which businesses may be formed to meet certain objectives of their organizers?

3. What are some of the objectives business organizers typically have with respect to ventures they start?

4. As agents of their clients, what legal obligations are traditionally assigned to interior designers and others when they act on behalf of clients?

5. What are the elements considered legally necessary to form a valid, enforceable contract?

6. Describe some of the specific laws relating to the planning of interior spaces for accessible, safe use of which a designer should be aware.

7. Define the legal terms *tort* and *negligence*.

8. How have individual states extended protection to consumers in ways other than through common law?

9. What body of laws specifically covers topics such as the sale of goods and the conduct of merchants?

10. Describe some basic legal concepts that should be familiar to an interior designer.

WESSEX

CHAPTER 5
PLANNING YOUR BUSINESS FINANCES

MENTOR MEMO

It has been my experience that clients respect interior designers who are not afraid to openly discuss fees and costs. Open up the conversations early and when you need to address issues around money. Know your facts, and don't be shy.

After reading this chapter, you will be able to

- Understand the financial environment in which interior design firms of any size operate;
- Define basic accounting and finance terms;
- Recognize documents used to relate the financial position of interior design firms;
- Evaluate the various means by which funding for interior design businesses may be obtained;
- Describe managerial accounting and its role in operating interior design businesses.

INTRODUCTION TO PLANNING YOUR BUSINESS FINANCES

This chapter seeks to make the basic financial principles applicable to interior design businesses understandable and usable. This chapter is important to you because it identifies three processes that, together, form a system that enables you, as a practicing interior designer, to easily administer, measure, and evaluate financial information about your business. Having this knowledge of basic financial principles is necessary for any professional. Understanding terms and concepts presented in this chapter will help you to form your own strategy for working with those whom you consult about

Successful clients understand the importance of sound financial practices in their business operations, just as interior designers should.

financial matters. Of course, your foremost interest is producing meaningful interior design work. However, nothing prevents you from also being a sound financial manager as well. This chapter explores the basic objectives of business finance by discussing three interrelated processes that, together, form a system for managing the financial matters that are necessary for the operation of interior design businesses.

OBJECTIVE #1: FINANCIAL ADMINISTRATION

Most discussions of financial concepts begin with lengthy definitions and other details. The approach of this chapter is to first ask you to think about the financial operations of most businesses. For example, most business owners and managers regularly establish and monitor methods for handling payments that the business owes or that is owed to the business. Methods of working with the available cash the business has acquired as well as ways of recording expenses and retaining receipts for payment are other important concerns. These are examples of activities that may be thought of as making up a process by which the business's finances are administered. Before the financial status of the business may be scrutinized and evaluated, there should be in place a specific process for generating and retaining the kinds of financial information required for those later tasks. Accordingly, this chapter describes what is involved in administering the finances of a business. Many large interior design firms or practice groups include staff members who are designated to carry out these tasks. Managers and business owners frequently call upon that group for information about financial matters that are critical in making important decisions, such as whether to work with certain clients or extend credit to them. On the other hand, in many small shops made up of only one or a few practitioners, designers themselves may be responsible for carrying out administrative tasks. These practitioners use the financial information obtained through administrative processes for largely the same purposes as their counterparts in larger firms. In both scenarios, interior designers rely on the financial information gleaned from routine administrative processes.

OBJECTIVE #2: FINANCIAL MEASUREMENT

After financial information is acquired and retained, it must be interpreted for use in ways that benefit a business and its ongoing operations. Understanding and recording the financial effects that result from operating a business (for example, determining whether the business made or lost money) require a distinct process. The role of financial accounting principles and practices is to provide such a process. Financial accounting is generally described as the process of recording, organizing, and interpreting information related to financial transactions and performance. To carry out these functions, financial accounting relies on the use of three different documents, known collectively as summary reports. These reports are referred to individually as *balance sheets, income statements,* and *statements of cash flow.* How exactly these reports are constructed is discussed in many accounting texts. This chapter is concerned with their importance in measuring the financial performance of an interior design business.

OBJECTIVE #3: FINANCIAL EVALUATION

Financial information may be used for measuring the periodic performance of a business or as the basis for making more complicated business decisions. Interpreting financial information with the intent of using those results to make decisions or to evaluate different options is a process distinct from measurement. Managerial accounting principles and processes provide a method for business owners and managers to analyze and interpret current or prospective business activities. Businesses can evaluate financial performance using a form of fractions called *ratios*. Depending on the components of these ratios, they may be used to measure three different kinds of financial activity: the ability to pay obligations; the ability of the company to generate a profit or economic surplus from the operation of the business; and the ability to use effectively the business's assets (that is, certain kinds of property that the business owns).

Interior design businesses, as you know by now, require a great deal of monetary resources to operate. Using financial management guidelines, for example, enables designers to fully understand the impact of expenditures on a business's ability to not only function but also to show a profit. Although financial processes of any kind may seem remote from what is involved in planning attractive, functional interior environments, the cost and labor-intensive nature of interior design work, combined with the very real-world need for any business to show an economic profit as quickly as practicable, makes your study of financial topics highly relevant.

Financial administration, measurement, and evaluation are skills that enable designers and firms to profit from large and small projects.

MORE DETAILS ABOUT CHAPTER OBJECTIVES

The following introduction sets the stage for exploring more detail about the preceding objectives. The following three questions begin that discussion:

1. What is involved in administering the finances of a business?
2. What are the methods of measuring the finances of a business?
3. What questions about business finance does the evaluation process answer?

How Are Finances Administered?

Think of all the bills, receipts, and related items you receive in your personal life. Now, imagine the number of such items received by a small business. When you give further consideration to the vast number of such items a larger firm or practice receives, the need for an organized, systematic approach for administering the business's finances becomes apparent. What is really involved in the task of administering the finances of a business? What kinds of issues can interior designers expect to encounter, and, more importantly, what can they do to make the administrative process as easy and useful as possible?

In a sense, every business is different. Some interior design businesses are small enough that the owner is able to handle the administrative details almost as if the business were an extension of the owner's personal finances. No matter how informally some businesses may be managed, once any business gains a degree of size and complexity, it becomes necessary to identify ways of handling its financial activities. There are several issues of financial administration common to most businesses: establishing procedures for handling cash coming into and going out of a business; handling the expenses a business incurs from its operation; extending credit to clients; and keeping records of a business's financial activities for later measurement and evaluation purposes. Consider each of these activities.

1. **Dealing with the cash flow of a business** Businesses of any kind require cash to pay for such things as inventory and operation expenses. Although it may be difficult to determine exactly what specific amount of cash will be necessary, business owners and managers can estimate what typical expenses the business has incurred in the past and would, based on that historical information, be likely to incur in the future. Gathering this information may require keeping extensive records of expenses and revenue on a monthly basis. The importance of cash management for interior designers becomes apparent in those instances where designers have good months and bad months financially. Some designers choose to work in locations where their business varies according to time of year, gaining more business in certain seasons than in others. Also, many designers face similar variability as their businesses gain a following of clients. Regardless of the reasons for incurring financially strong and weak periods, designers must know how to accumulate then marshal cash reserves accordingly. As noted, record keeping of financial activities from previous periods is important as is monitoring current levels of sales and expenses.
2. **Handling the expenses of the business** From an accounting perspective, resources such as cash described earlier are considered part of the assets of a business. However, there are obligations incurred by a business that must be satisfied in order for that business to remain in operation. These are typically referred to as liabilities and

may be thought of as obligations or claims against the assets of a business before any profit can be determined. The key to recognizing one form of accounts payable is to look to see whether the business has received, but not yet paid, for goods or services. Other forms of accounts payable include promissory notes (a kind of debt) for which a business has received a financial loan that it must repay, but has not, or expenses it has incurred but not yet paid. Operating any business is an expensive undertaking, and interior design being no exception.

Finding ways to monitor expenses, project their occurrence and plan for meeting those obligations in a timely manner is critical for the ultimate success of any business.

3. **Extending credit to customers** This practice forms another asset of the business known as accounts receivable in which sums are owed the business by others. A common example of accounts receivable occurs when an interior design business extends credit to its clients by allowing them to pay outstanding balances over a period of time instead of all at once. Usually, design firms charge for this by imposing interest charges. This is a general overview of some of the ways in which business decision makers administer the financial operation of their ventures. Apart from these very basic decisions, what are more specific ways they may measure the effectiveness of the decisions they make?

How Are Business Finances Measured?

Many creative people gravitate to careers in interior design because quantitative skills are not usually emphasized. However, you are also in the process of becoming an entrepreneur willing to assume the risks inherent in running a business. How can you assess such risks? An old adage states that "sometimes you just have to put pencil to paper to figure out what to do." You put pencil to paper when realizing a design concept; here is how you can do much of the same kind of preparation in order to realize your goal of establishing, managing, or functioning in a profit-focused design business. Becoming familiar with the context in which you will use these accounting and financial management skills is the first step in that process.

Many people refer to money-related determinations as simply *accounting* when in fact there are two distinct divisions within the accounting profession, each making its unique contributions to quantitative business decision making. Financial accounting is perhaps the more commonly known and understood. Every time you determine the balance of your checking account, by matching deposits (revenues) with deducted payments (expenses) using the actual sums of money you have deposited in your account, you are engaging in a simple financial accounting process. With that in mind, you know that financial accounting concerns the measurement (the balance you achieve as a result of the addition and subtraction of funds) and reporting (the entries you write down) of monetary resources available.

Financial accounting has two other characteristics. Financial accounting occurs periodically, that is, at predetermined times. Many people, for example, balance their checkbooks only at certain times during the month in order to ascertain whether any money remains in their bank account until they receive their next paycheck. Business owners and managers, on the other hand, may balance their company's accounts daily in order to maintain adequate funds for operation from one day to the next. In addition, although you may balance your checkbook only for your own information and use, many businesspeople employ financial accounting practices to provide necessary information to those outside their organizations. Financial accounting practices are thus usually used to generate information for review by external parties. For example, preparation of financial accounting documents is frequently done for review by prospective and current company stockholders and government taxing authorities. Others external to the company usually given access to financial accounting information include those extending credit or lending money to a business—a requirement you explore in some detail in this chapter's Strategic Planning Project—along with those either permitted by the company or otherwise required by law to have such information. Of course, those within the business may use accounting information for evaluative purposes such as determining the amount of cash available for business operations.

Every profession has its own, unique terms used to describe important concepts. Each entry, or transaction noted in your checkbook represents an account, or record of any increase (credit) or decrease (debit) affecting an overall balance. These transactions are usually recorded in chronological sequence as they occur in what is called a journal. Your checkbook is a type of journal.

Documents of financial accounting include the following:

- **Balance sheet** The purpose of the balance sheet is to indicate the financial balances—the relationship of credit to debit—for a company at a particular time.
- **Income statement** An income statement is intended to show the operating performance of a business for a specific year, as reflected by changes in the company's net income.
- **Statement of cash flows** This statement breaks down a company's monetary resources according to where it derives its income and how it uses its available cash.

What Questions about Business Finance Does the Evaluation Process Answer?

Of the two areas of accounting discussed here, managerial accounting is likely less familiar to you. Managerial accounting focuses on processing quantitative, or numerical, information for use within a company to evaluate options available to the business and then make decisions based on these assessments. What this means, simply, is that managerial accounting determines the financial picture of some aspect of a company's operation and then evaluates options for possible company action based on that information. Determining, for example, whether a company makes money, or is profitable from some activity it undertakes, is one important aspect of managerial accounting.

With this information, owners and managers usually make decisions about actions the company should undertake, continue, discontinue, or modify in some way. The primary method of processing financial management information is through the use of mathematical formulas. Although detailed, these formulas, you may be relieved to learn, are based on ratios, or fractional percentages determined through division. More complicated managerial accounting formulas combine percentages with addition, subtraction, and multiplication, all processes with which you are familiar.

You may have already employed a form of managerial accounting in your personal life without recognizing it as such. Your analysis of whether to work while in school to pay tuition—less time to study now, but no costs later—or, alternatively, to take out a student loan—more time to study now, but higher costs later—is a process involving managerial accounting. One specific application of this kind of decision faced by businesses involves determining the percentage of obligations the company owes to others compared to the assets, or things of value, the company has available to pay those obligations. The debt ratio is a simple fraction in which the total amount of these debts is divided by all company assets. Very high debt ratios, indicating that a company owes much more money compared to what it has available to pay those debts—a situation referred to as being *highly leveraged*—ultimately may endanger a company's survival.

Financial and managerial accounting skills are important for prudent business decision making. In this chapter, financial and managerial accounting principles are explored within the context of operating an interior design business, namely those concerning the amount of project income, the timeliness of its receipt, and the payment of project expenses. This chapter focuses on methods of recording and interpreting these items as they relate to the overall operation of the design firm. Think for a moment about what financial information would be of interest to you as you operate or manage your own interior design business. Wouldn't you like to know the financial picture of your company at any given time? Think back to the reasons why you balance your checkbook and the role financial accounting plays in that process. Don't you want to find out how much money you have on hand and what your expenses are? Business operators desire the same kinds of information; methods of managerial accounting allow them to evaluate the financial position of a business and make decisions based on those determinations.

These businesspeople use a process referred to as ratio analysis in which mathematical formulas usually in the form of fractions are used to interpret financial information. There are three basic kinds of ratios used: effectiveness ratios, liquidity ratios, and profitability ratios.

- **Effectiveness ratios** measure how well the company uses its assets, including how quickly the company collects payment on its accounts receivable (A/R). There are several commonly identified effectiveness ratios used in businesses, including the A/R turnover and inventory turnover. To see how these work, consider the application of the first of these effectiveness ratios. A low accounts receivable ratio, for example, in which the number representing a business's net credit sales is divided by a denominator representing the business's average gross receivables, divided by 360 (for days in the year), means the business collects payments in a timely manner. A high number that results from this formula can, conversely, mean those to whom the business has extended credit typically wait long periods of time before paying, a result that can seriously affect the business's ability to pay other obligations as necessary. That ratio is as follows: A/R turnover (days) = net credit sales/(average gross receivables/360).
- **Liquidity ratios** measure the amount of money a company has on hand to pay its obligations as they become due for payment. Typical liquidity ratios include the current ratio in which a business's current assets, or the property and financial resources it owns, are divided by the business's current liabilities, or obligations such as debts. Other examples of liquidity ratios include the acid test ratio, in which, the sum of the following three elements are divided by the current liabilities of a business: cash equivalents + marketable securities (such as shares of

stock) + net receivables (what is owed to a business by others)/current liabilities. If the effect of a business's current liabilities is to diminish the financial benefits of the other elements of the equation with a resulting low number from using the acid test, the business, it may be concluded, faces serious problems.
- **Profitability ratios** measure how well the company is able to generate profits from its activities. Perhaps, the most common example of a profitability ratio, one with which you may already be familiar, is that of gross margin. In that ratio, net income is divided by net sales. Net income is derived by subtracting all expenses from the total revenue earned by the business. Similarly, net sales are derived from the total of all sales less the costs to the business of generating those sales. Use of this ratio makes clear the extent to which the business is able to show a profit from that business's sales.

PROBLEM-SOLVING STRATEGIES FOR FINANCIAL PLANNING

There is yet another hurdle to cross on the way to becoming a design professional: obtaining the financial resources to begin your enterprise. If you are still debating whether a solo or small interior design firm is for you, this financial hurdle may help you decide if or when you might be able to start your first business venture.

SOURCES OF FUNDING FOR YOUR INTERIOR DESIGN BUSINESS

Essentially, there are two major sources of funding available to businesses. These may be classified as either public or private. As you might imagine, *public* sources are available to businesspeople and the business community at large. These include U.S. government-backed entities such as credit unions, traditional banks, and other lending institutions. The financial services offered by these sources are usually available to any businessperson or company meeting predetermined standards of acceptance. In contrast, *private* sources are financial resources that may be available to only one or a few people, based on friendships or family connections. Financing from these sources may range from outright gifts of money to loans with very lenient repayment terms; it also includes other forms of financial advantage not made known, much less made available, to the general public. Each type of financing, whether public or private, should be considered with care before you enter into an agreement that obligates you as a new business owner to someone. Most of these sources will impose some sort of obligation for repayment or exert some expectation that must be met by you and the business entity you seek to establish.

Regardless of which form of funding you ultimately choose—public, private, or some combination of the two—most sources will require that you present something in writing that explains your plan for establishing and running your business. You are already familiar with the role of business plans in describing your enterprise to others. Even if a business plan is not specifically required, application forms may ask questions that elicit the same kind of information contained in such a plan. When you examine the information requirements for a Small Business Administration (SBA) loan, you will notice its similarities to portions of a business plan.

Interior "design" is a client expense that requires an income that is sufficient, no matter how large or small the scale of the project.

CHAPTER 5 PLANNING YOUR BUSINESS FINANCES • 97

Even private sources of funding may wish to see your business plan in writing; however, in these circumstances the plan may not have to be as exhaustive as plans submitted to public sources. In addition to asking exhaustive questions about your proposed business and your plans for running that business, public sources of financing will also ask many exhaustive questions about you. In particular, these lenders will look at your preexisting history of repaying obligations such as student loans, credit cards, mortgages, and other debt that appears on credit reports compiled by credit-reporting agencies.

Before you apply for a loan or seek financing, it is a good idea to check your credit rating through any of several sources readily found in print and Internet media. Your credit rating is one of several factors lenders consider when deciding whether to grant a loan in the first place and also whether to charge higher or lower interest rates on the sums you borrow. Usually, the better your credit rating—showing careful stewardship of existing credit obligations—the better the terms of any new loan, all other factors, such as income stability, remaining constant. Fair, Isaac and Company at http://www.myfico.com is an example of a credit-reporting agency. The FICO score is mentioned and used by many lenders in making credit determinations. Although other agencies report historical credit data, such as the number of late payments over time, Fair, Isaac has developed a proprietary mathematical score, or scale, that predicts how well or poorly individuals are estimated to control their debt obligations. In addition to preparing a written business plan, an interior design entrepreneur should take into account a credit score before seeking financing.

Public Sources of Business Funding

Banks, credit unions, and savings-and-loan institutions are readily available sources for operational funds. Each of these entities offers loans to small-business entrepreneurs who can meet the guidelines imposed by the U.S. government and a particular bank's own lending policies. These guidelines include concerns such as the credit rating of a borrower and whether that borrower has any assets that can be offered to the lender as security for making the loan.

Loans from Banks and Other Financial Institutions

As part of the lending process, and in addition to the borrower's credit rating, virtually all public sources will require written documentation attesting to the nature of the business as well as the borrower's formal business plan. Some types of loans, known as secured loans, will also require the borrower to pledge some asset of value, such as equipment or real estate. This is considered security against which the lending institution may seek financial satisfaction in the event of the borrower's inability to repay the loan. Secured loans usually have lending terms and interest rates more favorable to the borrower than types of unsecured loans that require no pledge of assets.

In addition to considering credit scores and secured loans, designer entrepreneurs should also be aware of the financing options available at specialized lending institutions such as credit unions or cooperatives in which they may be eligible to participate. Many universities sponsor or are affiliated with credit unions that are available to their students. These institutions may offer better loan terms and rates to their members than might otherwise be found elsewhere in the community. Researching sources of funds for your design business includes seeking out all possible alternatives available in your community. It also means that you understand the obligations that an entrepreneur, as a loan recipient, has to the lending institution for repayment. You should understand the recourses that institutions will take to obtain satisfaction against debtors who cannot repay loans under the terms of agreement; this is critical for successful borrowing.

SBA Loan Guarantees

Banks and other public lending institutions make loans directly to qualified borrowers. However, in those instances where, for example, a potential borrower has established a business with a viable cash flow but does not yet have a strong credit history to qualify for a conventional loan, certain government loan programs are available to guarantee a loan or assume at least part of the lending risk should a borrower default. These public sources of funds are not loans from the federal government in the traditional sense. In fact, a borrower would seek these types of guaranteed loans from a bank or other lending institution and not from the federal government or private individuals. Such programs provide the federal government's insurance to a lender to make a loan it otherwise could not make on reasonable business terms.

These loan-guarantee programs act as another, although indirect source of financing to entrepreneurs. An overview of these Small Business Association (SBA) loans states the following:

> To qualify for an SBA guaranty, a small business must meet the SBA's criteria, and the lender must certify that it could not provide funding on reasonable terms without an SBA guaranty.... The SBA can guarantee as much as 85 percent on loans of up to $150,000 and 75 percent on loans of more than $150,000. In most cases, the maximum guaranty is $1 million.

Note the language in this statement about certification from the lender that financing on any reasonable terms is unavailable. In other words, for a variety of reasons, the borrower may not be eligible to receive any loan from any lender according to federal banking and lending policies. Poor credit, for example, may be a reason for many lenders to decline the loan, except for the assurance of the SBA. However, the addition of language stating that a governmental assurance can be based on broad criteria may make it possible for potential borrowers to obtain funding with the assistance of the SBA. Among these criteria for assurances is the following description of what the SBA looks for in a loan application: repayment ability from the cash flow of the business is a primary consideration in the SBA loan decision process but good character, management capability, collateral, and owner's equity contribution are also important considerations.

Finally, all but a few types of businesses may avail themselves of the SBA loan guarantee. The agency spells out what types of businesses are ineligible for its support. These include such enterprises as real estate speculation and pyramid schemes "in which proceeds gained from the financial contribution of later investors in a business are used to pay 'profits' to earlier ones." Careful review of the type of business being conducted is necessary on the part of the entrepreneur and lender before making a formal application.

Of note to interior designers is the prohibition against guaranteeing businesses that seek to use floor plan financing. Suppose a design entrepreneur sought to establish a retail store from which to operate an interior design business. The store, moreover, would carry a particular manufacturer's furniture that it obtained on credit from the maker. Retail stores may well be a permissible SBA-backed undertaking, but a store in which merchandise is obtained by the store owner on credit from the manufacturer may not be eligible for an SBA-supported loan. Essentially, the store owner, under this type of agreement with the furniture manufacturer, does not own the furniture that serves as the principle asset backing the loan. In the event of the store owner's inability to pay, the furniture manufacturer may be found to have superior ownership rights to the furniture in the showroom, leaving the lender with no other recourse but to seek reimbursement from the SBA. Again, it is important to carefully review the type of entity that an entrepreneur is seeking to establish through the use of an SBA-backed loan before obtaining governmental assurance.

Credit Cards

Credit cards and the use of debt are now relatively commonplace in life and in business practice compared with their use as little as a generation ago. Some have argued that perhaps it is now too easy for people, whether they are starting businesses, to obtain credit; many who do so now do not understand how expensive and potentially detrimental these financing sources really are. Nevertheless, the use of debt is widespread, particularly among those who are starting new businesses, precisely because credit cards are so easy to obtain. An understanding and appreciation of the effects of credit card debt on a new business is another requirement for the design entrepreneur. It is thus necessary to understand certain aspects of the operation of debt financing through credit cards.

Every source of money, except for an outright gift, will inevitably require repayment of the borrowed money, usually with the addition of some type of finance charge, known as interest. Every businessperson should therefore be aware of two important issues. First, the borrower must be aware of the percentage of interest the lender will charge for the use of its funds. Many credit cards tout the cash advance feature of their cards, which enables cardholders to obtain cash readily through automated teller machines (ATMs). However, most cards charge a higher percentage of interest for cash obtained in this way. Using credit cards to obtain cash advances is a more expensive way for a consumer to obtain funds than by means of a bank loan, for example. Debt and credit card calculators are readily available for businesspeople and can even be found on many Internet sites. Every businessperson, especially one who is working in an expense-laden industry such as interior design, should be aware of how much it will cost to obtain working funds.

Just as important as the cost of funding is the awareness of the length of time before sources require repayment of borrowed money. Credit cards require payment of some or even the entire amount borrowed approximately within a month of incurring the debt. American Express is one commonly used credit card that requires full payment at the end of the billing cycle for individuals and business patrons. Other sources may permit longer repayment times. Unfortunately, it takes time to establish any business, particularly one in which projects are obtained through professional networking and personal referrals, as is true of interior design. What this may create for a designer is a *cash flow* problem: Few, if any, new funds are available from projects, while start-up expenses accumulate and payments to creditors are due.

Many credit cards tout the low interest rates they apply to balances carried from one billing session to the next. Care should be taken not to fall into the introductory rate trap, in which low rates are charged for a period of time, only to be exchanged for higher rates later. It should also be noted that paying just the minimum payment may result in a long payment time until the entire balance of principle and interest are paid off. As a result, it may take as long as several decades for a cardholder to pay off a high balance just by paying those low minimum payments.

All cards seek repayment eventually. Unfortunately, these repayments may unhappily coincide with periods in which no revenue is earned and the business cash flow is compromised. As a practicing interior designer, beware of the temptation to "kite," which is where revenue earmarked for use in one project is used instead to pay items such as debt incurred in another project. Recognizing such problems before they arise is necessary so that a new business does not soon become mired in debt.

As careful as a professional must be in using credit card debt, the prudent use of credit cards may nevertheless become a type of asset for the business. Businesses may gain an increasingly favorable rating among the credit-reporting agencies that track credit card use and payment history. A long practice of prudent credit card use may result in issuers increasing the amounts of money that card users may borrow as well as in relatively lower interest rates applied to balances carried on those cards.

Private Sources of Business Funding

Among the basic sources of funding available to get a business started, perhaps the simplest source is personal savings. Unfortunately, for young designers getting started right out of school, there may be little or no savings after years of education. At some point, however, a design practitioner should accumulate an amount in savings to do such things as sustain their personal and professional expenses or pay accumulated debt.

Personal Savings

By saving, through practices such as putting a given amount of money from each project into an interest-bearing account or, as one recent author has suggested, cutting out only $10 a day of nonessential purchases, designers can begin the process of building a financial cushion enabling them to sustain both themselves and their active practice. The balance of income and expenses may be skewed in favor of the latter at some time during the designer's career. For that reason, a savings plan should be initiated from the start. Budgeting for expenses as well as estimating living and professional costs incurred over a six- to nine-month period will help in understanding not only why savings are important but also how much money is required for both daily living and work.

However, even experienced designers should approach using savings cautiously. For example, many practitioners have accumulated amounts in 401(k) or other retirement plans. Use of such funds may result in substantial income tax penalties in the event withdrawals are made before a certain age or scheduled payment date. Any plan to use these types of funds should be made only after careful consideration and consultation with knowledgeable financial professionals.

Savings account plans providing some payment of interest to the account holder are readily available at most banks and savings-and-loans. The percentage of interest paid to account holders should be researched to obtain the most advantageous rate. In addition, the frequency and number of withdrawals available to depositors using the plan should be ascertained by asking questions of the lender's account representatives and reading material related to the accounts. Many institutions have established savings plans that transfer certain amounts from a savings account into a checking account every month. The goal of your research should be to find the savings account that offers the most convenience but charges the least for fees or penalties.

Gifts and Related Agreements

Gifts of money may be one source of funds that can be used to establish a design practice. A gift, in the true sense of the term, is one in which the recipient does nothing in order to receive it—there is no consideration in legal terms for the making of the gift. In addition, a true gift is given with the intent or expectation on the part of the givers that it not be repaid (Merriam-Webster 1996). Outright gifts of the nature described here are, indeed, very attractive financial resources. However, gifts of any kind, particularly those of cash from one individual to another, should be memorialized in writing. All that may be required is a simple written statement to the effect that the sums advanced are a gift made without expectation of repayment, and for which the recipient did nothing to occasion it being made. Such a statement will prevent any misunderstanding later concerning whether the money was actually a loan to the person to whom it was given and for which the donor expected to be repaid. This is a common misunderstanding surrounding gifts. In addition, such written statements can serve to counter possible claims that the money was stolen or obtained through coercion. Legal counsel should be sought to ensure that the language of the acknowledgment mirrors the jurisdiction's definition of what constitutes a gift.

Gifts made to a married person are usually considered to be the property of the individual recipient, not jointly held by the couple as an asset of the marriage in most states; however, any monetary gift given to a married person should be drafted with the help of an attorney to make clear the ownership rights of the sums advanced. The more specific a gift acknowledgment is, the less opportunity for later misunderstanding about the reasons for the gift's donation, purpose, and use.

The requirement of writing down the specific terms of a gift become necessary in the event of gifts of great value, either cash or property. In general, these large gifts may expose the recipient to income tax liability. Any large gift should be made with the advice and counsel of relevant experts, such as an attorney and accountant or tax specialist. In general, an individual may give up to $10,000 annually to a recipient with no income tax liability accruing to the recipient. However, the income tax reporting requirements on these examples of largess are complex enough to warrant informed advice.

Monetary gifts may be of a more complex nature as well. This is particularly true in those instances in which the gift is made with the specific intent that either some or all of it is to be repaid, in which case the gift is really more of a favorable loan. Also, a more complex gift may be one in which the donor expects to have some measure of control, or say-so, in the operation of the business. It should be apparent that such gifts have substantial strings attached. In order to avoid any serious misunderstandings between the donor and recipient, a formal written agreement, possibly drafted by an attorney and notarized by a notary public who has confirmed the identities of all the parties to the transaction, should be executed—with the terms of the gift spelled out as clearly as possible.

In some instances where the donor is willing to underwrite an enterprise in its entirety or to some substantial degree, a formal partnership agreement should be drafted by legal counsel. Recollections and handshake agreements are imperfect, especially when surrounded by conflict or controversy. Offers of gifts of working capital, especially in those instances where lenient repayment or donor control of the enterprise is contemplated, should be very carefully thought out before agreeing to enter into them; under no circumstances should these agreements be left to the unwritten understandings of the parties involved.

Gifts made to a recipient through a will or a trust arrangement are other more complex mechanisms for obtaining funds to establish a business. These gifts involve legal and administrative steps to bring them about. As a result, the administration of wills and trusts usually requires the assistance of an attorney and, perhaps, an accountant to ensure that all legal and tax requirements are met. There are costs, sometimes substantial, associated with seeking the assistance of these professionals. Nonetheless, ready availability of financial resources is necessary for the establishment of any business enterprise, interior design included.

Successful interior design entrepreneurs work to establish business opportunities and find design solutions from challenges.

Suppose a worst-case scenario for your financial prospects when you leave school. You do not have a job or wish to be self-employed. Your savings are minimal after years of being in school, loans are difficult to come by for someone with little business experience, and gifts of the magnitude necessary to start your business are just a dream. What should you do? Remember the definition of entrepreneurs: They are described as those who organize, manage, and assume the risk of businesses.

Your job is to first organize your business's finances. In an interview, one designer noted that she began her decades-old practice with little available cash. To generate business and to obtain funds for further growth, she placed a series of small ads in her local newspapers. In these ads, she offered to help prospective clients choose colors and furnishings for their apartments or starter homes. She also offered to work with her clients' existing furniture and within limited household budgets. On the basis of these first ads, she started and grew a business that, as she also noted, grew with her clients. From their first homes to their retirement homes, she completed projects for repeat clients that she had met as a result of these early ads. In short, these ads proved to be not only a source of working capital but also an investment in her business's future. That's an example of an entrepreneur's strategic business planning!

ACCOUNTANTS IN YOUR INTERIOR DESIGN PRACTICE

This section aims to discuss practical ways of enhancing professional practice skills as you carry out interior design work and related business activities. Think for a moment about being an interior designer. You will be responsible for many, if not all, of the conceptual and organizational tasks involved, but you will also need the assistance of accountants. Consider these important business advisers and the various business issues with which they can assist.

The Role of Accountants

Practitioners in the accounting profession concentrate their work in two distinct areas. Financial accountants gather and interpret financial information according to guidelines known as *Generally Accepted Accounting Principles* (GAAP) as well as the appropriate federal and state tax laws. In the most general sense, financial accountants assist in periodically evaluating and reporting the financial status of a business or person. Those who have completed formal educational requirements and passed state professional exams are known as **Certified Public Accountants or CPAs**. Practitioners in the other area of accounting specialization, managerial accounting, have also met rigorous education and examination standards and are known as **Certified Managerial Accountants, or CMAs**.

These professionals use mathematical equations, usually based on fractions or ratios, to evaluate the financial performance of a business. In this chapter, you learned the application of basic financial accounting concepts and record keeping and will describe common financial-management ratios. Later discussions will help you to communicate with accounting professionals and to understand how you may best interact with them. When you consider engaging the services of an accountant, do some research and ask for referrals to accountants who have worked well with other interior designers. Not all accountants understand how interior designers work; find one with whom you can easily communicate and who can explain accounting procedures and practices to you in a meaningful way.

Questions to Ask Accountants about an Interior Design Business

At this early stage of your education in strategic professional practices, you should be aware of the important role financial accountants can play in your work. Following are several critical questions to ask a financial accountant if you are not seeking to start your own design business:

1. What kinds of documentation should I seek from my employer for tax purposes?
2. As far as taxes are concerned, what difference does it make if I am an independent contractor rather than an employee?
3. How should I prepare personal records for income tax purposes?
4. What do I need to do now so that I can own my own interior design practice or retail store or, for that matter, retire from work?
5. Is it economically feasible to open my own interior design practice?

If your plans involve immediately starting your own interior design business—or your ultimate plan is to open your own business after working for others to gain experience—then you will definitely need an accountant's assistance to answer the following questions:

1. Are my plans for a new interior design business financially feasible, or should they be modified in some way?
2. What kinds of financial records will I need to keep as a business owner, and how do I do so?
3. How much cash should I accumulate in order to sustain my business for the first year?
4. How should the business be best structured for income tax purposes?
5. Can I afford to hire other full-time designers, or should I hire freelancers as needed; and, if feasible, should the latter be classified as employees or independent contractors?

These are, of course, only a few of the questions that you might address to a financial accountant. Regardless of your ultimate career intentions, or even if you have a knack for numbers as well as design, the assistance of a financial accounting professional is critical if you want unbiased opinions about matters such as a business's financial status at a specific date and its exposure to the imposition of taxes by governmental authorities.

NOTES FROM THE FIELD

With respect to your finances, large projects have different issues than small projects. Every large project begins with a contract, or at least it should. That contract will outline the terms of payment that you will be expected to work within. Clients and their lawyers will understandably outline terms that are sympathetic to their needs. Some of those terms may suggest long windows where you (the design team) are not compensated for your work. Or they may insist that you meet certain criteria before receiving payment. In the case of large projects, sometimes those windows of financial drought can be more than a year. Know your limits and whether you or your firm can live with these terms.

Many small to medium-size firms do not have the financial means or total project turnover to withstand these terms. The first step is to communicate. Good clients do not want to see their projects suffer financial hardship, which only means less staff underperforming on critical details. And because salaries are still paid either every two weeks or monthly, and bills are monthly, these terms should be discussed with your client. Ideally, you will not be bearing that burden. Solutions include accessing funds put in trust by the client, or drawing down deposits against basic costs, or a requesting a simple retainer to mobilize and fund the work.

If you are a subconsultant to either another firm or an architectural team, be aware of "pay when paid," which in laymen's terms means you are not compensated until the primary consultant is paid. This can mean 120+ days after you have completed that work, and you are potentially tied to the primary firm's financial ups and downs. Most firm's bill interest against invoices that are over their term, knowing these parameters is critical to an interior designer's financial sustainability.

In the event you are managing the subconsultants under your contract, maintain the same level of transparent professionalism that you would like to receive. Review your subconsultant's contracts in detail. In the event their services are to be paid for on completion (verses pay when paid), you have a professional obligation to alert the client, their services will need to be prebilled in advance to avoid any unnecessary delays in the projects construction documentation completion. This level of communication and transparency will ensure that great subconsultants will always want to work with you.

Practical Activity

Finances affect all business. Describe how you will get started as an interior designer from a financial perspective. Do you want to have your own studio? Establish a "thumbnail," small budget for what you estimate basic expenses to be: rent, supplies, fees and dues, and utilities. Then, indicate what you estimate your income or cash available to operate your business. How long can you operate before you will need further influxes of cash in the form of bills paid by clients? Suppose you are interested in working for others. What will that employer provide and what will you have to purchase for yourself? How "far" do you estimate you can make your paycheck go to cover any professional and personal expenses? Share your findings with the class. With the pooled information, all will have a clear understanding of how important it is to plan your business finances, even before you are in business!

Review Questions

1. What are some of the ways of administering the finances of a business?

2. What is involved in the financial planning process for a business?

3. What are accounts payable and accounts receivable?

4. What general area of business finances is concerned with measuring the financial position of a business?

5. What is a transaction in financial accounting terminology?

6. Define the following: assets, liabilities, owner's equity, revenues, and expenses.

7. Identify the three basic documents of financial accounting, and state the purposes of each?

8. What is managerial accounting, and what purpose does it serve in business?

9. What information do ratios provide about a business's finances? Give some examples of several different kinds of ratios.

10. What ways of obtaining financial resources for businesses are available to entrepreneurs?

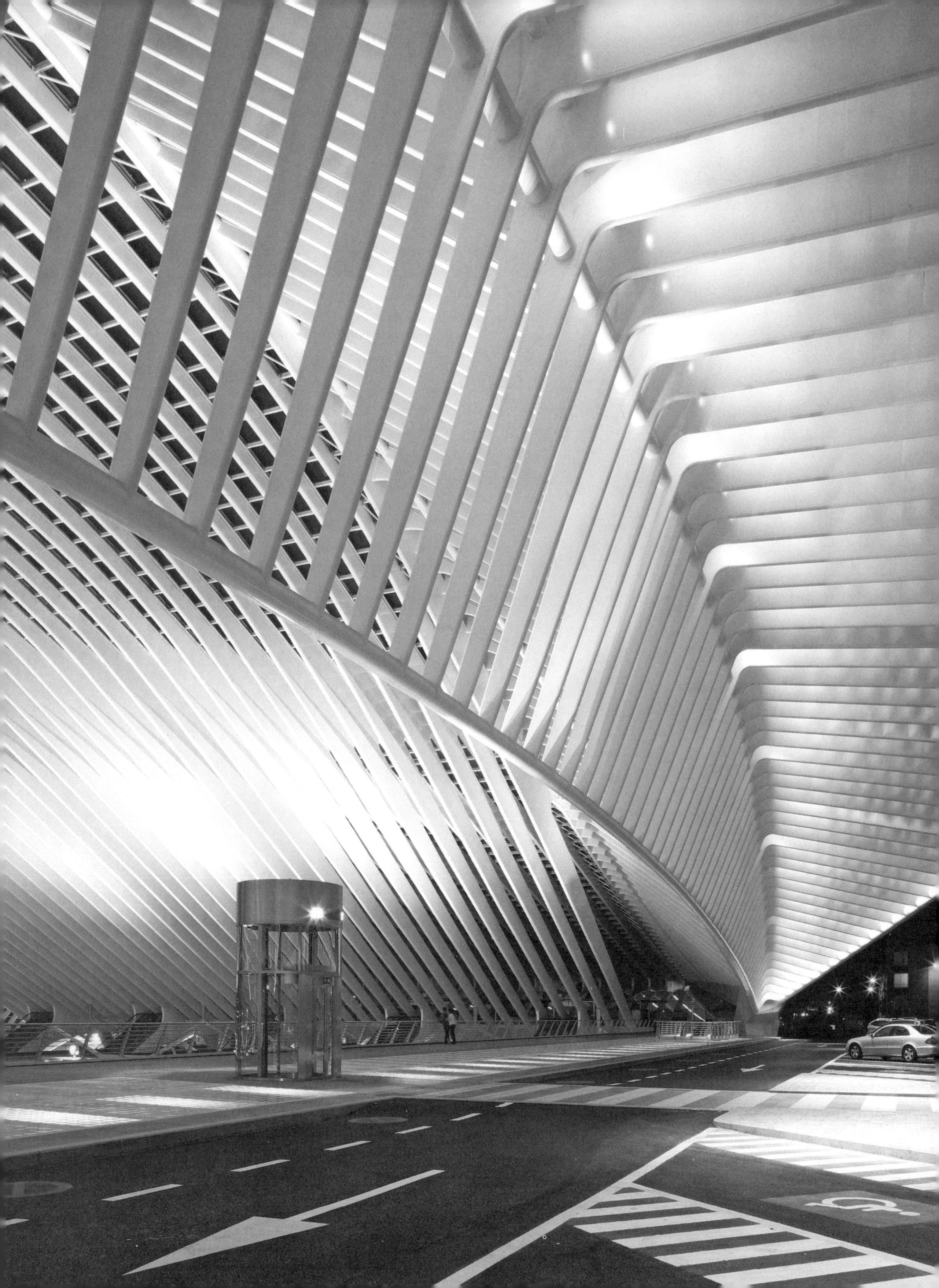

CHAPTER 6
MANAGING YOUR BUSINESS

MENTOR MEMO

It is the job of your manager to create the environment staff needed to do their best work. Your manager may need to reinvent the organization chart and create new descriptions for staff to thrive in. Shuffling the deck was a risk, one that resulted in outstanding success for both staff and our clients.

After reading this chapter, you will be able to

- Describe the management environment of interior design businesses of various sizes;
- Understand the role of the designer-manager when it comes to operating businesses and performing professional design work;
- Define the role of workers and others in interior design firms from a management perspective;
- Recognize the role laws play in the management of interior design businesses;
- Understand the contents of employee handbooks and related management documents;
- Explain the role and functions of teams in interior design businesses.

INTRODUCTION TO MANAGEMENT OF INTERIOR DESIGN BUSINESSES

Whether you work on your own as an interior designer or are employed by an interior design firm, you will call upon your knowledge of the topics discussed in this chapter to assist you in making business decisions. Perhaps the subject of management will be among the most important since at some point in your working life you may be personally responsible for managing the operations of a business, supervising workers, or having your own activities supervised by managers. Therefore, this

A designer's vision and a well-managed team are required to produce these functional and dramatic interior spaces.

chapter is important because it will make you aware of the various roles managers perform; the critical distinctions between managing businesses and workers; the kinds of issues that affect management decisions; the ways in which management policies are presented; and issues relating to the management of teams. These topics apply to the daily operation of interior design businesses, allowing you to develop your own thoughtful strategies for nurturing a sense of community in any business in which you participate.

As you begin this chapter, think about an interior design project you might be called upon to complete. That project will require you to plan and monitor many activities. To do so, you will have to assume responsibility for running the entire project, which involves coordinating the actions of others. In short, your management of that project will be similar to the ways in which business managers influence the operation of their businesses. This familiar scenario emphasizes your awareness of the activities performed by those holding management positions. Just as designers coordinate the complete design of interior spaces, managers plan, implement, and oversee activities related to the functioning of their businesses. This often includes directing the actions of individuals involved in the business. What skills do you think may be required of those who wish to manage interior design businesses and the workers in those businesses? There is much to be explored on the topic of management, including different philosophies of management and the federal and state laws relating to management practices. How might an interior design student, on the verge of becoming a practitioner, learn about these topics without becoming lost in their numerous details?

That understanding begins by establishing a helpful context in which business management issues arise. Entrepreneurs may choose from among several different ways to initially organize their businesses, some of which are sole proprietorships, partnerships, corporations, or limited liability companies, among others. As you begin this chapter you might inquire whether these different types of business organization affect how businesses are managed. After all, different ways to organize and structure a business indicate precisely those business activities in which entrepreneurs may and may not participate. How do management activities relate to the operation of the business?

Management activities involve relationships internal to the business—for example, the roles traditionally carried out by *staff* and *line* workers, terms you will come to know more about shortly. The business types analyzed in Chapter 4 refer to relationships external to the business, for example, to those who extend credit to the business or those who are in various ways harmed by the business. Laws unrelated to business formation, such as federal and state laws regulating employment practices, are some of the more important controls the legal system places on internal business operations. An overview of the influence of these laws on management practices is found in this chapter.

Internal management practices may be considered in two very general categories: those practices seeking to advance the goals of the business itself and those related to workers in the business. This chapter refers to the former practices in terms of *business management* and to the latter in terms of *personnel management*. The chapter's objectives are to explore fundamental concepts of both types so that you can recognize and utilize them when you participate in interior design business.

Management activities affect virtually all professionals in some way. Sole proprietors must engage in management activities on behalf of their businesses to prosper, even if doing so affects only themselves. In larger, more complex businesses, management practices are necessary to ensure survival of the business. This chapter identifies five basic questions you may have about management. When you conclude this chapter, you should be able to answer them:

1. What functional roles do managers play?
2. What are some of the different ways in which businesses and workers may be managed?
3. What are some of the ways management decisions may be influenced?
4. Where are management policies and procedures presented?
5. How are teams managed?

MANAGEMENT FUNCTIONS

"To direct or carry on business affairs" is the basic way in which Webster's dictionary describes the function of **management**. From your own experiences working with, or even as, a manager, you know that a great deal is required when directing or carrying on affairs related to a business. In fact, a list of the specific activities in which managers engage in any business setting, including the practice of interior design, would likely be quite lengthy. Many interior designers who operate their own businesses or have controlling interests in a firm—as might a principal in a large design practice—are responsible for performing a wide variety of tasks ranging from the seemingly routine job of paying the bills to the more influential function of instructing employees about company policies. Managers also perform tasks that are critical to business growth such as identifying and approaching potential new clients or formulating strategic plans for the future. Because of its seemingly all-encompassing nature and its ready application to most business practices, the scope of management and the work of managers have fascinated business writers. Many of these writers offer new theories about management practices, but one influential study conducted approximately thirty years ago is noteworthy today for having defined the working life of managers and delineated the roles managers play in business. That study is particularly instructive not only because it provides a useful context in which to discuss management but also because its findings are applicable to the practices of interior design businesses.

The environments in which managers operate require that they perform a great deal of work, often under tremendous time pressures. This finding underscores a major challenge faced by all professionals, including interior designers: how to accomplish their managerial duties and still be able to perform the work for which they were educated and trained. By now, you have a detailed understanding of the many activities that make up interior design work. Imagine combining those activities with managerial tasks, and you will have a better idea of how and why those in management positions in any line of work, including interior design, constantly face a time crunch.

A typical manager may perform many small tasks that fall across a spectrum of duties. Think of the previous example of a manager paying the business's bills and then working to develop new clients for the business. Even in an interior design business, it would not be uncommon for a manager to engage in a variety of very different tasks within a particular day. In general, managers prefer to handle issues related to the business that are current, specific, and nonroutine. Current issues require attention and resolution immediately or at least in the near future. Vague or undefined issues are difficult to both ascertain and resolve since they may not come to the fore as full-blown problems and will likely encroach on the manager's performance of more immediately demanding tasks. No one, including a manager, likes routine, repetitive tasks. Managers, according to this study, prefer to delegate repetitive tasks to others and to focus on those issues requiring a response to specific facts or problems that need to be solved. Think again of the managerial tasks that have been mentioned. Although paying company bills is a routine task, interior designers in small firms may have no one but themselves to whom they can delegate that responsibility; at the same time, they need to attend to a range of more demanding professional duties.

How might the functional roles of managers be described? We are not interested so much in an exact listing of every task a manager performs as if it were a template of general kinds of activities. Managers can be said to perform three basic types of roles when carrying out their work: interpersonal, informational, and decisional. Consider how each of these three roles may be performed by managers who work in interior design businesses.

- **Interpersonal** This managerial role encompasses three basic components: representing the business to those outside the business, acting as a leader who seeks to motivate and unify people working within the organization in order to carry out the goals of the business, and working with other managers. Refer back to the brief discussion of specific activities performed by managers. You will note activities such as meeting with potential clients (*figurehead* representation of the business to outsiders) and instructing employees about business policies (promoting a unified effort to carry out those policies). Working to define strategic business goals usually requires the ability to work with other managers in all but the smallest of organizations.
- **Informational** The informational role is perhaps the most visible and therefore most recognized role performed by managers. Consider the activity of instructing employees about company policies. Managers may disseminate information. One way in which managers hand down company policies is through verbal and written communications. This chapter discusses the latter in more detail, particularly in relation to preparing handbooks explaining company policies for employee reference and use. In addition to communicating company policies, managers also monitor the activities of employees under their supervision as part of their informational roles. Finally, managers act as spokespersons for the business, imparting information to others outside the business.
- **Decisional** Of course, managers have to make decisions about many issues. Planning the strategic course of the business is very much a decisional activity, as are activities such as formulating budgets that allocate the resources of the business to different activities and handling unique or difficult problems. It should be noted that decision making requires identifying goals, evaluating information, and then planning activities that will satisfy those goals.

The roles managers perform, the working environments in which managers operate, and even the purposes of management vary greatly according to the particular business being managed. A very small interior design business, for example, requires that a designer perform all of the managerial roles discussed here as well as the professional duties of an interior designer. In a larger interior design business, or an interior design practice group that is part of a large architecture firm, an interior designer may perform only a few management roles, depending on the internally determined division of work duties among managers. Although it is possible to compartmentalize particular management roles, in many instances all of them affect the nature of working life for managers and those whom they supervise. If you have given some thought to owning and operating your own interior design business, you should have an understanding of management basics as well as the general conditions under which managers work to determine whether, or to what extent, you wish to assume such responsibilities in addition to those required of interior design professionals.

PERSONNEL MANAGEMENT

After defining management and management roles, it seems logical to focus on the workers whom managers manage. First, it is important to recognize that management tasks focused on coordinating the activities of workers are frequently referred to as **personnel management**, to distinguish it from other management activities.

A discussion of personnel management requires a distinction between two different kinds of workers found in business: employees and independent contractors. An **employee** has been defined as "a person who works in the service of another person under an express or implied contract of hire, under which the employer has the right to control the details of work performance." Employees are entitled to benefits offered by the company as well as unemployment and worker's compensation insurance should employment end or on-the-job injury occur. On the other hand, the person hiring an **independent contractor** has control only over the independent contractor's finished product. Employers may either accept or reject the final results produced and may or may not pay the workers for their labor; but they cannot direct the *means* and *methods* by which they were produced. Independent contractors receive no company benefits, nor are they entitled to unemployment and worker's compensation benefits. Another difference between employees and independent contractors concerns whether an employer must withhold portions of earnings, known as deductions, for federal and state income tax purposes as well as deductions for Social Security and Medicare. These deductions are required for employees but not for independent contractors. Independent contractors are responsible for paying self-employment taxes on their earnings.

How is the employment relationship defined from a legal perspective? Would it surprise you that under most circumstances an employer can terminate a working relationship with an employee without giving prior notice to the worker or a reason for termination? Under what is referred to as the employment-at-will doctrine, which is recognized in most states, this can and does occur. Likewise, according to this doctrine, an employee may simply quit a job with no prior notice or reason given to the employer. There are, of course, limits on the application of the employment-at-will doctrine; for example, an employer may not terminate the worker for discriminatory reasons or out of retaliation for the worker's actions. Nevertheless, the employment-at-will doctrine is the prevailing viewpoint defining the relationship between employers and employees.

THE ORGANIZATION CHART

Within an organization, there are further distinctions made between workers, particularly employees. These workers hold positions referred to as either *staff* or *line*. You have likely seen organization charts for many businesses; in many respects, they resemble a genealogical family tree, since they often show tree-like structures bearing the titles of positions within the organization. In interior design businesses, these positions are usually listed, in descending order: design director, project designer, designer, and design assistant. Different firms may use other titles for these positions, such as Designer #1. Regardless of title, however, the position of these workers on the organization chart results in their being referred to as **line positions**. This distinction relates to the belief that holding a line position could result in moving up the line to positions higher on the chart with greater responsibilities, prestige, and, of course, pay. In a typical scenario, a design assistant, after gaining an initial measure of experience and the confidence of management decision makers, might ascend to the position of designer. The line is also important in the organizational structure because it establishes what is called the **chain of command**, or lines of authority within an organization.

STRUCTURE OF INTERIOR DESIGN BUSINESSES

Within most interior design firms of any size, or within interior design departments of architectural firms, the first line position is usually that of design assistant. This is most often an entry-level position held by recent graduates of design programs with little experience outside the classroom. After these designers gain experience handling projects that are relatively small in scope and have earned some amounts of revenue, they may progress to the position of designer. This next position may also be called staff designer; they work under the direct supervision of others. Nevertheless, the position is not a staff position since it is on the organization chart and requires the independent exercise of professional judgment that workers need in order to carry out tasks—characteristics uncommon among true staff positions.

Positions found on a business's organization chart pertain to those held by workers who carry out the principal function of a business, be it accounting, law, or interior design. People holding these positions do not rely on other line members to assist and support them in the conduct of their individual tasks; they rely on what are referred to as **staff members**. An administrative assistant is one type of staff member found in most businesses, while a drafter of design drawings and CAD specialists are examples of staff members particular to architectural and interior design firms.

Rising from the position of designer to that of project manager is the next step design professionals may take in their organization. Project managers not only have extensive experience carrying out their own complex and financially important projects, but also a demonstrated ability to supervise others effectively. These positions frequently call upon the worker to oversee the work of many designers as well as support staff and also to assume some marketing activities. Interior design professionals with extensive project experience, often gained as a result of years of practice, and who have demonstrated abilities to oversee others and attract remunerative clients may be eligible to ascend to principal in firms.

Firm principals may include entrepreneurs who initially founded the firms at which they work, or workers who rose to this high level from other positions within the organization. Usually, principals are primarily responsible for their firms' creative direction and for interacting with clients, especially important clients. Principals are also responsible for forming strategic plans concerning major firm activities, such as the nature of future projects and methods for charging clients for services. These individuals may sometimes be referred to as partners, although the organization itself may not legally be a partnership, perhaps having been formed as a corporation or limited liability company. The way in which the business was formally established will control management decisions.

THE TASK OF COMMUNICATING INFORMATION AND EVALUATING WORKERS

Organizational structure is important for several reasons. Hierarchical in nature, it also suggests an established route by which information is conveyed throughout a business of any size. In small businesses, the chain of command—the pathway that members of the organization recognize and follow when communicating business information to each other—may be quite truncated: a junior-level worker may be able to relay information directly to a firm principal, as can a principal to the worker. In more highly structured organizations, upper-management workers communicate through those in intermediate, or middle-management positions, to convey policies and instruction. Entry-level workers, under a formal chain-of-command structure, would report only to those directly above them in the organizational scheme—for example, assistant designers might direct questions to designers who oversee their work. In this way, the organizational structure within a business influences how communication of managerial information will flow.

An important activity in which managers engage is evaluating worker performance. Determining the degree to which a worker understands and adheres to established companywide communication procedures is often a consideration in these evaluations. In some businesses, chain-of-command and organization structure play a large role in determining how managers will conduct these evaluations. Chain-of-command and organizational structure are important when companies utilize what is referred to as **360-degree feedback**, in which colleagues situated in the organizational scheme above, below, and on the same level as a worker (as well as the workers themselves) prepare written statements describing their perceptions of the quality of work produced by that individual and their working relationship with that worker. This inclusive approach is gaining acceptance in large organizations, particularly those that utilize many layers of management. Its implementation depends on whether there is sufficient organizational structure in place to generate enough relevant information from which to draw conclusions about a worker's performance. Because this approach is expensive and time-consuming, it is less likely to be used to evaluate the performance of staff workers or of line workers who hold entry-level or low-level positions, although the institutional policy varies in this regard.

MENTOR MEMO

In my current job, I manage a large team of designers and project managers around the globe. Each of them is different, with skills of varying complexities. On my first day at the firm, I was handed an organizational chart completed by my predecessor. It was clear that each person had a title and level description of their current skills. It was a great place to start; every team should have one.

After a few months, my co-manager and I came to the conclusion that some of the designers were not working to their potential, whereas others were simply doing production with little to no exposure to design-related tasks. Were we doing something wrong? How could we motivate people to be further engaged with the tasks at hand? And then an idea begin to percolate. The design director and I decided to "shuffle the deck."

We choose ten staff in question and handed them each a roll of trace paper, and a program with instructions detailing what we hoped to see in return. Of the ten staff, we had production leaders, designers, and managers. Every person was being asked to step out of his or her comfort zone to try something new. This was indeed a design competition, and all solutions would be posted for team discussion in two days. The results were both shocking and enlightening.

The most established in their careers posted ideas that were safe, achievable, and, of course, buildable. Those with less experience were understandably more fearless, providing thought-provoking ideas with uncharted creativity. One junior designer produced forty-seven ideas on one continuous piece of trace paper, using the entire roll to get to the recommended solution, in an exceptional narrative. The results gave light to an idea, whereby designers would work in teams of two, with both experience and fresh ideas coming together for every finished product.

For our clients, this was a communication hurdle that we managed carefully. It was essential to share our plan, and to assure established clients that someone with very few years under their belt was there to challenge the norms and spark creative ideas. The more established designers continued to assist in a more hands off way, but they were still deeply engaged in the success of the finished product. For others who participated in the design challenge, it became clear that their skills were more about team management than design execution. And in their cases, a completely new job description needed to be crafted. Are you in the right chair, was the questions that needed to be asked.

In summary, and three years after the experiment, our success rate for landing new clients had increased, and our design quality had improved. This is not needed in every firm; however, it is the job of your manager to create the environment staff needs to do their best work, even if it means reinventing the organization chart and creating new descriptions for staff to thrive in. Shuffling the deck was a risk, one that resulted in outstanding success for both staff and our clients.

FACTORS INFLUENCING MANAGEMENT DECISIONS

Businesses management and personnel management are not activities that exist in a vacuum; rather they are influenced by factors both internal and external to the business itself. As you complete your education, you have undoubtedly thought about your future employment in interior design. Perhaps you have had conversations about the job market. In doing so, you have identified one of the external components that

Satisfied design firm employees and clients result from management actions attuned to "big picture" issues more than the "big chair" concerns.

influences management decisions: the economic conditions prevalent in the marketplace, both national and local.

National and local economic conditions profoundly influence management decisions, especially those related to hiring new workers. Individual sole proprietors—in essence their own managers—make decisions based on these conditions as well. Economic health determines the availability of new jobs as well as the longevity of those in existence. In good times, as in the late 1990s and early 2000s, national and most local economies expanded, so that individuals and businesses had greater monetary resources at their disposal. That availability of capital, for example, provided the financial impetus for the commission of new interior design projects, both residential and commercial. Managers, therefore, had more reasons to hire designers and create new design-related positions: There was a greater demand for the services of designers. As a result, those seeking employment in established firms and practice groups, or working in individually owned businesses, faced fairly good prospects for obtaining work.

Unfortunately, economic conditions changed and the demand for designers decreased, so that managers had to react by reducing, sometimes drastically, their existing staff. Employment figures for designers dropped considerably during the period ranging from 2001 to early 2004. Currently design jobs are slowly being added in the workplace. Employment of designers in sectors such as government work has grown in the interim, with increased demand for design services in governmental and military projects. Managers in these areas have responded by posting more government-sponsored jobs for interior design services; however, the extent to which managers in other sectors recognize the incremental advances in the economy and respond by hiring new workers remains to be determined.

Both businesses and workers are affected by economic conditions, whether good or bad. As you have seen, in expanding economies, management decision makers scramble to fill positions to meet the demands of many new projects. The challenge for managers then becomes determining the extent to which these added workers can be retained when economies contract. As you plan your career in interior design, ask yourself how you would enjoy the responsibility of making sometimes-difficult management decisions that stem from changing economic conditions, as many business decision makers are required to do.

MENTOR MEMO
Regardless if you work for a named star designer or a great team of selfless talented professionals, each with something valuable to bring to the table, you will need a plan for your projects to get you from A to B. A great work plan is your first tool to formulate a fee, its your reference tool to manage a team effectively, and sometimes it's your slide in the PowerPoint to explain to a client where and how their project will be completed. A good work plan will get you there. Your one-page plan, should list all staff, your schedule, and your project milestones. Excel is often the simplest tool for this effort, hours and hourly rates should be used to calculate the net results.

If you work through the plan, and the requested fee is higher than the market of competitive areas will absorb, you will be looking at refining the scope or the designer's hourly rates in order to reduce the fees at hand. In every case, and at all times, you are subject to the market where you are doing business. Very few designers are able to quote fees, without a firm understanding of market rates and a competitors' structures for fee ranges. Remember: "Work the plan . . . and plan the work!"

INFLUENCE OF EMPLOYMENT LAWS

Another important external factor that influences managers and the business decisions they make concerns personnel management, specifically the federal and state laws that relate to employment practices. A detailed survey of this topic could fill entire volumes and still remain incomplete. For the purpose of your study of personnel management, an overview of these laws along with a thumbnail description of their major provisions as they apply to interior design businesses should serve as an effective introduction. The formal titles of the major federal laws affecting employment practices are as follows:

- Civil Rights Act of 1964, Title VII (sometimes referred to as *Title VII*)
- Age Discrimination in Employment Act of 1967 (amended in 1990)
- Equal Employment Opportunity Act of 1972 (EEO)
- Civil Rights Act of 1991

The combined effect of these major pieces of employment-related federal legislation is that employers, especially those in businesses that have fifteen or more employees, cannot discriminate on the basis of race, color, gender, age, marital status, or national origin in hiring and employment practices. Business managers responsible for personnel decisions must not only be aware of the provisions of these laws but also incorporate these provisions in internal business documents, such as employment applications, to ensure that potential hirees know that the revelation of prohibited information is not required. Terms found in employment handbooks must also be crafted by managers to reflect provisions of these and other laws. In this context, personnel managers are also tasked with organizing employment practices, such as the conduct of employee evaluations and terminations, in equally compliant ways.

Other federal laws related specifically to employee pay and benefits have also influenced the actions of business managers. Prominent among them are the following:

- Equal Pay Act of 1963
- Family and Medical Leave Act of 1993 (FMLA)

According to provisions of the Equal Pay Act, employers must pay all employees holding the same or similar jobs and having the same kind of work experience the same starting salary. Provisions of FMLA require that employers of fifty or more employees (who must have been with that business for at least one year on a full-time basis) provide those workers with up to twelve weeks of leave in order to care for a parent, spouse, or child. In addition to these and other federal laws related to employment practices, most states have enacted specific legislation applying to businesses in their jurisdictions. Managers are, of course, responsible for knowing the provisions of state laws and incorporating them into organizational practices as well.

INTERNAL FACTORS IN BUSINESS DEVELOPMENT

Management decisions are also influenced by conditions internal to their businesses. Two particularly influential internal factors involve understanding the developmental stage of a business's life and the kinds of services a business offers. It is important to note that these internal considerations do not exist apart from the external factors affecting management decisions. Managers need to be aware of the interplay of all these factors when making business decisions.

Developmental Stages of a Business

Businesses, like the people who work in them and the products they sell, transition through different phases throughout their lives. Whether referring to an infant or an introductory phase, you may notice a parallel development in the lives of people, products, and businesses. Characteristics of these different phases affect management decisions. These stages of business development may be defined as early, middle, and late.

In the early stages of a business—for example, when it first opens—managers may be called upon to make relatively few personnel decisions. Small firms in particular may have only a few or no workers other than the owner. In many instances, an owner and an initial group of workers share similar beliefs about a company's purpose and direction, so formal management practices are of less concern. Instead, decisions made during the early stage are likely to focus on getting the business off the ground. Doing that may require that the owner and workers collectively decide to forego many benefits, or even regular salaries, to make adequate resources available to the business.

The middle stage of business life may be thought of as having two distinct phases: increasing growth and maturity, where the latter is sometimes referred to as a business's *peak*. As the terms *growth* and *maturity* suggest, management activities increase as the business becomes a viable entity and the need arises for greater internal structure to organize the business. In addition, management activities are increasingly required in order to assure compliance with laws regulating business and employment practices. Perhaps because of the services the firm offers or the economic conditions present at the time or some combination of these factors, after the services of a nascent business become recognized, managers have an incentive as well as a financial ability to add employees to meet the demand for services and to focus on strategies reinforcing a business's position in the marketplace. In short, with the success of a business and its resulting growth, management activities traditionally increase to handle this development.

The second phase in the middle stage of a business's development is its maturity, or peak. Management practices during this phase are directed toward identifying new areas for firm growth as well as finding ways to organize its increasingly complex structure. By this time, a business's founders may have been joined by others who may not share the same beliefs that held the original core group together. In addition, the need for workers at this stage becomes more specialized and compartmentalized. Managers are responsible for finding ways to integrate the different beliefs into existing business practices along with identifying, hiring, and retaining workers who satisfy organizational needs.

The final stage of business development is referred to as the late, or decline, stage. Management decisions during this phase may focus less on retaining new workers than on finding ways to accommodate a business in what by then would be a substantially different marketplace for its services than was present at its beginning. Winding up a business's activities in preparation for the retirement of its owners may be one focus of management, as might locating a buyer for the business's assets. Merging the business into another entity may also be an activity for managers of especially large firms or practice groups.

It is important for interior designers seeking employment to assess the stage of a business before applying to work there. Young businesses may offer the excitement and freedom of less structure, but they may also be riskier choices than work at a more seasoned firm with an established clientele and procedures. On the other hand, by choosing an established firm in which to work, a designer may be subject to more management supervision, especially with regard to business-development concerns. Many larger firms and practice groups place specific requirements on assistant designers seeking to become owners in a firm to attract profitable work.

In their later stages of development, firms may offer much in the way of name recognition and prestige; however, they may also have long entrenched practices and values that are not conducive to new or different points of view. Determining the stage of a business within its developmental life cycle can provide important clues about the working conditions, management practices, and opportunities to be found there.

Services Offered by a Business

Another important internal factor influencing management decisions involves the services provided by firms. Business managers must focus on the exact services firms provide and the extent to which the consumer marketplace recognizes the need for those services. Knowing the services their businesses provide enables managers to formulate strategic plans for their businesses.

Strategic plans identify business goals and define ways to meet them. Strategic plans may include determining the areas of practice on which to concentrate more or less attention. For example, many commercially trained interior designers, working in a crowded marketplace for office design, may choose not to work in that practice area but rather to apply their skills to designing healthcare facilities. Even within the field of office design, designers tired of simply "warehousing" workers may combine extensive research in corporate culture with their design skills in order to offer services that more creatively mesh a company's identity with the physical environment in which that company's employees work. These new directions for applying interior design services are often the results of strategic planning in which designers realize how their services can be differentiated from those of others in their field. After management decisions are made about the new direction of services, they can be followed by personnel decisions relating to the new business goals.

MENTOR MEMO
Do you work for a "star" or a "constellation"? This is a commonly used way to describe working practices in the interior design industry. If you are a "star," your name is probably on the masthead, and you undoubtedly are or were the driving force who the opened the doors and the original person who got the practice up and running. In some cases, clients only want to work with the individual star or ensure that singular driving force has a presence on their project. Many firms start and stop with this mentality because there was never room for the next generation of talent to find their way. Great stars simply represent a brand or a level of design or a style, and clients fully understand there is a pool of talent behind the game. The great stars gracefully hand the reins to their peers when the timing is needed on a project.

The opposite is sometimes referred to as a constellation. A constellation is cluster of bright shiny professionals who are less about one name on the door. Instead, they are, more representative of a broader team mentality for both problem solving and creative ideas.

 In either case, there is no wrong structure. With hopes to learn, many designers new in their careers target named design firms where there is a face to the driving force behind the company. Regardless, be sure to ask the right questions around team structure, mentorship, and peer review.

MANAGEMENT POLICIES AND PROCEDURES

Earlier in the chapter, you learned that one of the key roles a manager plays is as an informational source, disseminating knowledge about the company and its operations to workers. On a daily basis, much of that information is likely conveyed in an informal manner, orally, or in the form of e-mail messages. Businesses, especially those in later stages of their development, usually require consistency in the language and interpretation of management policies. To that end, managers are tasked with assembling and disseminating employee handbooks. Often published in the form of a spiral-bound notebook, these handbooks are intended to provide participants in a business, whether employees or managers, with a comprehensive source of information about company policies and procedures. As noted, one rationale for disseminating this information is to maintain consistency of policy; these handbooks are also a convenient source of company policy since they are usually made available to every worker through personnel managers.

As you might suspect, these books provide detailed information about the conduct of practices adopted for use by the business. That information, and much more, may be found in various sections of the handbook. Typically, these books contain sections defining employment and business practices such as the following:

1. The organizational structure of the business
2. The employment procedures followed by the company
3. The method the company uses to determine pay and benefits
4. The daily operations of the business
5. The termination procedures followed by the company when employees leave the organization

Most businesses provide their employees with handbooks and frequently require employees to acknowledge having received one. Think for a moment about the discussion of contracts in Chapter 4. In particular, do you recall the stages in forming a contract: offer, acceptance, and consideration? Referring to these characteristics, many employees have argued that after they signed off on receiving a company's employee handbook, an *implied contract* was formed between them and the company. The terms of this implied contract are those found in the employee handbook. In general, courts of law have recognized that claim as valid; courts have further agreed with employees in related claims that companies breached those contracts by, as is usually the case, terminating the services of employees without following the terms and conditions specified in the company's handbook. Managers of businesses need to be aware of the possible effects of distributing employee handbooks and should seek assistance from legal professionals to assess those effects.

PROJECT TEAM MANAGEMENT

Just as management practices do not exist in a vacuum, interior designers do not work in isolation. An increasing challenge for managers in interior design businesses is to find ways of managing the groups of professionals who collaborate in carrying out projects. The project manager is frequently responsible for coordinating the actions of these project teams. Because project managers must collaborate with, even motivate, other skilled professionals, their work requires a uniquely diversified set of skills. This section first identifies the professionals with whom project managers interact, and then defines some advanced management skills necessary for project managers.

Perhaps the most important of the advanced management skills required of project managers is the ability to foster a sense of collaboration among a project's constituents (Coleman 2002, 704). However, no amount of team building can ignore the fact that the project manager needs strong technical skills in order to convey the project's design intent and the means for bringing that intent to fruition. Project management and organizational skills, as well as interpersonal skills, are also necessary to integrate the various project components to successfully satisfy budget, schedule, and end-use requirements.

IS MANAGEMENT IN YOUR FUTURE?

In this section of your plan for your ideal interior design business, focus your attention on the specific position you wish to fill in the organization you want to establish. For example, do you wish to assume the full range of management and design responsibilities as design directors commonly do? Or do you wish to organize your own job in your ideal interior design business in such a way that others will assume management and administrative tasks and leave you to concentrate primarily on design activities? As you begin this project, think first about the balance you wish to strike between carrying out management and design-related activities. Some design professionals wish to focus their attention only on detailed activities such as product development, having little interest in business management and personnel supervision. Such professionals, especially those who started their own businesses, hire others to take care of managerial matters. However, many designers enjoy the management process since it allows them to mentor the development of other designers. At the opposite end of the spectrum are designers who have assumed many managerial responsibilities, retaining only those creative and design-focused projects that promise very high design commissions or much publicity. They have chosen this approach because often their very large firms require concentrated attention from senior members to address its many management issues. Which of these scenarios might be the right one for you?

NOTES FROM THE FIELD

Early in my career I went to work for a large firm, with exceptional leaders at the management level. They were great communicators, extraordinarily talented designers and fearless when it came to fighting for good design. This was a firm of approximately 700 staff, with plenty of depth and bench strength in the delivery of large complicated projects. Given that I was only ten years into my career, I was well aware there were levels ahead of me, which was reassuring. There were plenty of people around to answer my questions! This is the story of one disastrous situation, by one firm leader, with an unfortunate end result for all parties involved.

This firm secured a major contract for a billion dollar building and surrounding site. My job on that project was the lead of the interior design team for the building. There was a five-year contract on this project so I would have to attend many meetings where I would listen and understand the buildings structure and other meetings where I would be presenting or working with the client directly. But in summary, there were no less than twenty team members that worked hand in hand, ironing out every detail, tirelessly and for months on end. The older generation of architects were designing and teaching the next generation along the way.

After five years and many sleepless work nights, the building opened, with a smash. This was a high profile site and a global entertainment venue; the world was watching for the inaugural event. The principal for our firm was invited to give a speech to the press, and we all waited to see what he would say. We heard a long description on his particular inspirations; plenty of "I" and not much "we." Unfortunately, the team was never acknowledged for their years of hard work and effort, there was no thank you, and there was no recognition for the extended family of professionals that project required. Many left the venue, bruised and disappointed. Many of the talented people who worked on that building left the firm soon after. Every person deserves positive recognition where it is due. Those leaders who properly credit their teams will attract the best talent in the world not because their employees are seeking recognition but because a beautiful project of any scale requires more than one person. That principal who failed to recognize his peers found himself quickly without a team and perhaps a diminished ability to assemble another one. In the world of interior design, you may build a project in a year, or in many. In any and every case, acknowledging the team of people who assisted you—from product representatives to contractors—is important. Remember: There is no "I" in "Team"!

Practical Activity

This chapter has explored teams and their importance. What makes a good team member in your experience? You have undoubtedly worked in teams at school and at work or in an internship. Define general characteristics of a good team member and note how you might coach someone to become one. Use examples from your experiences to illustrate desirable team member characteristics and how you would counsel others to become such a valuable team participant.

Review Questions

1. Define management, and describe the working environment and functions of managers.

2. What are some of the noted functions performed by managers?

3. What is personnel management, and what are some of its functions?

4. What are some stages of development in business entities?

5. Describe some issues related to business and personnel management that occur during each stage of development.

6. What are staff and line positions?

7. Describe the roles design assistants, designers, project designers, and design directors play in interior design organizations.

8. How do managers formally present company policies and procedures?

9. How do laws impact the management of businesses and personnel?

10. What are some components of employee handbooks?

11. What are the functions of job descriptions and employee evaluations?

12. What are some issues that designers should be aware of when working in teams?

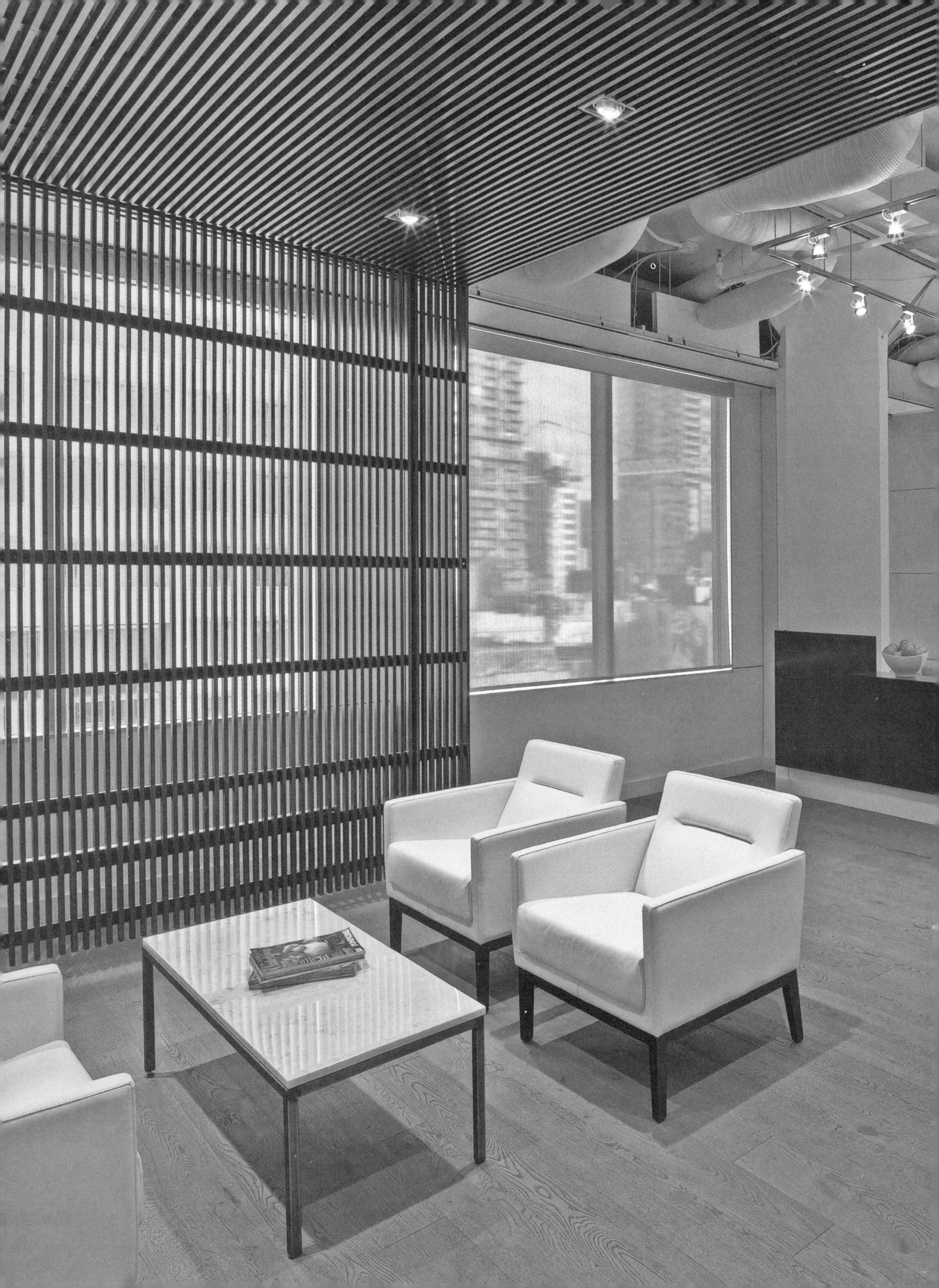

CHAPTER 7
MARKETING AND PROMOTING YOUR BUSINESS

MENTOR MEMO

Very few designers are good at sales. Sales means you are actively promoting to the clients you want. In the sacred church of design, if you are good, clients will find you, or so they say. But, I argue, times have changed. We are in an information society, and you will need help to become known. Very few clients will spend more than a few minutes considering the list of designers they will interview for a project. You will need to be one of the first designers that come to mind, when a client starts to think about who would be the best at solving this challenge.

After reading this chapter, you will be able to

- **Define marketing's basic concepts;**
- **Distinguish promotion and its related activities from marketing and describe their use;**
- **Describe what is meant by sales and selling and the necessity of both;**
- **Explain how interior designers may develop a multichannel marketing approach through use of Internet and social media;**
- **Explore how interior designers may meld their talents and marketing skills into brands, recognizable and sought after by potential clients.**

INTRODUCTION TO MARKETING AND PROMOTING YOUR BUSINESS

Traditional and technologically based marketing afford interior designers exciting ways to reach new worlds of prospective clients. This chapter first refreshes knowledge of basic marketing principles and promotional methods. Next, it considers ways interior

Interior designers' skills at marketing are responsible for attracting potential clients to their creative point of view.

designers may develop a multichannel marketing mix of traditional, Internet, and social media platforms. What foreseeable issues related to the use of technologically based marketing methods should designers be aware of? The chapter continues with a short survey of special issues related to technologically based marketing. Finally, it explores ways practitioners may combine their talents with marketing plans to build their own unique interior design brand.

MARKETING AND PROMOTION FOR INTERIOR DESIGNERS AND THEIR BUSINESS

Coffee. . .tea. . .or interior design! On at least every *other* street corner isn't there a coffee shop from which you might choose? Perhaps as a study break, you stopped in to your favorite coffee shop and had a drink prepared to your liking by a barista who knew just how to put that swirl of coffee through the foam to make your drink special or prepare tea "your way." As you sat down in the attractively lit space, you enjoyed music, appreciated free WiFi, and considered unique, colorfully packaged items on offer. Then, you relaxed, pleased with your choice. "Positive associations," "defined, recognizable identities," "variety of choices," "personalized service," "interesting products," and "personal satisfaction" are words that could describe your coffee shop experience.

Would it surprise you to know that your interior design clients might seek exactly the same things from you? How might you distinguish yourself professionally and your business commercially from others? How, in other words, might interior design clients come to you, and only you, just as you went to your own preferred coffee shop? This chapter explores marketing and promotional activities, both those now considered traditional and those now available through social media. These are concepts and practices interior designers use to differentiate their services, make them attractive to new prospects, and, ultimately, build a business of satisfied clients. The Mentor Memo notes that we are "in an information society." You are likely familiar with fundamental marketing concepts and terms, but added information about how they relate specifically to interior design will set the stage for other chapter sections.

BASICS OF INTERIOR DESIGN MARKETING

What will set interior designers apart from each other? To be sure, their creative perspectives and design talents will be the primary way they distinguish themselves in the eyes of consumers, but whether and how they market those skills will also be important. There are many different definitions of what marketing entails. Perhaps the most comprehensive is that promulgated by the American Marketing Association (AMA):

> [Marketing is] the process of planning and executing the conception, pricing, promotion, and distribution of ideas, goods, and services to create exchanges that satisfy individual and organizational goals.

How might interior designers use this definition and decipher its terms to form workable marketing plans?

Marketing Analysis

The "process of planning and executing," noted in the definition, usually begins with a *marketing analysis*. This first step identifies particular services designers and/or their businesses provide. For example, design consultation and space planning are often noted services for residential interior design; evidence-based solutions are services for hospitality or healthcare facilities in commercial interior design.

Marketing analyses also identify specific consumer groups to whom a designers' or a firms' services might appeal. As well, marketing analyses include surveys of services offered by other design professionals working in the same community. To be meaningful, marketing analysis should examine each of these components in detail, so that designers and firms can have a better understanding of who they are creatively and what they stand for professionally. With this knowledge, designers and firms (working with advertising professionals) are able to shape the marketing message. This may be an attention-getting statement indicating succinctly what the designer or firm represents such as their creative point of view or professional capabilities.

Marketing analysis should indicate market conditions for interior design services. For example, are there a great many residential interior designers already in the community, seeking the same clients and projects as the designer, or firm? Similarly, marketing analyses should indicate to commercial/contract firms how many others are engaged in the same kind of work. Since many commercial designers and firms have national, even international practices, the "community" aspect of marketing analyses may be worldwide to accurately inventory those providing similar services.

Marketing Plans and Budgets

Information gathered and organized in marketing analyses forms the basis for **marketing plans**. These plans define specific goals designers or firms have, provide an exact identification and description of services offered, and propose the promotional means by which designers or firms intend to achieve goals. Marketing plans typically include such information as budget amounts and schedules. They may contain such features as firms' current cadre of present clients, those clients sought (the target market), comparisons of the firm's rate with those of competing firms, and details about who in the firm will make marketing decisions and the means by which they will assess the results. Such means may be numbers of new clients obtained and/or how effectively the firm has utilized its resources in accordance with its marketing budget.

Marketing budgets indicate how the interior design business proposes to allocate its financial resources to make known the services it offers. These services can also be generated from marketing analyses, as they are often based on what competing designers and firms are estimated to spend. Marketing activities, from business cards to interactive websites, are business expenses. Decision makers for the design firm will, at this stage, determine what kinds of marketing tools they will use and set costs for them. What this means is that the principals operating a design firm might wish to run a series of print advertisements in either residential- or commercial-focused magazines. Determining the costs for producing and running such advertisements and then ascertaining whether the firm can afford some or all of those costs without jeopardizing other business activities is just one example of how a firm budgets for marketing expenses.

Designers with strong marketing strategies are able to attract clients with different spaces and needs.

Designers who understand return on investment concepts are better positioned to profitably grow their practices when competing with others for projects such as this.

Timing of marketing efforts is important if they are to be successful and not adversely impact budgets and cash flow.

Budgets describe what designers and firms believe are the best uses of financial resources available to achieve marketing goals. They are electing to spend their own money, but in ways that often do not have clearly defined results. Can, for example, there be a definite one-to-one financial (or other) return for every dollar spent on marketing efforts? There are no clear answers to questions about what marketing achieves for many designers and firms. Instead, most develop a *return on investment* (ROI) standard to determine what has been achieved from marketing. Characteristics of ROI analyses include assessments of whether there are greater revenues, increased numbers of signed clients both new and repeat, and the number of new prospects attracted from expansion into new practice areas. ROI measures link marketing plans and budgets, as the latter are often included in the former as a means of interpreting results.

Market Segmentation and Niche Marketing

Just as you might patronize a certain coffee shop, so, too, might clients work with one, particular interior designer, instead of another. Likely, they would go to a designer or firm they believed could best provide the services they needed for their project. In short, they would seek a design firm with talents and skills uniquely attractively to them and their needs. They might find out about such firms through that company's marketing efforts. In the course of preparing a marketing analysis, the firm may have described the specific design services it is able and willing to provide. In doing so, it set itself apart from others as part of its efforts at **market segmentation**, or **market differentiation**. The purposes of doing so are, of course, to establish the firms' practice area of expertise. Additionally, it seeks to attract the firm's **target market** of potential clients. This would be the subset, out of the larger pool of all potential clients, of individuals or groups to whom firms' specific design services might be appealing.

CHAPTER 7 MARKETING AND PROMOTING YOUR BUSINESS • 131

The target market for many interior designers are commercial clients with practical business needs related to space as these.

The target marketing process, another form of marketing analysis, can be highly detailed. There is no single factor alone defining a target market. In fact, many factors come into play to determine the individuals, or groups to which specific interior design services might appeal. Some of the more commonly used factors include

1. Demographic data-based interpretations of populations, ages, incomes;
2. Geographic locations of potential clients;
3. Psychographic profiles about lifestyle characteristics, including noting products and services identified groups would likely use;
4. Types of businesses in specific areas and the kinds of services they would likely use.

These target-marketing factors can serve as the basis for focused efforts by designers or design businesses to identify potential clients. Particularly in large firms with appropriate financial resources, designers often seek assistance from marketing survey firms specializing in demographic, psychographic, and other forms of consumer research.

MENTOR MEMO

It is absolutely critical to know your potential client's business almost as well as they do. Before you engage in a conversation with them, do your homework! Check what's driving their economy: Are they growing or shrinking? Research their competition, and digest key global trends that might impact how they use space and how their employees might interact within the space. Let's call it "niche research"!

These tasks are great additions to the job description of a librarian, or an intern. For example, if you plan to focus on landing law firms, find out what the average use of space is for partners versus associates, how many drawers their filing standards support, and what industry trends are around conference use and security. Look at all items that might impact their space, and note how much space they lease. Again, sector- and client-specific niche research is critical to securing more clients and doing a great job with the ones you have.

COMPETITION FOR INTERIOR DESIGN SERVICES

Market research includes assessing other interior design businesses. This is often referred to as the *competitive landscape*, or, informally, as the competition. Others in the profession, especially those designers and firms with similar professional specialties, are vying for new work among each other, seeking the same clients. This fact makes differentiation of services all the more important because potential clients often do not perceive or understand the unique subtleties characterizing one design firm over another. Promotional activities, such as advertisements, reflect and emphasize differences—in creative point of view, scope of services offered, types of previous projects completed—one designer or firm has from among competitors so that practitioner may attract clients in crowded markets.

How many coffee breaks have you had like the one suggested? Has every drink been *exactly* the same? They were similar, yet likely there were subtle, or maybe not so subtle, differences among those in past. Perhaps there were times the server was new or hurried; on other occasions, the server was more experienced or had plenty of time. These disparities resulted in different qualities in your drinks; it may have been hotter, colder, or blended more or less strongly. Such variety in how your drinks were made underscore marketing's service versus product distinction. This differentiation applies to interior designers and their work as well.

The AMA definition of marketing notes it applies to the "pricing, promotion, and distribution [of goods, ideas, and services]." Interior design is a service profession. The "goods" and "ideas" designers provide are part of an overall package of services they provide. Marketers note services have definitely different characteristics than those of products. Consider those in light of the designers' work.

Perhaps the most notable characteristic services have over products is their *intangibility*: It is not possible to physically touch or feel services. Prior to hiring designers for their services, prospective clients are in a similar position as you were in the coffee shop placing your order. They cannot "hold on to" what you will do for them. They have only images from other projects and other marketing materials to guide them. When it comes to marketing for services, marketers stress focusing on explaining or demonstrating to prospective clients results such as benefits: Will the designer be able to complete the project on time and on budget, for example? As designers gain increasing experience and commercial and professional recognition, the benefit to clients may be their agreement to work with them at all! The concept of benefit is noteworthy as well. Clients receive the benefit of work with particular designers or design firms; they receive financial compensation from client for doing such work. The AMA definition of marketing, noted earlier, refers to this as an *exchange*, or the mutual giving of something of value.

Inseparability in another characteristic: services cannot be disjointed from their providers. Who else but you can conceptualize interior spaces and establish design plans in the exact way you can? Successful marketing efforts are those establishing designers as thought leaders. They are the ones other professionals respect and clients actively seek. They have "something," based on their talents, personalities, and ways of doing business, that prospective clients desire and that no other designer can provide. This mystique is considered by marketers to be part of designers' *brand identity*, or those impressions or feelings associated with them. Branding and brand management is discussed in subsequent sections of this chapter.

Another differentiating characteristic is *inconsistency*, or variability. No service provider ever gives exactly the same service in the same way each time they work. Different circumstances and desires of each client will cause designers to work in different ways. Each project site, for example, has different features. Some clients will want to play active roles in the design process, whereas others are less interested in doing so. For many prospective clients, the idea of inconsistency is concerning. They seek—and will pay for—unique, cost- and time-aware solutions to their design concerns. No client wants to feel processed or to have the finished project unusable, or unremarkable. The marketing challenge for designers is to convince clients that the inherent inconsistency of interior design work does not mean they are unqualified, or incapable of handling new projects. Therefore, marketing and promotional efforts often stress their experience and qualifications.

Services involve time and expertise to make available. This means their providers do not have ready stocks of *inventory* for just their services alone although they may have inventories of goods available for sale. It is possible to set monetary costs for those goods. Might it be so for services? The costs associated with services are known as *idle production capacity* and may be thought of as their carrying costs. Service providers may not be able to quantify exactly overhead costs when it comes to services; they may vary widely and may not be clearly obvious. Yet, it is also true that each day designers do not work "costs" them, as they still must be able to pay such expenses that do arise.

Services are differentiated from products by their characteristics of intangibility, inseparability, inventory, and inconsistency—all of which offer challenges to designers and design firms as they seek to market their services. Promotional methods provide the means by which those challenges are addressed.

PROMOTIONAL METHODS

Marketing, as a discipline, has long been studied and analyzed. One definition of it has guided this discussion. Found throughout that description are references to such topics as product, place, and price. For example, you have explored differences between products and services; learned that place can refer to where target markets for designer services may be geographically located; and found that price refers to amounts designers propose to charge for their services. According to many marketers, those terms comprise three of the "four Ps" of marketing and are considered to form the *marketing mix*. Promotion, the subject of this section, remains to detail. Four broad categories of promotion traditionally used by interior designers are advertising, sales promotion, personal selling, and publicity.

Advertising and Sales Promotion

Advertising is a term often misused as a synonym for *marketing*; yet the two are decidedly different in what they seek to accomplish. *Advertising* is the paid transmission of a marketing message to arouse desire in potential clients to buy goods or services offered by the advertiser or to produce a favorable image of the advertiser on the part of those exposed to the message. Advertising may be considered one of the techniques marketers use in an overall plan designed to facilitate exchanges of goods and services. Marketing budgets often include substantial allocations to pay for the creation of advertisement concepts based on marketing messages, advertisement production costs, placement fees (i.e., costs associated with getting ads in the media before the general public), website creation, search engine optimization (SEO) consultations, and consultations related to social media participation. Broadcast advertising includes television, Internet, and radio. Interior designers typically favor newspapers and magazines, particularly "shelter" magazines, or those with established bases of readers of potential new clients, interested in seeing examples of finished projects. Within the realm of commercial interior design, request for production (RFP) responses are a form of advertisement for designers and firms.

MENTOR MEMO
The corporate commercial interior design world operates in an entirely different fashion (from residential interior design), when it comes to business development. In the corporate world, work comes from two streams—either directly from the end user or from the real estate brokerage. In both cases, you will be competing for an interview. There are bid sites that, due to procurement proceedings in government or public companies, put the RFP process out for public bid. This is a blind bid, and you may or may not know the number of people you are competing against.

If the RFP (request for proposal) comes directly from the end user, it will typically outline the specifics of the requirement and ask for a very specific response. You will see the requests for company history, size, insurance, and disclosure of any pending lawsuits. They will also ask for your PA (project approach) or process methodology. Asking to outline a project approach is your opportunity to share with the client in a step-by-step way, how you will get the job done without errors and omissions. Case studies and detailed photography that is professionally done will be requested.

If the opportunity is coming from the (commercial real estate) brokerage community, your chances normally improve because you are already on the short list of preferred designers with that broker. In order to sign a lease, the tenant must know how much space to take. The real estate broker is responsible for getting those leases signed; that is how he or she makes a living. As a result, the broker will assist the client with the issue of an RFP for interior design services. Usually three firms are invited in to meet the client first and to provide an introductory presentation before submitting a fee. This is always the preferred situation because the client knows your value because they have met you before you submit a cost for your services. All designers are not the same, and the client needs to know what makes your team unique.

Fees are discussed over a number of chapters. There are many ways to calculate, track, and monitor fees. In the submission process, when being considered, be clear; it is better to itemize and fully disclose where you are making money on the project. If quality of the team and the design are among the priorities of the client, fees will become less of a concern and more of a conversation. It's important to help a client understand what percentage of the total project budget the fee represents. In my experience, clients are keen to negotiate the designer's fees, given they are one of the first numbers they see and are keen to discuss. However, given that the designers' fees often represent less than 10 percent of the total projects budget, and those same designers are in charge of the remaining 90 percent, clients should want you to have enough time to be both thorough and focused on the work, without mistakes.

Brokerage Services

Before you enter into the picture, it is recommended that you fully understand what a brokerage company has sold the client. Many good brokerage teams offer product buying agreements, project management services, procurement and even space planning. Ensure you know, what their services are, so as not to step on any toes, in your pitch for the work.

Before the lease is signed, a great broker will invite designers in to pitch for work so that all parties will understand the pros and cons of site selection and to qualify the general square footage. It is NOT recommended that designers provide RSF (rentable square footage) for the purposes of a lease. In the event you are even one square foot off, you could impact the value of your client's lease; your liability is tremendous. Providing the USF (usable square footage) is common; however, you must have a firm grasp of local regulations for capturing that square footage, and how the landlord chose to represent that space.

Because of the incredible expense of print and television ads, the concept of *cooperative advertisement* came about. Interior designers may team with one of their vendors, such as a rug manufacturer, and use images featuring that company's products, followed by designers' business name and contract information; both (or one) of the businesses might pay to run the ad on local television or in print media. Usually, this form of advertising is used by residential designers associated with large retail businesses, such as furniture stores, or commercial design firms in professional design journals.

Sales promotion is another term sometimes confused with marketing. It can be part of the marketing mix, but is a method determined by marketing analysis, set forth in marketing plans, and funded via marketing budgets to attract clients. Some residential interior designers offer coupons in magazines. Often, these take the form of "dollars off" or "complimentary" initial consultations. This method may be used, certainly, to bring in new business. It may also be used as a measure of advertising effectiveness and whether publications physically reach target markets of interior design consumers.

Interior designers may be called upon to work with business partners like real estate brokers to help them understand particular client needs.

Selling

Selling involves making known attributes of goods or services to potential customers or clients with the intention of bringing about an exchange. The goal of selling is to convert prospects into paying consumers. It is an important part of the marketing process, not only because it is a source of revenue but also because it is often the first and only contact businesses may have with potential customers or clients. Selling is often accomplished through personal presentations.

Personal selling mostly involves spoken presentations given one-on-one, or in small, controlled groups in which the attributes of goods, or services are touted and offered. It plays an important role in the overall marketing efforts of any kind of product or service. It first involves identifying specific consumers, their needs, and resources. This is referred to as *qualifying* sales prospects, those that are most likely to be interested in and able to afford products or services offered. Then, it involves explaining or demonstrating why and how those products or services should be chosen to address such needs. The sales process concludes with what is called a *close*, during which the person making the *pitch*, or ask, requests the prospect's business in the form of purchasing an item or signing on as a client. As simple as that process may seem, the idea of "selling" is difficult for many, including interior design professionals. This may be because there are risks involved with selling. Rejection, of course, is among them, but so, too, is reluctance. Is selling really necessary for interior designers?

Creative professionals view their work product very differently from consumers of their products and services. Consumers, for their part, may desire design solutions that meet their immediate needs and require (or want to pay for) nothing more. Designers, in contrast, have studied the processes behind the work they do from different perspectives and view their solutions as representing or being inspired by those studies. For some designers, results they produce from their training and experience should need no further explanation, much less touting for the purpose of obtaining work. However, the merits of a design solution, while obvious to a trained professional, may not be so apparent to nondesigners. The reality is brilliant ideas may remain forever on drafting boards if designers are unable, or unwilling to "sell" them to prospective clients and show them how such ideas best meet their needs, over those of others. Personal selling skills are perhaps the best way to make clients aware of the merits of a designer's solution. To be sure, most clients are extremely sophisticated consumers of professional services. However, selling skills on the part of designers can help ensure that prospective clients interpret correctly (and understand the merits of) designers' work products and the ideas informing them.

Word-of-mouth (WOM) marketing is the mirror image of personal selling. Instead of designers touting their services and explaining the value of their skills, it is their clients—past and present—speaking to others about the designer. It is a truism that people talk, especially in interconnected social and professional worlds. Those who desire and can afford services of residential interior designers probably know and socialize with others who also desire and can afford these services. Commercial clients behind large-scale contract interior design projects also know and network with others. Interior designers, with either kind of practice, should be aware of the high possibility that they, their personalities, their work and business habits, how well the project came together, and any number of other issues (good or bad) are possible topics of this kind of informal marketing. Inevitably, designers will discover these discussions have taken place. After all, people talk! What should they do?

First, positive WOM marketing can be highly effective. It can pave the way for introductions to future clients. If possible, designers should thank sources of positive *referrals*. Referrals are vital to the growth of any business; those making referrals are personally vouching for the designers' expertise and are willing to direct others to them.

MENTOR MEMO

In residential work, personal referrals are everything, and not every interior designer will make a great residential interior designer. In this area, you are dealing with a person's personal space, and decorating plays a much larger role. You will need a great photographer and publicist to capture the work the moments it's done and preferably before the client moves in. The process of properly photographing a project deserves a chapter unto itself, but in short, hire a professional. Proper lighting and staging are common. Yes, every project receives a liberal amount of Photoshop work to remove small items and improve contrast or color. After a project is photographed, a great publicist or marketing team is hopefully at the ready to publish the work, or target electronic market to clients you would like to work with that might see this work as interesting.

Less-than positive comments need to be addressed as well through *damage control*. Again, it is suggested, designers should, if possible, address the source of comments, acknowledge disappointment at any dissatisfaction, and then ask what might have been done differently. Of course, there is no way to really prevent people from talking or knowing what they will say. It may, in fact, be surprising what catches clients' attention. Complaints include fairly minor concerns like designers not returning telephone calls as promptly as desired. Others are of concern, as these go to designers' integrity. Residential interior design clients have been known to express their belief that designers "kite" orders; that is, the designers wait until they receive payment from one client before they place orders on behalf of another client. Contract clients often express concerns about final project costs and wonder (aloud) why designers could not keep them lower. Such client impressions, whether valid or not, nevertheless, should be addressed constructively by designers. Negative WOM "marketing" by others can undo much of designers' planned, expensive efforts done on their own behalf.

Publicity

Publicity, as another form of promotion, seeks to inform, not persuade, and involves making known information about products, persons, companies, or events that may be of interest to the public. In contrast to advertisement, which can be expensive to produce and get out, there are no costs usually associated with getting publicity-intended messages before the public. Radio, television, and print media resources, often seek out and transmit in their communities such information as those about special events, local personalities, visiting notables, occurrences, and special interest news not otherwise covered.

An example of publicity might begin with a studio hosting a workshop about current interior design trends, free to the public. Information about such an event, where and when it will occur, who is slated to speak, and what topics are planned would be the subject of a *press release*, or written statements. These are issued by businesses and sent to local media contacts. They contain information that the designer wants disseminated, such as the workshop event and its details. Releases further contain specified dates during which the item should run in order for its subject matter to be timely and relevant. If the contact deems it appropriate for transmission or publication (and there is space and time for it), information about the interior design trend event will appear. Press releases are one way for interior designers to build relationships with journalists and others such as media planners and buyers and magazine and newspaper publishers, among others. These professionals can be useful contacts for designers as they develop their businesses.

MENTOR MEMO
Getting your name in print is not a simple task. Every designer wants to be recognized and on the cover of a major magazine. Here are two points of advice on that topic. Assuming your projects are great (and they will be!), connect with the publications you think might

be interested in the work, and inquire what the specifics are they look for in publications. Some have a specific number of shots or an orientation that is preferred (landscape versus portrait). Other publications like to see the work before, or in process, in order to build a great story around the work. Just being pretty is not enough. You will need more of a hook to get on the page. Second, plan for what you are going to do after you get published. Now, you must target market to other similar clients who might see your recent work as intriguing and want to hire you for a future project. Regardless, press is marketing that makes business development easier.

MULTICHANNEL MARKETING FOR INTERIOR DESIGNERS

The Internet's impact and importance are ever growing. Numbers of websites proliferate as evidence. People the world over are now gaining access to it such that the Internet is their "go to" resource for information and purchases. Social media continues to fascinate. Much of that interest is due to its ability to build communities. By permitting information sharing, social media fosters participation among users. Social media may mirror or negate mainstream marketing messages, or even create its own. As "virtual" groups, their members come together, joined by common interests or causes though not always personally acquainted. Interior designers are finding ways to get in touch with each other and with potential, future clients through such platforms as LinkedIn and Facebook. Of course, advertisement and other traditional means still remain viable. What does all this mean? Together, all these methods, if well-coordinated, afford interior designers at every stage of their careers tremendous marketing options.

The Internet and social media have been much discussed in terms of functionality. As a student, you probably have taken on-line classes, or "tweeted" friends about what's going on in class. You and your family keep up with each other through Facebook, perhaps. Through your personal experiences, you know a great deal about Internet and social media use. Think about what you know and consider what fashion retail marketers are now doing: developing *multichannel marketing* strategies, which is sometimes referred to as *omnichannel marketing*.

Basically, multichannel strategies in the fashion retail world involve finding ways to build positive customer shopping experiences across physical stores, Internet sites, catalogues, and mobile devices such as apps. You may not have a store, or even an Internet site, or for that matter a catalogue, or an app. How might this relate to you? Think about what these marketers and promoters have discovered about consumers.

Fashion retail marketers have found customers like having multiple shopping avenues available to them. They have also found consumers appreciate it when those channels have the following attributes in their multichannel experience: convenience, consistency, engagement, and authenticity. As you go forward promoting your interior design services, how might you incorporate these characteristics?

Can potential clients find you and your Facebook page, or full-fledged Internet site? In short, how *convenient* are you to find? The next section addresses that concern under search engine optimization. After prospects do find you, do your Facebook pages appear cluttered, or have so many scripts pages take a lengthy time to load, or are they even able to load properly at all! Images are designers' stock in trade when it comes to promotion; imagine having your work appear "off" because there is simply too much loaded onto your pages. Are you on Pinterest and Instagram for users who like those photo resources? How do your images and written content appear on these? Thus, do you take a *consistent*, or "whatever" approach to how you present your work? The following brand-building section addresses another reason why consistency is important for interior designers.

Continuing with these thoughts, does your content interest and entice potential clients; in other words, does it encourage *engagement*? Blogs (Web + log), or on-line diaries, are one way to get your content out on the Internet, to reach the world. But think about this: Are you using your website or your Facebook page to get business, share your personal life? Instead, why not offer information that viewers might be able to use in their own decorating; you could take them somewhere they don't, or can't, usually go, such as inside "trade only" showrooms or project construction sites? When you do provide written content, how does it read? Does it sound like you have just written a formal letter, or is it in your own natural style? Can viewers get a sense of you and what you stand for creatively when they visit any Internet, social media, or encounter any form of traditional marketing methods you use? Fashion marketers have found consumers respond to *authenticity*; "real" seeming messages and language echoing their own interests and needs as well as being in language they would use themselves. These elements can be helpful to interior designers as touch points, goals to seek when planning promotional strategies.

WHAT INTERIOR DESIGNERS NEED TO KNOW ABOUT "TECH" MARKETING

Changes in technology occur breathtakingly fast. Keeping up with them (if possible) and what is new in their own industry can be daunting, because designers are expected to be innovative, including knowing how to work with developments across the spectrum of products, technology, and media. The following are, to date, among recent technology issues designers might ask techies to explain and their short explanations as they affect interior designers and their marketing efforts.

What is search engine optimization, and how can it help me market my business? Say you go to GOOGLE and enter your name; where did it show up on the list produced? Search engine optimization, or SEO, works with programs running search engines to position your name as among their first results. If your name is unique OR there are few others like it, you may be okay. But what if you're way down the list of results and there are other interior designers above you? It's not good. So, to fix, you need to edit, even change website names, modify content titles appearing on it, and maybe go back to your site's designers and ask them to change its HTML coding. Remember, the Internet is *inbound marketing*, users come to you, not the other way around as with *outbound marketing*, like print ads you run in magazines. Words users type in have to be found by search engine programs to be more "relevant" in order for your name to appear as near the top of the list as possible.

I'm worried about Internet security. Is it safe to use WiFi and Cloud technology? Of course, it's convenient to be able to work anywhere, anytime, and anyplace, but there are risks with WiFi and Cloud technology,. Hackers can get to your credit card information if you are not purchasing from a secure, encrypted site and your own is not protected. If you intend to do much purchasing through WiFi, seek out the newest, most comprehensive encryption for your office and don't give out personal information when using public WiFi. The area of security is tough; everyday hackers find ways around encryption solutions. With Cloud, you just don't' know how many, or what kind of servers are involved, their speed, their security, nothing. No matter the risks, however, you usually have to agree to them in the providers' terms of service or else miss out on being able to get on line. So, what this means is that you must assess the degree of risk as best you can. Probably, most Clouds will not present problems, especially if there are multiple levels of password protection involved, but there may not be!

What does net neutrality mean, and is it only important to techies? When you go online, the speed at which you are able to navigate around depends on your cable connection, or whether there is wireless service. It doesn't matter what you are looking for, whether you are shopping, updating Facebook, or simply surfing the Web, you can do so as fast as possible and so can everyone else once you are on line. Also, the only "costs" to obtain Internet service is how much cable subscriptions costs, if you even have one, because many people access and navigate the Internet for free. Right now, we are in a mostly "net neutral" environment with fast, free access to content available to everyone. But suppose you were charged for both the speed at which you could navigate the Internet and the content you were able to access? For that matter, suppose you were changed for just about anything else: for accessing the Internet using a mobile phone, or for using an app (application), or for any and all other reasons? These issues are currently being discussed. They are important to consumers because they will have to pay to do what they can now do for free, should net neutrality be eroded. For businesses, isn't it difficult enough for consumers to find your business? Suppose they do, but the service is so slow it takes a long time just to load your homepage with all the images of your interior design projects! That might be the reality, as well. What this means, of course, is that businesses will have to pay more out of their marketing budgets to allow searchers and users "premium" access. It is unclear how this issue will play out, but at present, many are not even aware it's being discussed.

BRAND BUILDING FOR DESIGNERS AND THEIR BUSINESSES

How might you, your creative point of view, your talent for interior design, and your newly acquired knowledge of traditional and technologically based marketing be combined into something wonderful? What might that even be? How about Brand You!

To set some context, recall the products and services you go back to again and again. Items like your preferred kind of running shoes. Places such as your favorite coffee shop. Why do you like them so much? One reason, of course, is that they fulfill your expectations about them: the shoes wear well; the coffee tastes great. But there is something that brings them to the front of your mind when you make purchasing decisions. That something is their brand identity and the positive associations that image carries with you.

Brands are names, terms, designs, symbols, or any other feature that distinguishes one product or service from another. Look at your shoes and the coffee cup. Likely you recognize them as being by a particular company and will find such elements such as special colors, logos, or taglines. There is something more. Successful brands are those that evoke opinions and emotions. Again, recall your shoes and coffee shop experience; you definitely have opinions and emotions about each. The issue becomes how to make your interior design services successful through brand practices just as the major companies did to produce your shoes and provide your coffee shop experience.

Brand identity is the sum total of what a brand stands for, both good and bad, in the eyes of consumers. Your work, as represented in your portfolio and images of completed projects, is one element of your brand identity, of Brand You. It is, by analogy, your version of the shoes and coffee shop. The words, colors, statements, and other items form what will become your brand elements. These physically represent Brand You and are the means by which potential clients will recognize you and your services. They will also be able to differentiate you from other designers through them.

Establishing Brand You is a detailed task. As you put together your initial promotional materials, from business cards to Internet sites, and then develop your social media presence and put out your on-line portfolio, collect press releases, and the like, think about developing consistent themes. What creative vision do you have? What point of view do you want to project? What statements might you make about your work that is easy for others to remember? What colors and symbols (such as logos, or typefaces) best embody that point of view? Will potential clients be able to distinguish your work apart from others just from seeing images of it? They may well need something more—phrases that describe the lifestyle you were trying to evoke or how well the public environments you originate satisfy human and business needs. How do you want to present yourself and your work through social media? After you have addressed these initial brand characteristics, it is possible to develop consistent themes that can be used across promotional activities. Brand You begins with vision. The following Notes from the Field underscore the importance of having a creative—and business—point of view when building your interior design brand.

> **NOTES FROM THE FIELD**
>
> Great design leads to more great design! Every designer I know wants to build an outstanding résumé of great clients. Clients that are loyal, hire you over and over again, and understand our sometimes-fickle creative process. Let me start by saying that not every client starts out being a wonderful client . . . you simply need to know how to get them there. You will need to maintain their trust and have the courage to be honest, even when something did not go as expected. Finding those client gems is a gift unto itself, and throughout this book you will find many hints to assist in the process.
>
> Step one is always, make it great! There is never an excuse for bad design, and everything needs design, even the toilet paper dispenser. Years ago, I booked a trip to New York City (Mecca for us creative types) to see the soap dispensers in a world famous hotel; they were custom designed by the architect for the project, and everyone wanted one. I digress. A lengthy plane trip to view a washroom detail is a bit extreme, but consider the conversation the architect had with the client, to convince them to build it! Why is this important?
>
> Great design, in whatever form it takes, can attract attention and foot traffic (if that's the goal) and will receive positive press. Pretty soon everyone will want to go there. But if the design is forgettable, poorly detailed, badly executed, or lazy in the thought process, no new work will come your way. You will argue with contractors and fight for your ideas, but if it's worth it, be prepared to make a good case.
>
> It is normal on a project—residential or commercial—that a client will say, "I don't like blue," but regardless of the color, your clients opinion should always be heard. However, if you had started your presentation by outlining the psychology of color, alluding to the number of gray days in the client's country, detailing the ties of color to productivity and happiness, and then all of a sudden personal opinions on highly subjective project details make take a different point of view.

Practical Activity

Do you have your own "app"? Why not? A quick Internet search will uncover many sites offering users the ability to create their own app . . . for free! First, think about what you want the app to do and what you want it to accomplish. Perhaps you would like to put your résumé and portfolio in an easily accessible format for others to find. Maybe you would like to document what inspires you. Develop a title based on that goal. Then, locate images and materials supporting that result. Have them available for easy download. Select a site offering free apps and follow the directions for making one. How many classes have you left where you have something you can use, share with others, and can use as well?

Review Questions

1. Define marketing as described in this chapter. In your own words, draft a short statement noting what you understand marketing should accomplish.

2. Define promotion and its goals, as explained in the chapter.

3. Distinguish among types of promotional methods.

4. What is selling, and what steps are there in its process?

5. What are the ways in which the marketing process is organized?

6. How might marketing plans and their components be defined?

7. What role do marketing budgets play in the marketing process?

8. What is contact management, and what does it seek to accomplish?

9. What is a prospect, and what does it mean to qualify them?

10. How is a sale closed, and why might interior designers consider personal selling as part of their marketing efforts?

11. Describe social media, and give an example of how interior designers might use its platforms to market themselves and their businesses.

12. Explain how branding is related to marketing; how does each one benefit the other?

13. What is cooperative advertising, and why might it be important to designers?

14. What does word-of-mouth marketing involve, and what is its relationship to referrals?

YOU AND YOUR CLIENTS — PART 3

This part of the text discusses objectives and processes that will enable you to achieve goals that are specifically related to the work of interior designers.

Chapter 8. Defining Your Services: Introduces and explains the scope-of-services concept, which correlates results clients seek with designers' creative and management skills.

Chapter 9. Charging Clients for Your Services: Describes how you may derive profitable compensation from your scope-of-service analyses of projects.

Chapter 10. Managing Your Client's Project: Explores project management techniques in greater detail, this time from the perspective of scope-of-services analyses and formal project management practices.

Chapter 11. Defining the Client Relationship: Demonstrates how design contracts may be constructed on the basis of scope-of-services analyses to include terms related to charging for services and project management.

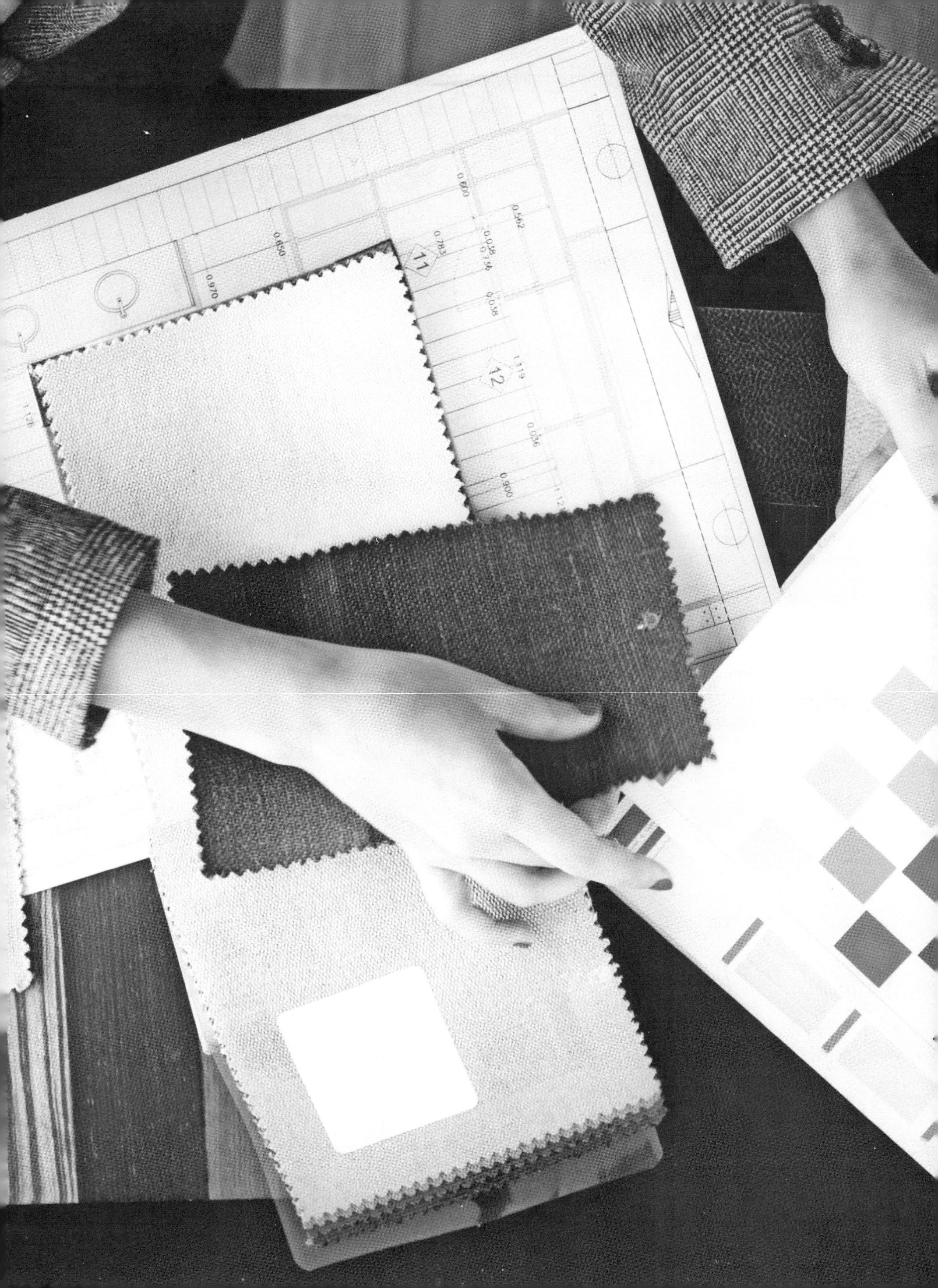

CHAPTER 8
DEFINING YOUR SERVICES

MENTOR MEMO
As interior designers you first task with any client will be defining what you do, and how you will do it, in a simple and elegant way. It is true that most people don't clearly understand these basics. Take your time, try not to rush through these first initial meetings, this is the client's turn to share their thoughts and dreams with you.

After completing this chapter, you will be able to

- Define scope-of-services analysis in your own words;
- Explain designers' functions to someone who is unfamiliar with their work;
- Discuss how interior designers traditionally gained information about their clients' needs for projects;
- Describe some modern ways of information gathering about client needs, and explain their interpretive processes;
- Learn how the global arena for interior design services impacts how designers define their scope of services to clients.

INTRODUCTION TO DEFINING YOUR SERVICES

"The term *analysis of scope of services* has such importance that it should be posted prominently in every interior design office and planted firmly in the mind of every designer," so noted one professional practices expert in the 1970s. Such a statement along with the observation found in this chapter's opening Mentor Memo underscores the importance of defining the exact services you will provide to your clients as an interior designer.

You are now acquainted with four fundamental sets of skills required of interior design professionals who participate in businesses. And you have learned the ways interior designers incorporate those skills into their own practices. This chapter is important

Interior designers bring an authoritative use of color to interior spaces.

to you because it will explore ways to identify and describe the interior design services you provide to clients. The description of the scope of your services is one key aspect that defines your working relationship with clients. To help you perform this important task, this chapter will explain

1. How the term *scope-of-services analysis* may be defined and its place in the project management scheme;
2. How designers traditionally—and now not so traditionally—obtain project information in order to determine the services they provide;
3. The importance of carefully negotiating a scope-of-services analysis with your client.

A CONTEXT FOR SCOPE-OF-SERVICE ANALYSIS

Ask yourself how you might go about defining your services and what information you need to know about the client, the site, the environment proposed for the project, and even the "feel" of the project itself. For that matter, how have designers traditionally analyzed their clients' needs and wishes to determine what services they need to provide, and how is this activity changing?

As you will come to learn, the kinds of services offered greatly influence the methods designers use in seeking compensation for their services. Scope of services also affects management of the projects. Finally, a definition of services must be included in the written contracts for design services entered into by designers and clients.

During the course of your design education you have probably come across the term *scope of services*, or perhaps you have heard of a designer preparing a scope-of-services analysis. Maybe you wondered about the meaning of this term, since it seems so integral to the work of an interior designer and is so frequently mentioned that it seems to need no definition. First, the scope-of-services analysis is not necessarily a formal project document, although it is a part of the contract with the client for design services.

What is important for you to know is that the **scope-of- services analysis** is an evaluative process necessary for the designer to understand the client as well as the client's wishes and needs for a proposed project. After a designer determines that it would be appropriate (and potentially profitable) to participate in the project, the scope-of-services analysis may then be formally incorporated into the written agreement between the designer and client.

Designers also use scope-of-services analyses as ways of anticipating problems that might possibly hinder project completion (an underlying project consideration). With this context in mind about the scope-of-services analysis, how might a working definition of the term and its related process enable you to better understand and apply it?

MENTOR MEMO

Designing your process is actually your first design job! If you are starting your own business, this will become part of your pitch to a new client. If you are joining an existing process, there will already be determined tools and approaches that you will need to understand in order to establish yourself and your own role within the firm. The design process is linear, and if you skip a step, it will haunt you later.

Interior designers define their services to correspond with their clients' needs and goals and to contribute to their own profitability.

EVALUATION OF CLIENT NEEDS

When designers and clients initially meet, designers need to translate what clients are really asking them to do in realizing proposed projects. Sometimes that translation involves determining what specific activities will be required of designers to bring the projects to fruition after interpreting the emotional nuances of and solving concerns expressed by the clients. This is certainly true of residential interior design, in which a designer and client often build a close personal relationship. In these circumstances, the practicalities of carrying out a project may be underemphasized by designers and lost entirely on clients, all of whom may have their own reasons for wanting to see the projects realized. Contract interior designers, alternatively, may seem to be code breakers in understanding a prospective client's needs. Often, these designers have only a request for proposal (RFP) in front of them from which they must decipher the clients' most important concerns about projects. On that basis alone, contract interior designers must intuit how to practically address those needs as they carry out the project. Designers in both areas of practice rely on the scope-of-services analyses in planning how to transform clients' ideas into finished spaces.

MENTOR MEMO

What questions should you ask clients first?

What are you looking to accomplish with this project? Start the questions very high level, over time they will become much more detailed. It's critical to understand why you are there, and what the grand idea really is. In some cases, the answers may be confidential (i.e., a merge, or layoff). In which case, be mindful of the room and context

CHAPTER 8 DEFINING YOUR SERVICES • 149

where you inquire. If you are speaking to the client, they already have a goal in mind; Your mission is to find out what that goal is and to start defining the guiding values of this project. To ensure that you are on the right track, you will go back to these two mission statements over and over.

How would you measure success, on this project? Before you got there, the client is already bubbling with ideas and preconceived thoughts around the project. This applies to both residential and commercial installations. Making something more aesthetically pleasing is one answer, but hopefully there is more information to digest. For commercial clients, they may be looking at return on investment, increasing connection and engagement, competing for and retaining higher-quality staff. They may have a lease that is up or could be quickly running out of space. There may be competing agendas between the CFO, CEO, IT and HR departments, which is normal and expected at this stage in the onboarding of a new team.

On the residential front, more space or a more calming space or a space that just works or looks better is no less important. This is where we rest and raise our families! The desired end results may be less involved, but should no be undervalued.

Are there major hurdles to overcome? This item is a constant on any project, regardless of sector, region, or scale. It's critical to know where the client sees the potholes. Are staff members not willing to move? Will they lose staff if the location is too far away? Stylistically, are people divided on the amount of space or number of functions needed? Are they rolling out new global standards, and the existing employees are not informed of the changes that lie ahead?

Have you ever worked with an interior designer in the past? Chances are that large corporate clients have, and you will be contacted by representatives from their real estate or facilities departments. If it's residential, they might not have had the experience. In either case, if the answer is no, your onboarding and extraction of kickoff building blocks might be slower. Reviewing the basics around roles and responsibilities and presenting a checklist of activities to come is a good place to start.

ELEMENTS OF THE SCOPE-OF-SERVICES ANALYSIS

A scope-of-service analysis may be thought of as having two basic parts: a description of the physical space, often referred to as the subject space or property, and a description of the specific results the designer is agreeing to bring about on behalf of the client. The latter part may be thought to have two inherent considerations, creative and financial, both based on client expectations.

MENTOR MEMO

Manage your client's expectations! Depending on your client's goals and agenda for their project, managing their expectations is essential on two primary fronts; creative and financial:

Creative Expectations The most successful designers in our industry are all GREAT designers. They are published because their solutions are unique, and chances are they are quite sculptural and poetic in their execution. Picking up any design magazine, you get the picture. There is a reason very few magazines show those finished interiors as a work in progress or the steps that lead up to the final product. The mock-ups, the teardowns, and the reconstructions are all part of the ART of our profession. Many great designers do a design only once, and never again, as it is site and client inspired. Any client will be anxious to see the end product and will need to be told what to expect and how long this process, which involves a highly creative solution, might take.

Financial Expectations As previously outlined, if your process and solution are highly unique (in either residential or commercial), your budget and schedule will need to allow for mock-ups, use of nonstandard materials, and potentially unusually long wait times. All of these items come at a cost that needs to be built into the project's financial projections and contingency. As discussed previously, your project budget is below the contingency line on your master budget. Many clients want to see the contingency as not necessary, and only needed if the designer has made a mistake, in which case the designer can pay for those mistakes. This is not the case. There are simply too many variables in the orchestration of bringing multiple trades together on a project that can't be anticipated. Or, a client walks the space in the middle of standing studs and after seeing the actual scale, would like to make a room bigger. It is best to make those changes early, rather than regret not making them later. The contingency is there for that purpose. If there is a change midconstruction, an appropriate CCO (contemplated change order) would be issued and presented to the client, prior to any decisions on the financial implications being made. Regardless, having a transparent conversation around what the contingency is and maintaining a healthy budget will only benefit the process and your relationship with your clients.

Practically speaking, descriptions of physical spaces can be a statement reading simply "the entire home," as in the final version of some letter of agreements for residential interior design. Of course, a description of subject property for a nonresidential project is often much more detailed, with references to spatial dimensions quoted on blueprints or schematics. The description of subject space or property, whether destined for private or commercial use, should be as specific as possible to avoid any misunderstanding or confusion. If spaces flow into each other or opinions could reasonably differ about what is, in fact, the subject space—for example, a residential living room that segues into an entryway or an office waiting area leading to an attached hallway—then the designer's description ought to include a statement about the project's underlying intent. If the client intends to have design work in only the living room, for example, that should be specified in the initial scope-of-services analysis and finally in the language of the contract between a designer and client. Similarly, a scope-of-services analysis for a commercial space should note the physical coordinates of the subject space.

THE DESIGNER'S DUTIES

As soon as the physical description of the project space is finalized, the designer needs to consider how to realize the client's goals for the project. At first, this description of duties may be very informal, even presented orally to clients. The better practice would be for the designer to write out the project activities in list form. As designers gain experience in handling projects, the informal outline may take a specific form in which project tasks and the designer's duties are organized within the context of formal project management phases.

MENTOR MEMO

Once small piece of advice: before you jump into a new adventure, consider whether you have the staff, résumé, and skills to anticipate all the challenges this project could present. If the answer is NO, consider entering into a strategic partnership or joint venture with other team members who might be able to bring something to the table. If the skills do not exist closer to home, working together in a smart team tends to net the most exciting end result and value to your clients.

PROCEDURES AND PROCESSES FOR DEFINING YOUR SCOPE OF SERVICES

What do you think is involved in carrying out the first of these objectives? Conducting an informal evaluation of the project and its characteristics is an important threshold concern a designer should address. At early client meetings, there are likely to be numerous suggestions and comments about client goals and project requirements. In the excitement of undertaking a possible new project, it is important for the designer to gather this information and record it in such a way that it may be easily referenced and evaluated later. The many forms found throughout this text enable you to easily record project information as you obtain it. Another easy way to record information is to take written notes during these early discussions. The main thing is to record the information in a useful way since you will refer back to it countless times during the development of the project.

Evaluation of a Project and What It Will Entail

What information about a project should be of special concern as you begin to assess what it involves and how to bring it to completion? As part of the scope-of-services analysis process, you should focus on the following two factors in completing information worksheets or taking notes:

- The kind of project that is being proposed and its size
- The amount of research and resources required to understand project concerns or to meet client wishes or needs

MENTOR MEMO

What are the tasks and issues to consider? That information would be good to know! After all the questions are answered and thought through, you are on your way to determining a scope. What are we starting with? Are there existing drawings? Are there existing relationships with vendors that the client would like you to maintain with care? Have they had bad experiences with any vendors or general contractors that you should avoid? Is there existing furniture or pieces or equipment that need to be considered when you get started?

Without using "arch-i-speak" (words foreign to your client) start building a menu of services that you can offer your client, that respond to what you have just learned. If the new project is coming to your attention via a request for proposal (RFP), chances are that these basic questions will be outlined in the project overview. In our business, it's not unusual to see requests for qualification that ask you to respond with your history and a team of résumés to be considered for the work. In an RFP, most clients ask for what they think they need, but a good designer will also include what they as the professionals can expect might be needed, in addition to the basic scope. These line items are often called optional or value added services.

Type and Size of Project under Consideration

Certainly, there is no hard-and-fast rule for determining what kind of project is easier to complete than another. For example, the design of small retail spaces clearly intended for nonresidential use will likely take much less time and effort on the part of a designer than residential projects of any real magnitude. However, small projects are not always easy projects: A living-room concept requiring only custom-made furniture and elaborate built-in features may be extremely difficult to realize, and large projects such as hotel installations utilizing existing items may be fairly easy to implement. The purpose of identifying both the kind and size of project being proposed is to determine whether a designer is realistically able to handle such a project.

A designer's ability in this regard may depend on several factors, including the timetable for completing the project. A designer involved in multiple projects within the same time frame, even if they are in different stages of administration, is quite simply a busy designer. Such a designer might conclude that he or she is not able to take on another project after conducting an informal scope-of-services analysis. Other concerns relate to a designer's ability to work within the time and budget constraints proposed by the client. A designer may not be able to accomplish what the client wants given the time and budget available.

Furthermore, a client may require inordinate amounts of the designer's time while vacillating about design choices or, worse yet, second-guessing the designer; the client may simply demand the designer's involvement excessively. As a result, the designer may conclude that he or she does not have the ability to juggle the client's demands along with the project's demands. Subjective impressions formed in these early assessments are also important to consider when deciding whether to take on a project. For example, a designer may conclude that he or she would not be able to work with a client in a business relationship.

From an objective perspective, however, designers need to conclude, during the course of these processes, whether they have the professional ability to carry out a project without jeopardizing either the project or their reputations in the community. While conducting your initial scope-of-services analysis and learning about the client's project goals, ask yourself whether you are able to complete the project given your education, experience, time commitments, and perceived relationship with the client.

With respect to the research and resources required to both understand the project and meet client goals, both are important concerns answered during the early scope-of-services processes. Many times, clients will seek designers' services because of their expertise or the style for which they are known. Such renowned designers usually have firsthand knowledge of what it takes to complete similar projects and do not require much specialized research of products or tradespeople. They frequently have available a network of suppliers and contractors on which they can call.

Whether a new project will permit designers to draw from their network of sources is also addressed in the scope-of-services analysis. What this means for the less-experienced designer is that client goals requiring a great deal of research into territory with which the designer is unfamiliar may result in problems later during the course of the project. The scope-of-services analysis reveals the extent to which the project requires a strong research component among its other tasks.

Projects bring out all the client's hopes, desires, and fears. The designer's task is to sort out the client's desires from what is actually needed to complete the project. The issue of supervision offers an example. Clients may want designers to provide a level of project supervision that is unwarranted by the actual nature of the project. In that circumstance, a designer has to persuade the client that such oversight is not needed.

On the other hand, clients sometimes wish for the installation of features requiring extensive modifications to, or reinforcement of, the original structure. For function and safety of the space, the designer should point out to the client the necessity of including additional provisions for less obvious support mechanisms and to also engage the assistance of other professionals—especially architects or engineers—to aid in that task. Reaching conclusions about project requirements requires designers to understand the implications of what clients wish for and to convince clients of their necessities.

Methods of Gathering and Assessing Project Information

Interior design projects require information in order to come to fruition because varied and specific information is required to determine the scope of a designer's services on a project. To meet the changing demands of modern interiors, designers must be familiar with innovative ways of collecting this information. This is a vanguard area of interior design.

Useful information gathered in developing a scope-of-services analysis usually includes the physical dimensions of a project's subject space, the project goals, its end users, and how they are anticipated to use the space. Designers then analyze these factors to produce spaces that are functional and attractive at the same time that they take into account health, safety, and welfare needs. Recent trends, however—in fields as far-ranging as technology and interior design education—suggest that, increasingly, there are other goals to meet. These goals require yet additional information for designers to consider when developing a thorough scope-of-services analysis on a project.

In identifying these additional goals, IDEO, the noted design firm based in Palo Alto, California, has become an innovative force in many different disciplines, including architecture, consumer product innovation, and technology. Its influences can be seen in a diverse number of business settings including retail, communication technology, and, in particular, healthcare. The firm's approach is to enhance the experience of consumers in using the products and facilities it researches as a consultant.

Toward that end, IDEO strives to imbue these items with characteristics their research has identified as desirable. For example, the group found that young automobile drivers perceived authenticity as a desirable characteristic of their car buying and operating experience. To arrive at these insights, IDEO developed unique information-gathering methods to pinpoint how to imbue their products with such experiential qualities. It is important to recognize that consumers now expect products and services to provide positive, authentic experiences. How has the interior design industry responded to such trends?

"Environmental poetics"—"creating memorable and inspirational spaces that address aesthetics and humanism," or "the 'art' of design that focuses on the meaning, emotion and spirit of place"—has been identified as an important concern that should be addressed by interior design education, according to ASID. The relevance of this concept is in line with the IDEO approach of meshing experience with product and facility design. This trend of imbuing experience or emotion into product and design offers great opportunities for expanding an interior designer's scope of services. The issue for designers, however, is whether traditional ways of gathering information are sufficient to achieve these intangible, but nonetheless very real, design results. How might one, for example, identify emotions that could then be translated into usable interior spaces?

Traditionally, interior designers have asked clients to simply tell them about the qualities they want the completed design to feature. Designers also usually rely on their own detailed observations of their clients' current environments and objects to identify what elements to retain or further develop. Other ways of gathering information include the use of questionnaires or personal interviews—particularly in contract interior design projects, when large numbers of employees will inhabit a workspace, much information is sought out regarding the uses to which the space will be put.

As entrenched as these methods are, they are not without limitations. Clients and employees may not understand the full implication of the questions asked of them and so give partial or meaningless answers. And personal biases may skew the interpretation of results. Or, quite simply, the subjects participating in this type of research may not feel like they are a part of the overall design process and thus may view it as cumbersome and annoying rather than as a means for bringing about a positive outcome.

To gather information that is both useful in achieving a project's end results and flexible enough to engage interview respondents, something more is required. To that end, the IDEO developed a series of observational and prototyping techniques that hold particular promise for use in developing interior design that is responsive to the physical and emotional needs of end users. Techniques such as the ones described here permit interior designers to gather information that they can use to expand their scope of services and produce spaces that are also experiential. Following are some of these approaches developed by IDEO.

- **Behavioral Mapping** In this technique, spaces are photographed for a series of days to understand how a space is being used and to catalog the range of emotions elicited by users in the space. One important implication of this approach for interior design is that it can serve as a neutral, objective way to report the actual uses to which a space is put, free from subjective interpretations. Used as a way of evaluating existing spaces and identifying problems that will be addressed in the scope-of-services analysis, this technique also has the advantage of being less intrusive than interviews and questionnaires.
- **Extreme User Interviews** This technique involves having those who know very little or a great deal about a product, service, or, in the case of interior design, a space evaluate their experiences with these items.
- **Shadowing** This technique involves following subjects as they interact in spaces.
- **Storytelling** This technique prompts people to talk about their own experiences in using an item.

- **Unfocus Groups** In this approach, the traditional focus group—usually made up of a target group—is modified so that many different kinds of people, not only a targeted few, are interviewed.

These unique ways of gathering information can be incorporated within the context of interior design so that interior designers can expand their scope of services to account for factors such as emotion and experience. After information has been gathered and assessed, it is important that designers obtain what is referred to as client buy-in, which is when clients agree to designers' scope of services before finalizing everything in contracts for design services.

PROBLEM-SOLVING STRATEGIES RELATED TO SCOPE-OF-SERVICE ANALYSIS

Since you are a professional, your clients will expect you to solve problems for them. Also as a professional, you will have to understand and solve problems that the client creates for you. Suggested changes offered by a client to a designer's scope of services are one such problem area. Resolution of these concerns in large part depends on which stage in the designer-client relationship the modification is requested and how well the designer is able to negotiate with the client. Many of the questions regarding changes to a designer's scope of services are addressed in the design contract or letter of agreement binding a designer and client. But what of suggested additions or subtractions made by a potential client before a contract is signed?

Consider these kinds of changes to a scope-of-services analysis commonly requested by clients and some strategies for resolving them.

Problem Prior to signing a contract for design services, a client asks the designer to omit the task of installing items at the project site; the clients' reasoning is that he or she can follow the designer's layout without having to pay installer's costs or pay for the designer's time (when the designer is being compensated at an hourly rate).

Strategy Clients understandably do not want to pay more for services and goods than absolutely necessary. Because a designer and client have not yet formally agreed to work together, designers (theoretically) could agree to this limitation in their scope of services as part of the give-and-take of precontract negotiations. The issue addressed here is the timing of the change. No final bargain for services has yet been struck that requires the designer to take part in the final installation of the project. A designer could agree to this proposed limitation on his or her services and have the contract written to reflect it.

As a point of negotiation between a designer and client, a designer may need to first empathize with the client about the need to keep project costs low but then simply refuse a subtraction of this kind. Eliminating some number of fundamental tasks in an attempt to save some money can and probably will endanger the project's outcome. How a project looks after final installation is a crucial test for designers. Agreeing to a provision of this kind, even at a client's request, is likely to result in disaster for both the project and the designer's reputation and should be refused even at the precontract phase.

MENTOR MEMO
Be careful describing the project budget. It is not an "estimate"! Estimating in the commercial arena can be risky. Why? You are doing more detailed quantity takeoffs, and unless you are speaking to subtrades often, you might not have your finger on the pulse of costs in the industry. Unless you have specifically been training to estimate a project, tread carefully. It is typical however for an interior design team to complete a budget with the assistance of a licensed construction manager. There are four large areas of a budge: construction costs, furniture costs, soft costs (consultant fees), and relocation costs if required. What is important about a budget is it must be thorough, and it must have a contingency. Contingencies in a first budget should be around 20 percent; as multiple budget exercises take place, the contingency will be reduced. When you explain the need for a contingency to a client, emphasize that there are millions of pieces of information on a set of construction drawings. And, even if a set of drawings is perfect in every way, there could and will be surprises in the walls that might have to be addressed during construction and after demolition.

Are there any kinds of changes, notably subtractions, to which a designer might agree during the precontract phases of a project? Of course, there are. Facts and circumstances vary greatly according to a designer's area of practice and geographical location. One situation in which designers might consider limiting their scope of service (assuming they are compensated on a basis other than commissions earned from goods sold) occurs when the client has greater buying power than the designer. Institutional and government clients may have far greater procurement abilities than the designer. In such instances, the designer may agree to evaluate the institution's cadre of vendors to identify those most likely to provide appropriate goods. In addition, the designer may also write product specifications and review received merchandise for compliance to the specs. Again, the designer should carefully evaluate suggested subtractions to the scope of services, even at the precontract stage, based on their reasonable effect on the overall project.

Problem During early negotiations, the client requests the designer's presence at the project site daily, a requirement the designer does not feel is necessary or even possible to provide.

Strategy Suggested additions to a designer's scope of services, if ultimately agreed to, may be as onerous as subtractions, especially if their inclusion is not really necessary in order to complete the project as agreed and scheduled. The Residential Interior Design Project Simulation considers this very topic. As a point of negotiation, the designer should attempt to find out the reason for the client's requests. Perhaps this is the first time a client has engaged the services of a designer and is insecure about the outcome. Addressing the source of the suggestion as soon as possible may be the designer's best strategy for coping with unnecessary additions. To conclude, consider the following steps as starting points for developing a project scope-of-service analysis:

1. Conduct an informal evaluation of the project and what it entails.
2. Select appropriate methods of gathering project information and identifying relevant information according to tangible and intangible goals.
3. Obtain client buy-in before finalizing the scope of services in contract form.

NOTES FROM THE FIELD

A few years ago, global scope of service was not even a conversation. Interior design services were perhaps city to city, not country to country. And, understanding the subtle regional differences can be critical to your success, just as sometimes not offending your client is the key to success. Some context; If an RFP for five floors is issued in North America, chances are you will receive an overview, scope, and request for fees. Your submission to such a request will involve a detailed APPROACH to delivering the work. That begins with listening and learning before acting and creating anything.

Our professional associations across North America frown and discourage work for no compensation. In other countries, however, it would be expected for that same RFP of five floors, that an entire schematic design solution be submitted just to be considered. Those responses would not be submitted on paper, but rather on boards and mounted for the companies' leaders, or chairpeople to consider. If they like what they see, you are hired. If they do not, the investment was yours to make. You might never get the chance to meet the client or even explain your submission; it must speak for itself. These are general assessments, and there are certainly anomalies to the norm, but these differences must be considered and navigated with caution given the time, cost, and expenses involved.

If you are selected to continue, and you are providing the solution on North American soil, there will be a drawing team locally required in the country where the project will be built. You will need to understand the regulations around local drawing institutes, taxes and your role once the creative decisions have been made. You may have a role, but in many countries that role can be managed by a general contractor and the design revised at the leisure of the contractor.

Regardless of what country you have the pleasure of working in, embrace the local vendor and contractor community. You will have products and prospects that only that country can offer, and you will have different selections and opportunities unknown to you at the time you secured the contract. The scope of service analysis is, indeed, global now!

Practical Activity

Pick a country other than your own. It can be anywhere. Do a bit of quick research on the Internet about potential locations and services available there. Delineate in step-by-step fashion your own approach as to how you might plan, deliver, and install a small-scale project in such a location. Suppose, for example, you plan to install a kitchen/communal dining area in an office, nonresidential space in your chosen country. From just such an example, can you see how complex it is to both define your services and work with local sources? Exercises like this are good practice for later, real-life work, performing the same task for clients.

Review Questions

1. Define analysis of scope of services in your own words.

2. Note some of the ways to obtain and evaluate client needs as part of an interior design project.

3. What are some of the client expectations interior designers might be expected to "manage"?

4. Note several concerns or impressions designers might have regarding a potential project.

5. What are environmental poetics, and why might they be important for designers to consider?

6. Describe some of the ways to gain project information, such as those proposed by IDEO.

7. Note some concerns around use of the term *estimate*, and describe what interior designers can do to avoid them when preparing project budgets.

8. Why might an interior designer not want a client to install items ordered for a project space? What should they do if clients insist on performing that task?

9. Should designers visit project spaces every day during its completion; what strategies might designers do to ascertain whether or not to do so?

10. What might designers do to better ensure they can work with their scope-of-service analyses on a global scale?

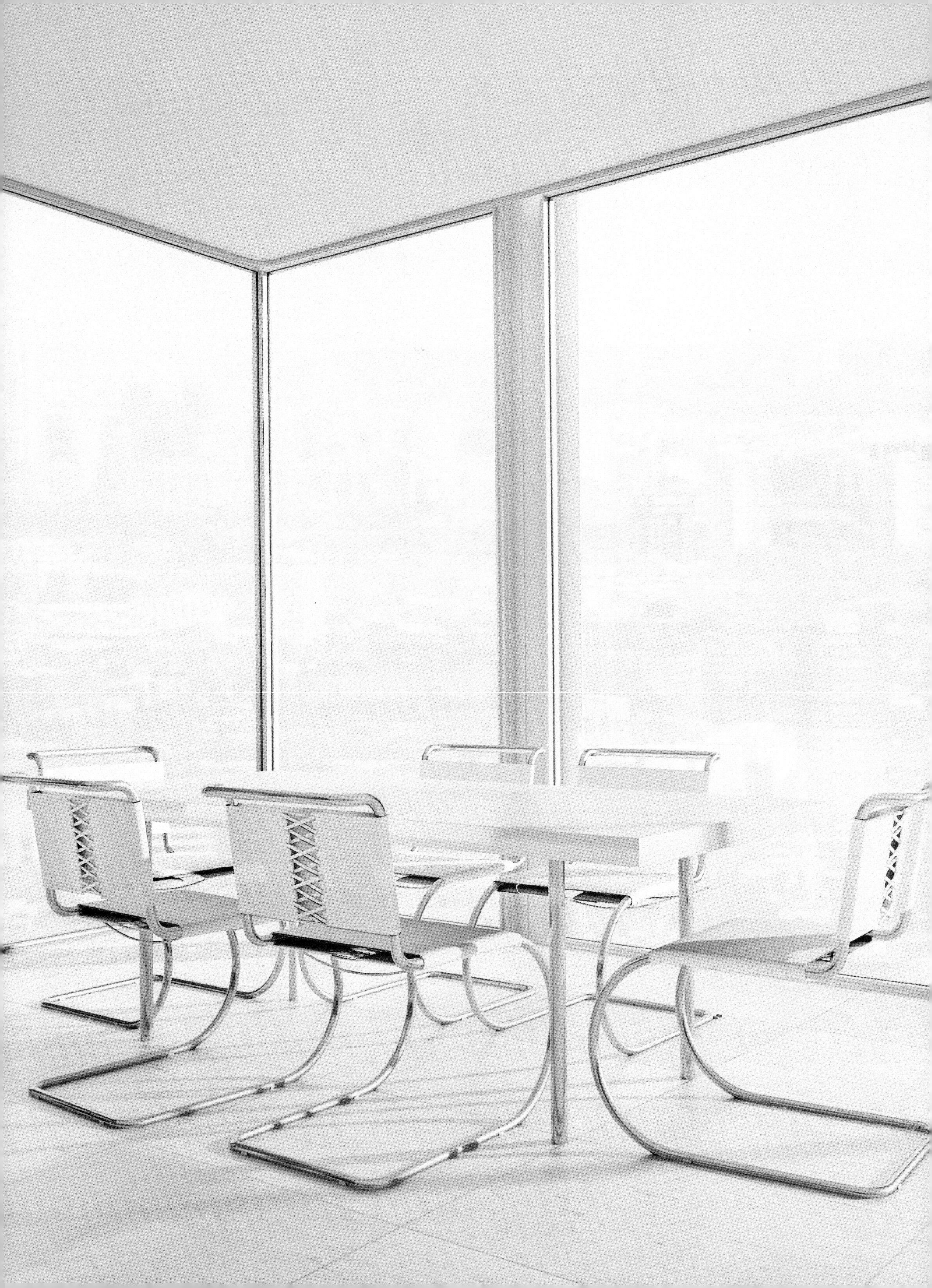

CHAPTER 9
CHARGING CLIENTS FOR YOUR SERVICES

MENTOR MEMO
On more than one occasion in my professional career, I have met clients at the permit office to receive an unpaid invoice in exchange for submitted contract documents.

After reading this chapter, you will be able to

- Explain basic ways in which interior designers may charge for their services;
- Understand the different methods used by designers to calculate their own costs and those related to their projects;
- Demonstrate knowledge of different kinds of expenses designers incur during the course of their work;
- Define basic accounting terms as they relate to interior designers and their businesses;
- Explain why it is necessary for designers to understand collection and charge-off procedures for outstanding account balances.

INTRODUCTION TO CHARGING CLIENTS FOR YOUR SERVICES

Designers generate revenue for their businesses by charging and collecting fees from clients. These fees are usually determined by things such as the services rendered by designers, the merchandise they specify and "sell," or a combination of these things. This chapter is important because it proposes a three-part strategy for you to use in setting your design fees, based on your business's needs and the specific services you provide. Using this suggested strategy should make the process less of an unprofitable art form and more the sound professional practice it can be. The fee arrangement is just

---

As an interior design professional you will develop space identity and usage concepts and find ways to charge clients for those ideas.

one of the ways in which designers define their working relationships with clients. This chapter explores how fee arrangements, along with other issues, may be included in contracts entered into between designers and their clients.

A STRATEGY FOR CHARGING FOR YOUR SERVICES

As you begin this chapter, envision yourself in the enviable position of having been selected as the designer responsible for the interiors of what, under your guidance, will become an impressive commercial space or private home. The design concept you proposed for this environment was deemed the best among all the presentations. Next, your new client asks how you will be compensated, or paid, for the activities you will perform to make that client's project a reality. How will you respond? What do you need to know about the needs of your own business and about the project itself before offering the most appropriate response?

MENTOR MEMO

How do you make money? That's a great question! And, if you learn nothing more from this chapter, know that how you make money needs to be disclosed and transparent to your clients. Accepting favors or bribes along the way (gasp!) will catch up with you, and you will lose a client in the process. If a client thinks you only specified a carpet because you were compensated behind their backs, they will always wonder if it was the right carpet for their job.

The following objectives are profit-conscious and project-focused in nature. As such, they typically form responses designers give when asked about or presenting how they charge for their services.

1. The first objective to master when determining design fees is knowing what to charge for your services. Simply put, what do you need to charge clients to satisfy your business's expenses and give you a *profit*, or financial surplus? In this context, determining the expenses your business incurs from its operation is a logical beginning step to take in planning for profitability. Are you aware of these expenses and the terms used to describe them? This chapter will identify these necessary expenses so that you can better understand the importance of choosing a financially appropriate method of charging for your services.

2. After you have determined the costs of your business expenses, your next objective is to consider the methods typically used by designers who determine their fees. You should also understand how certain characteristics of a project can and should inform your final decision about which of the eleven methods discussed in this chapter to use.

   Most designers eventually select one approach for charging clients that they think is most suitable for their typical projects and that best enables them to earn profits. Knowing the range of methods available for determining fees for services enables a designer to select the most profitable fee structures in carrying out a range of different projects. After you have ascertained your expenses and the range of methods available for charging for your services, you will know how to evaluate a project's potential for earning your business a profit; the expense obligations that need to be satisfied before any profit can be realized; and what characteristics of different kinds of projects could limit, or even eliminate, any possible profit. Understanding the relationship among these important considerations is necessary before selecting and applying a particular method of charging clients for your services.

3. Receiving payment of fees in a timely manner is crucial to both the designer's business and the project's orderly progression. Specifying appropriate times for the payment of fees and understanding the options available to designers with late-paying clients are important aspects of charging for your services. The following detailed discussion of these three objectives demonstrates how you can master their challenges.

THE FINANCIAL NEED OF YOUR BUSINESS

To determine what to charge for your services, you need to become familiar with several important financial accounting concepts and terms. You need to know whether the method you select for charging clients will adequately pay for the costs of providing those services as well as other business expenses. So you need to know how income, or financial increases, and expenses, or financial decreases, are handled and described.

How Businesses Calculate Revenue

During the course of their operation, businesses receive amounts of money paid by consumers for the goods and services produced by that business. These amounts are generally referred to by terms such as *income* or—for purposes of completing financial accounting reports, such as *income statements*—**gross revenue**. Of course, there may be other sources of income for a business, such as reimbursement for expenses or incentive payments. What is important is for you to be aware of these general terms used to describe the financial increases produced by a business. Income for an interior design business is typically derived from the design fees it charges and the merchandise it sells. Fees earned (and collected), proceeds from the sale of goods, and any other financial increases are added together to arrive at an amount referred to, for income-reporting purposes, as **total gross revenue**. Consider the following excerpt from the annual income statement of a small interior design firm:

Gross Revenue Fees for Services	$375,000
Sale of Goods	$225,000
Total Gross Revenue	$600,000

Amounts noted as being gross revenues from fees for services are typically calculated using one of the methods described in this chapter. Contracts for the designer's services, discussed in detail in Chapter 11, contain provisions related to how designers will charge for their services. Gross revenue derived from the sale of goods may also be determined using one of these methods or, when designers sell merchandise "off the floor" in a shop setting, it can be obtained from that source.

The amount of gross revenue is then decreased by a sum total of all financial adjustments. For example, interior designers who accept returns of merchandise from clients would note the dollar amount of that return, and then add it to other such adjustments to reach a total sum for all adjustments. That total is then subtracted from the sum of gross revenue to reach a sum known as net revenue.

Gross Revenue	
Fees for Services	$375,000
Sale of Goods	$225,000
Total Gross Revenue	$600,000
Allowances and Adjustments	**$ 25,000**
Net Revenue	**$575,000**

The amount of net revenue is important because it represents the sum, or total, of the financial resources produced by a business. This amount will be further decreased when both the costs of providing services and a business's operating expenses are considered.

How Businesses Calculate Expenses

Perhaps you have heard the saying, "It takes money to make money." The money it "takes" is more formally referred to in accounting terms as **cost of sales** or, in businesses that primarily sell merchandise, *cost of goods sold*. These costs are added together to produce the total cost of sales.

Gross Revenue	
Fees for Services	$375,000
Sale of Goods	$225,000
Total Gross Revenue	$600,000
Allowances and Adjustments	$ 25,000
Net Revenue	$575,000
Cost of Sales	
Fees from Services	$ 65,000
Fees from Sale of Goods	$ 35,000
Total Cost of Sales	$100,000

It is important to highlight the fees from services amount, listed here as $65,000. This amount is also referred to as the **direct labor expense**. What is involved in determining this expense, and why is it important that designers understand this concept when determining design fees? It may be simple to explain this concept if you first assume that the designers in this example are employed by a design firm or are independent designers who have specified their own annual salaries. In this case, further assume that such designers receive the following as their total annual compensation from their respective firms:

Annual Salary	$25,000
Other Benefits (holidays, paid sick leave, health insurance)	$ 5,000
Total Designer Compensation	**$30,000**

Why do you think the amount shown as the direct labor expense is $65,000 and not $30,000? Take a moment to consider what is involved in determining designers' compensation as expenses to their firms. How might these costs be calculated for income-reporting purposes? In this scenario, a designer works for a business a total of forty-eight weeks a year, or roughly eleven months, for a weekly cost to the firm of $625. This amount is often referred to as the **direct personnel expense** or **DPE** incurred by a business for having a designer on staff. Annual salaries for designers vary greatly as do amounts spent by businesses on employee benefits. Here is an example of such expenditures for a hypothetical interior design organization.

Annual Salary	$25,000
Other Benefits (holidays, paid sick leave, health insurance)	$ 5,000
Total Designer Compensation	$30,000
$30,000 annual salary/48 weeks of work	$ 625

As you can see, the designer "costs" the business a total of $625 a week in salary expenses: Given a typical forty-hour workweek, the salary expense incurred by the firm for employing the designer is $15.63 an hour.

$625 weekly rate/40-hour workweek

It should be noted here that this hourly rate is not the $15.63 billing rate for the designer's services. *Do not confuse a designer's hourly DPE with the employer's billing rate.* The billing rate is the dollar amount charged per hour to clients for the services of a designer. The billing rate is customarily applied when a designer and client have agreed to the hourly rate fee method. While the billing rate uses the hourly DPE rate, its calculation is more complicated. As a very general rule, the billing rate is approximately double the DPE, if that can help you better understand billing rate in relation to hourly rate.

During the course of a project, designers keep (or should keep) records of the amounts of time they devote to working on each of their projects. These amounts of time are then totaled and multiplied by the specific dollar amount determined to be a designer's cost to the firm. Here, for simplicity's sake, assume that a firm employs ten designers, each of whom costs the firm the same amount of salary, namely $15.63 per hour, and each of whom works the same amount of time.

Designer 1: 416 hr × $15.63	$ 6,500
Designer 2: 416 hr × $15.63	$ 6,500
Designer 3: 416 hr × $15.63	$ 6,500
Designer 4: 416 hr × $15.63	$ 6,500
Designer 5: 416 hr × $15.63	$ 6,500
Designer 6: 416 hr × $15.63	$ 6,500
Designer 7: 416 hr × $15.63	$ 6,500
Designer 8: 416 hr × $15.63	$ 6,500
Designer 9: 416 hr × $15.63	$ 6,500
Designer 10: 416 hr × $15.63	$ 6,500
Fees from Services	**$65,000**

Savvy students will note that 416 hours of work, assuming a usual forty-hour workweek translates into these designers each working about ten and a half weeks, that is, approximately one-fifth of the year. This conclusion would mean that each designer received $35,000 for his or her work. More complicated income statements and discussions of costs would include larger numbers, of course. *The point of this example is not the amount of time the designers worked or the amount of money they received, but rather to illustrate that the services of the designer cost the designer's employer a certain amount of money.*

This concept is very important to whatever method is used by designers to charge for their services. Without knowing the costs to the business, designers cannot realistically determine which method will be most satisfactory. Cost of sales also includes supplies consumed during the course of the business's operations, telephone usage, amounts expended but not yet reimbursed, cost of goods purchased for use on projects, and transportation costs of those goods—in short all sums expended to provide design services and merchandise. It is important for you to be aware of the term **gross margin**, which is the difference in amount between net revenue and total cost of sales; here, that amount is $475,000.

Gross Revenue	
Fees for Services	$375,000
Sale of Goods	$225,000
Total Gross Revenue	$600,000
Allowances and Adjustments	$ 25,000
Net Revenue	$575,000
Cost of Sales	
Fees from Services	$ 65,000
Fees from Sale of Goods	$ 35,000
Total Cost of Sales	$100,000
Gross Margin	**$475,000**

It is from gross margin that all remaining costs of a business are paid. These costs are referred to under the general term **operating expenses**. These are all the expenses required to operate the business, including the salaries of workers who support the activities of the design staff; rent paid for the office or studio space; utilities; and office supplies, to name just a few. You should also be aware of what is known as indirect expenses. These are the expenses a designer incurs in the course of completing a project that usually come about because of events or situations outside a designer's control. For example, a designer assumes responsibility for a project of a kind they have not done previously. Who pays for the time the designer spends researching unfamiliar design issues and learning to make appropriate decisions?

Often, a designer cannot bill a client for time spent in activities such as these unless a client has agreed to pay a fee. In cases where a client has not agreed to pay a said fee, the time and costs to a business are absorbed as indirect expenses. You may better remember the concept of indirect expenses by noting time is only money to designers' businesses when they are able to adequately charge clients for it; if they are not able to do so, then time becomes an expense to those businesses and a limitation on the amount of gross profit they ultimately earn. Interior design is an expensive profession to pursue. Keeping each of these expenses as low as possible to be able to function and attract new clients is a key concern of managers in large firms as well as individual practitioners. Their success at managing expenses becomes evident, or appears lacking, when the total of all operating expenses is subtracted from the amount of gross margin. As a final note, the amount of net income is further reduced by taxes levied on a business.

Gross Revenue
    Fees for Services $375,000
    Sale of Goods $225,000
Total Gross Revenue $600,000

Allowances and Adjustments $ 25,000
Net Revenue $575,000

Cost of Sales
    Fees from Services $ 65,000
    Fees from Sale of Goods $ 35,000
Total Cost of Sales $100,000

Gross Margin $475,000

Operating Expenses
    Non-billable salaries $ 40,000
    Rent $ 25,000
    Supplies $ 5,000
Total Operating Expenses $ 70,000

Net Income   **$405,000**

This overview of the accounting concepts used in calculating and describing the financial needs of a business is important when setting design fees for the following reasons:

- You need to know how the sometimes-considerable amount of net revenue generated by a designer or an entire design business can be substantially eroded, or even eliminated, after cost of sales and overhead expenses are calculated. You now understand the meaning of accounting concepts such as *revenue, cost of sales, operating expenses, gross margin,* and *net income.* These terms and concepts are intrinsic to the charging methods described in this chapter.
- The concept of *direct personnel expense* is important in determining the hourly rate that a designer or design firm charges clients for design services.

Understanding the full scope of a business's financial needs is a lengthy process. This discussion has placed less emphasis on categorizing the many possible examples of overhead expenses and how they may be calculated. Accountants and office administrators with responsibility for the finances of a design firm can and do provide guidance to practicing designers on how to handle such issues. Above all, taking active measures to reduce or keep these expenses as low as possible is an important goal for achieving greater profitability for a firm. Enhancing the profitability of interior design businesses is an important goal to consider when establishing design fees, as further discussed in the following section of this chapter.

WAYS TO CHARGE FOR YOUR SERVICES

The second major objective of this chapter is to introduce you to the specific methods designers use to charge for their services and assess potential projects for profitability. The latter process requires that designers recognize typical characteristics of projects

How well you understand charging, billing, and collection issues may well determine your success as a practicing interior designer.

that can and do influence their completion and also indicates whether a commitment to that project will prove to be a profitable use of designers' time and resources.

To help you to learn and recall the different methods of charging for your services, they can be categorized according to their four general characteristics as follows:

1. Rate-based methods
2. Sale of merchandise-based methods
3. Combination methods
4. Other methods

The following discussion provides a capsule explanation of each method, including a phrase to help you recall it. The text then presents a more complete explanation of how each method operates as well as the kinds of projects most appropriate for each method. Finally, the advantages and disadvantages of each approach are noted.

Is there any one method of determining how to charge for services that is best for a designer to use? The answer to this frequent question depends on many factors. The method that is best understood by a designer may not be best able to satisfy this chapter's first objective—namely, meeting the expenses of a designer's business and producing a financial profit. Be receptive to the benefits of each of the following approaches. As you gain experience working with clients and projects, you will be able to recognize situations where one method rather than another will allow you to earn a greater, but still reasonable, profit from the expenditure of your time and talent as a design professional. For that reason, think of the methods described here much as you might a book of textile swatches: They are materials available for use on the project for a reason. When you understand the nuances involved in using each method and have learned the financial needs of your business by calculating its various expenses, you may form your own strategy for determining how to charge clients for your services.

168 • PART 3 YOU AND YOUR CLIENTS

RATE-BASED METHODS

Two major ways of determining fees for design services are considered in this category, notably the flat or fixed fee method and the hourly fee method. Their names give you a sense of how they operate. What may be less obvious, however, are the nuances distinguishing how they are calculated and how they are used.

Fixed Fee

Using this method, designers receive an agreed-upon amount, or flat fee, usually paid in increments, for their services. This approach is based on a designer and client agreeing at the outset that the designer will receive a defined fee as compensation for his or her services. Usually, this amount is stated in the designer's contract for services as a total dollar figure not to exceed an agreed-upon amount. Typically, the fee is paid in installments as successive phases of the project are completed, and it does not include costs for the designer's purchase of merchandise. In addition, reimbursable expenses, which can include travel to the project site and incidental expenses that may be incurred in many ways, are typically billed separately. The designer who selects this method must have experience with similar projects in order to accurately estimate the single price to place on the services necessary to complete the project and to provide a gross profit to the firm when costs and expenses are subtracted from the fixed amount of income earned.

When to Select the Fixed Fee Method

The fixed fee approach is usually considered when two factors are present. First, a client wants to know the cost of a project before work on it begins. Second, designers who choose this method will have such a thorough understanding of both the scope of the proposed project and the costs and expenses involved in running their businesses that they can estimate the appropriate fixed fee that they can afford as compensation. Designers who routinely work on similar kinds of projects—for example, restaurants—maintain records of their costs in terms of salaries paid to design staff members, the time it took those designers to complete prior restaurant projects, and the business expenses incurred in implementing those projects. These records are sometimes referred to as *historical records*, since they document project costs over a period of time. Records of this kind are extremely valuable to design businesses, especially those that meticulously record the amount of time spent by members of the firm in completing projects.

As a side note, as a new practitioner, you will probably dislike the process of keeping time records. It takes time to write down what you do and how long it takes you to do it. As an experienced interior design professional, however, you are more likely to understand the value of such records, since they provide valuable information about the time it takes you and members of your staff to perform various project tasks—time that costs the firm in terms of salary expenses. These costs must be more than compensated by revenues earned by the business if it is to earn a profit.

Advantages

It is appropriate to use the fixed fee method when designers are aware of the historical costs of completing similar projects. If designers use that data well, they can earn their businesses a profit by seeking a flat fee that more than covers costs and expenses. Furthermore, accepting a flat fee might be an incentive to a prospective client to do more business in the future. In short, the fee structure may allow the firm to distinguish itself in a particular marketplace.

Disadvantages

The fixed fee approach requires a great deal of preparation to use. The success of this approach is also very dependent on the accuracy of a project's budget. If designers have a wealth of data about the costs incurred by similar projects, they can conclude whether the client has set aside a viable amount for the project under consideration. This approach will probably not adequately compensate a designer if the project requires excessive purchase of merchandise or if the scope of services that a designer will have to perform has not been precisely defined. When a project requires that a great many purchases be made, other methods for setting design fees would likely result in greater profits. Situations in which a designer will be called upon to complete many tasks on an ad hoc basis or projects that require a designer to spend a lot of time with a client are not likely candidates for use of this approach.

Hourly Rate

Using the hourly rate approach, a designer receives a fee based on the amount of time spent working on a project multiplied by the billing rate. This method of charging for services is perhaps the most familiar to those who have engaged the services of other professionals. Designers charge clients an amount determined by multiplying the number of hours they spend working on that client's project by a billing rate, a dollar amount calculated to compensate for firm expenses and desired profits.

When to Select the Hourly Method

The main reason to use the hourly approach in charging for your services is that it compensates designers for their time spent working on all aspects of the project. Thus, it is appropriate in situations that require large amounts of time to be spent in providing design services, consultation, or preparation for the project.

Advantages

This approach has the chief advantage of flexibility for a designer. At the start of a project, it is often difficult to adequately assess the amount of time or the kinds of activities that will be required of a designer. Using the hourly approach, designers receive compensation for their work despite these uncertainties.

This approach has one advantage not readily apparent, but related to its flexible nature: It can provide a way for a designer to more easily exit a project. Of course, legal counsel about the effects of contract provisions should be consulted, since laws differ among jurisdictions. However, by carefully drafting the hourly rate provision in contracts for design services, designers may be able to simply bill clients for services rendered as of a particular date, without further obligation to continue working for those clients.

Disadvantages

The flexible nature of this approach can be intimidating to clients who fear design fees may become quite astronomical. For this reason, designers using this approach should insert not-to-exceed clauses in contracts for their services. This approach in particular requires designers to keep extensive time records, a process that is antithetical to some.

MENTOR MEMO

Your firm, large or small, will have a timesheet process. I do remember thinking these horrible documents were my worst nightmare. But, take a breath. You will come to welcome their data as you grow through your career. A timesheet is often logged every hour. Projects and their phases are assigned a number(s) and you log, electronically, how much time you spend working in each phase. Interior design firms typically bill monthly in North America, but in other parts of the world they bill at completion of a phase. This means you are carrying your staff, for monthly or years, without getting paid. Only big firms can usually work this way, but that is even more reason to have an accurate log of time spent. My recommendation for any newcomers to the industry, make it a habit to write it down every day, no exceptions, your employers will thank you for it.

SALE OF MERCHANDISE-BASED METHODS

Historically, interior designers have used the merchandise they specify and sell to clients as the basis for determining their compensation. The following four methods are classified in this way:

Retail Method

Under the *retail method*, fees for a designer's services are derived from charging clients the manufacturer's suggested retail price for project merchandise—typically, double the net price paid by a designer. The fee for a designer's services, such as programming activities and schematics, is derived from the difference between the amount a designer initially paid for merchandise (the *net* price, also referred to as the *cost* price) and the price at which a client purchased that merchandise from the designer.

When to Select the Retail Method

As you would suspect, projects in which large amounts of merchandise will be purchased would be ideal candidates for use of this approach. However, even if a proposed project requires a designer to purchase many items, it is important to fully consider the scope of services. Any profit that might have been earned from proceeds derived from large purchases may be more than offset by the extensive amount of time required to provide other project services.

Advantages

This approach can offer the greatest possibility of earning designers the most profit, assuming the designers' scope of services do not include lengthy hours of their own time engaged in programming activities and contract document preparation.

Disadvantages

Interior designers, especially those with residential practices, have historically used the retail method for setting fees in which they specify both products and the final prices that their clients will pay for them. However, some question the practices of selecting and setting prices for design merchandise, as reflected in the following statement: "The practice of selling furniture and accessories as the key compensation method is under attack by many sources. . . . The issues of protecting the health, safety, and welfare of the public are in conflict with the segment of the profession that is compensated primarily through the sale of products." What do you think is the conflict to which the writer refers? Consider, again, this chapter's Mentor Memos to help you get started.

Implicit is the idea designers using the retail approach have an incentive *not* to specify the most appropriate product if it will not garner the most profit for them. This criticism may seem valid when it appears that designers can take advantage of clients because they have superior access to merchandise offered by a manufacturer. This criticism may even apply to designers who charge an hourly rate for their services, especially when they routinely sell so much of any one manufacturer's merchandise they receive substantially preferred pricing and considerations such as expedited delivery. Even when these designers pass on some savings to clients or when clients themselves place orders directly with manufacturers, there is still an incentive for designers to use a single manufacturer's products. If certain products are especially pleasing to clients they may patronize a designer who provides them even if other products may be more appropriate for client needs, or are more readily available or produced in a more ethical manner.

Cost Plus Percentage Markup

The fees earned by designers using the cost plus percentage markup method are based on increasing net cost of project merchandise by a percentage typically less than the percentage used in the retail approach. When learning about this approach, remember designers increase the amount they paid for merchandise before reselling it to clients. The retail method is extremely expensive for clients, many of whom may be less interested in using a designer's services without having some concession in the pricing of merchandise. Using the cost plus percentage markup method, a designer adds a percentage amount to the merchandise cost that is substantially less than the 100 percent used in the retail approach. Interior design businesses that set fees this way decide which percentage best fits their needs and will provide them with an adequate profit. Otherwise, this approach is similar to the retail approach.

Discounting of Percentage Off Retail

Designers who use the discounting of percentage off retail method to determine design fees decrease the manufacturer's suggested retail price of merchandise by a set percentage. Designers lower the retail cost when using the discounting of percentage method, whereas they increase the retail cost when using the cost plus percentage method. Typically, a designer's cost price is much less than the manufacturer's suggested retail price. Under this approach, designers lower the manufacturer's suggested retail price by some percentage; this is the equivalent of putting the merchandise on sale for the client.

As with the retail approach, this method is appropriate when large quantities of merchandise need to be purchased. It shares with the retail method the same advantage of earning a large gross profit for a designer's business provided that the fees also satisfy the costs of services provided for the project.

Percentage of Merchandise and Product Services

To determine fees using the percentage of merchandise and product services method, a designer estimates an appropriate percentage of the cost of project merchandise and services and multiplies it by the amount of a client's budget for the project.

COMBINATION METHODS

Cost Plus Percentage Markup with Fixed Fee

Designers who use this approach charge a set or fixed fee as compensation for their services and increase the price of any merchandise they sell by some percentage amount above the cost they paid.

Cost Plus Percentage Markup with Hourly Fee

Designers using this approach charge an hourly fee as compensation for their services and increase the price of any merchandise they sell by some percentage amount above the cost paid by the designer.

Designers using the combination approaches essentially have chosen two methods of charging clients: a fixed fee or hourly rate they believe will cover their expenses and that will pay them for the merchandise they provide.

When to Select These Methods

These methods of charging clients may be appropriate for projects that involve many activities on the part of the designer. When designers understand the financial needs of their businesses, particularly expenses, they can accurately estimate what flat fees at hourly rates will cover those expenses.

Advantages

These approaches probably best compensate most designers, who usually provide both services and merchandise.

Disadvantages

These approaches can be confusing for a designer who does not understand how their use can affect his or her business's profitability. They can also be confusing to clients who believe they are being charged twice for the same services or merchandise.

OTHER METHODS

Square-Foot Method

In the square-foot method the amount of project space—square footage multiplied by a calculated dollar amount—is used to determine a designer's compensation. Using data from previous projects, it is possible to derive a monetary amount that a firm could charge that would provide a profit to the firm; that amount would then be multiplied by the project's square footage to arrive at a designer's fee.

Advantages

When accurate records can be used to determine the dollar amount to be charged, and market conditions allow for use of this approach as well as the specified dollar amount, it may be profitable for a firm to use this method.

Disadvantages

This approach may be extremely lucrative in locations where the services of designers are so highly valued by consumers that the monetary rate per square foot can be kept high. On the other hand, market conditions may be unfavorable when the rate that designers would have to charge for their services in order to show a profit would be unattractive to potential clients. In addition to geographic factors, economic downturns also determine whether to use this approach.

Value-Based Method

The value-based method allows designers to charge a premium for their services based on some intangible benefit they are perceived to provide to the client for the project. Such benefit might be the designer's expertise, or the fame that the designer enjoys. According to Nila R. Leiserowitz, this method of charging clients will be the preferred approach in the future:

> The interior design profession will develop value-based compensation. The traditional fee model of cost per square foot has not worked well for our profession. . . . Interior design fees will be divided into two portions. One portion will be fees for delivery of design from programming through construction administration. The

second portion will be fees based on value-added services and work environment performance. (ASID 2004)

A PROJECT'S POTENTIAL FOR PROFIT

You must be aware of more than just the needs of your business in order to determine what to profitably charge for your services. Of course, you need to completely understand the demands of your project and to estimate what will be required for you to complete it. Think for a moment about two important factors that affect the work of interior designers: the time at their disposal for professional activities and the merchandise their clients purchase from them. Assessing a proposed project's potential for earning a designer a profit involves balancing these two factors to find an approach that best compensates a designer.

Considering the following questions as you approach each newly proposed project can give you a better idea of how your time will be spent during the course of a project—time for which you should find a way to be compensated. Before determining how to charge for your services, consider which methods of charging clients will best pay you for engaging in your interior design activities. What other factors are critically important for the project and should also be considered when assessing a potential project's potential for profit?

1. **What kind of project is contemplated, and how many project stakeholders are involved?** Interior design work may be applied in either residential or commercial installations. In residential work, there is usually only one or, at best, a few stakeholders who have an interest in and input into the project. When approaching residential projects, the designer needs to assess the magnitude of the project and the extent to which stakeholders wish to be involved. Large-scale interior design projects can involve either the construction of a completely new structure or substantial renovation of an existing building. In both instances, it is highly likely that the designer in charge will be required to meet frequently with the clients as well as many other professionals, such as architects and general contractors, during the course of the project. Small-scale projects may involve only selected spaces in an existing dwelling and thus require the designer to spend less time meeting with other professionals and clients.

2. **How experienced are you with projects of the kind you are considering?** If designers have a great deal of experience with certain kinds of projects, they will need to do less initial research to undertake it. Often, time spent on initial preparation is not time the designer can bill to the client as a direct expense.

3. **How experienced are your potential clients in working with you and with the process of interior design?** Clients who have not experienced the scope of interior design projects or who want to be extensively involved in the process are clients who will demand the greatest amount of a designer's time. The expenses required for such large expenditures of time can make a project unprofitable for a designer.

4. **Will buying merchandise be necessary to complete the project, and if so, who will be responsible for making the purchases?** Large purchases of merchandise can be profitable sources of revenue for a designer. In those instances, a designer should consider using any of the purchase of merchandise-based methods of charging for services.
5. **What is the scope of services offered by a designer?** Projects for which a designer has agreed to provide a full range of services, from programming to contract administration, will require substantial expenditures of time. In those circumstances, a designer may wish to combine an hourly or flat fee with a purchase of merchandise-based method.

A STRATEGY FOR CHARGING AND COLLECTING FOR YOUR SERVICES

Any strategy related to determining business revenue must take into account the timeliness of payments. Few interior designers can (or should) allow unpaid invoices to accumulate after billing clients for the services they provide or the merchandise they sell. Unfortunately, clients may not be so concerned about paying the balances, or totals, listed in their designers' receivables accounts. For these reasons, you should be especially aware of the need to specify to clients—before it becomes problematic—when you expect to receive payment of the fees you charge. Most contracts for services entered into by designers and their clients spell out payment terms, as you will note in Chapters 10 and 11. You should also know when and how to initiate payment from clients and how professionals charge clients for permitting them to delay payments, as well as basic aspects of formal collection practices.

ACCOUNTS RECEIVABLE, CREDIT, AND INTEREST

Amounts due to designers from clients are classified according to accounting principles as designers' accounts receivable (accounts payable, from clients' perspective). Each design business develops its own policies for handling situations where clients owe a design firm for services or for merchandise purchased on the clients' behalf. Many firms cannot financially afford to allow any balance due from clients to remain unpaid, whereas others are able and willing to allow the client to pay these balances within a certain amount of time. Usually, firms not able to provide extended payment terms require payment of amounts due when billed. Firms extending credit to clients by allowing them to delay payment typically request it within thirty, sixty, or ninety days after the balance is billed. Why might these firms extend credit for a specified period of time?

State laws often allow businesses that extend credit to charge for this service by charging interest, or a percentage of the total amount due, as compensation to the business for allowing these amounts to remain unpaid. Theoretically, had the amounts been paid, the design business could have used the monies for other opportunities, which were lost when the business extended credit. This interest expense can be a viable source of revenue for the business, since amounts collected can be added to the business's gross revenue amount to increase its net revenue.

BILLING AND COLLECTION PROCEDURES

Interior design businesses intent on maintaining profitability through timely receipt of fee payments develop effective billing and collection procedures. The billing process involves preparing invoices and making them available to clients for payment as soon as possible after the fee for service or for merchandise is incurred. This is followed by initiating follow-up procedures with clients when payment is not received within a specified time. Attempts to obtain payment for amounts due are generally referred to as collection practices and are further controlled by the laws of the state where the interior design business is located.

Collection practices may be implemented informally by a designer or the financial administrators of a designer's business. This usually takes the form of letters and phone calls to a client to request payment of fees due or to make other arrangements for payment of at least a portion of the amount. These practices may be more formally implemented by attorneys or collection agencies that have expertise and success in collection. Usually, businesses that resort to using formal collection services pay for doing so in the form of an hourly rate to attorneys and a percentage amount to collection agencies.

As important as it is for designers to know the financial needs of their businesses, the methods they use to charge for their services, and the project factors that affect profitability, receiving timely payment of fees is crucial for designers since their own expenses have to be satisfied whether fees due them are paid on time. Assessing the ability of clients to make timely payments of fees charged is another factor designers should consider when setting their fees.

HYPOTHETICAL BILLING SCENARIOS

Consider the following scenarios, and then suggest the method of charging for a designer's services that you believe would be most appropriate based on your understanding of this chapter. More than one approach could reasonably be applied. State your reasons for making your choices. As you consider these scenarios, you may discover similarities to your own ideal business.

1. "I have clients who just want ideas and suggestions about how to design a few rooms in their homes. How might I charge for providing that service?"
2. "My client's project will likely involve the purchase of a great deal of new furniture, but little of my time in other matters, since we agreed that the scope of my services on the project would be limited. What method of charging for my services might I specify?"

3. "Help! My clients are new to interior design and are not even sure what they want me to do. The project is one that promises to be quite extensive—if the clients ever decide on anything. What method of setting fees might work in this case?"
4. "I am a well-known specialist in small-sized medical facilities such as day clinics. I have expertise in completing these facilities quickly and less expensively than most of my competitors, who lack my education and experience. What methods might I use to determine my fees that take into account the valuable contribution I make to my clients' businesses?"
5. "Are there any advantages to charging on an hourly basis for my time, as do lawyers, accountants, and other professionals? It does seem like a lot of work to keep track of the time spent on projects."

NOTES FROM THE FIELD

What does the fine art of getting paid involve? First, you can't discuss timesheets and billing for your work without the second half of the money puzzle, collections. Also known as AR (accounts receivable). Accounts receivable can be good for a firm, but it can also be very bad if left unchecked. Walking through a project, you will bill periodically for your work. If you have a good client, your invoices will be paid between thirty and forty-five days, sometimes sixty for larger clients with layers of their own. If an unpaid invoice goes past sixty days, it's time for a polite phone call to ask, "Did you get my invoice? Did you have any concerns?" Don't assume you are in trouble as a first response. In my experience, many invoices do get lost in the system or land on the wrong desk.

Here are a few ideas that have worked in the past.

Invoice for $1. What? When you start a project, immediately invoice the client for a few dollars, a random minor amount, to work out the invoicing bugs that will occur. With new clients, there is often a supply chain management process to navigate, and the paper trail should be established early. When you send your first major invoice, it will work through the clients payment pipeline much faster.

Consider your terms for final handover of work. In my professional history, my most successful approach has been to inform clients that final construction documentation will not be issued for permit until invoices are current. Clients can be tardy with payments during the process, but they tend to catch up quickly if they realize the project permits are dependent upon the outcome. All said, you must tell your client this is your policy. If they know in advance, you will have no issues.

Relative to bad debt and "writing off" work, occasionally, you will have a client that is not happy or refuses to pay fees for your services. Often this is a result of bad communication or managed expectations. If this occurs, you must discuss you tax and AR provisions for write-offs. **Writing off bad debts** is not a good thing, but it is not an unusual occurrence in any business.

Practical Activity

Find a space that needs your attention as an interior designer. It can be any space, but identify one you believe you realistically could work on. Describe which of the following methods of charging for your services you believe most applicable to such as space. Note why you believe as you do. Are there any special characteristics of the space that you believe affect your determination and about which a client-owner of the space should be aware?

Review Questions

1. What are direct/indirect overhead expenses?

2. What is a billing rate?

3. What four basic methods may designers use when determining how to charge for their services?

4. In addition to being paid for their services, are there any other payment concerns that designers should be aware of?

5. What is an invoice?

6. What are accounts receivable? Are they related to accounts payable?

7. Describe the process of billing a client for services you provide.

8. What does it mean to collect payment?

9. To what extent do you believe the services of an interior designer add value to a project? How might you explain it to a client, and what concerns do you think the client might have about using such an approach?

10. Identify the charging method that you think will be most applicable to the kind of interior design practice in which you intend to participate. What factors about your business and the specific method of charging led you choose that approach over others?

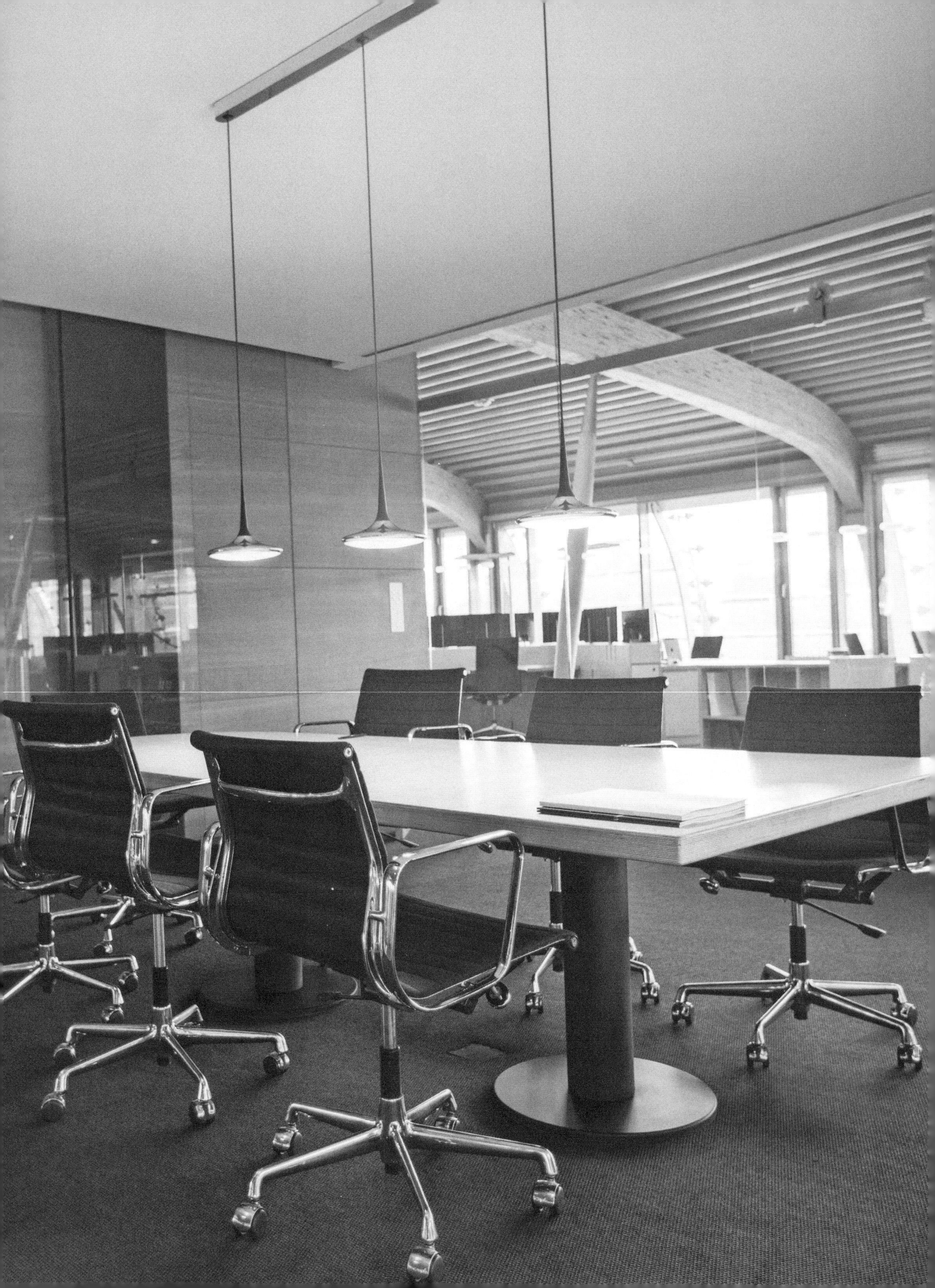

CHAPTER 10
MANAGING YOUR CLIENT'S PROJECT

MENTOR MEMO
Many clients will bring their experience with their decorators, into the boardroom and expect the process will run the same way. Or the reverse occurs, they expect that the commercial process is how their residential process should unfold. If you pause and communicate, you will have a happy client.

After reading this chapter, you will be able to

- **Define project management from the perspective of interior designers;**
- **Relate the concept of design intent to project management;**
- **Describe the various phases of interior design project management using characteristics of each;**
- **Analyze and explain constraints imposed on interior designers related to project management;**
- **Explain the relationship between interior designers and project managers in terms of their duties and obligations;**
- **Understand the importance of frequently used construction documents;**
- **Contrast construction documents with other kinds of schematics usually used in interior design projects;**
- **Distinguish from among different types of specifications and know when and how they are used;**
- **Explain how specifications relate to and may be used in contract documents;**
- **Gain awareness of common client concerns occurring during projects as well as ways interior designers may address them.**

Project design intent, client budget, and space requirements make managing each project unique.

INTRODUCTION TO MANAGING INTERIOR DESIGN PROJECTS

Managing interior design projects effectively requires that practitioners orchestrate the completion of a series of detailed, interrelated tasks. Throughout this process, designers must not only undertake or initiate specific activities but also know how to document the initiation, progress, and completion of the tasks. This chapter is important because it will explain why designers need to use project management skills in their practices and what tasks and documents are necessary in carrying out each of the five project phases typical of all but the most unusual interior design projects. As a practical matter, understanding the process of project management should better enable you to define your working relationship with clients when preparing contracts for your services, the focus of the following chapter. From the perspective of a designer's working relationship with clients, proficiency at project management and the ability to communicate its intricacies are tremendous business skills.

Such skills begin with this chapter, which will provide an overview of the phases through which an interior designer guides projects from initial information gathering to final installation and project closeout or completion. What are the reasons that interior designers might have for using a formal methodology such as the one described here? Aside from the most obvious reason—to get the job done—gaining perspective on more subtle rationales for employing formal project management procedures can be insightful.

INITIAL PERSPECTIVES ON INTERIOR DESIGN PROJECT MANAGEMENT

Using project management procedures to organize tasks and practicing effective interpersonal communication allow designers to better inform their clients about the sometimes lengthy and complicated processes required to complete projects. Clients in both residential and commercial projects want to know the status of their projects at any given time, including what activities will occur next. Perhaps the worst response designers could give to their clients is to say they don't know what is happening next. Being aware of the sequence of project demands within the scope of the project management procedure explained in this chapter enables designers to clearly explain a project's progression to their clients.

Professionalism and Project Management

Another important reason for working within an organized project framework is apparent in contract interior design projects. When business decision makers allocate a portion of a company's financial resources to interior design projects, those resources are no longer available to address other business concerns. A designer should be able to allude to project management techniques in justifying the use of company resources and ensuring those decision makers that they will obtain tangible results from the project. For example, designers rely on project management techniques to gain information about working conditions and activities in order to demonstrate to stakeholders that project results will promote worker satisfaction and efficiency.

Profitability and Project Management

Undertaking projects should be financially profitable for an interior designer. Knowing what is required to complete each phase of a project can help designers determine how to charge for their services. Consider, for example, a designer who routinely relies on an hourly rate for compensation. In this method, the time required to carry out project management tasks, such as preparing contract documents, determines how design fees accrue. However, not all projects require the same amount of work from a designer; for example, he or she may have to perform very little formal project management in some projects. When designers ascertain that a project will require less time to manage its phases through completion, they can then better assess which method of charging for their services, as previously described, might be more profitable. Lack of knowledge about project management tasks may mean that a designer is working for extended periods of time without being compensated because he or she could not foresee necessary expenditures. In such cases, the project will not likely be financially profitable for the designer.

In addition to these financial concerns, designers develop ideas and concepts that inform and guide the vision of the project shared by both designers and clients who are working together. How might project management techniques influence the development of these intangible, ephemeral, yet significant aspects of a project such as design intent?

Design Intent and Project Management

Interior design projects typically can be divided into five phases. During the course of a project, designers initially conceive and, considering client input as well as time and budget constraints, continually refine the design they have selected to meet the goals of the project. **Design intent** is a concept best defined as making up the set of decisions made by designers to address the aesthetic and functional issues that are critical in the project. These issues are identified as a result of the factual information gathered by a designer as well as a client's input. Obtaining this necessary information is one of the goals of the first phase of project management.

PHASES OF INTERIOR DESIGN PROJECTS AND THEIR MANAGEMENT

Interior design projects begin with what is usually referred to as the project's **programming phase**. At this stage, designers gather information about their clients' goals for the project and the reasons for selecting those goals. After discussing the project and the terms of their working relationship, designers and clients formally agree to work with one another by entering into a contract for the designers' services.

The **schematic design phase** sets in as soon as designers and clients formally agree to work together. It is at this stage that a designer uses the information gathered during the first phase to develop the initial design intent, or concept, on which the entire project will be based. As you will see, there are many tasks involved in developing a responsive, factually based concept for an interior design project.

Finalization of a project's design intent occurs during the subsequent **design development phase**. At this stage, the options presented for consideration during the schematic design phase take shape as specific features of the design to be completed. Also during this phase, designers prepare written specifications for merchandise to be purchased, reflecting final product choices made by designers and clients. Designers also inform clients of the costs likely to be incurred in ordering specified products and services, and decisions may be adjusted as a result. The final expression of a project's design intent is thus subject to financial constraints.

The **contract document phase** is, as the name suggests, the stage where appropriate documents are drawn up to communicate the design intent to those providing the labor needed to complete the project. It is also the stage in the project where purchase orders for the merchandise specified during the prior phase are submitted to vendors, along with any additional specifications and instructions. The project's design intent at this stage is considered to be fully determined, since any subsequent changes are likely to affect the schedule and cost of the project.

It is during the **contract administration phase** that the design intent of the project is realized. At the conclusion of this phase, a designer's efforts to program the project to meet the needs of a client become apparent. All products and services, as specified and ordered by a designer and approved by a client on the basis of estimated cost and schedule, have been brought together for the benefit of the installation and realization of the project. However, this phase does not typically end with project installation; it continues until all invoices and bills have been certified and paid and project evaluations have been conducted. The process of project management, especially the role of budget preparation and scheduling, can thus influence the final expression of a designer's intent, as well as any number of design decisions made during each of the project phases. A knowledge of the phases of project management, including the appropriate junctures for decision making, will benefit a designer's ability to bring the project to fruition as well as to recognize when to assess or recommend options, or propose alternatives, that satisfy the project's design intent.

THE ROLE OF THE PROJECT MANAGER IN INTERIOR DESIGN PROJECTS

Project management thus far has been presented primarily as a function of a designer in charge of the project. It is true that designers frequently are the designated professionals "of record" who agree to carry out the management responsibilities required to complete a project. Particularly in large projects, however, specifically designated, "outside" or third-party project managers may be responsible for carrying out project management tasks. These professionals frequently—although not always—have expertise in construction practices and in working with other professionals, such as technical consultants, who provide highly specialized services.

Although designers who accept project management responsibilities and designated project managers ultimately have many of the same goals in mind, notably completion of the project in a timely and budget conscious way, project managers perform specific tasks that may be distinct from those assumed by a designer managing a project. These specific tasks include the following activities:

- Working with the in-house design team responsible for the project to ensure timely and correct submission of project documents, such as specifications and construction documents.

- Identifying other professionals, such as contractors and consultants, and assisting in soliciting and evaluating the proposals, bids, and other documents they submit for consideration.
- Acting as liaison with the client by obtaining information relevant to the project. In many instances, the project manager acts as the linchpin between a client and design team, contractors, consultants, and others retained for the project.
- Where indicated by applicable state and local laws and by the terms of the agreement between the client and project manager, evaluating the quality of the specified products and supervising the completion of required work.
- Maintaining project budget and schedule documents and providing status reports as needed or as called for in any service contract.
- Performing administrative duties, such as maintenance of project files and documents.

Project managers typically are *not* called upon to provide services such as space planning, product research, or specification writing; those fall within the purview of interior designers. Whether the designer or a specially designated project manager is responsible for completing the actual project, both must be aware of their specific duties and attuned to the tasks and documents characteristic of each phase of the project management process.

MENTOR MEMO

What does a third-party project manager do? In interior design, project management by a third party is the new normal. It can, however, be a point of contention and duplicated services if not properly outlined by the team. If you were to look back twenty-five years ago, this was a service provided by the design and architectural professionals directly. This service has migrated, and so to have the fees associated with that work. Project managers can be independent or embedded in either the client team or the real estate team. And, given the growing number of consultants and sustainability, they can be a huge asset. If a client adds a project manager to the project, ensuring that he or she is qualified is a necessary and delicate step, as is outlining clear roles and responsibilities for the new project manager.

A good project manager, in my opinion, should take complete responsibility for the project schedule, meeting minutes, and work plan. They should be managing the RFP process for all consultants, their contracts, and the client's expectations and schedule relative to making decisions. I am sorry to say, there are many project managers that push all of those tasks onto the designer, but again, a transparent meeting to discuss roles and responsibilities will clear that up right away.

THE FUNCTIONS OF PROJECT DOCUMENTS

This chapter also presents documents that designers may use throughout the course of managing an interior design project. These documents, such as notes taken to help with decision making, are kept for a designer's own use in facilitating project tasks. Other documents, such as detailed construction drawings, concept boards, or other forms necessary to communicate a project's design intent to a client and others are usually referred to as deliverables, since they are intended to be shared with users other than a designer or design firm. With this basic overview of the project management process in mind and an understanding of some of its more relevant terms and concepts, this chapter will consider the specific objectives of each phase of this process in greater detail. In so doing, the discussion will focus on

1. Tasks that designers must accomplish in each phase of the project;
2. Documents that designers employ to manage each stage of the project, enabling them to record and interpret data and information as well as the project's progress.

PROGRAMMING PHASE OF INTERIOR DESIGN PROJECTS

The *programming phase* may be defined as the stage at which a designer obtains and interprets information in order to develop a project's design intent. How can designers accomplish this critical task and prepare for the phases of the project that follow?

Associated Tasks of the Programming Phase

Interior designers have a great deal of information to accumulate, record, and interpret during the course of a project. This is particularly true at the very beginning of a designer's association with a potential client. During the programming phase, a designer engages in some of the following typical tasks:

- Conducting interviews with residential clients in order to ascertain the project's functional and aesthetic needs. With regard to nonresidential clients, the designer may prepare and evaluate written survey forms completed by project stakeholders, such as office workers, in order to gain insight into the project's organizational demands.
- Obtaining existing floor plans, construction drawings, or related media that can help a designer prepare space plans during subsequent phases of the project.
- Identifying any existing items that may be used with appropriate modification in the design space or to obtain information needed to specify new items. In residential projects, for example, it is common for clients to request that designers use some of the existing furnishings or objects owned by the client. On the other hand, items used in commercial spaces may not be suitable for use in the new project, although they can inform designers about their efficiency and appearance.
- Conducting visits to the site of the proposed project, measuring the space, and assessing its present condition and location for later project-planning purposes.
- Preparing budget and schedule estimates based on the goals of the project and the level of design and construction skills it will require to be realized. For example, completing an elaborately detailed suburban living room or a historical restoration can and probably will require substantially greater amounts of project resources than most public spaces intended for commercial use. During the programming phase, the designer takes note of these issues and shares them with the client.

Detailed project documents ensure wayfinding, security, safety, and human concerns are addressed when creative approaches differ.

- Conducting research in order to ascertain how—and whether—designers will assume responsibility for the project. An important activity for designers at this stage is to ask themselves what knowledge they will need to obtain in order to complete the project. Certainly designers gain expertise over time in handling specific kinds of projects. However, each project is different and has different restrictions placed on its completion by a host of applicable laws, as well as building and safety codes. The needs and requests of clients also differ from project to project.

During the course of early project programming, designers also indicate whether services provided by other professionals, such as artisans, craftspeople, and expert consultants, will be necessary to carry out aspects of the project that a designer is not able to perform. In summary, the programming phase includes the following tasks:

- Reviewing initial project requirements
- Documenting project requirements
- Preparing project budget/schedule
- Determining physical/budgetary feasibility
- Providing written program of requirements

Documents Related to the Programming Phase

In earlier chapters, you were introduced to some of the activities designers perform during this phase of project management. You were also acquainted with a number of forms that might be used to facilitate those tasks and enable you to gauge the progression of a project from its inception to conclusion. Given this basic knowledge, you can now consider in greater detail the documents that are typically generated during this first project phase. As you are aware, a major purpose of the programming phase is to accumulate and retain project information in assessable ways. Many designers now enter such information into their computers as text narrative or on electronic

Designers add value to their services when they are able to inform clients of better uses of available space.

spreadsheets for later retrieval and possible transmission to others involved in the project. Documents associated with the programming phase usually serve the following purposes:

- Note taking and information gathering which may be used throughout the entire project-management process.
- Defining the working relationship with the client such as letters of agreement developed by the designers that will be used in contracting their services on the project. Chapter 11 fully sets out the provisions of these documents as well as gives rationales for their inclusion.

Unless designers and clients have agreed that designers will conduct programming activities as part of a design study separate from their contract for services, the programming phase in residential projects usually begins when the two enter into an agreement for a designer's services. In nonresidential projects, especially when a designer has submitted a proposal in response to a published RFP, the programming phase may begin after a designer or design firm has been retained by a client. This first phase of project management is distinguished by its focus on information gathering. The use of that information by designers is the subject of the subsequent phase.

MENTOR MEMO

"I know how much space I need!" Do you really? Law firm clients are one of my favorites. Although I treat every client's time as intensely valuable, I recognize that a law firm partner's is even more precious. The message being, be on your game at every turn. I received a call from a large national law firm, asking me to come in for an interview. New spaces with appropriate budgets are exciting as a starting point. My team and I prepared a detailed PowerPoint that outlined our process of discovery, strategic planning, programming, and square footage confirmation. These steps are followed by the creative steps of visioning, schematic design, design development, and 3D analysis. Lastly, we reviewed the documentation, tender, permit, and construction phases. We finished the presentation with an overview of relevant case studies of similar clients and testimonials of how we had exceeded their expectations. Step one of this process, of course, is always the confirmation of space and how much is needed.

We won the bid and got to work. At our first meeting, which I refer to as the onboarding and discovery meeting, where all known facts about the project are put on the table for discussion, the client shared that their lease was signed for 75,000 RSF (rentable square feet). And my first question was, "How did you know, that was how much space you needed?" They responded, "It's what we have now, plus 10 percent."

Learning that fact, we started asking a number of questions around workstyle, the impacts of technology, the number of articling students, and the rate of retiring partners—all facts completely relevant to how their space will need to work in the future. We completed an in-depth trend analysis, finalized the high-level and deep programming, and looked at what the competing law firms were doing to attract and retain valuable new associates. In short, once we completed the analysis our assessment of what they needed for space, was closer to 65,000 RSF.

Testing the theory, we applied the program to the base building background plates. Our suspicions were confirmed, and we shared them with the client: They had signed a lease for far too much space. The lease did not have a clause allowing them to sublease or to give back to the landlord at market rates. The financial implication of that decision was millions of dollars.

The only way we could assist with the new landscape was to advise they engage a real estate broker to assist this firm is shedding the expensive piece of real estate. If you were to ask this client what they would have done differently, I suspect there would have been language to protect their investment, and to qualify their needs with their designer before the ink was dry on the lease.

THE SCHEMATIC DESIGN PHASE OF INTERIOR DESIGN PROJECTS

Once the relationship between a designer and a prospect has been formalized by means of a contractual agreement, so that a prospect has now become a full-fledged client, the interior design project enters into what is referred to as the *schematic design phase*. At this stage, designers use the information they have obtained in order to develop the first comprehensive design concept for the project.

Associated Tasks of the Schematic Design Phase

As this phase begins, a clear division in project-related tasks become apparent. In addition to those tasks necessary to actually complete the project, there are tasks required to support project completion. For example, this phase is usually considered the stage in the project when designers start to prepare preliminary diagrams and drawings indicating their design concept. Designers also make initial selections of furniture and other merchandise that will be submitted to clients for approval. As part of this process, designers prepare the first series of time and cost estimates for the fabrication or procurement of these items. That task is an example of an activity necessary to support the project's completion. The tasks associated with the schematic design phase may be summarized as follows:

- Preparing preliminary functional diagrams
- Reviewing alternative approaches to the project
- Preparing space allocations/utilizations
- Preparing design-concept studies
- Submitting preliminary cost estimates

Documents Related to the Schematic Design Phase

During this phase, designers are responsible for preparing initial design sketches and floor plans, as well as sample boards showing selections for products, colors, textures, and finishes. In addition, designers prepare initial estimates of the materials, labor, and associated costs necessary to complete as accurately as possible a budget for the project in its next phase. Designers may prepare estimates, or initial determinations of project-related costs, for a wide variety of products and services they intend to incorporate in the project. As a practical matter, a designer should make clear to a client—by means of informal communication as well as the specific terms of the written agreement for a designer's services—that estimates of project costs are approximations made by a designer using the best, most recent information available. Final costs of these items and services may vary as a result of many factors outside a designer's control. The schematic design phase is perhaps best characterized as the stage when the designer makes initial design decisions and takes action to support those decisions. The next phase involves further refinements of those tasks.

THE DESIGN DEVELOPMENT PHASE OF INTERIOR DESIGN PROJECTS

This phase is, in essence, the stage in which the project is refined and finalized. The *design development* phase of a project begins as soon as the client approves the plans and estimates generated in the previous phases. The main goal of the previous stage is to establish the concept or design intent of the project; the purpose at this stage is to fine-tune those details and establish the final set of project characteristics.

Associated Tasks of the Design Development Phase

During this stage, a designer presents the updated cost estimates for items and services needed to complete the project as programmed and planned. From a practical standpoint, this is the time when a designer should also review with clients the project costs related to delivery and installation. At this stage, the costs of the project become more apparent to the client. In addition, estimated arrival and completion dates for desired goods and services may not coincide with either the project budget or the schedule. The challenge for the designer here, in order to receive the approvals necessary to move the project into its next phase, may involve further research to find products and service providers more appropriate for the actual project budget and schedule.

Whether the project is residential or commercial, the designer must attend to many external details, such as the constraints related to project compliance with public health, safety, and building codes. Only after such details are considered do designers make final presentations to clients of their refined selections and plans as well as revised budgets and schedules. Although adjustments are made throughout the duration of the project as designers and clients gain more information, it is at the conclusion of the design development phase that the major creative, functional, and technical aspects of the project become set. The tasks associated with this phase include the following:

- Preparing documents to fix/describe the final project
- Completing documents to reflect final project appearance/function
- Recommending colors/materials/finishes as necessary
- Preparing presentation boards and related materials
- Advising on cost-of-work adjustments

Documents Related to the Design Development Phase

During this phase, designers are required to complete drawings and schematics indicating space allocations and placement of furniture and equipment. They should also present their accumulated swatches of textiles and other project merchandise. Interior designers typically produce three kinds of documents, construction drawings, schedules, and specifications during this phase. Construction drawings are items such as floor plans and elevations that depict the location of geographical landmarks defining the subject space. Schedules, with which you may also be familiar, are graphics that convey information about project characteristics not readily apparent from construction documents, such as architectural finishes to be applied or location of light fixtures. In addition, designers note in the specifications the exact characteristics of labor and merchandise destined for application in the project. Consider this latter aspect and how writing of project specifications fits within the larger context of managing an interior design project.

Labor and merchandise for a project may be obtained through any of two basic means. These include contracts entered into with specific service providers or vendors by the designer or client at the suggestion of a designer. Alternatively, the scope of the project (as with publicly funded projects sponsored by government or military entities requiring it) may call for use of a process known as competitive bidding. Under this approach, different service providers and vendors submit binding offers (known as bids) to provide requested goods and services. The project's client then selects from among those bids to choose those resources to be used. Regardless of which approach is used, designers are responsible for describing in writing the merchandise and services planned for use. Usually, designers perform this task during the design development stage. From your other interior design studies and related experiences, you may already know these written directives are referred to as specifications, or less formally as specs. According to one source, specifications are "written to describe the details of the materials to be used, delivery and storage of those materials, installation methods, and acceptable workmanship for installation. Specifications work in concert with the graphic information presented on the drawings." Because of their prevalence and, hence, importance to interior designers, the different types of specifications and the manner in which they may be organized should be noted in addition to their relationship to other contract documents.

Specifications may be classified as *descriptive, performance, proprietary,* and *reference*. Considering the most basic characteristics of each should make clear how and why these different approaches are used. A descriptive specification is one in which designers provide detailed written notations about the tangible, physical characteristics of items or features sought. These specifications are made without a designer's reference to any one particular manufacturer or source, only to required features. A written instruction for a "black plastic laminate counter top 3' wide by 8' long with a 1" bull nose edge" in which a particular brand or manufacturer name was not further specified, would be a simple example of this kind of specification. This form of specification allows a vendor or service provider, not a designer, to choose the source for the item or service.

The performance specification is similar to descriptive specifications in that both make no mention of any one particular source for an item or service. Whereas the descriptive specification relates physical attributes of items and services sought, the performance specification notes what the selected item or feature must do, that is, what function it must carry out. If, in the preceding counter top example, a designer further noted that the countertop must be able to withstand the application of heat up to a certain degree, again without specifying a source or brand name, then it would be a performance specification. To gauge the appropriateness of the selected item or feature, the required performance criteria should be ones capable of measurement and evaluation. In this example, that might include noting the specific degree of heat tolerance required for the project.

Often, laypeople refer to items by a commonly used brand or company names. Designers carry this practice further through the use of proprietary specifications in which they particularly describe a product, by its specific name or model number. You can probably think of several examples of proprietary specifications just from recalling design products you like. Due to the exact nature of this kind of specification, by necessity the name of the maker or source as well as the exact way in which that resource refers to its products must be included in the specification.

Reference specifications rely upon characteristics and standards set by such sources as the American National Standards Institute (ANSI) or the American Society for Testing and Materials (ASTM). These sources set minimum performance requirements for acceptability of a variety of products. For interior design purposes, these standards include flammability of textile products or wear resistance for floor coverings.

With the knowledge of the basic types of specifications used by designers, it is next important to consider how those specifications are organized. Within the professional interior design community, the most commonly used way of organizing product specifications is with the approach developed by the Construction Specifications Institute (CSI). Discussions related to the preparation of contract documents include a more lengthy description of the CSI approach. This approach utilizes three categories, or levels, to provide first the basic requirements and information about project products in the General Requirements section. Next, in a section devoted exclusively to the desired products for use on a project, a detailed description of those to be used is noted. Finally, the manner of installation of the product is noted.

As you can see, designers consider a great many details during this phase of completing a project. What is important for you to remember, however, is that the information about a project in the drawings, schedules, and specifications should act together and be conveyed consistently and without contradiction or omission.

THE CONTRACT DOCUMENT PHASE OF INTERIOR DESIGN PROJECTS

As the name implies, the *contract document phase* of the project is largely devoted to the preparation of working documents. The construction documents prepared at this time are "created to communicate a design project to contractors for pricing and ultimate construction," and thus "provide clear, complete, and accurate communication regarding the design intentions of a project," as one resource notes. This phase may be best thought of as the stage when the design intent is carefully communicated to the service providers and vendors involved in the project.

Associated Tasks and Documents Related to the Contract Document Phase

The documents related to the contract document phase are more highly detailed and technical than those created during the design development phase. Drawings at this stage are usually drawn precisely to scale, with each sheet precisely and consistently organized so as to prevent any misinterpretation. These documents may illustrate the plan of ceilings and placement of mechanical systems, other equipment, and partition walls. Schedules in rendered, not written, form and other construction documents are generated at this time. These typically indicate where surface finishes will be applied and the placement and direction of doors and windows. Great care must be taken in preparing these drawings since they are used not only as models to guide the construction of the space but also as the basis for seeking competitive bids for construction services as well as bids for fixtures, furnishings, and equipment destined for the project. These documents are thus considered as part of the contracts for services and FF&E.

Interior designers working on small projects may suggest which general contractors are able to provide the construction necessary to complete the project. In more complicated projects, where designers are retained to work as designer/specifier, for example, they prepare all final deliverables, such as construction drawings, for use by the project manager. Note that designers who place orders may do so at the conclusion of this phase. Alternatively, they may defer until the project moves on to its next phase. Designers should be sure not to place purchase orders for merchandise until they have been presented to and reviewed by clients and all necessary authorizations and initial payments have been obtained. In this way, designers will not incur any financial liability for purchasing items without full client authorization if some change in a client's situation should occur. If clients are responsible for placing project orders, designers may instruct them to do so at this time or during the next phase. Such decisions depend on project circumstances and how designer and client have structured their relationship. After the designer receives formal client approval for necessary construction work and purchases, the final phase of the project begins and can include such steps as

- Preparing final working drawings/specs,
- Advising on further cost adjustments,
- Obtaining necessary approvals/permits,
- Qualifying vendors/suppliers/contractors,
- Assisting clients in assessing bids for project,
- Assisting in preparing/awarding FF&E bids,
- Placing orders for FF&E, given final client approval.

THE CONTRACT ADMINISTRATION PHASE OF INTERIOR DESIGN PROJECTS

The contract administration phase is where it all happens! It is the stage during which the entire project is completed and its outcome evaluated. Unlike other stages of the project, which a designer of record is primarily responsible for completing, the role of a designer during this phase may be limited. The first constraint imposed on the activities of designers during this phase is contractual in nature. In some instances, designers agree to be responsible only for developing the project's design intent or concept and for preparing construction documents and their attendant specifications. Given that scenario, responsibility for completing the project rests with a project manager, an individual or business hired to implement a designer's plans.

The other constraint is imposed by laws. Usually, laws of the state in which a design project is sited control issues such as whether a designer who is not a licensed general contractor may assume responsibilities for supervision of construction and project installation. In instances where designers are not allowed to perform these functions without a license, it is usually the role of an appropriately licensed general contractor to complete contract administration activities. In states where a designer is legally able to perform these tasks, there may be other legally based reasons for wishing an appropriately licensed general contractor to complete them. For example, designers may wish to limit any liability they might incur in supervising the work of others. Many clients seek legal recourse against designers when construction tasks are not completed correctly, when injuries occur, or when there is property damage. As a result, some designers stipulate in their contracts that the client—not the designer—is responsible for the selection, retention, and payment of fees to any general contractor or subcontractor that the client wishes to employ. Within this framework, designers work with clients to review the progress of construction work. They also advise clients about necessary changes, adjustments, and repairs, which need to be implemented by the project's general contractor.

Associated Tasks of the Contract Administration Phase of Interior Design Projects

At this stage of the project, the activities of others are required to bring about its completion. Usually in small residential projects, designers may either strongly suggest project workers, such as general contractors or subcontractors whose previous work designers have seen and deemed satisfactory, or they may ask clients to locate these service providers. As projects gain in complexity, however, and especially in projects where governmental agencies are the client of record, service providers are retained through what is referred to as **competitive bidding**.

The competitive bidding process begins when a client solicits responses from service providers—sometimes from any who wish to respond in open selections or from only those previously identified and qualified to respond in closed selections—by publishing an invitation to bid containing project details. This is usually followed by a series of instructions to bidders about the required form of submitted bids. Designers are usually responsible for assisting clients in this aspect of contract administration by preparing and evaluating bid documents for publication and approval. In a typical project in which a designer is responsible for preparation of bids but not the actual supervision of construction, the role of a designer may be more consultative in nature as designers and clients work together to assess the progress of the project. In some cases, a designer may be tasked with only supervising the ordering and delivery of products destined for project use whether those products are procured by a designer, provided by bidders, or purchased through resources, such as in-house governmental purchase offices directed by a client.

When a project is at or substantially near completion, designers conduct what is referred to as a *walk-through* with a client—or representatives of a client—to note any errors in workmanship that need to be corrected. Usually stickers or pencil marks are used to mark the location of a problem, which is then indicated on a document referred to as a punch list.

Contract administration is the phase of a project where its many facets come together to build, install, and appoint the space in accordance with the project's design intent. To determine the effectiveness of these efforts, many designers, especially those working on commercial projects for the use of a variety of people, conduct postinstallation evaluations of the completed environment. These evaluations typically assess user's perceptions of the space and seek input about any adjustments or refinements that could enhance user efficiency and enjoyment. For your reference, the contract administration phase typically includes the following activities:

- Assisting with final bids
- Managing the job site if no project manager is required
- Placing orders for FF&E, given final client approval
- Maintaining project management records
- Visiting the job site periodically to review the program
- Supervising the installation process
- Assisting in determining substantial completion of tasks and payments/releases
- Conducting postoccupancy evaluations/adjustments

MENTOR MEMO

The process of delivering a project is step by step, and it is linear. Not fully completing one step, before proceeding to the next step, will result in gaps and holes that will need to be filled later, prompting lost fees and increased liability. To help your clients better understand this process, you will need to dedicate one full meeting to onboarding a client to the process, especially if they have never been through a design process before. A client will be anxious to see what a space looks like, and a great rendering or sketch will be able show them that dream coming to reality, but if you have done your job well, that inspired end result will come at the conclusion of a thoughtful stage of strategic planning, the two stages of programming, and a brilliant creative process.

You need to define your process in the RFP (request for proposal) and in your pitch. The first step in landing a new client, in the commercial world is responding to an RFP. These come directly from either the occupant or the real estate company that is assisting with lease negotiations. In an ideal world, an outline of their challenges would be sketched out in the RFP. If it's a major hospital or P3, that outline of needs may be 200 pages long. Regardless of the scale of the sector, you need to be clear with your potential clients what your specific process will be. Chemistry with your clients should not be underestimated. You will win some and lose some just on the basis of not connecting with your clients at a level that resonates with their needs. Your clients are addressing their real estate needs either because they are growing, shrinking, or facing a lease that is expiring. Change is scary, and a clear and concise process that minimizes disruption in their day is priority one.

Project discovery Increasingly in today's projects, there is more that is unknown than known. Prior to finalizing the scope of work, one suggestion to designers is to engage in project discovery. During project discovery, the team will be asking investigative questions about the future plans of the business and what is driving the changes that will drive their future. If their business needs are clear, the existing realities of their space may need to be qualified. Spot demolitions, question and answer with engineers or a trusted code or estimator may be what is needed.

Programming involves two steps in the process—snorkeling and deep diving. Snorkeling? Think about it. You are skimming the surface but not diving too deep. Prior to qualifying the project's final scope and size, a high-level program qualification needs to take place. This is tied to project discovery. Reserve the right to revisit your fee submission, if you find something you were not prepared for. "Snorkeling" is designer-speak for skimming just the surface information to confirm lease, scope, consultants, and the big blocks to get your process moving.

After you have the high-level information and the space location has been determined (or in residential, the scope is clear), you can further investigate the finer details, such as inner working or copier machine power consumption, lineal inches of filing needed, and the security requirements of the front door. These are all items you will need to address, but none of them are necessary to assist in site location or lease negotiations. If you are joining an established firm, chances are you will have available a great toolkit of questionnaires and Excel documents, with every question listed that you will need to ask a client to design their space.

FACTORS TO CONSIDER WHEN MANAGING INTERIOR DESIGN PROJECTS

Project management is a process complicated by the interplay of many different factors. Designers must understand not just the details related to identifying and specifying tangible goods for use in the project but also how to provide detailed written and drawn instructions in ways understood by other professionals. In addition to the technical aspects of project management, there is also a decidedly interpersonal factor: that related to working with others.

During the course of a project, designers may be called upon to work with clients, architects, engineers, consultants, general contractors and subcontractors, among hosts of others, each with differing levels of education and expertise. Designers are assisted in their work in such complex environments by first learning project management information of the kind described. Then, they need to develop their own strategies based on that information for organizing the progression of events, tasks, and documents that result in successfully completed interior design projects.

Residential Interior Design Concerns

Residential interior designers should ascertain whether clients have reasonable expectations about the outcome of projects given their ability to bring about desired results. For example, do clients understand the expensive and time-consuming nature of interior design? Often, potential clients have seen and been impressed by finished projects, but they have little idea of the time and money required to produce highly customized items or dramatically finished spaces. Designers should listen for clues that indicate whether the budget for the potential project is in line with the desired results. Designers should also pay attention to clues about desired completion times, as many prospective clients foresee schedules that may be patently unrealistic considering their expectations and the resulting demands placed on designers. Simply, are expectations realistic, given a designer's abilities and the projected budget and time constraints? The answer to these questions may either bless or doom the project before it has even begun.

Factors Related to Residential Interior Designers

Designers should not agree to accept a project when they do not have the expertise to complete nor assume responsibility for a project when they lack the experience and knowledge required to complete it. Yet, how can designers gain experience and learn new professional skills if they don't take on projects that present some new challenge or difficulty?

Some writers have suggested that designers consider the 80/20 rule when deciding whether to take on a new project. According to this rule, designers should accept projects in which 80 percent of the required work is readily familiar to them from past experience, and no more than 20 percent requires unfamiliar work. This approach is based on the idea that a designer's financial profitability diminishes the more the designer assumes new project tasks, such as background research required to learn about a project. Nevertheless, in many instances, designers may not be able to adequately bill a client for all the time required to learn about new sources or to perform new tasks. Designers' final decisions to undertake any one project depend on their comfort level—financial and otherwise—with it.

An easy project probably does not exist; moreover, no two projects are ever exactly alike. As a result, even well-educated designers, who have extensive prior experience working on residential projects may find themselves having to solve unforeseen problems during what may have looked like the most innocuous project. Thus, effective skills for designers in charge of accepting or managing residential projects can include advising clients about such concerns as

1. Whether a designer believes that he or she is able to accomplish the project and can perform tasks such as keeping the client routinely informed of a project's progression, given constraints placed on a designer's time and energies by every project for which a designer is responsible;

2. Whether the proposed budget is adequate for the amount and kind of work the project will require;
3. Whether the time schedule proposed for completion is realistic given the project goals;
4. Whether the designer will have to spend a great deal of time researching particular products or services necessary to complete the project;
5. Whether the method of compensation proposed is appropriate, given the tasks a designer needs to perform and the amount and kinds of merchandise a designer needs to procure to complete the project;
6. Whether any project management issues—for example, potential project delays— appear relevant based on goals a client wishes to accomplish;
7. Whether clients are aware of possible project delays that might occur when a designer specifies a particular item around which an entire design concept depends—a large custom-made rug, for instance, destined for use in either a hotel lobby or residential living room. If that item is delayed or becomes unavailable, the entire installation process planned for the space in the latter part of the contract administration stage may be delayed as the site sits empty.

The major objective of project management is to address the needs of a client. These needs may be explicitly expressed by a client—"I want a blue living room"—or inferred by a designer from facts about a project—"From what you've said about needing a large conference room, we'll have to reconfigure the room using space from the entry area." However project goals are determined, accomplishing them in an objectively reasonable manner is an important task requiring project management skills. Another important objective of project management is to enable designers to earn a sufficient, reasonable profit that justifies the use of their talents and time.

NOTES FROM THE FIELD

A great project manager can be an outstanding asset to the project. I have had the pleasure of working with great project managers, and the creative end result was wonderful and rewarding. This is not that story. Unfortunately, the term *project manager* (PM) is not a regulated part of our industry. And, from time to time, those lacking the experience and letter behind their title, are guiding a complicated process with huge opportunities for failure, due to uncoordinated details.

A client brought me and my team on-board to complete a full-floor tenant improvement out of town. My team does about fifty projects of this scale a year, we were well equip to handle the project and fully understood the details required. The client inquired whether our team would be working with a project manager, in hopes the PM would be able to minimize their (the clients) involvement. Our answer to this was, no problem, and we welcomed the PM to the team.

The project unfolded as any good project does, creative was running smoothly, the renderings were approved, and the budget was on target. The next step for the team was to begin the private office furniture selections and assemble the procurement documents for the client. Just as we were getting started, a letter arrived from the project manager informing us that the furniture portion of our contract would not be necessary and our work was done. Pardon? The team was mortified and deeply concerned we had done something wrong. Immediately we called the client, whose response was "you guys are great!" and proceeded to inform us the project manager would be providing the furniture selection and procurement services, saving him a step. What a problem. We politely suggested to the client, please ensure the correct due diligence is done as furniture needs to be cross-checked against the electrical drawings and put onto the plans for scale, door, and thermostat coordination. Given the project manager did not have access to our drawings, we were concerned for our client and responded with our own letter (copied to the project manager) simply outlining the steps that should take place. The client proceeded with the project manager's advice, and the furniture was ordered without the steps we had outlined for the client. The end result was unfortunate, the furniture was too big for the space and was not wired properly for their use. The client called our team, and we assisted with a remedy for the client, returned the furniture the PM ordered, and reordered the correct pieces.

The client was more than gracious, and deeply apologetic for not understanding the subtleties of the process due diligence, and of course we responding with the assurances it is our job to make this look easy. Why is this important? Document your concerns as they arise, and they will. We clearly outlined to the client where they were at risk, and when things unfolded badly, we had a letter outlining our concerns and position. When the project wrapped, we learned that this project manager had a purchasing agreement with the furniture dealer and further profited from selling the client furniture. That project manager is no longer in business, and the client is still my client and has become a most trusted friend. I truly hope this story in an anomaly. There are great third-party project managers in the industry that would have succeeded in this situation.

Practical Activity

You undoubtedly have a special interior. Perhaps it is a public building, a church, a library, even an airport or train station with soaring, inspirational, or evocative spaces. Maybe it is a private residence realized by a designer you especially esteem. Identify one such meaningful space, gather an image of it, and research how that space came about.

Where is it? Was it new construction or a renovation? What was written and said about it before, during, and after its construction and installation? Prepare a five-minute oral history of your selected space to present to your class. Be sure to emphasize the design-build aspects of the process of how the space came into being. What steps had to be completed before others could begin? What hurdles had the designer overcome to finish the project? How did—or did not—the client help? Tell about the process that brought about your selected space.

Review Questions

1. Note some perspectives related to interior design project management. Why are these important concerns for practitioners?

2. What is entailed in the concept of design intent? Why do think it is important for designers to be able to explain this concept to others?

3. Through what phases are interior design projects considered to transition? Identify at least two issues practitioners usually address during these phases.

4. What are some tasks interior design project managers often are called upon to perform?

5. Define the difference between tasks interior designers perform and those of project managers.

6. Note several documents and their contents associated with each phase of a "usual" interior design project.

7. Note the different kinds of specifications identified in this chapter, and explain their characteristics.

8. What is the competitive bidding process? What is it comprised of, and how do interior designers assist clients during it?

9. What is a walk-through, and what does it seek to accomplish?

10. What are some concerns interior designers should consider before agreeing to accept or manage a project?

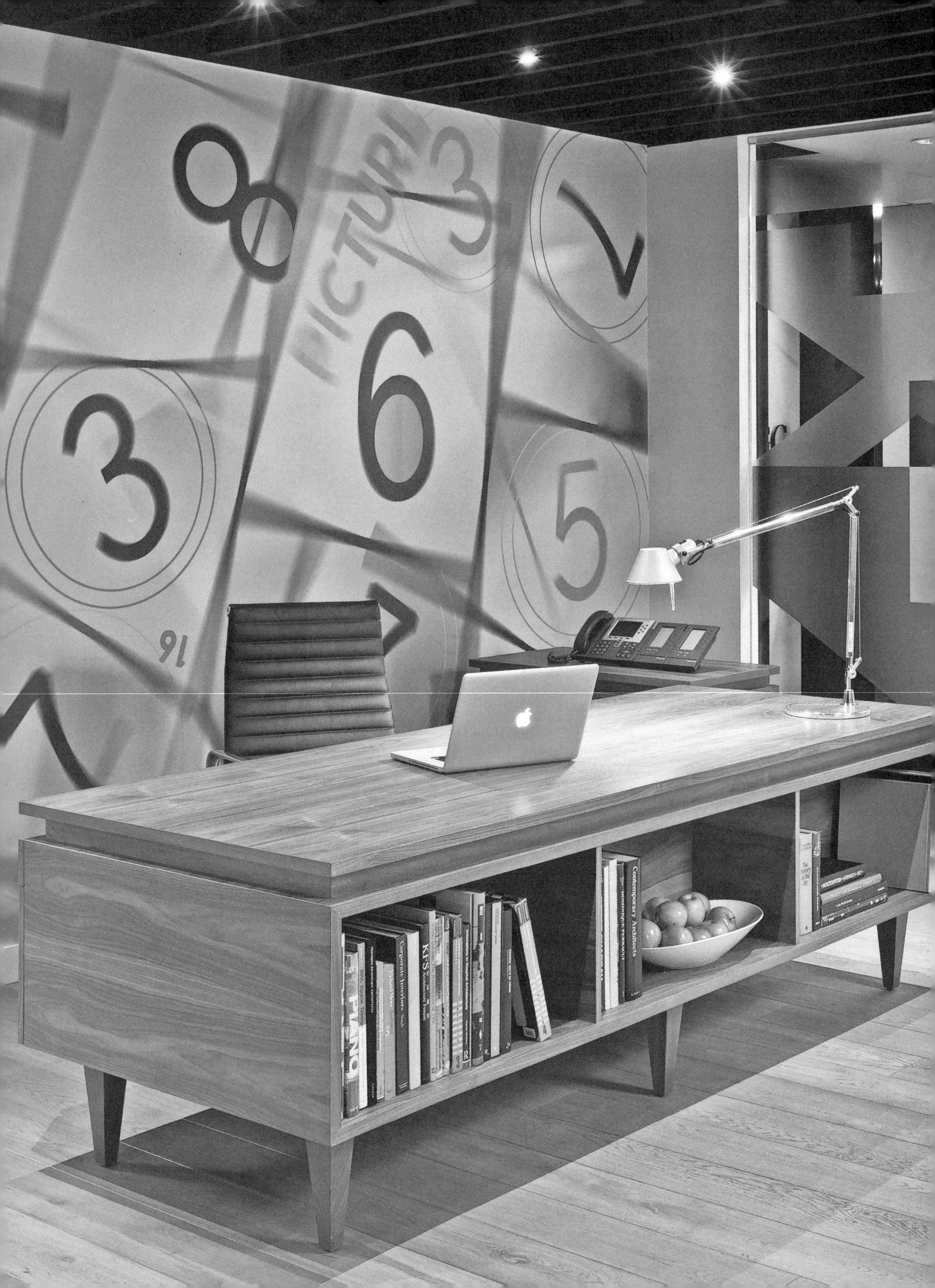

Contemporary Architects
Corporate Interiors
PIANO

CHAPTER 11
DEFINING THE CLIENT RELATIONSHIP

MENTOR MEMO
Managing expectations is critical to any project.

After reading this chapter, you will be able to
- Know better the forms of contracts interior designers typically use;
- Understand basic contract concepts and specific provisions related to the work of interior designers;
- Present and negotiate contract terms with potential clients;
- Be comfortable with the practical business realities and how they may be reflected in contract terms.

INTRODUCTION TO THE DESIGNER-CLIENT RELATIONSHIP

No matter sizes or budgets of interior design projects, there must be workable—and working—relationships between designers and clients for them to be successful. How might it be possible to describe, much less define, the complex interests and needs of both? Interior designers use **contracts**, or legally binding agreements, to establish responsibilities they and their clients will have as they work together. You are already familiar with basic contract concepts and terms from previous chapters. This chapter expands on those to describe how designers use contracts to establish and carry out their work with clients. Contracts for designers' services are not just "paperwork" but results of careful assessments of projects and negotiations with clients. As well, they are reflections of the practical realities facing today's global interior design profession. This chapter explores the process of defining designer-client relationships through negotiations and contracts reflecting them. Working with contracts and defining the designer-client relationship begins with considering the systematic approach found in this chapter.

The purpose of this chapter is to help you explain to a client a design concept such as this and then put that information into a written contract.

CONTRACTS AND THE CLIENT RELATIONSHIP

What are interior design contracts? Even though practitioners may be knowledgeable about contracts, those learning about the working world of interior design may be less familiar with them. Before discussing *substantive* issues related to contracts, such as elements required for them to be upheld legally, consider *forms* interior design contracts can take. This should provide context for contracts' requirements and contents, as well as how they may come to represent integrally the designer-client relationship.

Forms of Interior Design Contracts

Basic contract forms interior designers use for their services include the following:

1. **Letter agreements** Perhaps the most informal, often shortest types of contracts are those taking the form of letters, passed between designer and client. These are usually presented after designers and clients have developed relationships and

---

BOX 11.1

LETTER OF AGREEMENT FOR INTERIOR DESIGN SERVICES

[Date]
[Name of Interior Design Business]
[Address]
[Contact Information]

Dear [Prospective Client]:

Thank you for selecting [name of interior design firm] for your interior design project. The purpose of this letter is to describe the terms and conditions under which we will render interior design services. Before signing, please read this letter fully and carefully. You are welcomed and encouraged to consult with an attorney of your choosing should you feel further clarification is necessary. If the terms of this letter are satisfactory to you, please indicate your choices as appropriate throughout this agreement, sign on the line above your printed name under the word "Agreed" found at the conclusion of both copies, and return one copy for our records. Once signed, this letter will become a binding contract for services between you and this firm.

Cordially,

[Name of individual representing the firm]
[Name of interior design firm]

Agreed: _____   Date: _____
_____
(Prospective Client's Printed Name)

---

202 • PART 3 YOU AND YOUR CLIENTS

discussed projects. The body of these letters, following the opening salutation, sets out terms such as scope of service, methods and times of payments, and other details. After the parties sign the agreement, these seemingly simple letters define the contours of their relationship; their terms are binding on both.

2. **Standard-form agreements** Informal, letter-style agreements may work well with residential projects and those where designer and client have established rapport. In other instances, large-scale projects and/or times where designer and client feel more comfortable precisely knowing what is expected, standard-form agreements may be used. These often take the shape of blank forms in which designers fill in requested information. These are published by and made available from professional organizations such as ASID and IIDA for members' use.

   These are previously prepared, preprinted forms in which designers (who are members of these organizations) and clients enter specific information but otherwise do not change terms they contain. A brief scan of these forms indicates that for a contract to benefit from the court's ability to enforce all of its terms, that contract must, at the very least, contain a date, identify the parties to the contract, spell out the scope of services to be performed, state the amount and method of compensation, and be signed. After the contract is signed, contract performance is usually initiated.

   Standard-form agreements are proprietary to such organizations and require payment of fees each time they are downloaded for use. In general, these forms are thought to favor interior designers with the terms they contain. For example, they set forth specific ways in which designers are to be compensated for their work and provide for remedies, or monetary penalties, when clients do not comply with agreement terms.

3. **Custom contracts** In very large interior design projects, especially commercial ones, designers and clients may request their own attorneys to prepare custom-drafted, project-specific contracts. Lawyers with experience drafting design-build contracts, knowledgeable about their complexities, and able to anticipate events that might occur during a specific project are usually called upon to draft these agreements, which can contain numerous pages. There may be back-and-forth negotiations between legal councils for designers and clients until final provisions are agreed upon.

From simple to complex, contracts for interior design services may appear contradictory. How can documents that are able to take so many different forms do the one thing they claim: define relationships between designers and clients? Two further aspects about contracts are helpful to consider in resolving that question. These include describing requirements legally necessary for *any* contract, regardless of form, or length. It includes setting out provisions specifically applicable to interior design work. Together, these issues provide insight into how and why interior design services contracts come about and, in doing so, define relationships designers have with clients.

General Contract Requirements

Contracts are agreements courts of law will enforce, meaning they will hold responsible any party that does not do what they agreed to do. Courts may do this because certain requirements have been met. Those requirements may be summarized as

1. An **offer** to do (or not to do) some specific activity;
2. An **acceptance** of that offer by another on exactly the same terms as was offered;

3. **Legal capacity** of all involved and the contract itself for a **legal purpose**;
4. **Mutuality**, where the parties agree—and understand they agree—on all terms;
5. **Consideration**, or something of sufficient value exchanged between the parties.

Specific Requirements for Interior Design Contracts

//

MENTOR MEMO

In a typical contract outline, we would clearly state how many options the client would receive, before additional service fees or hourly work would take over.

Contract basics seem straightforward enough. How might these legal necessities required for a valid, enforceable contract be "translated" into the work—and language—familiar to designers? What suggestions, as indicated in the preceding Mentor Memo, might designers be most interested in? Using this guidance, specific provisions for interior design contracts include

1. **Names** of all parties to the agreement such as the designer and client, usually as representatives of their businesses;
2. **Descriptions** of what the designer will do. Legal experts refer to this as the subject matter of designer-client agreements; designers refer to it as their scope of services. This part of contracts often includes well-articulated descriptions of exact locations on the client property where designers will undertake their work and specific activities they will perform during programming, schematic design, project management, and contract administration phases;
3. **Compensation** for the services of the designer. This refers to the consideration requirement for contracts: the agreement to perform design services in exchange for payment of those services referenced earlier. This section contains provisions specifically stating how and when designers will be compensated, including amounts

Does your client contract provide for continually refining of the project space and its concept? If so, is it at their cost or yours?

required to retain designers' services, methods by which they will be compensated (rate-based, sale of merchandise method, or combination method), due dates, and reimbursement payments;
4. **Date of signatures** by parties to the contract;
5. **Signatures** of parties (designer and client) to the contract.

Other Interior Design Contract Provisions

In addition to elements required of all contracts, those for interior design services have unique provisions related to the practices—and realities—of the profession. The following terms are often found:

1. **Client responsibilities to designer and project** One of the clients' responsibilities is timely payments to designers. Another includes cooperation with the designer throughout the project to effect its successful conclusion within the time frame set by the contract and to provide the designer with reasonable access to the subject property;

2. **Project document ownership rights** Many designers claim to own project drawings, graphics, and written specifications (among other documents). As the argument goes, these are their work product. Increasingly, however, clients state they "own" project documents because they paid for them. They also cite privacy and security issues as other reasons they should belong to them. Presently, many contracts for interior design services include provisions giving designers ownership and reproduction rights to the documents they prepare. Clients may ask designers to remove the clients' names or identifying information associating them with the project but permit them to own and publicize drawings and images. A related issue concerns nondisclosure agreements. Many clients require designers, even service providers such as general contractors, to agree they will not let others know about matters related to the clients' projects. Usually, this is done through agreements separate from design services contracts and prohibits designers from giving out details as client names, personal information, and project budgets.

3. **Mediation and arbitration agreements** Contract disputes can be lengthy, expensive affairs to resolve if left to the formal court system. Less cumbersome ways of resolving issues are usually desired. Usually, provisions of this kind state both parties agree to resolve matter without going to court through mediation and arbitration. *Mediation* refers to nonbinding negotiated resolutions, whereas *arbitration* refers to binding resolutions. Many contracts for design services specify a two-part procedure for both parties to follow in the event disputes arise. The first part of the process usually calls for the dispute to be heard by a neutral, third-party mediator who will gather information about the cause and nature of the dispute and then negotiate a resolution between the parties. In the event the mediator fails to resolve the issue, these contract provisions further allow the matter to be considered by an arbitrator whose decision determining the outcome of the dispute is binding on the parties.

4. **Force majeure and impossibility of performance** There are events neither designers not anyone else can control. This provision addresses what legal experts refer to as "acts of God" (*force majeur*). The occurrence of natural disasters such as floods, hurricanes, and tornadoes are examples of this, as are incidents of labor

strikes, or events such as riots. These render impossible designers' abilities to do their work. Provisions of this kind state that designers shall not be responsible for the occurrence of these events and any delay to, or impossibility of completing projects that results from them. In the event these do occur, designers are excused from performance of their duties as set out in the contract.

5. **Disclaimer of liability** Designers perform their work in tandem with other professionals such as architects, engineers, and general contractors. Should designers be responsible for their actions and possibly have to pay for problems they create? Fairness and contract terms addressing this issue provide they are not.

6. **Assignment and delegation of contract** What might happen if residential clients sold homes for which they had contracted for design services? Similarly, what might happen if a commercial client becomes part of another company during the course of a project? This can occur with corporate mergers and acquisitions. Provisions related to these occurrences state that neither designer nor client may allow another party to "stand in" for them without the written consent of the other.

7. **Integration of contract terms** Should oral information, expressed between the parties but not otherwise found in the written terms of contracts, be considered persuasive as to what they mean? Legal tradition for centuries has held it cannot be; provisions of this kind mean the contract, as written, contains all the terms its parties have agreed to.

8. **Severability of contract terms** These provisions mean that should one part of the contract "fail," or be found to be legally unenforceable, any and all other provisions remain valid, unless otherwise determined.

9. **Contract termination or suspension** Interior design projects are complex undertakings. There are those instances where clients may not be able to complete projects. For example, they may no longer have the financial ability to pay for the project. Nevertheless, designers should not be left uncompensated for their work. Termination provisions state contracts may be stopped permanently and designers paid in full for services rendered to that date. *Suspension* is a concept related to termination since clients become unable to continue to participate in an interior design project, although they intend to finish the project. Provisions of this kind usually apply when clients have not paid for design services within set times; the contract suspended until they do so.

10. **Contract amendment** Usually this section provides that any change to agreements between designers and clients must be in writing to be valid; oral modifications are not sufficient.

11. **Controlling jurisdiction** This provision refers to what legal experts call *choice of law*; it means, simply, designers and clients agree the laws of a particular area will govern the contract and be applied in the event of disputes.

CONTRACTS: PRESENTATION AND NEGOTIATION

Designers should be aware of how to present and negotiate contracts with potential clients. Procedures used in residential interior design work differ from those in contract/commercial work.

Residential Interior Design Contracts

Within the context of residential interior design, designers and prospective clients may meet and become acquainted through any number of means. Usually, designers are referred to prospective clients by past ones, or clients seek out designers whose work they have seen and liked. During this early stage of a possible project, residential interior designers will interpret the needs and wishes of prospects and make suggestions about what could be included in any future project. These early-stage services teach designers a great deal about both the client and the potential project that might lie ahead. At such a preliminary stage, designers do not, as a rule, receive compensation unless they enter into a **design study fee agreement**. These kinds of agreements are usually reserved for large-scale residences, or ones with special concerns, such as for interior work on historic or architecturally significant houses.

At early, preproject stages of getting to know each other, designers learn about the project budget and proposed time frame for its completion, and whether the designer will have to generate working documents because of the absence of blueprints. Designers may request financial information from prospective clients, even going so far as to request a credit check or other background financial information. Lacking a credit assessment, designers should consider whether they feel comfortable going forward on what might be a very expensive project not knowing if the client can afford it.

During this time, as well, designers usually indicate the terms by which they structure their working relationships with clients. This can be done, of course, informally, through oral communication with prospects, or designers can provide a blank contract form (of the kind described earlier) for them to review with their legal advisers. After contract signing, typically, the project's schematic design phase begins. During this, designers make initial design choices based on information gathered previously.

Contracts and the Contract Interior Design RFP Process

Designers with commercial, nonresidential practices obtain clients differently that those described previously. Usually, contract interior designers will respond to a formal written **request for proposal**, or **RFP**. These are issued by entities, such as businesses and governmental agencies, seeking interior design services. Such requests may be found in journals of record, or though specific institutional sources. RFPs may be found by perusing journals devoted to commercial architecture or construction as well as the websites of U.S. and state governmental agencies. Responding to these requests can involve lengthy preparation and research to decipher and interpret the needs of these prospects. Again, designers and their firms are not likely to receive compensation for these initial preparatory activities.

After prospective institutional clients receive all RFPs by the specified deadline, they review submissions, interview successively narrower and narrower sets of respondents, and then offer the project to the one candidate determined to be most appropriate for and capable of completing the project according to requirements. At this stage of the process, designers and clients enter into an agreement, formalized with a written contract. Designers usually begin formal programming activities such as interviews and focus groups with project stakeholders to determine their needs further as well as prepare schematics and review site blueprints.

Thorough programming by the design team ensured that the client image was reflected in both the design intent and the final imagery for this project.

//
MENTOR MEMO

You want me to use what as inspiration? Every day clients who have extraordinary challenges place unrealistic expectations on my desk and ask me to solve them. This is typical, sometimes fun, and at times we feel more like magicians than designers; however, we have a responsibility to be clear about what we can do and what is not achievable.

This story involves fish, lots and lots of fish. I was hired to complete the design of a public facility, with animals as the main attraction. In the event you do get a chance to work on a zoo, aquarium, or vet, your challenges will be many. In this case, the technical challenges of the project had been met. Thanks to a great team of specialty consultants, the health and safety of the animal environments was well under way. And since the facilities for the animals were almost done and complete, we were now dealing with the aesthetic elements of the project, and our target demographic of visitor to this site was under the age of ten, young busy eyes and hands that needed a specific design concept.

With the creative team, I traveled to middle America to tour other similar sites, built by this client, large animal zoos and small animal aquariums, were on the agenda and my rubber boots fit in well. I was taken to the tropical fish aquarium, which if you stood in front of and squinted, every color of the rainbow came swimming by in a flash. The client stared at the tank and said that the interior of my new building should look like the tank. Every color was required, and I wondered if I was up for the challenge. Where do I start? How do I capture this in a built environment?

The client felt strongly that this project needed to be inspired by the colors of every tropical fish; it needed to be flashy and colorful, with lots of energy. But if the interior of the building had the same colors as the fish, would visitors actually see the fish? No, they would not. The animals were the stars of the show, not the tile, carpet, or ceiling colors. Therefore, any design decisions needed to be about showcasing why people were coming to this facility; plus it had to be cleanable and easy to care for.

Given that the client was so adamant, we felt the best thing to do was a split screen with both options shown, one fully colored and one more neutral, both with the colorful fish rendered into the tanks. This tactic clearly made our case but gave the client the ability to choose. When the client saw the two ideas, we ended up with a great hybrid of the two ideas. Downplaying the aggressive colors where the animals were present, allowing the beautiful natural colors to shine through, and the remainder of the facility being in keeping with a great experience for kids, and grown-ups alike; it was filled with energy and color in the right places and made the right statement.

Why is this important? Going into the design challenge, the client had one very strong opinion. Leaving the design stage, the client felt empowered to accept some new ideas, and we made sure that he had true authentic ownership in the decision making and end result. It is important to keep in mind that the client has been thinking about this project a long time, long before the designers have been brought on board. Because ==you do not want to squelch the client's passion for the final product, we need to listen and pay attention to the "fish" in every scenario, allowing your ideas to become their ideas, in a graceful== and professional way.

Contracts reflect how interior designers will work with many different client needs to produce creative, realistic, and profitable solutions.

PRACTICAL REALITIES OF CONTRACTS AND INTERIOR DESIGN

Contracts do not exist apart from other business practices and day-to-day realities faced by designers. These give rise to various issues related to the how and why contracts are so important. What kinds of questions might you, or any other designer have about them?

Must There Even Be a Contract?

Practically and legally, it is better professional practice for interior designers to have written contracts for their services before doing any work. For that matter, it is sound policy for designers to not place product orders without having written authorization from clients. Without written documentation, it is possible that clients may refuse—on grounds there was no "real" agreement—to pay for designers' time, efforts, and knowledge, much less for any items ordered. As well, Uniform Commercial Code requirements related to sale of goods may also require written memorialization in order for them to be valid and enforceable.

Is a "Perfect" Client Contract Possible?

Given the emphasis on the many different forms contracts may take and the importance of their provisions, is there such thing as a "perfect" contract? In other words, is there a way to draft a contract that will be the best at protecting interior designers' interests? Many legal writers agree there probably is not. Facts, circumstances, laws, and their application vary too much for that to be possible, realistically. However, what is possible is for designers to have their own legal counsels advise them about any and all arrangements for their services and alert them to any potential issues that might arise.

What Tips Are There for Working with Contracts and Clients?

When working with clients in a "graceful and professional" way, as mentioned in the preceding Mentor Memo, how might designers do so when working with contracts and clients? The contract negotiation process is challenging for even the most experienced designers. They—and you—want to make a difference in the design world and to remain in business. However, at what professional and personal expense? What red flags should alert designers to proceed cautiously, if at all, with prospective clients and projects?

1. Clients have unreasonable expectations, budgets, or time constraints. Interior design work is expensive and time-consuming. Finished spaces can enhance lives and functionality. They cannot, nor should not, be expected to "solve" greater,

internal client problems, such as unhappy marriages (as with residential work), or make faltering businesses sound (as with contract work). Designers should anticipate they will need to educate clients about what it will take to finish projects. As well, they should make known the extent of their responsibilities to and for the client and project;

2. Clients do not wish to negotiate on terms can be another problematic issue. Established designers, those with ready streams of projects, may simply walk away from such clients. Other designers who need the project to remain in business may consider going ahead with client and project. How can the designer decide? In general, clients who do not want to negotiate terms are not clients it will be productive or positive to work with. This is especially true if terms the client will not talk about include "cost saving" ones. Clients who want to do their own purchasing of items, work only with particular trades people, do their own project installation, or other activities impacting designers' work, reputation, and profitability are prospects designers should decline as clients.

Prospective clients are usually not fully aware of what designers do. Also, they will likely share their concerns regarding projects of any kind and scale. Educating prospects, anticipating their concerns, and finding ways to address them through transparent lines of communication are important skills, ones inherent in the negotiation process. Having information available is key to handling most concerns as they arise.

What Tips Are There for Working with Contracts and Legal Advisers?

A common goal of businesspeople is to protect their businesses and property from the effects of any legal claims brought against them. Accordingly, designers often consult legal advisers about the following issues:

1. Laws or other regulations that might prohibit, limit, or otherwise affect them and their interior design practice.
2. The terms of proposed agreements, which may favor either the designer or the client, and what ramifications there might be for working under such terms. For example, how encompassing are limitation of liability provisions in protecting the designer?
3. The form of business organization that would be most appropriate to protect the interior designer and the design business, such as limited liability company (LLC) or corporate form. The organizational form of the interior design business along with carefully worded contracts can protect both designers and their businesses from the effects of legal claims brought against them.
4. The types and amounts of insurance coverage appropriate for designers and the work they do. They may also suggest tax and investment experts since most of these matters relate to and involve contracts.

NOTES FROM THE FIELD

When can a bad contract happens to good people? Working around the globe is a pleasure, and a gift on so many levels. In my professional career, I have delivered work in dozens of countries to clients who spoke a different language and lived in disparate cultural landscapes, and I can assure you no two are the same. In North America we deliver design one way, and in Asia or the Middle East is it entirely a different process. Assuming the same rules apply is an innocent but expensive mistake.

At the time, our practice had a team that specialized in large hotel and entertainment complexes. It was not only a fun and interesting area of practice but also highly creative and fulfilling. Our group had delivered dozens of five star hotels for the industry veterans; we knew what needed to be done and how to do it, or so we thought.

Normally the creative process truly begins after you are on-board and have connected with the client on the measurable and nonmeasurable goals of the project. In this country, different rules prevailed. In order to get the project, we were to generate a complete design concept, prior to meeting the client, place our ideas up on the wall, and walk out. We had no chance to explain or sell our ideas to the "chairman." Our work was being looked at, alongside many other firms without the benefit of designer in the room to explain it. Every other firm, all great firms, was asked to do the same. It was simply a beauty contest.

As you have been reading in this book, a great process should involve getting to know your client well enough to allow a solution that is inspired by them, reflecting their goals, their wishes, and their culture. This situation is the exact opposite; that was red flag number one! Surprisingly, we guessed correctly and were awarded the work. We were notified via a letter; no conversations took place. A schedule of this clients expectations was forwarded to us, and we were firmly requested to start work. Given that this client was half way around the world and the schedule was tight, we proceeded in good faith, but with caution.

The contract was sent to our legal counsel, and at the same time the designers got to work. Why is this important? For large projects, contract conversation can continue well into the design process; this is not unusual, as long as it is close behind. Had this project been on home soil, you would not be reading about it as a case study. In the country where this project and this client were residing, their contract was what we would abide by.

The team was struggling, a number of creative concepts were sent with no response or constructive feedback. Hearing "I don't like it. Keep working" from the client is not helpful or productive. But, given that we had little connection to the client and no ability to ask questions in person, we had no choice but to accept the bruises and keep trying. We were defeated with every step: We were not good enough or creative enough to secure the approval of this client. There were millions of dollars on the line, we needed to get this right.

Here comes the interesting part. One month later and creatively no further along than the day we won the work, our in house lawyer informed us of the contract's fine print. We would work until the client was happy, providing as many options and revisions as they felt required. In a typical contract outline, we would clearly state how many options the client would receive before additional service fees or hourly work would take over. In this case, we could be working indefinitely until the client "liked" the work. We immediately put our pens down.

In this situation, we should never have proceeded without fully digesting the fine print in the contract, especially given this foreign country's unique cultural norms. In their view, this as a contract approach was normal. With the help of our lawyer, we crafted an amendment to the contract outlining a detailed summary of what we would provide and that we would need a deposit to draw against for the upcoming work. The client did not respond well to our request, and we all agreed (both the design team and the client) that we would not work well together.

I had never resigned from a project before; the defeat was overwhelming. That said, had we chosen to proceed, we would have been contractually obligated to work indefinitely, with no means of getting the feedback we needed to deliver a world-class destination hotel.

Practical Activity

This chapter has brought together the basics of contracts, as previous chapters detailed, and applied them to the actual work of interior designers. It has done so by delineating typical provisions found in contracts for design services. Consider the following three such clauses in more detail:

Disclaimer of Responsibility
Limitation of Liability for Acts of Third Parties
Mediation and Arbitration Provisions

Consider the various Notes from the Field you have encountered in the text as well as your own knowledge gained over the course of your interior design study. State why inclusion of these provisions is necessary to protect interior designers; use examples from your studies and work as well as research to support your opinions.

Review Questions

1. How would you define a contract for interior design services?

2. What is the Statute of Frauds, and how is it related to interior design contracts?

3. What are two common forms of contracts for interior design services?

4. To what does the concept of enforceability apply, and what must be present?

5. What are three basic objectives to consider when working with contracts for interior design services?

6. When should proposed contracts be presented and negotiated with prospective clients?

7. What is contract negotiation, and what is involved in the process of negotiating contract terms?

8. What basic elements are necessary for all design contracts?

9. What contract terms represent the importance of defining the services you propose to offer?

10. What contract terms represent the important ways in which you propose to charge clients for your services?

11. Describe terms such as *arbitration*, *disclaimer of liability*, *assignment and delegation*, and *integration of contract terms*. State why they are included in contracts for interior design services.

12. What is the difference between mediation and arbitration?

> **BOX 11.2**

> # SAMPLE "STANDARD FORM AGREEMENT"

> **1. The names of the parties to the agreement**
>
> It is important for both the designer and the client to be specifically and recognizably identified by name and to include information such as the address where they may usually be found. Most agreements provide spaces in which to insert this kind of information about all parties to the agreement:
>
> > The parties to this agreement are (*insert name of designer*), "Designer," and (*insert name(s) of client*), "Client."
>
> **2. The specific services the designer will perform**
>
> Recall that a complete and detailed analysis of the scope of services must be completed by a designer and agreed to by a client. It is helpful to organize this section in terms of project phases. The sample contract excerpted here is by no means inclusive of all this section might contain. Rather, it is included to show you how this provision may be organized and the type of language commonly used in a contract to express the scope-of-service intent.
>
> > **Scope of Services**
> >
> > Designer agrees to perform the following work:
> >
> > *Project Phases in Scope of Services:* Designer agrees to perform the following services in order to plan, manage, and complete the project described above:
> >
> > > *Program Stage* (information and planning stage): Designer agrees to meet with Client to determine project objectives, observe and record existing characteristics of subject area(s), measure dimensions of subject area(s), and prepare drawings or renderings depicting proposed design plan for subject area(s). Recommend merchandise purchases and identify construction work necessary to carry out proposed design plan. Other services Designer agrees to perform for this project include:
> > >
> > > > Unless specifically requested, Designer will not prepare a proposed project budget. If Client requests a proposed budget, Client agrees that any such budget prepared by Designer is for estimation purposes only and is in no way a guarantee of availability of goods and services so noted, nor is a guarantee of final price of those goods and services and, furthermore, is no warranty of fitness of those goods and services for any particular use or purpose or guarantee of quality.
> > >
> > > *Schematic Design Phase:* After acceptance of proposed design concept, Designer agrees to prepare working drawings for use by others describing the following areas of subject property:
> > >
> > > > Upon Client's approval of these drawings, Designer agrees to submit drawings for competitive bids to contractors of Client's choosing made after consultation with Designer. Designer agrees to prepare orders for project merchandise and construction tasks. Designer agrees to submit those orders to Client for Client approval prior to making any such purchase or engaging any such construction professional. In addition, Designer agrees to perform the following tasks at this stage:

Project Management: Designer agrees to make on-site inspections of project progression on the following basis: _____

Designer agrees to be available to consult with Client about project progression, status of orders and contractors, and conformity of purchased goods to specifications made. Designer agrees to be available to consult with Client about the conformity and suitability of project construction to plans and whether such construction is of suitable quality. Designer agrees to the following as well:

Designer agrees to make project presentation within days after this agreement becomes effective, or alternatively within days after Client provides the following:

After final approval of design concept, Designer agrees to do the following (please indicate):

___ Begin project and undertake all reasonable efforts to continue project OR

___ Undertake these steps:

Projected date of completion of project and availability for occupation is scheduled for:

Contract Administration: "Designer agrees to make any reasonable effort to carry out the completion of this project within the time set for its completion . . ."

3. **How the designer will be paid for services**

    This can be quite a lengthy provision in a design contract. As you recall from Chapter 9, it important for designers not only to select a method of charging clients for their services but also to take care to see that payment from clients is received in a timely manner. The purpose of the billing and collection process, also described in Chapter 9, is to ensure that the designer is paid or that the designer is compensated for delays in payment by receiving additional fees known as *interest*. Considering these factors, this provision should contain:

    - *The amount of retainer paid for the services of the designer*
      Client agrees that Designer's project retainer for services to be rendered will be in the following amount:

    - *A description of way(s) in which the designer will be compensated*
      Refer to earlier discussions of charging methods (see Chapter 9). Those methods may be based on several different ways of computation, and their provisions would appear here. Frequently used methods of charging the client include the rate-based methods such as fixed-fee and hourly methods; sale of merchandise-based methods, including the retail, percentage of merchandise and product

services, cost plus percentage markup, and discounting of percentage off retail; combination methods involving cost plus percentage markup with fixed fee and cost plus percentage markup with hourly fee; and other methods of compensation, including the square foot, value-oriented, and consultation methods.

A sample of this contract provision might read:

> Client agrees that Designer's compensation for project services rendered will be calculated according to the following method: The difference between any discount Designer may receive for merchandise purchases and the full retail/list amount, plus % of any project construction costs.

- *Timeliness of payment*
  This section should also contain a statement to the effect that the designer expects payment for services or purchases within a specified period of time after being billed. Typically, interior designers require payment upon receipt, or specify a set number of days within which they expect to receive payment.

- *When and according to what percentage interest payments on outstanding amounts owed are due and are to be computed*
  Usually most design contracts consider interest charges to accrue after a certain number of days from the date of the invoice and specify a percentage rate such as 1.5 percent of the outstanding amounts due, although that rate may vary according to the cash-flow needs of a designer's practice as well as general business practices in a designer's community. It is important to note that without including such provisions, designers can be prohibited from charging interest.

4. **Date contract was signed by designer and client**
   Stating the intended duration of a project is also useful, as noted in the previous excerpt from a sample contract.

   Projected date of completion of project and availability for occupation is scheduled for:

5. **Signatures of parties to contract**
   It is especially important that any contract for interior design services contain the signature of the party to be charged, a term taken from the Statute of Frauds. Since it is usually a designer who offers his or her services, and a client who then accepts and agrees to pay for those services, it is the client who is usually considered the party to be charged under the terms of contracts for interior design services.

PART 4: YOU AND YOUR RESOURCES

This part of the text addresses your relationship with vendors and service providers. Who are these professionals on whom you will rely to make your concept for an interior design project a reality?

Chapter 12. Working with Vendors: Identifies important objectives for you to consider, among them learning how to access merchandise vendors, many of whom may not sell to the general public, and understanding policies and terms that define how vendors price and deliver merchandise.

Chapter 13. Working with Service Providers: Explores how to develop and manage your relationship with the different service providers typically used in interior design work. This chapter further contains intriguing images of completed interior spaces that show the successful results interior designers seek when working with service providers.

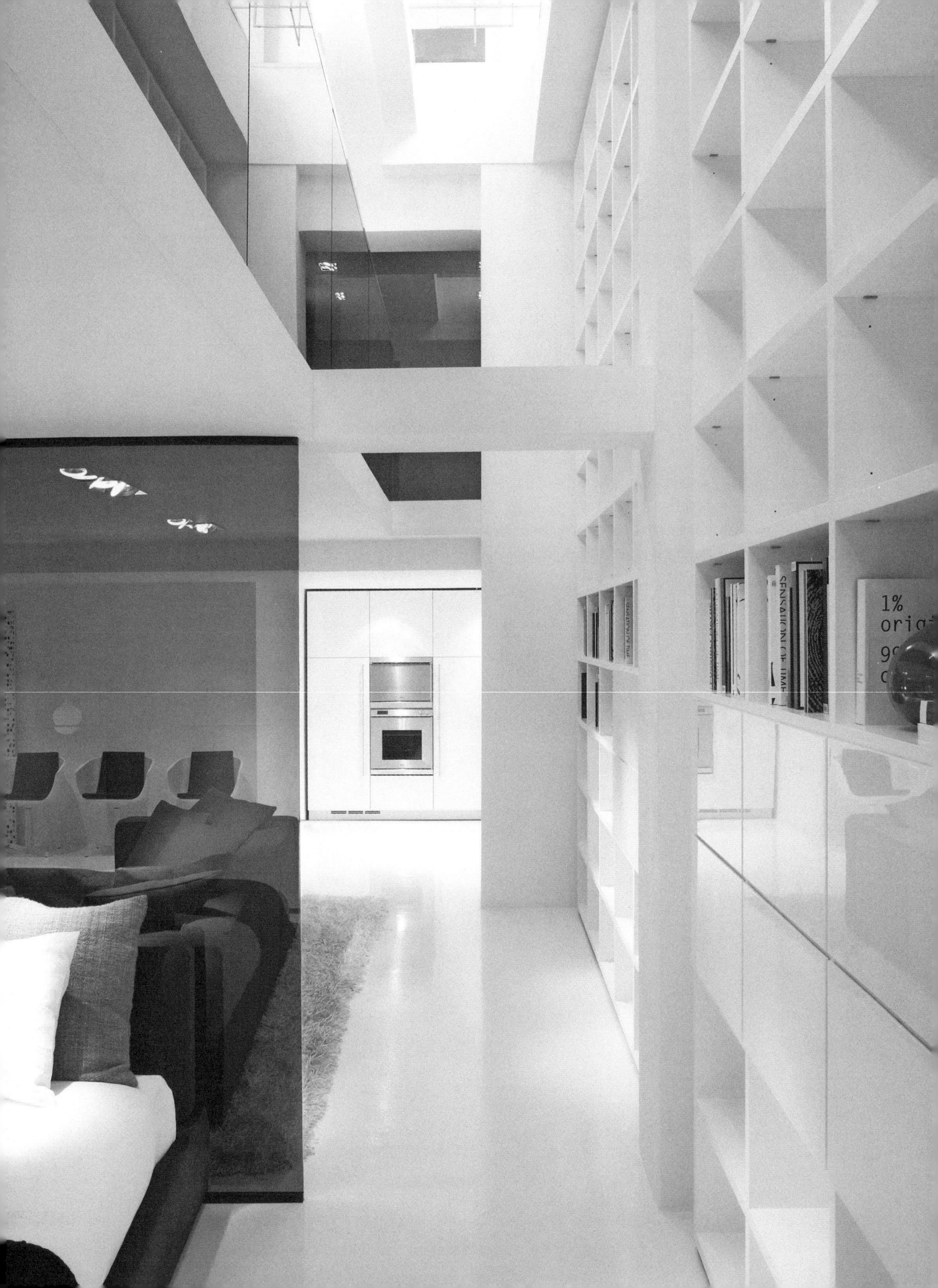

CHAPTER 12
WORKING WITH VENDORS

MENTOR MEMO
It does take a village of professionals, consultants, product reps, and constructors to deliver a project of any scale as complete transparency is critical in our profession.

After reading this chapter, you will be able to

- Describe how to access vendors providing project merchandise;
- Understand how vendors' pricing, discounting, and other policies are determined;
- Understand ordering and delivery procedures, as they are typically used by vendors;
- Recognize and know how to apply basic terms and conditions found in sales contracts;
- Explain, even anticipate, problems that may arise with vendors, their products, and clients' expectations.

INTRODUCTION TO WORKING WITH VENDORS

Whether developing specifications for private residences or multistory, commercial buildings, knowledge of design-build materials is expected of designers. In addition to understanding *what* "to spec out," designers further need to be aware of *where* and *how* to obtain items they require to complete projects successfully. To do this, designers work with **vendors**. These are professional sources offering for sale textiles, surface coverings, furniture, fixtures, works of art, and accessories, among other products. These sellers are educated about and experienced with ordering and manufacturing processes. Interior designers should know vendors' policies and procedures, interact positively with them and their own clients, and work profitably on behalf of their businesses.

Detail, detail, and more detail! That describes best what it will be like working with vendors. This chapter describes a systematic approach to building successful working relationships with interior design trade resources in light of the many details involved in doing so.

Professional product vendors are capable of following designers' specifications to produce results such as this.

AVAILABILITY OF VENDORS AND PROJECT MERCHANDISE

"To the trade only," a statement seen in print advertisements and on showroom doors and, perhaps, whispered about by clients, signals that there is something different about where and how merchandise is available to interior design professionals. Whether the focus of designers' practices is on residential or contract/commercial work, obtaining appropriate products for project use is critical. One factor contributing to the success of any kind of project may well be designers' ability to locate and obtain project-appropriate furniture, textiles, lighting and other fixtures, surface coatings and coverings, window treatments, flooring and floor coverings, works of art, antiques or collectable pieces, accessories, among other products. Thus, identifying where vendors of these items may be found as well as learning procedures for accessing and ordering them are necessary strategies for designers.

Furniture and design products showcases have a long tradition in the interior design industry. What were once occasional exhibits became permanent, full-time venues serving the design-build professions and retail stores. These places are known by different names, but they are often referred to as *merchandise marts* and *design centers*. These are where designers research items, consult with vendors, and seek out those products best able to fulfill project objectives and provide design solutions for project issues. Marts and centers are also venues offering the very products architects and interior designers have conceived, produced, and made available. Two characteristics distinguish professional marts and centers from the kinds of stores and malls with which most consumers are familiar.

Perhaps the most significant feature of marts and centers is they are only accessible to members of the design-build profession, those seeking project-related products, and/or proprietors of shops looking for items to resell to retail consumers. Like "regular"

Showroom samples and, increasingly, online catalogs enable designers to specify correct items for project use.

shopping malls, they contain the places of business of individual companies. Inherent in this professionals-only format are various requirements patrons distinguish themselves from general consumers. Thus, they must have valid, verifiable credentials as members of the design-build community and/or are legally permitted to resell merchandise and collect mandated taxes from purchasers. This means designers able to show valid state-issued certifications, or registrations, or memberships in organizations like ASID may obtain admission on those credentials. Specific requirements vary, but mart and center patrons

> **NOTES FROM THE FIELD**
>
> Want to create your own furniture line? It is a dream of many designers to conceive and make available furniture and other items, the kinds of products found in design marts and centers. What do you think that might be like? Consider the following as how such lines come about.
>
> Launching a furniture line of your own sounds so easy doesn't it? In 2002, I launched my own furniture line, with the help of a manufacturer, and that product is still in production today. Here's how it happened. As designers, it's our job to bring creativity to every project. I was working with a client whose business had a large amount of paper and brochures that were always in the reception area. After visiting their offices and seeing the situation firsthand, I couldn't help but think that there had to be a better way to contain this paper? I went looking for a great table, with a recessed drop to hold these brochures, and couldn't find anything. Then a light bulb went off—let's make one!
>
> With a full sketchbook of ideas, I researched three furniture companies whose product was not dissimilar and set up meetings to present my ideas. Prior to my presentation to each, I asked each company, about their process to view and consider new furniture pieces. Two of the companies had an organized process that involved an NDA (nondisclosure agreement), which was intended to protect all parties. I needed the assurance that my idea would be protected. I chose one of the two companies and flew to present my ideas to their head of industrial design. (However, some advice given to me by my mentor: Don't leave your sketchbook and take everything with you when you leave the room! You never know where your ideas might end up and you receive nothing in return).
>
> The company liked my ideas! And, felt there was a market opportunity worth exploring, past the one table required for this particular client. They provided me two options—first, sell my idea outright for $10,000, giving the home company the complete right to do whatever they wanted to do with the design, or royalties for life making a small percentage of every piece of furniture that I sell. If the table line never sold, I would make very little. Giving it some thought, I chose the second option and went into production with the manufacturer to guide me.
>
> **Why is this important?** I knew nothing about bringing a table to market, and I knew nothing about industrial design. Therefore, this was my opportunity to learn something new, without the liability of doing it entirely on my own.
>
> The next step was to fly to Italy to meet with the company's industrial design team. I had designed a table that was too heavy to produce and ship and too expensive for the buying market. Since I wanted to sell more than five tables, I needed to brainstorm with the experts. After two weeks (and plenty of great Italian meals), the design was redone, I had signed off on the creative changes the product needed to be viable, and it went into final drawings and production.
>
> Typically furniture companies do not accept ideas from interior designers because we simply do not know enough about the industrial design process. Our education path is different, and industrial designers generate thousands of ideas in the timespan it took me to hatch just one. I was grateful to have had the chance to learn; it was humbling on every level.
>
> The coffee table eventually made its way into the hands of the client, who graciously agreed to wait the eight months for it to arrive, knowing their project was the catalyst for a broader idea. Today the line now includes twenty-six pieces and is marketed nationally by the same company that walked me through the process years ago. As it turned out, many clients were looking for a similar solution, and thousands of tables have sold around the country, thanks to a network of vendors and reps they promote the line.

Designing an item, such as a table, or an entire product line that becomes widely adopted is a goal of many interior designers.

operating retail establishments usually must show they hold current, state-issued certificates permitting them to collect state and local sales taxes—perhaps showing proof of use tax permits as well. Credentials of all professionals seeking access to marts and centers are verified. Then, designers, architects, and retailers receive documentation permitting entry.

Individual vendor showrooms, whether located in marts and centers, or freestanding, may have slightly different admissions policies. *Open* showrooms allow general consumers in addition to professionals and function more like retail stores, some even selling to customers directly through Internet and mobile retail channels. *Closed* showrooms, admit only professionals, but may permit designers' clients to enter and browse (but not purchase) after their designers' letter or personal introductions. A significant number of marts and centers and individual vendor showrooms remain resolutely "trade only."

VENDOR'S PRICING AND OTHER POLICIES

Another characteristic of these businesses is they are usually *wholesale* establishments. This term means these are places where merchants sell to other merchants and has several implications.

List Price and Manufacturers' Suggested Retail Price

Prices shown, or quoted in these places are not *list price*, or *manufacturers' suggested retail price*. MSRP, as you may be aware, are those prices shown every day to consumers in retail shops. Wholesale prices are typically much lower than retail prices. Depending on the compensation arrangements designers have with clients, they may pass on the cost benefits of obtaining goods at wholesale by selling them to clients at these reduced prices. Otherwise, interior designers and/or retailers add a percentage amount to what they paid for each item in order to obtain the eventual price charged to clients.

In general, list prices and MSRPs are double the wholesale price, although merchandise pricing policies differ widely. Further, companies selling merchandise to others for resale cannot require (under U.S. federal law) any subsequent vendor to charge the list price/MSRP. Those prices, therefore, may or may not be final ones charged to consumers. Many interior designers will offer items to clients at prices lower than retail prices (but not as low as wholesale) in a practice referred to as *discounting from retail*. Designers who take that approach to pricing items typically select a percentage reduction amount and apply it to list price/MSRP to determine what they will charge clients. The *net price* is the amount typically representing one-half list price/MSRP.

Designers' Markups and Vendors' Discounts

Markup from cost is another way designers may determine eventual costs charged to clients for goods purchased in marts and centers. Historically, interior designers earned their entire compensation through this method of pricing. Then and now this approach can be quite lucrative, especially when a great many items (and/or a great many expensive ones) are purchased for projects. Quite simply, designers would add a percentage amount to what they paid and then charge clients that increased amount. For example, products costing designers $1,000 at wholesale might then be doubled (assuming a 100 percent markup from cost) with clients charged $2,000 for it.

Other related issues to consider include *gross margin*. This refers to the differences between the prices of those items sold by designers and the costs paid by designers for those items. When those amounts are divided by final selling prices, gross margins are determined. Gross margins are important for designers who base their compensation solely on selling merchandise since this amount represents compensation for their labor and is the only source of income to pay operational expenses. Designers who rely solely on the sale of merchandise for their compensation, logically, would choose to earn the highest gross margin amounts possible.

Designers may select whatever percentage amount they choose when setting prices for products obtained in trade showrooms (among other places). Although there is a movement toward fee-based compensation arrangements, many designers still earn most, if not all, of their income from selling merchandise. The difficulty with any method of establishing selling prices is determining how much the market for interior design services in any location, at any given time can bear the ultimate product costs. Even though 100 percent markup from cost, of the kind referenced here, may be beneficial for designers, there may not be enough clients willing or able to sustain that practice.

Whether wholesale, retail, or any price at all, interior design merchandise is expensive for all involved. To incentivize business from interior designers, many vendors offer *discounts*. These are price reductions off list price/MSRP offered to wholesale purchasers. Three common forms are *trade discounts*, *volume discounts*, and *cash discounts*. All serve to reduce final costs of merchandise purchased by interior designers. For their part, designers may, or may not, "pass on" trade and/or discount savings to clients in the form of lower merchandise prices; they may add their desired markup percentage to list price/MSRP in order to maximize profits for their business. *Trade discounts* are price reductions offered to design professionals; 25 to 30 percent reductions are examples. *Quantity discounts* refer to those reductions given on the basis of numbers of items ordered. Fairly large numbers of purchase items are usually needed to trigger this price reduction. Frequently, the more items ordered, the larger the percentage discounted.

Cash discounts are reductions for prompt payment. Frequently terms such as 5-10 Net 30 or 2-10 Net 30 appear on invoices if cash discounts are offered. Respectively, these terms mean purchasers may take 5 percent or 2 percent from totals if bills are paid within 10 days of receipt; the total amount of the invoice due within 30 days of receipt. *Cash discounts are taken only after all other discounts have been figured.*

GENERAL TAX ISSUES RELATED TO MERCHANDISE SALES

In the usual course of purchasing goods, it is inevitable there will be tax consequences for which someone will be responsible. Countries, states, and local governments levy taxes for their ongoing financial support. There are three forms of taxes that those who deal in merchandise sales, like interior designers, should be aware of.

State and local governments assess taxes in order to earn revenue to support the function of these entities. They do this through the imposition of sales and use taxes. **Sales taxes** are percentage amounts added to the total purchase price of goods and paid by consumers. Holders of government-issued **resale licenses** are obligated to pass those amounts on to the entity from which the license was obtained. Thus, in areas that impose sales tax, retail stores and those holding licenses are obligated to impose taxes on purchases. Sales tax is collected from the final purchasers of goods, as when clients, end users, purchase items from interior designers.

If you have purchased goods out of state to be shipped to your home or, as is typical today, have purchased goods on the Internet, you probably did not pay any sales taxes. You are also not subject to paying tax for using such items in your home state, or area. The situation is different, however, for businesses that purchase goods out of state or on the Internet. States impose a **use tax** when the same goods would have been subject to sales tax in the user's state. In addition to sales tax licenses, businesses also need to obtain use-tax permits, or certificates.

Whether to tax goods purchased over the Internet is a lingering issue. At present, none are imposed unless retailers also have a physical presence, or "nexus," in states where purchases are made. This situation can make some interior design goods less expensive when bought "on line." Continued pressures on governments to find new sources of revenue may eliminate the current lack of Internet taxation on purchases.

VAT, or **v**alue **a**dded **t**ax, and GST, or **g**eneral **s**ales **t**ax, are another form of taxes about which designers should be aware. These taxes are consumption taxes and are imposed by governments for the purposes of raising revenue. These are, also like sales taxes, additional percentages added to selling price of goods, paid by purchasers. Those percentages vary according to the area imposing VAT and GST. These tax schemes are more complex than sales tax-based ones, especially for providers of taxable goods and services. That said, however, what should designers know about these taxes?

Interior designers selling items to clients are obligated to collect VAT/GST, or sales tax, depending in which is required by law. Those, of course, increase costs to clients. Designers have an obligation to account for and remit those taxes properly, an increase in administrative costs and responsibilities. Contracts, or letter agreements, between designers and clients should spell out exactly who will purchase—and pay taxes on—project-related goods. Designers, as best as they are able (often with vendors' assistance), should provide for estimated taxes in projects' budgets.

PRODUCT DELIVERY ISSUES IN INTERIOR DESIGN

When is project merchandise "owned"? If the interior designer orders it, when does the client pay for it? Does the client own the items after they are produced at the factory, or after they are delivered at a designated location? Questions such as these are important because they determine who is responsible for such items. For example, if it is determined that a client owns an item when it leaves the factory, the client is responsible for its delivery costs and bears any risks should it be lost or damaged in route to its destination. Three notations are important for interior designers to know related to this issue. The first is referred to as **FOB**, or **free on board**. This term comes from the Uniform Commercial Code, mentioned previously, and is followed by either "factory" or a specific destination place. In the former instance, ownership of merchandise passes from sellers to buyers at factories where made or finished, usually when items are placed with carriers. This means buyers must pay transportation as well as insurance costs to get goods from factories to sites. FOB notations followed by specific, named locations, such as *FOB New York*, are usually interpreted to mean that sellers retain ownership of items after they leave the factory and throughout the transportation process until they are received at the buyers' location. The purchaser usually bears no associated delivery costs since sellers pay for delivery under this FOB notation. Sellers pay insurance costs as well. **Freight prepaid** is another delivery term of note. This term indicates ownership of goods passes from sellers to buyers once sellers place them with transportation carriers. Buyers in this instance assume liability for damage that may occur to goods during transport (and may still be responsible for insurance charges), whereas sellers agree to pay transportation costs to get goods from factories to the buyers' locations. Such payment of costs is considered incentives for buyers to assume transportation risks (and pay insurance) in exchange for having actual transportation costs borne by sellers.

Forwarding, Storage, and Installation Issues

After merchandise has left its originating source, it must be transported yet further (forwarded), stored for use, or installed. These activities add to final product costs. Storage and related insurance costs depend on where, under what conditions, and how long merchandise is held until use. Charges further accrue for the costs of the physical labor necessary to transport merchandise to project sites, unload and uncrate it, and then place/install it. Simple placement of items requires workers to consult charts and follow instructions prepared by designers. Installation, however, usually implies specialized labor or knowledge of product application is required in order for the product to function as intended. For example, overhead light fixtures are not considered fully installed if removed from shipping cartons and left on the floor.

Terms and Conditions of Sale

MENTOR MEMO

When working with suppliers and representatives, communication protocol is important. Please be clear with your valued and trusted product reps, and outline what is expected of them relative to communication. Typically designers meet with reps first, be it in the office or in the showroom. We discuss which products we are interested in for a project, and the budget (if known) we are trying to achieve. If the intention is to bring the client to the showroom, a good manufacturer's representative will follow your lead and stay on topic.

If specifications are large and complex, it is important to consider a full specification manual that provides a more robust write-up about the product. If a librarian is part of your firm, spend the time to fully understand what you specifying and how it will perform over time. If a product is difficult to install or has a long lead time, communication is key.

ANTICIPATION AND RESOLUTION OF POTENTIAL PROBLEMS

Working with vendors is undoubtedly one of the more fascinating, if at times frustrating, aspects of the interior designers' work. It is fascinating because as interior designers they see, touch, and experience objects available to few others. It is, however, "quite maddening," as one designer put it, when issues arise. No matter whether your practice is residential or contract interior design, or whether you or your clients completed the purchases, as the interior designer, you will be expected to anticipate potential problems and resolve them when they do. Designers serve as intermediaries between vendor and client. Issues to consider, therefore, relate to those project stakeholders and ways designers may facilitate positive outcomes. What, then, are specific problems; how might they be avoided, or at least minimized?

Issues with Vendors

The adage "There are no guarantees in life" also applies to work with merchandise sources and other vendors. Specification concerns, order cancellations, and damaged goods are three common issues interior designers may likely have with them.

> **BOX 12.1**
>
> ## TERMS AND CONDITIONS OF SALE OUTLINE
>
> As you read the terms and conditions of your chosen vendor/company, consider its provisions. Describe in your words what each section seeks to do.
>
> After you have completed this form, explain to friends what each section provides, and answer any questions they may have about how it might affect them if they were your client.
>
> **Introduction to Terms and Conditions Forms**
>
> *Purchaser/Orderer/Buyer* Designer or client, depending on the agreement between the two
>
> *Company/Vendor/Seller* Entity selling merchandise
>
> *Limitation of Liability* In what ways has your chosen company defined the kind of relationship it is willing to have with those seeking its products?
>
> *No Alternative Terms* How does this phrase appear to affect purchasers? What importance does this place on purchase documentation?
>
> *No Cancellation Policy* Do you see the importance of obtaining your client's sign-off on your final design concept?
>
> *Quotes, Prices, and Payments Policies* How long does your chosen company honor quotes?
>
> *Sales Order, Acceptance, Payment, and Deposits* When are payments due with respect to orders?
>
> *Incomplete Sales Orders and Production Scheduling* What constitutes an incomplete order?
>
> *Change-Order Specifications* Does your chosen company permit change orders? If so, under what conditions?
>
> *Abandonment and Collection* What do these terms mean with respect to purchasing products?
>
> *Shipping and Delivery* Who is responsible for these activities?
>
> *Storage Fees* Do you see how this provision can add to product costs and the importance of delivery scheduling during the contract administration phase?
>
> *Return Policy* Under what conditions, if any, will your chosen company accept returns?
>
> *Claims* Does your chosen company permit arbitration of disputes? What other claims provisions are there?

Merchandise Specification Problems

Delivery date arrives and with it an item that seems "off". Perhaps fabric color differs in gradation on various sections of a sofa, although it might still be said to be the one specified. Expect clients to come to you and ask how the problem might have been prevented and, then, what you can do to fix it! Troubleshooting this type of problem with vendors requires planning on your part. First, be sure to prepare your specifications with extreme care, and, if possible, select vendors you know will work *with* you, not against you, to correct problems. Vendors assume you, as a professional interior designer, understand and can follow specification and ordering procedures. Troubleshooting problems requires knowing questions to ask vendors before and after specification preparation. First, gain access to the best information available: Ask vendors for the most recent swatches of textiles, leathers, and finishes, still fresh and not yet overly handled. Look at samples from different angles and, if possible, in different lighting. Some light causes colors to fade to near-invisibility, whereas others make them appear garish. Pieces of "classic" furniture, as well, may look awkward when viewed from certain angles or positioned in certain ways. If possible, really get to know products from more than a photograph or tiny swatch as early as possible. Also acquaint clients with the look of the products so they will not be surprised should they happen to see items before properly applied, or installed.

After you have identified the products you wish to order, ask the vendor's representative how best to ensure their arrival as specified. One simple, but not foolproof, way is to make sure items are specified (or otherwise identified according to vendor methods) in all documentation. For example, the products' specifications should read identically on written order forms and invoices, among others.

This attention to detail also extends to specification preparation. With textiles, this may mean reserving particular quantities of fabric from dated, or numbered dye lots. Leather-based products can be particularly troublesome, as delivered products can appear and feel unlike swatches. Alert clients to the fact that skins differentially absorb tanning treatments, dyes, and other processing. Then, request that the vendors supply cuttings from available hides for final approval before placing orders. Many vendors obtain goods from a variety of makers and then sell them under their brand. Fabric houses, for example, may obtain trimmings from smaller producers according to availability and pricing. These makers may produce items that are very similar, but not exactly alike. In other words, ask about your sources' own sources! Request information about how best to obtain identical items when this is the case. With custom, highly expensive furniture pieces, it may be possible to specify items from particularly consistent craftspeople, or workshops. With less-expensive case goods, which are often produced in factories, it may be possible to obtain items from the same production run as a means of assuring consistency. Finally, ask whether sources have had problems producing items, due to unavailability of raw materials or necessary labor. Further, inquire about (or research) complaints about products under consideration. Responses to these may be warnings to consider alternative products.

MENTOR MEMO

When looking at international specs, nothing is typical; ask to see everything, and know they are not governed by the same tolerances of product ranges for items such as veneers and stones. Similarly, consider where the product was produced. For example, if the product was assembled in an area of the world that is particularly humid, and your intentions are to ship the product to a dry climate, it will not perform as expected. It will delaminate, peel, or worse fall apart. If these issues can be navigated with caution, and you have a shipping broker that can readily assist you and is trusted to deliver, you will do just fine.

Order Cancellation and Merchandise Return Issues

Among the challenging issues that may occur during a project are those related to cancellation of merchandise orders. An order may have to be cancelled because a project's budget or schedule required reassessment, or the client (even designer) may have decided to change direction. This problem usually arises after the vendor accepts the signed order form and initial deposit payment. No matter why and when the need to cancel, you need to determine what can be done. To further compound the situation, language found incorporated in vendors' terms and conditions of sale often states very explicitly that once they accept orders, purchasers are liable for entire amounts due. In short, there is a provision for someone who wants to back out of a contractual agreement. This is a highly problematic situation for designers who are caught between clients who are unlikely to pay such balances and vendors who will not honor cancellations.

Several strategies are available to avoid this situation. First, it is absolutely critical for designers to receive written and signed confirmation from clients regarding every planned project purchase before vendors become involved. This is done with a formal document referred to as a **confirmation of purchase**, or sales agreement. The purpose of these documents is protection: They legally obligate clients to pay for goods ordered by designers. Second, designers who have a long, successful history of working with particular vendors may be able to negotiate a resolution to the cancellation issue. Vendors usually want to accommodate designers and continue to receive business from them. To that end, they may permit order cancellations, but designers may not always be able to recoup any initial deposit. Vendors may (and probably will) keep any deposits, considering them *liquidated damages*, or payments for unfilled orders. Ultimately, vendors' decision to consider, much less grant, order cancellations may depend on where the merchandise is in the "pipeline." It may be easier to convince vendors to cancel recently placed orders when their own preparations for its production or shipping have not yet begun. To be sure, order cancellation is a challenging issue for designers, one requiring skillful negotiation to resolve.

Merchandise returns can be another vexing issue for designers. At issue is whether vendors will take back otherwise acceptable items after delivery. Vendors whose products are in demand may accept merchandise returns (and from cancelled orders) as long as the goods are in condition suitable for resale. Items such as door and plumbing hardware, light fixtures, and "trophy," or name-brand appliances are among those that may be accepted for return. Vendors that do accept often impose **restocking fees**, based on percentages of returned items' retail prices; 15 percent is commonly used, although percentages vary among vendors. Clients should be informed it is uncertain whether vendors will cancel orders or accept returns. Both issues can have an impact on the projects' costs and completion time and the client's satisfaction.

Damaged Goods on Delivery

Most vendors do not ship the goods they sell, often relying on shippers and freight forwarders to move merchandise. Some large manufacturers will ship goods directly to designers, or project sites. Another difficult issue for designers arises when goods are damaged in transit by either third-party movers or direct-ship vendors. This is the typical situation: Upon arrival, a piece appears to be flawed in some way, a scratch, or "ding" that spoils an otherwise acceptable item. What follows is an exchange in which the manufacturer claims the goods were in perfect condition when turned over to the shipper. The shipper (or the company's shipping department) usually makes claims such as the goods must have been damaged before they arrived for transit or were unloaded incorrectly. No matter how such damage occurred, designers must address what to do.

One way to troubleshoot this issue is for designers to make sure they work with reputable vendors, those offering lenient return policies for goods damaged in transit. Alternatively, they should ascertain whether shippers (or vendors themselves) carry insurance for goods damaged in transit. As well, designers may purchase insurance as an additional project cost to be borne by the clients. Insurance is important because as soon as products are produced and paid for in full, their purchasers, not the makers or the shippers, own them. Merchandise is owned before it reaches its purchasers in the usual course of business. Insurance policies assume all, or some risks vendors, designers, or clients might otherwise have from the potential perils of shipping goods they already own. Without these policies, project clients, perhaps designers, may have no recourse, no way to "make good" financially for merchandise that ends up damaged. In instances where project merchandise has to travel long distances, or for extended periods, designers should consult legal experts for guidance about how best to insure against damaged, even lost, merchandise.

MENTOR MEMO

Out of respect for your valued relationships with vendors and product representatives, order only the samples you need. Samples cost money and should not be wasted. Nor should you order enough samples to tile your bathroom (believe it). Be mindful of professional practice in this area. I include this because samples, and in particular those that come from Mother Nature, vary wildly once viewed in larger scale. Marbles and large-scale veneers should be treated with caution. Ask your reps where best to see samples installed or in quantity, go there, take the time, it may change your mind about a large portion of the project.

Samples for furniture hold the same priority. If you are specifying large quantities of any product or piece, take the client to see the products installed. If it involves out of town travel, or mock-ups, be mindful of the costs undertaken by the manufacturer and, if possible, compensate suppliers by paying a portion of a mock up.

Client Issues Related to Vendors and Merchandise

Interior design, as a profession and in its practices, occupies an unusual place in the public mind. It is unusual in the sense that many believe they understand the work designers undertake and how rooms, homes, even vast commercial spaces are "decorated." Thanks to popular shelter magazines, HGTV and television shows on other channels, Internet sites, and countless Tumblr blogs, it can be argued that interior design knowledge has become marginalized for its entertainment value. The reality is that most nondesigners are unaware of even basic product specification guidelines and

Clients look to interior designers to work with vendors to ensure detailed products and complex projects come about exactly as specified.

interior space construction methods. Furthermore, they have no idea of the actual costs or the production time involved in the items prominently portrayed in print articles or proudly installed on shows.

This background shapes the reality designers face when working with clients. Some clients may be well experienced with interior design and acquainted with its processes; they could be extremely sophisticated about business matters related to the buying and selling of goods. Yet, designers will encounter clients who are neither. Then, it will be necessary for the designers to educate clients about what to expect, but the designers must know how to communicate that information in order for successful project completion to occur.

Communicating Cost Issues to Clients

Client expectations can differ from reality when it comes to merchandise costs. What initial questions might designers consider to ascertain client expectations related to costs? Are clients new to the design process as well as to you and your style of working?

Are your clients familiar with your work and undertaking their second (or more) project with you? Your responses to these questions may make your communication with clients easier when dealing with merchandise costs and issues related to them. Common sense should prevail. No client, however affluent, desirous of a particular item, or amorous of particular makers' products, enjoys unexpectedly expensive surprises. Designers, therefore, should establish with clients realistic expectations about costs, how they are determined, and can change.

There are some clients who are, or become, very apprehensive about prices and want detailed information and estimates before they agree to any purchases. By asking them such questions as "Are you comfortable with how expensive this item will be?" and, then, actively listening to their responses will help ascertain their degree of understanding. Another approach with such clients, particularly corporate clients on commercial projects with strict budget constraints, is to show a range of options. Many interior designers develop *value ranges* of merchandise they show to clients, grouping different maker's goods together according to price. For example, these designers may develop a budget-range list of vendors offering goods of acceptable quality, likely intended for shorter-term use. They may also develop a list of vendors with premium-priced, or custom-made merchandise, intended for longer-term use. With designers' assistance, clients can then choose from among those vendor lines that are within their project budget. Contract interior designers frequently use this approach, making sure to receive client *sign-off*, or authorization, as protection from budget-issue claims later. As unappealing as it may be, designers, both with residential and contract practices, often have no choice but to find less-expensive product sources when they believe clients will balk at prices or refuse to pay them.

Vendor prices may not be final even after products are ordered. After-the-fact price increases, thus, are another area of potential concern for designers. Compounding that fact is the fact that such changes can and do occur without any prior notice. Vendors may include in order forms language that states prices are subject to change without notice. Nevertheless, this can put designers in a difficult situation when these price increases do occur, leaving them to convey that news to clients. For their part, clients, often believing they have kept their side of the bargain, may refuse to pay the difference between the price originally agreed to and the newer, higher price. To avoid having to assume what may be a substantial cost overrun themselves, or sue the client in court for restitution, and, ultimately, put at risk the outcome of the project, designers often include a "mirror" provision to those of vendors. In their agreements with clients, designers require the client be responsible for all product costs, including those incurred as a result of vendors' price adjustments after products were ordered and before delivery.

Interior designers may find themselves in a quandary about merchandise prices and how to discuss them with clients. Few clients truly understand why products cost as much as they do, and after they learn those costs, that information can scare them from authorizing purchases. To circumvent this occurrence, many interior designers remain vague about merchandise prices. In all fairness, however, designers themselves do not know what final costs may be. Designers working in competitive bidding situations also face this concern as the interplay of factors such as the project's overall budget and type of specifications (*open* or *closed*) will be influential in both the final selection and price of merchandise used. Designers, no matter their practice focus, or clientele, do need satisfied clients to remain in business. Client satisfaction with designers may be enhanced if they believe merchandise costs were disclosed as fully as possible and prices of products were commensurate with their quality.

MENTOR MEMO

Tender transparency and procurement liability are issues. If an interior designer is only charging for his or her time, this needs to be openly disclosed to a client, in writing, and I recommend within your contract, especially if you are in a competitive bid environment for design services. In the commercial design arena, procurement of products is not typical; therefore, charging only for services is the norm. If one of your competitors, is being compensated in a no transparent way, from either the contractor or the manufacturer, the client may be paying much more than they realize for the same services.

If a client is under the impression you will be purchasing products on their behalf (procurement), in the event there is a problem with the product, you have the potential to hold the liability and the costs. In residential interior design, it is very typical for a designer to act as purchaser for a client and often there is a markup on product for that effort.

Often residential designers purchase at cost, and sell at retail, which is part of their compensation structure. If that is the case, you have a professional obligation to disclose. In the commercial world, it is not typical for designers to act as buyers. The structure and volume of product would make this cost prohibitive for the designers.

Informing Clients about Time Issues

In addition to issues related to product prices, few clients really understand the amount of time involved in preparing products of the quality specified by designers. Often, an item will pass through many different hands during the lengthy course of its creation. Alternatively, many items may take considerable amounts of time to produce in specified quantities. In either case, the amount of time may seem unreasonable or unnecessary to clients. As a result, designers should be aware of the need to communicate with clients about time issues before they become problems. Again, one constructive strategy is to ask clients whether they would be willing to wait for a particular product and choose vendors accordingly.

One practical way to work around time concerns raised by clients is for designers to specify products on-hand, or that are ready-made, available for immediate delivery. This approach may work for projects on extremely tight time schedules, for example. Doing this may prevent project delays, but it may not endear either finished projects or designers' talents to clients. It can make finished projects seem generic and designers' efforts minimal. Usually, designers note to their clients the degree of complexity and customization items require to complete, physical distances they must travel, and facts about vendors/makers (such as unusual production schedules) that contribute to long production lead times.

Determining Whether to Shop with Clients

One issue facing interior designers is whether to take a client along on showroom trips. Even in this day of smart phones able to take near-professional quality images of items and WiFi Internet connections, sometimes it may be necessary for clients to accompany designers in order to get a sense of certain products or prototypes available only in showrooms. For example, they may want to sit in chairs or see surface finish textures. Many designers have no problem with their clients' presence on such excursions and even encourage it. On the downside, however, some clients may use these trips to bargain shop. In this instance, they may attempt to purchase goods on their own (with the "help" of the showroom) and bypass the designers' markup.

Designers should gauge whether clients and/or vendors might act duplicitously. Do you, for example, know both the client and the showroom vendor well enough to be assured they will not cheat you? This issue can arise in the context of visits to art galleries and antique dealers, sellers of one-of-a-kind items, or sources that offer items for sale to both the design trade and the general public. It can also occur in showrooms where products are sold *off the floor*, meaning not custom-made. At the outset of designers' relationships with clients, any contract or letter agreement should specify that once those designers introduce clients to a vendor, clients are obligated to pay them a percentage commission based on prices of items purchased.

Clients may consider shopping a pastime, but it is work for designers. Work, moreover, for which designers should be compensated. Interior designers are often surprised that clients refuse to pay them for their time when both go to showrooms, especially if no purchases were made. One tactic interior designers use to address this issue is to indicate to clients such trips are the equivalent of going to the office. To this point, designers add language to their letter agreement making it clear time spent with a client visiting vendors will be billed separately at certain rate per hour, even if the designer also receives a commission based on merchandise purchases, or charges a flat rate for services. In this way, designers protect themselves from clients who believe designers' time is freely available to them, especially for something clients may not consider work.

PERSPECTIVE ON THE VENDOR/CLIENT/DESIGNER RELATIONSHIP

Vendor and client issues, as explored here, may, indeed, be isolated events. Examples such as goods found unacceptable do arrive occasionally, and some project clients can get frightened when "real" interior design is not like that depicted on television shows, as examples have shown. Yet, to get a perspective, consider that these issues ultimately do have a relationship to each other: the project interior designer. Specifically, the working relationship designers have with vendors. In the next chapter, you will come to see the importance of the working relationship between designers and service providers, as well. Developing a sense of partnership among and between stakeholders by designers can be a systemic way of preventing problems and a potential benefit when they do occur.

A fundamental way to troubleshoot issues of the kinds described here is to develop solid, business-like relationships with vendors. Granted, this may be difficult to accomplish as furniture line and other kinds of representatives frequently enter and then leave the profession or move to different companies. Vendors, for that matter, may be less than scrupulous, as the following Notes from the Field explains. However, designers who correctly specify products ordered, pay bills on time, and work to accommodate vendors and their production schedules by ordering as timely as possible are desirable clients. Reliable clients may be few and far between for some vendors, especially for up-and-coming, or small-scale makers and showrooms. Established, reputable showrooms like to work with the same kinds of designers and businesses. Many trade resources will try to work to accommodate conscientious designers with sound track records purchasing from them.

The importance of developing good relationships with vendors is underscored by considering the situation facing designers who do *not* have positive working relationships with them. Some vendors will flatly refuse to work with, or offer credit to designers with a history of sketchy payments. Other vendors will work with such designers, but only on a pro forma basis, that is, requiring payment in full for any and all merchandise ordered with payment cleared before orders are put into production. In these instances, designers are left with fewer vendor options from which to choose. As well, clients do not have the luxury of paying over time, as full payment is required upfront for project purchases.

Most transactions with vendors will begin and end satisfactorily. Clients will usually respect the integrity of the purchasing process, as well. Most, in fact, have neither time nor inclination to cheat a trusted designer. Your own projects will have positive outcomes because of your efforts to troubleshoot issues explored in this and the following chapter. As you begin, certainly as you grow, your interior design practice, network with other designers to become familiar with their best and worst experiences working with vendors. Also learn how other designers prevent and solve problems with vendors. Further, find those vendors that consistently support the design community by working collaboratively with its practitioners. Should you have reservations about the integrity of a vendor, discuss you concerns with your clients. Document in writing that you have done so, and request written confirmation *they* want to do business with a particular vendor about whom you have expressed concern. Receiving clients' written authorization in this way is one way to troubleshoot liability for yourself.

As in most aspects of interior design, education and experience are keys to beneficial interactions with vendors. Recently graduated interior designers and those with years of experience can benefit from vendors, as sources of practical information and real-life experiences. Equally important is the human factor: vendors' representatives and all others involved in making, selling, and transporting goods are people, too. Open, honest lines of communication among all stakeholders can prevent misunderstandings and help to resolve issues addressed in this chapter.

NOTES FROM THE FIELD

Let's discuss transparency and trust Issues when it comes to working with vendors. Because complete transparency is critical in our profession, you should find this story troubling.

I was delivering a very large project in a foreign country, with a performance specification that would rival any phone book. For clarity, a performance specification is a detailed narrative, outlining specifically the performance requirements of your needed interior design product for a precise purpose. Issuing a performance specification on a project suggests that multiple manufacturers can submit, and multiple product lines could suit your needs. This is the right tool for the competitive project outlines, where price is critical and quantities are large. This does not work when you are looking at proprietary materials with very specific design intent.

Back to the story: with the help of our contractor, a great client, and our project manager, I issued the RFP (request for proposal) performance spec, to three manufacturers, with request for submission in three weeks. We had already seen the product ranges available from the three manufacturers and knew, beyond any doubts, all three could provide comparable products and competitive pricing for this project. To put this into context, the value of this order would be between seven and nine million dollars; therefore, it was worth working through and putting their best quote forward. As a team, we had spoken at length to all parties involved and instructed all suppliers what was acceptable within the bid and what was not permitted.

In a bold move, after receiving the RFP, one of the chosen manufacturers, contacted the client directly, leaping past standard bid protocol with the hope to improve their chances.

Why is this important? In a bid process, it is absolutely critical to outline communication protocol with any manufacturer. In an effort to improve their position, sales driven representatives may attempt to sway a client, which could have a negative impact on both your budget integrity and the fairness of your bid process. Any communication outside the process, no matter how innocent, can influence the bid process.

The client, who was approached by this manufacturer, contacted the design team immediately, informing all parties of this manufacturer's offer – which was to compensate the client directly in exchange for an exclusive specification. These types of exchanges should not be tolerated in any business environment. After discussing this with the client, our first step was to ensure that this was not a misunderstanding and that we had all the facts. We quickly concluded the information was correct, and we contacted the manufacturer with a request to remove their product in 24 hours from all shelves, of all of our offices around the world for three years. The client supported this decision, and we quickly went out to market, to replace this manufacturer with another. Perhaps the lesson for this manufacturer—more damaging than the loss of one specification—was the loss of support by our global practice for this product line, and the loss of trust for how they respond in a professional bid.

Practical Activity

Do you have a favorite vendor? Perhaps there is a furniture manufacturer, fabric house, or some other interior design product for which you feel a special affinity. Identify this source and explain to the class, orally, or in a short written memo what services that vendor provides *to* interior designers. Do they have, for example, designated sales reps, who work only with designers or architects? What pre- and postsales services does this vendor offer to support the design community? What, in your estimation, does this source do well, now? What services might they add to assist designers even better?

Review Questions

1. Where are typical venues interior design merchandise may be found by professionals?

2. Describe a closed showroom in contrast to an open one.

3. Detail some of the issues that might be encountered when designing a line of furniture, as set out in the Mentor Memo. Do you see product development as part of your interior design career?

4. Note some of the most common ways vendors price their goods for purchase by interior designers.

5. What are some tax-related issues interior designers must address when buying and selling merchandise?

6. Describe some of the UCC provisions related to sale and delivery of goods. How do such provisions affect ownership of those goods?

7. Describe several issues that may arise when interior designers work with vendors. Give examples of how those issues might be avoided or resolved.

8. What are some issues of concern interior designers might wish to communicate with their clients? Give suggestions as to how such issues might be resolved as well.

9. Contrast open and closed specifications. When might one be more appropriate than the other? Further note what a performance specification entails and when it might be used.

10. Describe to a prospective client how interior design merchandise is identified, specified, ordered, and delivered in a step-by-step way.

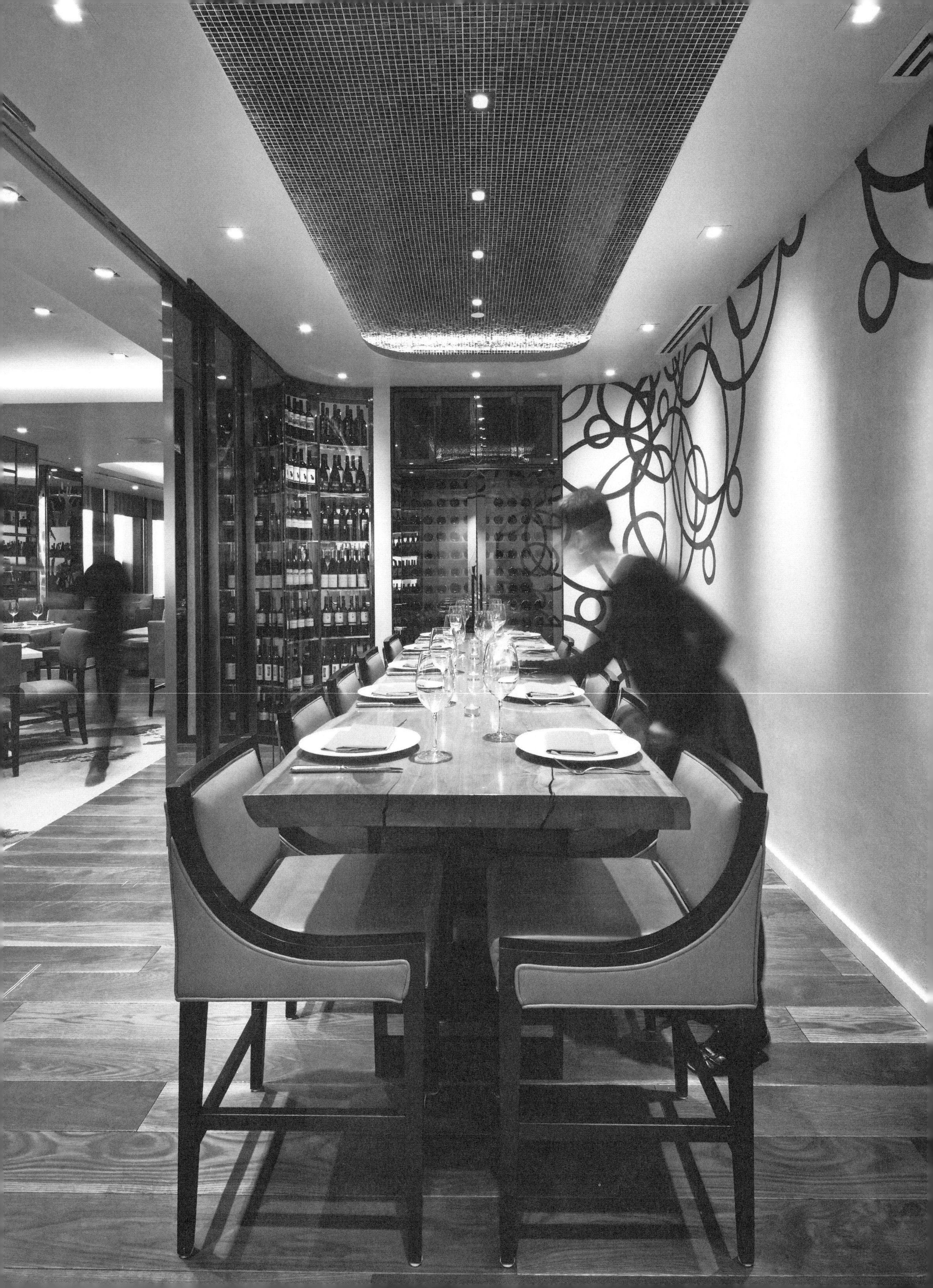

CHAPTER 13
WORKING WITH SERVICE PROVIDERS

MENTOR MEMO
You will not be in control of every aspect of the project. Maintaining eyes on the project, as expected and even on the simplest project detail is necessary and your client will thank you for it.

After reading this chapter, you will be able to

- Identify and locate interior design service providers;
- Understand how to work with contractors and others who provide expertise and labor to interior design projects;
- Troubleshoot problems related to work with service providers.

Working with service providers, such as general contractors and others identified here, requires that designers adopt a detailed, sequential approach because specifying and observing the professional efforts of others are complex tasks, so much so that maintaining complete project control is largely an unrealistic goal. However, becoming the knowing "eyes" of a project is possible after first identifying and then appreciating tasks performed by service-oriented stakeholders.

INTRODUCTION TO WORKING WITH SERVICE PROVIDERS

Designers enhance the function and appearance of interior environments. They do so by specifying physical attributes that will characterize completed spaces. To accomplish such objectives, designers work with service providers. These are the *professionals whose labor, skill, and expertise are necessary to convey designers' concepts into practical realities*. This chapter provides an overview of service providers, who they are and what

Take a moment to think about the many service providers responsible for realizing this sophisticated hospitality environment.

they do. Furthermore, it defines the concepts, terms, and issues necessary to understand the working relationship among interior designers, service providers, clients, and each other.

IDENTIFICATION AND LOCATION OF SERVICE PROVIDERS

Who are the service providers who help carry out interior designers' plans? Among these professionals are general contractors, craftspeople, and independent contractors.

General Contractors

Perhaps the most common example of a service provider with whom interior designers work is the **general contractor**. A GC, as they are often referred, may be an individual operator or even an entity such as a business employing large numbers of people. General contractors usually perform the following tasks:

1. Enter into contracts with design professionals, home owners, and building owners/managers among others for the purpose of erecting a new physical structure or modifying an existing one to contractually defined terms and as otherwise required by law.
2. Retain the labor of others service providers with specialized skills and knowledge in some aspect of the construction process. Those hired by general contractors are usually referred to as **subcontractors**, or subs. These professionals are responsible for completing tasks such as structural framing; installing plumbing systems and fixtures; wiring electrical, cable TV/Internet, and other systems; putting in heating, ventilating, and air conditioning (HVAC) systems; and applying surface coatings and finishes, such as paint and wallpaper, tile, and carpet. General contractors are responsible for hiring and scheduling subs, assigning tasks to them, paying them out of the "draw" of funds, and resolving issues arising with them.
3. Engage in the lawful, ethical practice of construction and construction management. This means that they follow the laws of the state(s) and area(s) where they operate. For example, many jurisdictions, including cities and towns, have laws specifically related to general contractors and the work they are allowed to perform. At the very least, these laws require general contractors to have a current, state-issued license relating to their work.
4. Operate as a business in legally recognized ways, not casually or "out of the back of a truck." General contractors frequently organize their businesses as a form of corporation, such as a limited liability company. This form is often selected in order to protect the personal assets, property, of its founder(s) from financial claims arising from legal and other actions.

Craftspeople

Craftspeople, or artisans are service providers offering highly customized project elements. Think of an interior space with richly ornamented architectural surfaces. Likely, a craftsperson or artisan was responsible. This group of service providers might include muralists, "Venetian" plaster and Trompe L'oeil workers, and stained glass and wrought iron metal artisans, as well as hosts of other professionals producing unique interior design features. Interior designers, general contractors, and even project clients often directly hire these providers because of the desirability of their work. They may also be paid from them and separately from subcontractors.

Independent Contractors

This term, familiar to interior designers and businesspeople, includes general contractors, subcontractors, and craftspeople/artisans. Interior designers themselves may be classified as independent contractors. An independent contractor is a worker who meets certain Internal Revenue Service (IRS) requirements. Unlike employees, whose work is defined and controlled by others, independent contractors control the kind of work they do, whether or not they agree to undertake work, *and* the manner and method by which they perform any work they do agree to take on. Only the entity, individual, or company engaging the independent contractor controls whether or not to accept (and pay for) the final result of their efforts.

Identification of Service Providers

Clients frequently ask interior designers to suggest service providers best able to carry out an entire job, or, at least, some aspects of it. Designers themselves may have a cadre of service providers with they have previously worked successfully. In fact, so reliant are they, they will make it an express condition of their working relationship with clients they use their own "team" of workers.

Knowing service providers and the quality of work they are capable of performing are important parts of designers' work. How, then, might designers go about locating these all-important service providers? Among the ways to find contractors and other workers, designers often rely on their own experiences—whom have they worked successfully with before—and then they typically research others.

General contractors are responsible for bringing together subcontractors capable of executing the details that ultimately reflect designers' concepts.

In most communities, the work of residential contractors and craftspeople is on display and fairly easily ascertained: signs in yards of homes being built or renovated, charity-sponsored tours of private homes where contributions of the many workers involved are acknowledged, advertisements in local home and garden periodicals, and word of mouth. Previous clients, happy or not, are often eager to share their experiences working with contractors.

The identities of nonresidential, commercial contractors can also be fairly easily ascertained. Completed buildings usually acknowledge on their cornerstones service providers such as general contractors, as do the large signs bearing names of construction companies and contractors seen at most building and renovation sites. Building owners and managers frequently maintain lists of service providers who have worked on original construction or subsequent renovation projects there.

Many times, the issue with respect to locating service providers is not just finding them but finding the right one! Both residential and commercial contractors advertise in communities where they operate and often prospect aggressively for business. That, coupled with designers' own files and experiences and providers' overall presence in the community, can make it difficult to winnow down the choice of service provider to just one. Experience and research are, therefore, required to make such a choice.

Evaluation of Service Providers

After identifying individuals or companies offering interior design-related services in their community, designers usually conduct further research to find those providers whose work is most applicable to a project. For example, a residential interior designer may require the assistance of a service provider capable of precisely installing European-made kitchen cabinets or complicated plumbing fixtures. An interior designer with a hospitality and restaurant professional focus may seek a service provider capable of installing large industrial appliances without damaging what is likely leased property. In addition, designers usually consider those service providers whose working and communication styles are best suited to their own. On the basis of this ongoing research and evaluation, interior designers often develop lists of service providers whose work they deem appropriate and acceptable for the kinds of projects in which the designer engages.

Although affinity between designers and potential service providers is extremely important, it should not occur in a vacuum. Rather, designers should be aware of and interested in client input about characteristics *they* desire in project service providers. Together, designers and clients might agree important selection criteria include a service provider's overall reputation in the community, ability to complete jobs in a timely manner without excessive cost overruns and project delays, whether the service provider requires assistance from unionized (i.e., more expensive workers, usually) and has necessary skills to work within any unusual project constraints. Not to be overlooked is the ability of the service provider to communicate regularly, accurately, and truthfully to others involved in the proposed project.

The importance of ongoing research and evaluation of this kind cannot be overemphasized. The designers are responsible for making the best possible recommendation they are capable of. Doing so involves learning as much as is reasonably possible from available sources about the service provider and the work they have completed previously. To be sure, designers cannot predict (nor should they be asked to) exactly how well a service provider might or might not complete a new project based on previously completed ones. It is not clear whether or not designers might incur legal liability as a result. Much would depend on the facts and circumstances involved. However, designers who fail to research the abilities of the service providers they recommend, especially if they lacked any real knowledge about them and the nature and quality of their work, could possibly be found negligent legally.

Referrals, Recommendations, and Bids

Many interior designers develop close working and personal relationships with service providers. Within the design and service communities, obtaining steady amounts of new business is critical to long-term success. The ability to refer profitable business to each other is a factor in fostering development of both business and relationships. This symbiosis is especially prevalent and necessary in the area of residential interior design. Residential work in any particular community is cyclical in nature: It comes and goes with economic conditions and other factors beyond any obvious control. Referrals, even casual recommendations, can be sources of continued livelihood.

Referrals may also be of importance in nonresidential interior design work. However, because of the special decision-making process involved and the many stakeholders responsible for decision making in this specialty, personal contacts may have less influence. In contract interior design work, for example, decision making rests with groups of people. A committee of designers and others, many of whom may not have heard of a particular service provider, may be less impressed by oral recommendations and personal referrals. Projects in this practice area are awarded on the basis of written bids, a process discussed later in this chapter. Generally speaking, they are awarded to those service providers whose bids meet specified requirements.

WORK STRATEGIES FOR SERVICE PROVIDERS: RESIDENTIAL INTERIOR DESIGN

Interior design projects come about sequentially. A logical way to develop a strategy for working with service providers is to consider expected activities of client, designers, and service providers; what they are; and the project phase they frequently occur. Residential interior design work offers insights into this concept.

The service of providers has to be obtained before any work can begin. Designers' first objective, then, is to learn how general contractors and subcontractors are retained; suggestions for that have been discussed in other chapter sections. Once selected, these providers must work together or work directly with the clients or the designers selecting them.

With those in mind, interior designers should next be aware of ways in which service providers are usually thought to organize and carry out their tasks. Many of these workers are considered independent contractors, or those who have sole control over how they work. Those who hire independent contractors, however, do control whether they accept and pay them for their work. Thus, designers also need to be aware of how, on what basis and at what milestones during projects, providers are paid for such services.

As soon as projects are underway, having clear work strategies is critical. During the *design development phase*, designers typically complete project specifications and prepare budgets. Once that phase is completed and designers receive final client approvals, projects enter the *contract documents phase*. During the *contract document* and *contract administration phases*, designers, clients, and service providers interact. Essentially, the creative part of the project, where aesthetics and functionalities are determined, is complete once the contract administration phase begins. To be sure, changes can and do occur. You will come to see how in the following c sections in this chapter. The main goal is to organize the most expedient pathway to complete the project!

During the project's build time, activities of project stakeholders become actively involved with each other. The actual time of retention of service providers, of course, may vary depending on when they are needed, the circumstances of the project itself, and their availability. Particularly popular service providers, for example, or those few available in a particular area, or artisans requiring long lead times between commissions, these kinds of professionals may need to be obtained months in advance. Waiting until projects have begun may be impractical for their timely completion. Thus, service providers may have to be reserved and deposits paid for their services as early as projects' initial programming phases.

These thoughts provide a general overview, a beginning way to form a work plan. What, however, are some of the specific ways interior designers and service providers interact during projects they work on together? As the contract documents phase evolves, interior designers and clients typically decide on how to retain service providers for their project. With small to average-sized residential projects, for example, clients may simply go with providers recommended by designers. The following section will explore work strategies related to service providers and the competitive-bidding process, as typically occur within the context of large-scale residential and most commercial interior design projects.

With these kinds of projects, interior designers usually prepare written specifications for service providers to follow. They may, however, not participate in actually hiring those providers. Client may enter into agreements with providers, including providing by contract to pay them directly. In these instances, designers usually contract with clients to serve as consultants in matters related to the project. In some states, designers are legally permitted to do no more than that, unless they are also licensed to work as general contractors. The following troubleshooting section explores issues arising from designers' involvement with service providers.

When designers work as consultants, they may check on whether the task undertaken by service providers has been completed, reviewing the progression of dry wall installation, for example. They also check to ensure that completed work has been done according to their specifications and "cleanly." Designers undertake these kinds of tasks during the contract administration phase but may continue to do so throughout project duration.

WORK STRATEGIES FOR SERVICE PROVIDERS: THE COMPETITIVE BIDDING PROCESS

A highly structured process is often used to obtain the work of service providers on large residential and commercial interior design projects. This process is sometimes referred to informally as the *bid*, or *bidding process*. These terms refer to the *competitive bidding process*. This procedure allows a project client—be that one person, or a group of many—to assess availability and quality of many service providers at one time. In other words, this process enables project decision makers to evaluate whether service professionals may be able to perform construction-related tasks within project financial and time constraints. This chapter focuses on the bidding process as it relates to service providers; however, the same process and steps set forth here may be used when dealing with vendors of project merchandise as well.

Bidding is a formal procedure with schedules and requirements for submissions. The process may be administered by a project's interior designer or design team, if they agree to perform those services. Otherwise, clients may oversee the bidding process. The objective is to solicit offers, or *bids* from service providers. Bids state a dollar amount a service provider will charge to complete a specifically defined task, or many of them. Once accepted by the client, the selected service provider becomes obligated to complete project tasks according to the financial terms of the bid.

If a project's budget is to satisfy completion costs, service providers must perform work at costs stated in their bids. Due to such factors as unforeseen delays and product and labor unavailability, it can become extremely difficult for service providers to comply with their bids. They may be unable to perform work for the agreed-to amount. As a result, clients may require a form of insurance called a **bid bond**. This is financial protection for clients. Bid bonds are issued by specialized companies or banking institutions known as a **surety**. A bid bond, then, is the surety's guarantee bid work will be completed at the price stated; the insurer taking the risk they will not be obligated to pay more than the amount in the service provider's bid.

Interior designers may, or may not be involved in the bid process. Likewise, they may or may not be involved in another aspect of the contract documents phase, procuring state and local permits and other needed documentation for planned projects. Often, architects, engineers, and contractors are responsible for obtaining such documents as building permits. However, interior designers are often called upon for information needed to complete the lengthy, detailed forms required to obtain them. Because of this, designers should estimate the extent to which they might well be involved in such matters and seek compensation accordingly.

The three major steps in the competitive bidding process include:

1. **Invitation to bid** Publication of an invitation for competing construction and other service providers to submit bids for a project is the first step in this process. Usually, a *statement of general conditions* is made available in which clients provide information such as their business name and the legal right and responsibilities of the parties to each other after a bid is accepted and a contract awarded, or *let*. Invitations to bid specify qualifications required for consideration and provide deadlines for receipt of bids. Standard forms with preprinted general conditions are available from design-build trade groups such as AIA and ASID.
2. **Instructions to bidders** To ensure uniformity and fairness in the bid process, an *instruction to bidders* provides information about the form in which bids should be received.
3. **Tender (or bid) form** The form on which a service provider offers a formal price for completing a project is called a **tender**, or *bid form*.

The competitive bidding process seeks to ensure cost-efficient vendors and suppliers are project participants.

As you are aware, much can change before and during a project. Changes and corrections may be necessary to documents tendered for consideration. Any changes made by clients prior to awarding a project are usually referred to as an **addendum**. These usually modify contract documents and are necessary when discrepancies, ambiguities, and incorrect information are found in any of the original project solicitation documents. Each identified bidder usually receives notification of addenda terms. Changes made by a client after a project contract has been let are referred to as **change orders**. Change orders impact projects. Some may be relatively "easy fixes," perhaps modifying the choice of electrical plug plate. Large-scale changes, once the project is underway in particular, can greatly affect project budgets, time schedules, and ultimate completion dates.

MENTOR MEMO

Construction Management versus General Contractors. Most projects require a constructor. And large projects are even more particular with who are qualified to perform this role and often go through a detailed prequalification process to determine who can even bid. There is a difference between a CM (construction manager) and a GC (general contractor). Construction management is the service designers often need prior to bid process to fully estimate a project. What clients truly dislike, is coming to the end of the creative process and realizing a project is over budget. As a result, you will have a very unhappy client. Hiring a construction manager to work with you through the design process to estimate and reestimate the project will keep it on target to meet your budget needs. If you do bring on a CM, that does not mean you won't be competitively bidding this project to the subtrades. Often the CM will be one of the bidders. He or she may have a distinct advantage over the competing GC if this is the case, but most often the CM proceeding forward into the GC role continues to bid the subtrades, from the bid set provided by the design team. Affording the client the competitive process, with cost management along the way.

TROUBLESHOOTING PROBLEMS RELATED TO WORK WITH SERVICE PROVIDERS

The interests of many different people with many different skills and schedules come together during projects, so difficulties can arise. One way to address difficulties is to understand with whom and how they can occur.

Designers should understand, based on their own research and experiences, what will be involved to complete projects successfully before agreeing to do anything. Comprehending this will enable them to better draft their own scope of services and negotiate financial compensation. Among the options designers have might be to perform only design-focused activities such as programming, design development, and product selections. With this approach, designers and clients agree the designer will not assume full, or even any, responsibility for contract administration-related activities. They might, at most, prepare spec documents that will be made available to service providers after client approval. On the other hand, designers and clients may agree that the designer will do all those tasks and remain involved through the project, even, as legally permitted, supervise construction. As you can see, these options require different kinds and amounts of work on the part of designers. Failing to recognize those differences early on can be a source of problems for designers. Why? Changing the nature of the working relationship during the course of the project is difficult and fraught with the likelihood of misunderstandings. Attempting to adjust compensation methods after the fact opens up designers to the possibility of being underpaid for the work they do perform.

Thus, a first "troubleshoot" is in order: Designers should make every effort to be sure about actual project requirements and client expectations. . .and whether they will be expected to work with service providers. Project selection by interior designers can be a difficult task: there simply are clients and project with whom it would be desirable to work. That, and the always-present need to generate business revenue make for difficult decisions. However, designers have the obligation to educate potential clients about what they, as designers, can and cannot undertake.

Consultants are available to assist designers with such issues as physical ergonomics and lighting if needed.

MENTOR MEMO

I need more consultants? In order to gain some perspective, who besides yourself, will you need to complete a project? It will take a village! If you are completing residential work, a good designer with his or her constructor of choice and the product representatives might be all that is necessary. If you are working on a commercial project, the village becomes a small town. Here are your typical consultants:

- Base-building architect
- General interior designer
- Medical planner (if it's healthcare)
- Mechanical engineer
- Electrical engineer
- Lighting designer
- Communications engineer
- IT consultant
- Audio visual consultant
- Vertical transportation consultant
- Code consultant
- Artwork coordinator and artwork inventory specialist
- Building envelope
- LEED or sustainability coordinator
- Furniture dealer
- Project manager
- Estimator (if construction management or a contractor is not on the team yet)

Depending on the scope, scale, and complexity of the project, all of these professionals might be under contract. The architect of record can manage all of these consultants under their contract. In which case you (as the interior designer) are being paid for your work, after the architect has been paid. In calendar terms, this could mean 90 to 120 days before you are paid for your work. If this is unmanageable, be clear with your teams what your terms of payment are. Many interior design firms manage the consultants under their main contract; however, there are administrative costs and additional overhead required in doing so. It will be critical to be clear with your clients, if it costs them for you to act as the bank. Consultants can contract directly with the client, and they often prefer to do so as it speeds payment of invoices. However, given that all of the consultants' work is rolled into a construction set, the architect of record should be aware of how fees are running through the project.

CHAPTER 13 WORKING WITH SERVICE PROVIDERS • 249

Nothing usually prevents designers from doing walk-throughs during and after construction, informing clients of what they have observed and of any necessary changes. However, designers' abilities to do much more than that, such as hire workers and schedule and plan their activities, as well as supervise the actual construction process may be controlled by various state and local laws. California and Florida require those interested in construction-related work to hold a valid, unexpired state general contractor's licence before engaging such work. Because states impose serious legal penalties on those who engage without appropriate licensure in activities defined as supervisory, it is critical for interior designers to understand how laws in their areas affect them.

Successful completion of this hospitality space came about because the designer and the design team were able to work with such myriad stakeholders as building management, contractors, and local authorities.

NOTES FROM THE FIELD

What might it be like to work on a large-scale interior design project, one of international scope? The following case study gives an idea of what might—and might not—occur.

Being hired to complete a large renovation project, within a commercial tower, is fulfilling on every level. In one respect, you are updating the existing building to reflect new products that are undoubtedly more sustainable or healthier. And, you will be completing a project that might indeed outlive you. Over my career, I have had the pleasure of restoring quite a few iconic structures, and if I did my job well, it would look like I was never there. Sometimes you are working to make a statement, and at times you are not, be mindful what roll you play in either scenario.

For this specific project, I was tasked with base-building stone replacement for the interiors of the lobby and multi-tenant areas. This was indeed an iconic structure with historic significance. When you are dealing with any quantity of product, you need to be completely aware of the specification for both integrity of product and the specific needs around installation. Many stones from around the world were viewed, researched, and vetted with our specifications department. Large samples were brought to the stone yards, and we traveled to view and sign off on the product. Per our contract, once a product was approved, we completed the design drawings, and the construction drawings and the IFC (issued for construction) set was provided to the approved contractor. So far, so good, right?

Per contract and professional practice, designers need to provide field review of their work in process. This process is designed to ensure that the projects are built to your specifications and the design intent is being maintained. Per this requirement, I made a trip to the site specifically to see the stone, mid installation. When I got to the site, I flipped over the product to see the manufacturers stamp and country of original, but I found another country of origin instead. What!

My first step was to ensure everything was in order with the specification in the first place. Were we open to substitutions? Did I miss something? Did the client opt to accept a lesser-quality product and receive credit from the supplier? The product looked the same on the surface, so what happened? I called the supplier directly to inquire: "We purchased stone from Country X and on site is says Country Y, can you help me understand what has happened?" We knew that Country X mined the product as it should be, and the method of extracting the product from the earth preserved its integrity. The substituted product was mined differently, faster, and with the use of explosives; it was put back together with adhesives, versus continuous slabs cut to specifications. The investigation continued, with a thorough review of the supplier's fine print. Did we miss something? Was it disclosed to us somewhere that this product was coming from Country Y but marketed as Country X? The answer to all of the above was, no. Therefore, our specification had been tampered with. When asked, here is the answer we received: in order to maintain the competitive price, the manufacturer shipped its mining equipment from Country X to Country Y. The equipment was from country X, but the product was from country Y. Therefore, the manufacturer thought it was appropriate to represent the product was from another country. Sound like bad business?

Following a long legal battle, the client and our firm were found to be correct in our assumptions and the manufacturer was asked to replace all of the lower-quality product at their cost. The uncharted costs were the continuous disruptions to the valued tenants of the building, with a now-extended construction schedule that was years longer than expected. all parties wasted legal costs and valuable time.

Practical Activity

This Notes from the Field emphasized product substitutions that were unethical and wasteful. Unfortunately, tampered specs are not limited to the interior design industry, and their occurrences are occurring more and more across all industries. Consumer goods and fashion products have long been plagued with similar "substitutions." Research examples in current events where either an interior space, a product for one, or a fashion item were found to have been subjected to the kind of treatment described here.

Review Questions

After completing this chapter, you should be able to answer the following questions. Because of the prevalence of these terms, phrases, and concepts, you may want to keep these questions and your responses at the ready, to refer to, until you are sure of their meanings and uses.

1. Who is a general contractor, and what roles might he or she play in completing work specified by an interior designer?

2. Who is a subcontractor? What is the relationship to the general contractor?

3. If you were speaking to a client who did not understand the contracting-for-services process, explain how the process typically operates.

4. Why might an interior designer decline responsibility for hiring and supervising the activities of service providers, including general contractors and subcontractors?

5. Why should an interior designer use care when recommending the services of others?

6. What is competitive bidding, and how is it conducted? Why might a client be interested in this method of retaining service providers?

7. What documents are associated with the competitive bidding process, and what role do interior designers have in preparing them?

8. Distinguish an addendum from a change order and when each is used. . Who is responsible for each kind of document?

9. When, in the course of a project, are the activities of service providers typically called upon? How might these be scheduled?

10. What ways can interior designers prevent, or at least limit, potential problems that might occur when working with service providers?

11. To what do the terms *bonded* and *insured* refer? Why are these important from the perspective of interior designers?

12. What is a chain of command as it relates to project management and relationships with service providers? Why might an interior designer be interested in establishing a communication process involving project workers and clients?

YOU AND YOUR CAREER   PART 5

Your formal education may end when you graduate from college; however, you will need to have strategies for beginning and advancing in your interior design career. What kinds of activities will you have to engage in as you make the transition from student to professional?

Chapter 14. Beginning Your Work Life: Addresses those concerns. Accordingly, it focuses on topics you are probably interested in right now, such as completing a résumé and cover letter, compiling a portfolio, preparing for an interview, and participating in internships.

Chapter 15. Planning Your Career: Identifies career options for designers in a variety of professional settings from retail and wholesale establishments to architectural and independent interior design studios and academic institutions.

Interior design as a professional endeavor has a fascinating developmental history, an evolving present status, a foundation built on solid, ethical business practices, but, more importantly for young practitioners, a future filled with infinite possibilities. Contents found throughout these pages are intended to help you find your place in the excitement and challenges to come.

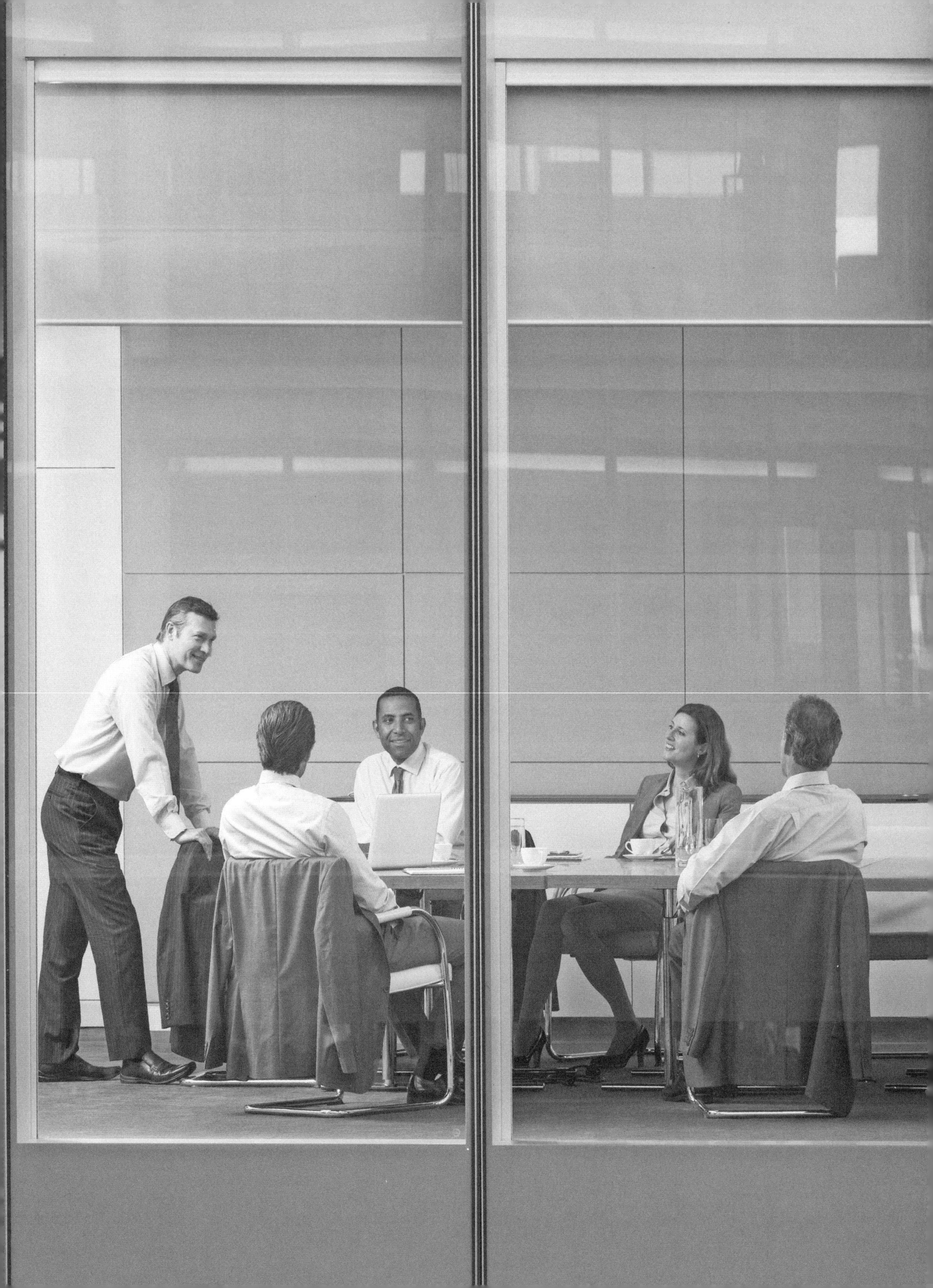

CHAPTER 14
BEGINNING YOUR WORK LIFE

MENTOR MEMO

Welcome to a global club of talent where the competition is fierce. How do you secure the job you want that fills you up and provides the foundation that every designer needs and wants? What do you need to do for a potential employer to notice you? What are employers looking for and how can you prepare for the interview process? What questions should you ask? Note that the questions you ask are an indicator to your employer of how you think. What is critical to remember is your employer is running a business. They will be looking for a blend of both professionalism and creativity.

After reading this chapter, you will be able to

- Describe résumés and cover letters as they relate to interior designers and relate how they are usually prepared;
- List contents of design portfolios and be able to explain why they are important to both job seekers and employers;
- Understand the place internships have in the professional development of interior designers and be able to describe that role;
- Prepare for initial or subsequent job interviews knowing procedures and questions likely to be encountered.

INTRODUCTION TO BEGINNING YOUR WORK LIFE

Are you ready to join that global club of talent now comprising the interior design profession? As a student, it may seem an intimidating goal, but it needn't be. Step back, and ask what basic element defines designers' work. The answer is projects. As a practicing interior designer, your career will depend on and be defined by projects. Your first project should be to prepare to take those first challenging, but admittedly, exciting steps into your interior design career—to become a full-fledged member of the industry's

As you transition from student to young professional, be prepared to meet new people and be in new work situations.

talent club! Take heart, nearly all professionals undertake the process and activities described here. With purpose and plan in mind, you will be prepared for this rite of passage and to begin your work life.

How and in what order you will have to address these topics will depend on your own circumstances, career timing, how you process this information, and on other developments as yet to unfold. Perhaps you have a résumé already in place but are seeking ways to better circulate it through social media? Maybe you are looking for that "something extra" to make your portfolio or yourself stand out to a prospective employer? Many considerations inform the progress of Project You! To begin, recall what you have accomplished already, and then prepare for how best to describe yourself to the interior design community.

THE RÉSUMÉ AND COVER LETTER

If you have applied for jobs previously, you are aware of the next tasks: preparing your résumé and accompanying cover letter. Simply put, **résumé**s are written summaries of education and work experiences. With them, it is often necessary to prepare a cover letter. This is the way to entice a prospective employer to read your résumé and convince them you are "the one" for the opportunity offered. Social media has markedly changed ways to present your résumé. You can reach the world of potential employers through its means. However, with its opportunities, social media brings issues about which to be aware. What are these? How might they affect you?

True enough résumés may be defined formally as "a summary of somebody's educational and work experience, for the information of possible future employers." That definition, however, describes only "nuts and bolts" résumé content, but not their subtle details. There are other elements, seemingly intangible, but no less important aspect that résumés should contain. For example, interior design hiring professionals seek candidates with "clarity and imagination." Beginning with a guide to practical content, you will discover here a multifaceted approach to preparing résumés and accompanying cover letters.

Developing Your Résumé's Content

Prior planning pays! When you consider all that you have accomplished, it first makes sense to organize your personal, education, and work-related information. With your life, literally, in front of you, written down, sorted as to academic and other achievements, developing résumé content and selecting its format becomes easier.

Résumés focus on the both academic and work-related accomplishments. Their writers typically emphasize achievements in such areas to varying degrees. For example, young professionals, those not far from graduation, often emphasize academic achievements, honors, and awards. More career-advanced interior designers include educational information, of course, but usually emphasize projects in which they were involved, projects they completed, and experiences they gained through work. As you proceed through this chapter, start to think about your accomplishments, large and small, in both school and work. Write them down and include their correct dates, order of occurrence, and relevant contact or reference information. Soon, you will be preparing a document describing these for other, either potential employers, or prospective clients.

As you know, résumés typically contain specific kinds of information. Such facts are anticipated by those receiving and ultimately considering them. The physical layout of your résumés should also follow recognized and accepted guidelines. Although creativity and problem-solving design skills are hallmarks of interior design, these talents are subordinate to the ability to describe yourself clearly through well-organized wording.

You may have noticed résumés typically contain the kinds of elements identified here. The emphasis accorded to one element, say educational information, and where placed in the résumé depends on the résumé form writers choose. Those methods are discussed next. To begin, however, consider résumé basics and their importance.

- **Contact information** Usually, the very top of the résumé will present your name and address. Although this may seem obvious, if you are a student living on campus who will soon be moving to a different location, you need to consider carefully what contact information to present. Your goal should be to include personal contact information permitting an interested employer to communicate easily with you during the time you remain on campus and afterward. If you are not yet sure of your address after graduation, include the most accurate contact information available as of the time you send your résumé. Perhaps you might include both your current address and the permanent address registered with your school. It may be necessary to retain a mailbox at a post office or a mail service in your new location, before finding a set place to live. You should indicate the personal nature of this information, so that you are not contacted at any current place of work.

    E-mail addresses and cell phone numbers can travel with you under some circumstances. Include these, of course, if they will remain active as you seek employment. Social media such as Facebook seem a good way to update contact information quickly and easily. However, doing so presents significant safety and privacy concerns. Any personal contact information should be placed in protected, nonpublic areas of your profile. Allow access to such information only to those to whom you give passwords.

- **Objective or professional summary** Many students seeking an early-career job list an *objective*. Job hunters with more experience typically include a *skills* summary beneath their contact information on the résumé page. Job objectives usually indicate the position sought—for example, an entry-level position as a member of the design team or a position as a junior designer.

    More experienced professionals, on the other hand, may focus on skills or accomplishments such as length of time in practice, design-team leadership, successful project completion, or abilities to market their skills and attract new clients and lines of business for themselves and their firms.

- **Education** Most job postings contain very specific educational experiences required of candidates. To make it past initial candidate screenings, your educational qualifications should be set out as accurately as possible. This means they must, of course, be truthful and understandable to those reviewing your résumé. Degrees obtained, for example, should be stated in full title as set by the institution granting them. Remember for jobs with very high numbers of expected candidates, your résumé likely will be screened by computers, set to find specific information. Your degree designations, therefore, should be able to be read physically, clearly by nonhumans as well. New professionals should list their academic achievements (in reverse chronological order) directly following career objective, whereas more seasoned professionals list their work experience (also in reverse chronological order).

- **Work experiences** More and more prospective employers are requiring more and more experience from candidates! When it comes to stating work experience on your résumé, this may mean asking you to list every job you have held, or all those within a specified number of years. Whether or not related, even relevant, to specific jobs sought, employers seek to determine candidates' employment patterns. Do workers, for example, go from job to job within fairly short times, or do they tend to stay? In short, is there evidence of continual (start and stop), or continuous (non-\stop) work? Because employers devote a great many resources to employees, such scrutiny is understandable. It does, however, place a larger burden on job seekers to maintain records of their employment and retain verifiable information of it. Social media such as Facebook, Myspace, and LinkedIn are areas where many post career and job information. Double-check the information you include on social media to make sure it matches that on your physical résumé.

- **Skills** Most employers state the technical skillsets sought, often mentioning exact brands and versions of software programs candidates are expected to know. Usually, this information is included in the "qualifications" sections of job postings. As truthful as you should be about stating education and work background, you should be equally truthful when it comes to describing skills of which you are capable. As noted in the following Mentor Memo, you should "be prepared for a technology test" as part of the interview process. This will include exhibiting your expertise with graphic and visual design computer programs. Note the exact experience you have and state realistically and demonstrably your level of proficiency. If you have received specialized software training and/or passed performance proficiency exams, note that training, the dates completed, and any certificates or diplomas received.

- **Activities and honors** Volunteering, elected or appointed offices held, student chapter membership of national and state organizations, and honor society inductions should all be included in this section of your résumé, which presents you and your academic and extracurricular interests and achievements.

- **Professional affiliations** Professional affiliations such as membership in national, state, and local interior design associations indicate job candidates have sufficient interest, qualifications, and interpersonal skills to join and remain in organizations representing designers' career interests. Membership in them, therefore, can be a further indication of candidates' accomplishments and should be included here. Note that professional associations usually have a definite point of view (often found in organizations' mission statements) about what they seek to accomplish. Such goals might include seeking greater regulatory oversight of the interior design profession, for example. Others may have views differing in degree or kind from these positions. Thus, memberships in professional organizations indicate some degree of "politics" of alliance with groups' tenants. Group memberships can give professionals, beginning or established, opportunities for advocacy about such beliefs. Have you stood up as a representative of a professional group and spoken before governing bodies about its concerns? This section of your résumé would be the place to include that!

- **References** Employers, as noted, seek as much information about prospective employees as possible. This includes asking for references. Candidates may be asked for any number of references. These may be individuals who are familiar with them personally, who have worked with them professionally, or both! Usually employers ask for a specific number of references and specify the relationship—personal, professional, or both—these references should have with candidates. Then, they will follow up this information to confirm details candidates have included on résumés. Former employers may only confirm employment dates and positions held, citing potential privacy and libel concerns. Of course, it is difficult to know exactly what a reference will disclose to prospective employee. However, references should have actual knowledge of the candidate, worked with them, or supervised them in some direct way in order to be credible.

Selecting a Format for Your Résumé

According to experts, résumés follow a variety of formats, but the most common are the reverse chronology résumé, the functional résumé, and a combination, or hybrid résumé.

- **Reverse Chronological Résumé** This is perhaps the most commonly used method of organizing a résumé, describing both educational accomplishments and work history in the reverse order in which they occurred. In this approach, the most recent experience is listed first and the earliest experience is listed last. Typically, younger professionals place educational accomplishments before work experiences, since school activities have been their major and most recent focus. Professionals further along in their careers who decide to use this approach list their work experience prior to their education, since many professionals have been out of school for some time and instead wish to highlight their work history.

  The primary benefit of this approach is its wide acceptance. It is an effective method for designers who are staring out their careers to highlight their educational accomplishments and note relevant extracurricular activities. At the same time, however, this approach highlights educational or employment gaps. This could be problematic for professionals with gaps in their histories.
- **Functional Résumé** The functional résumé shows those skills the applicant has acquired through education or work experience, or both. Typically, résumé writers using this approach identify a series of skills or abilities and list them in their order of importance.
- **Combination or Hybrid Résumé** This résumé combines the two previous approaches, typically focusing on skills, as does the functional résumé, and placing less emphasis on the sequential career development of résumé writers. The list of academic accomplishments usually appears towards the end of the résumé and is organized in reverse chronological order.

Completing a Cover Letter

Perhaps you are new to the process of preparing résumés and cover letters. What could entice a prospective employer to consider reading your résumé? A *cover letter* is intended to interest decision makers in the skills and abilities you acquired during the course of your academic and professional life. Simply put, the cover letter should engage readers' interest in you as a professional and as a potential employee. Using the template provided, consider drafting a letter to accompany your résumé. Once you find an employer with whom you would like to work, read about their business, point of view (mission), and goals. Then, recraft your cover letter to reflect how you would be a valued employee.

BOX 14.1

COVER LETTER WORKSHEET

Use this template to draft a résumé cover letter.

Your Name
Your Address
Area code and phone number
Other contact information

Date:

Dear Mr./Mrs.:

The first paragraph should tell the reader:
1. Why you are writing ("In response to your advertisement, website posting, etc.), I am writing to . . .")
2. What you are seeking ("to show my interest in and application for . . .")
3. The specific position you are interested in ("the position of [use the specific position title used by employer] . . .")
4. Your ability to practice interior design relevant to the state in which your registration/license will be held.
5. How you heard about the position ("I read about this opportunity . . .")

The body of the letter (two to three paragraphs, unless you have extensive experience to note) should spell out for the reader your education and experience and how they directly relate to the available position. One way to approach this may be to
1. Explain how your formal education is appropriate for the position ("I have earned a bachelors of art degree in interior design, as required in the posting"). Explain further details about your education, such as honors and awards.
2. Explain how your previous internship experiences are appropriate for the position ("As an intern with Co. X, I gained experience relevant to this position by doing . . .").
3. Explain how your early formal work experience is appropriate for the position ("While working as a (name position), I performed the following tasks that enable me to perform this position's task of . . .").
4. Explain how your recent work experience is appropriate for the position ("As manager of projects similar to those referenced in the position, I . . .").
5. Address any concerns that might be provoked by your résumé or that your otherwise need to address. (This may be necessary if, for example, there are considerable gaps in your work history.)

The final paragraph and closing should
1. Thank the readers for their time and interest;
2. Express your availability for an interview, either in person or on the telephone;
3. Add a conclusion, such as "sincerely" or "thanking you for your consideration";
4. Leave signature space so that you can sign your name;
5. Type your full name;
6. Add the following notation when sending a résumé: "Enclosure: résumé."

Getting Your Résumé—and You—Known

The effects of social media have been tremendous. We have become a world of individuals and businesses brought together by technology and common interests. Yet, we come to use this powerful force in our own way, at our own speed. Those who never knew a world without the Internet instinctively turn first to such platforms as Facebook to post résumés and as a place to become actively engaged in seeking jobs. Others may include social media later in their job-hunting strategies. Whether accustomed to or coming to grips with social media and its use, it never hurts to think about ways to use it to get your résumé and you known, and then hired! In your job search, also consider that interior design is a business about understanding people and their needs. This involves making contacts, building a cadre of personal contacts, and building networks between you and each contact based on mutual interests. Social media can help in this process, just as personal networking can. Each benefits from the other, and both should be reflected in your strategies to get your résumé into the hands of interested, prospective employers.

If you have a personal website, you have already taken a big step toward integrating technology into your job search. Through search engine queries, prospective employers may be able to find you through GOOGLE, Bing, and other portals, just by knowing your name. Even if you have not yet launched your own site, take heart. There now are many inexpensive services and independent providers available to consumers and able to get sites up and running quickly.

There are many ways to utilize the Internet, social media, and interpersonal means in your quest to get your résumé in circulation. Suggestions include these gleaned from various sources:

1. Let people—family, friends, and as many as possible—know you are looking for a job and ask if they have a copy of your résumé.
2. Use Facebook networks.
3. Find ways to hyperlink your résumé and portfolio images so that those interested in knowing more can access your information quickly.
4. Comment on influential blogs and on-line conversations hosted by interior design trade groups.
5. Establish a blog of your own, one expressing your own creative point of view, as shown by images from your portfolio and any completed projects.
6. Find out as much as you can about interior design firms in your area (or the area in which you want to work), what kinds of skills they are looking for in new hires, and the key decision makers in these firms and their contact information. Use this information to craft a thoughtful introduction to send via mail or e-mail with your résumé.

MENTOR MEMO
In my experience as an employer, the quality of the résumé is a direct indication of the persons creative DNA. We expect that a student freshly out of school or a younger professional, from anywhere in the world, is not going to have a built a project client list. What we are looking for is clarity and imagination. Please consider that your future employer might be viewing your (resumé and) portfolio on a PDA, or, yes, even on an airplane.

We are still in an industry, regardless of the sector, where showing your creative process, is a direct indication of how you might approach a challenge as a young professional. Be proficient. Be clear, be concise, and be specific. If you are submitting to a well-known firm, a good human resources department is trained to vet the strong résumés and immediately get those résumés into the right hands. Most importantly, you are making a first impression. Consider the statement you want to make. Please see the checklists within this chapter that outline the specific needs an employer looks for in a résumé, but the art of the assembly has equal weight.

Knowing What Skills the Market Needs

Embrace the future. We know, as employers, the skills of young professionals are often cutting edge, but the edge continues to draw nearer. We are looking for a marriage of new skills to our existing great experience. Chances are that your potential employer, were educated as hand-drawing specialists or AutoCAD experts in the craft of delivering a commercial design project. New programs are closing in and changing the landscape of how we deliver, technology turns over every eighteen months in the market and we look for tech savvy professionals. REVIT and others are the new normal and we as employers welcome new thinkers that bring technology to the forefront. Be prepared for a technology test. It is typical that an employer will ask you to demonstrate your skills during the interview process. Many designers exaggerate their skills on a résumé, and, when put to task, will disappoint new employers. It is in your best interest to share with employers specifically where your skills lie, be clear which programs you are proficient in, but do not misrepresent yourself as an expert.

At the end of the day, how best can you communicate your design in the most efficient way? Your need to choose the tool that best articulates that to an employer. Often as professionals we have one chance, one meeting, to win over a client to the aesthetic. In some cases, we are not in the room to communicate those ideas so they must speak for themselves, not unlike, how a résumé must speak for you.

YOUR PORTFOLIO

Preparing a representative, engaging design portfolio is highly important. No only do they exhibit your creativity and your ability to solve evidence-based issues through design solutions, but they also demonstrate your technical skills. From actual physical sketches to personal Internet sites, portfolios may be made available in many forms. There are classes specifically focused on portfolios included in the curriculum of most interior design programs. This chapter seeks to work with such courses or proceed independently in an effort to set out how best to present your skills as an interior designer across a variety of media.

A **portfolio** is more than just a set of pictures, as a dictionary might describe it. For interior design work, it may be considered a visual synopsis of projects you have completed using the creative and technical skills of which you are capable. Preparing interior design portfolios, therefore, is an ongoing, progressive work because the level of your skills and project responsibilities will greatly increase over time. Initially, such important career documentation might contain

- An entire project from early sketches to completed renderings, including programming and schematic development references;

- Freehand sketches showing the progression of how you reached specific design conclusions;

CAD renderings;

Perspective and elevation drawings and isometrics;

Furniture-placement floor plans; space planning drawings;

Color boards;

Evidence of lettering abilities;

A copy of your most up-to-date résumé.

Most interior design programs now include a class devoted to portfolio preparation under Foundation for Interior Design Education and Research (FIDER) accreditation standards. This emphasis reflects the important role portfolios play throughout designers' careers. This chapter's discussion cannot take the place of an entire course devoted to portfolio preparation. It can, however, prepare you for such a class by encouraging you to gather and organize materials and provide convenient reference about assembling or updating your portfolio.

What good is a tremendous portfolio if no one ever sees it? Technology has enabled interior designers to show their work to the world with just a click or through an app. CD-ROMs allow designers to leave their work for prospects to review again and again. That is, if the designer does not already have a personal website. Established interior designers feature examples of work on their companies' sites. Often, they insert a link away from the home site to their personal one so those interested in their work may pursue further. Other options for getting your portfolio circulating include ways with which you are likely very familiar: social media. Pinterest and Instagram are two possible platforms for showing off your portfolio as you would your résumé.

INTERNSHIP PARTICIPATION

During your interior design education, you will likely be involved in an internship program. After all, internship participation is required for successful completion of many undergraduate degree programs. What realistically can you expect to gain from working with actual, professional interior designers before your leave school, while you are still learning? Why do businesses and firms make internship opportunities available? What are sponsors of internships looking for in participants?

According to its common dictionary definition, an intern is "an advanced student, or graduate usually in a professional field gaining supervised, practical experience." Internships then may include any programs providing hands-on work, directed by others. From your perspective, internships are exciting ways for you to get a taste of actual working life and conditions while completing your education. Like many students, you are probably already anticipating the day you can begin your career. A successful internship should ground that understandable excitement with an honest appraisal of how ready you are for the work life of an interior designer.

Reasons to Participate in Internships

It may seem obvious that the chief reason to participate in an internship is because it is required. Yet, there are other reasons, those having to do with what motivates you to become an interior designer. You probably have many design ideas you want to try out: thoughts about different kinds of projects you would like to complete or ideas about

Internships afford students a look at professional life and what it entails before they leave school.

working with other designers and different kinds of clients. Since you have been planning your ideal interior design business during the time spent with this book, you have ideas about the kind of business—particularly its focus and creative point of view—in which you want to be involved. Along the same, line, you may have an idea about pursuing a particular career path or working with particular individuals or organizations.

To be honest, most interns are not usually allowed to make important decisions. Some intern assignments may not seem very significant at all, in fact. Nevertheless, interns *do* get an inside look at interior design businesses, at how and why they function as they do. This is the case even if they are responsible for correctly returning vendor catalogues to the shelves or answering office telephones. Internships also permit students to have access to the expertise of experienced, successful designers. When approached in the right way, at the right time, those professionals are often happy to answer student intern questions and listen to their ideas.

Reasons Organizations Sponsor Internships

Why might firms offer internship opportunities to students? Practically speaking, they do so because they are willing and financially able to share their knowledge and skills with a new generation of soon-to-be practitioners. From the firms' financial point of view, work performed by interns is not (except as a portion of overhead costs) billable to clients. As a result, design businesses require sufficient income to justify sponsoring interns instead of, say, upgrading the office color copier. Additionally, interns require support. The firm must allocate a portion of a regular employee's time to serving as an internship supervisor, a managerial task involving direct interaction with interns themselves and program coordinators at their schools. Thus, internship programs are not "cost neutral" for firms; they give up much in the way their own resources to make the opportunity available. True, firms receive the benefits of interns' labor and time, often paying nothing or very little for them. Nevertheless, both firms and students continue to benefit from internship programs.

As noted, you are going through a rite of professional passage as you prepare to enter the interior design profession. Many established designers were in exactly the same position you are now in. They remember those experiences, good ones and not-so-good ones, of transitioning from student to professional. The desire to make those processes beneficial (not just easier) for future colleagues motivates designers to be educators and mentors. They are also on the lookout for new talent. Students who show promise, those who are creative and technically proficient and who demonstrate the ability to work with others, as a team member, during their internship are likely to make promising entry-level hires.

Student Considerations about Internships

Compensation and contacts summarize two important student considerations about internships. Some internships provide financial compensation to participants while others do not. Financial considerations, therefore, are likely to inform whether you participation in them. As a student, your disposable income is most likely limited. Tuition and supply costs, not to mention living expenses, probably consume most of your financial resources. Although some internship positions do provide monetary compensation, often that salary will be more than offset by increased taxes, transportation, and other costs associated with your participation. Receipt of a salary, as well, may impact amounts of need-based financial aid available to continue your education. If no salary is offered, students should determine whether they have the financial ability and desire to take on the added costs and effort of participating. "Run the numbers," meaning ascertain the financial impact the internship will have on you and check with appropriate financial aid sources about eligibility. Whether or not an internship offers remuneration, the desire for experience should motivate your interest and desire to do well.

"It will look good on my résumé!" Many students give this as a reason for selecting internships especially with well-known interior design or architecture firms. A positive internship experience, one that allows you to become involved in the work of the firm, should be the goal, not a shopping expedition for names and titles with which to accessorize your résumé. Those involved in running internship programs routinely stress that the experience should be used to build a network of contacts with established design professionals; to demonstrate consistent, thoughtful work habits; and to demonstrate the ability to solve problems no matter how simple or mundane. Using these as your goals, you will then be able to secure heartfelt references from established designers who genuinely want to help advance your career.

Internship Documentation and Activities

Because internships involve relationships among you, your school, and any sponsoring business, what might the latter two expect of you? In other words, what are the ways in which internships are structured, and what tasks might you be expected to perform? To be sure, each internship is unique. You may face a list of specific tasks you will be expected to complete each day, or the program may be very open-ended, with tasks assigned as available.

After you have been offered an internship position, you should ask for and obtain an internship handbook or other reference detailing activities you will have to perform and by what specific dates, to receive academic credit. You are already familiar with a number of people with whom you will have to interact. These include an academic internship coordinator and a business intern coordinator or on-site program supervisor. You may also have to consult with an academic adviser at your school to ascertain your qualifications for the program. As well, you should ascertain how your internship will affect your future coursework or graduation date.

Generally, you will be required to complete timesheets and other worksheets or logs to document your internship experience. In addition, a written report, or several of them, may be required. In a typical academic program, at least two reports may be required of internees. Usually, these are due at the midpoint and end of the program and vary in length and complexity of requirements. During the internship, students are often required to keep a journal, detailing their impressions and experiences. This might include noting events that occurred at the intern site and evaluating the sponsoring business, as well as stating an overall, objective critique of the experience. Similarly, interns can expect to receive written evaluations by program coordinators.

A gamut of possible activities await internees. These include catalog and sample/swatch filing; updating product catalogues; researching and estimating material amounts; sitting in on meetings with different stakeholders; and engaging in physical measuring, rendering, manual drafting, CAD and blueprint work, space planning, furniture arrangement planning, and project installation. Time spent in these pursuits and days on which they were performed are. Interns should expect to be called on to do a variety of tasks, some admittedly more interesting and satisfying than others—a characteristic of the working life of most professionals. Internships provide a way for students to experience this reality and develop ways of handing it.

Your experience with the details of internship documentation will benefit you throughout your working life. Graduates are increasingly required to complete the Interior Design Experience Program (IDEP), administered by NCIDQ to be eligible to take that group's credentialing exam. Participation in IDEP exposes graduates to the extensive activities NCIDQ has identified as comprising the practice of interior design. Most of those tasks are spelled out on the intern timesheet. Journals about the internship experience are required as are completing verifiable worksheets signed off on by supervisors.

PREPARATION FOR AN EMPLOYMENT INTERVIEW

Congratulations! Thanks to your organization and preparation, you have been called for an interview with a prospective employer. You may have been informed by mail, e-mail, phone, or, who knows, maybe by text message, or "tweet." The important thing is you have the interview. Now what? You need to do more preparation! What kinds of questions might you be asked during the process? What will be expected of you from prospective employers' perspectives?

What to Expect during an Interview

With a date and time for an interview with a potential employer set, you need to prepare for the big day. The structure of interviews and how they are conducted varies by employer. In some instances, one person conducts the interview with the job applicant. In other cases, two or more interviewers conduct a team, or group, interview. Applicants will not usually be informed beforehand about which approach they will face

BOX 14.2

INTERNSHIP TIMESHEET

Intern Name _____   For Week Ending _____

Intern Coordinator _____

Intern Supervisor _____   Internship Location _____

Please indicate the amount of time you engaged in the following tasks during the subject week.
Use only the hourly method approved by the internship coordinator.

Tasks	Monday	Tuesday	Wednesday	Thursday	Friday	Overtime	Total
Catalog filing							
Sample/swatch filing							
Telephone reception							
Correspondence							
Updating product information							
Processing orders							
Office-wide meetings							
Workroom meetings							
Senior-staff meetings							
Rendering							
Manual drafting							
CAD work							
Blueprint work							
Researching materials							
Est. material amounts							
Physical measuring							
Space planning							
Furniture arrangement							
Color/material selection							
Concept board construction							
Construction-site visit							
Contractor meetings							
Installation time							
Assigned research							
Professional practices							
Other *(specify)*							
						Total hours	

Notes:

during the interview. Therefore, if you are an entry-level candidate, come mentally prepared to meet any number of interviewers. Many times, the person directly supervising the position for which you have applied and, perhaps, their manager will be present.

As you progress in your design career and seek positions requiring greater managerial authority and business decision-making skills, it will become more likely that you will face multiple interviewers over the course of several interviews. For example, more experienced professional designers seeking lateral career moves (that is, going from one mid to senior-level position without having to start again as an associate) can expect to meet with a series of interviewers such as firm managers, partners, and even the staff and work groups they might oversee once they have obtained the position.

Despite all your preparations, you may be surprised at the interview itself. Some interviewers may appear to be less well prepared than you expected. Many are likely to have had to squeeze the time for your interview into their own already busy schedules and, therefore, have not been able to become acquainted with the details of your file prior to the interview. In such circumstances, work to make the interviewer understand your accomplishments as easily as you can. Interweave in the conversation what you know of the firm and its priorities with what you have learned and already experienced. Make the case for your being a good fit with the firm, if you truly believe that. Furthermore, it may be helpful for you to review your résumé, section by section, before the interview is too far along and if the interviewer indicates doing so would be helpful. Regardless of the specific interviewer or number of interviewers you speak with, it is important to stay focused on what brought you to the interview in the first place—the position you seek. Another area of surprise may be where your interview takes place. Perhaps it will occur in a quiet conference room or office, or maybe not! Semipublic areas of workrooms, lounges, and even coffee shops may be venues for job interviews. Stay focused even as other activities and voices vie for attention.

Interview Formats

Not just whom, or how many interviewers, nor where the interview takes place, the kinds of interviews you may experience could also vary. In other words, there is no set form for job interviews. Prepare to be flexible in this regard, too.

Some interviewers use a dialogue-based approach, or a conversational style of interview. Others can seem more like being questioned in a court of law! Between these extremes are several other kinds of interviews to note and to be prepared to experience. There are approximately four generally recognized kinds of job interviews.

- **The conversational interview** These may not seem like interviews at all. During conversational interviews, the applicant and the person or group conducting the interview talk about a variety of topics that may not seem to have anything at all to do with the available position or even with the job. The thinking behind this approach is to get the applicant to open up, allowing interviewers to get a sense of the applicants' abilities to organize and take control of a seemingly random situation. If you encounter an interviewer who appears to use this approach, interview experts suggest turning these open-ended conversations into collaborations. For example, ask the interviewer about job responsibilities, the number of people to whom you would report. In other words, turn unfocused questions into dialogue about the position and its responsibilities. By doing so, you may be better able to discuss your education and experiences in the context of stated job requirements.

- **Stress interview** This approach is intended to be intimidating. The thinking behind this approach is that the interview in some way simulates actual conditions experienced by those working in the position for which you have applied. For example, many new designers must contend with unyielding time pressure and the demands of conflicting interpersonal relationships in the workplace. There will be clients unhappy with project progress calling, contractors complaining about the work of others in front of you, and team members who have not produced needed deliverables. You need to deal with issues such as these all at the same time. The ability to handle confrontation and pressure of the kind this example represents may be what the interviewer is seeking to ascertain. Are you up to these kinds of tasks?

    In this type of interview, you are asked confrontational questions requiring you to explain and justify every aspect of your résumé and portfolio in excruciating detail. Although all interviews seem to be challenging, the stress interview is especially designed to test how applicants respond to grilling, or to rapid-fire questions about what the interviewer perceives as inconsistencies in statements made or claims asserted by the applicant about his or her accomplishments or skills. Detaching yourself from this admittedly trying process and viewing it as something other than a personal attack are suggested coping strategies. Knowing your résumé content and being able to justify your technical skills thoroughly are further strategies for success.
- **Behavioral or psychological interview** As you advance in your career, you may come across other forms of interview techniques as you move from job to job. For more senior management positions, you may be confronted with highly sophisticated questions based on behavior profiles the employer has developed to identify personal and professional characteristics believed to be most appropriate for a particular position. This is the essence of the behavioral or psychological interview.
- **Case study interview** Should you choose to apply your interior design background in a business, rather than a design studio setting, you may encounter lengthy interviews known as case study interviews. Interviews of this type, in which you are presented with a series of facts about a business, are used to gauge your ability to solve business problems.

Questions an Employer May Ask You

Once you are in an interview, what might you expect to be asked? Basic kinds of interview questions include the following:

1. Tell us about yourself and why you are interested in this position.
2. What do you know about our business (or firm)?
3. How did you learn about this position and about our business?
4. Tel us why you believe you are qualified for this position.
5. What are your career plans or goals, and how do you expect to accomplish them?
6. What would you consider to be your greatest strength and greatest weakness?
7. What do you consider your largest achievement and your worst mistake?
8. What did you do to overcome your weaknesses and to correct your mistakes?
9. What about the interior design profession (and interior design) excites you?
10. What got you interested in interior design in the first place?
11. Whose design work do you admire and why?
12. How do you feel when your work is criticized?
13. Why should we hire you?

Are there "good" answers to these questions? Every interview is unique, as are the position sought, the location and situation of the event itself, and the people involved. What one person might say, might come across differently, might sound stilted or contrived in another. What might be your guide?

It may help if you remember two concepts: *focus* and *needs*. Quite simply, remain focused on the position itself, *not* on the person conducting the interview, his or her personality (or your perceptions of it), and even your anxieties, which are naturally present at such times. You are there to do a job: get a job! Think about the needs of the employer, and present enthusiasm in learning what the employer expects and needs from anyone holding the position. Appear, in other words, to be looking for whether there is a "fit" with you and the potential employer.

Many times, interviewers will run through a list of tasks and activities the successful job candidate will be expected to perform. If the interviewer seems unclear about what those needs are and what is expected, make sure you ask for more detail about job requirements. Is there a final takeaway about how to handle job interview questions? Consider that your response to any interview question should demonstrate how your personality, knowledge, and technical skill—you—will make their choice obvious. You are the right person for the job!

Questions to Ask an Employer

Employers expect you to ask questions of them and their businesses as well. In fact, most like to see candidates exhibit an interest in and appreciation of their firm, or studio *as* a commercial enterprise. When it comes to questions candidates might ask, consider a balance. On the one hand, it is not a good idea to appear to immediately want a job with responsibilities beyond those specified for the job sought, such as those a high-level manager mind have. On the other, it is equally unwise to appear unconcerned about the business and its future. Stating you would like to grow with the business—then explaining how—may be one way to indicate you understand this balance. Finally, consider that potential employers are listening to and considering questions job candidates ask. With these thoughts in mind, consider the following questions as possible ones you might ask a potential employer:

1. What specific responsibilities are expected of someone who holds this position?
2. To whom will the successful candidate report?
3. What are your plans for the future of this business, both in the near and more distance future?
4. What characteristics do you think are important for a candidate to have to be successful in this position?
5. How many people are employed by the company, and how is the organization structured (i.e. as a partnership or corporation)?
6. What resources and opportunities does this company provide to employees to enable them to grow and develop as professionals?
7. Are you interviewing many other candidates for this position?
8. Do you need any other information from me to help you make a decision?
9. Can I clear up any questions about my résumé?
10. When and how do you plan to announce your decision about filling this position?

With these questions in mind, you now have a better idea about how to interact with interviewers. Yet, after reading the previous questions, can you think of an important one that appears to have been omitted? Continue further and the next section will provide the answer.

Key Interview Issues

This text identifies three general areas of concern when it comes to handling interview questions. These issues relate to salary discussions, questions employers are prohibited from asking job candidates; and some obvious but overlooked actions that employment experts universally agree should not occur during job interviews.

- **Salary discussions** Should you mention salary, the one question not considered previously? If so, when should you bring up the topic? Should you simply take any amount offered? First, consider this issue as it relates to the employment application and them to the interview itself.

  Many employers state they will not consider applications that do not include current salary information. Others hiring are silent on this matter. In the former, applicants may have no choice, realistically, but to state the salary amount they currently receive or expect to obtain, if the employment process with that particular employer is to go any further. Many employment experts advise against providing this information if it is requested and not to volunteer it if not. Prospective employers can ascertain salary information when checking applicants' backgrounds. Since outright dishonesty about this, or any other verifiable information, will likely be discovered, attempts to inflate your current salary in an effort to raise salary amounts offered for a future position are discouraged.

  More commonly, applications ask job seekers to supply expected salary figures for the position they seek. Such inquiries may even be made on the spot, during employment interviews. What should you do then? This aspect of employment negotiations requires previous research on your part. What is the pay scale for the job you seek in the geographic area in which you are looking? For information of this kind, it may be necessary to turn to interior design career professional resources. These can include the ASID (and Canadian) Internet resources.

  As you conduct you own salary research, consider your prospective employer's location (salaries may be lower in smaller cities with less demand for interior design services). Also, take note of the size of the design firm where you are seeking employment (many larger firms may offer more in the way of salary but expect more of their workers). While not perfect, another way to find out salary information is to network and ask others about what to expect in the way of pay.

- **Prohibited interview questions** According to federal and state laws, it is considered illegal for future employers to ask job candidates some questions. Enforcement of these laws, should a complaint be filed, is carried out by U.S. agencies such as the Equal Employment Opportunity Commission (EEOC) and state employment and human rights agencies.

  In general, these laws prohibit questions related to applicants' ages, ethnicities, religious beliefs, and gender. For example, specific questions about such topics as applicants' exact ages, locations of birth, or religious beliefs, or any question pertaining to gender, marital status, or family size plans fall into these prohibited categories.

  Employment advisers suggest you either ignore such questions (by refusing to answer) or ask why any such question might have any bearing on qualities necessary for the job under consideration. If applicants believe they were denied the job, that is subject to discrimination, based on any of the grounds noted here, they should consider seeking counsel to determine their legal options.

- **What not to do in interview settings** Remember the focus should be on your accomplishments and abilities during an interview. Any employment candidate is advised not to engage in two general kinds of activities. The first involves the use of body language that distracts the attention of interviewers away from the applicant. Poor posture, slouching, large arm or hand gestures, and swearing are just some examples. Wearing extremely avant-garde, out of the ordinary, highly revealing, or otherwise provocative clothing, garments distract attention, probably will have the same distracting effect as body language.

  The second category of what not to do in interviews involves falsifying previous educational or work-related experiences. This includes providing fictitious references in order to create false impressions about either kind of experience. Virtually all employers perform background checks through which they will uncover such falsehoods. Typically, employers will reject applicants, or dismiss them if already hired, when such issues come to light.

What perspective might help you mentally prepare for the rigors of finding a job and of taking part in interviews? Consider the following excerpt as you set out on your interior design career.

NOTES FROM THE FIELD

This chapter has explored those issues employers consider when reviewing intern and job applications. But what about issues you should explore about such internship sponsors or employers? The following case study addresses this perspective.

What should you look for in potential employers?
My hope is that all young professional have an outstanding experience with their first employers. I did! It colored my view of the industry in an insightful and positive way. It would be a credit to our industry if this were the norm. Some advice: Start by researching potential employers. What firms are doing the type of work you are interested in? What makes them tick? Where is the industry heading, and what can you add to the conversation? Interior design is a business, and that business is fueled by other businesses. Understanding what feeds those areas of industry cannot be underestimated. Interior design firms promote their work for two reasons: to draw new clients and to attract world-class talent.

Timing is everything. If you have a true focus on working for a firm, keep them in your sights, but don't pester them. Our practice interviews many talented students every year, but only a few positions are available. Many firms have a minimum number of years of experience entrance requirement, this would be important to know in advance.

Do not underestimate small firms as first jobs.
Many professionals early in their careers place a great deal of focus on landing in a large firm. A large firm by today's standards would include multiple offices, typically more than one hundred staff. There are benefits to both large and small firms; allow me to expand on both. Larger firms tend to be more established and have refined a mentor program that has been proven over time. There are more layers to navigate. Larger firms also tend to have more breadth in their service offerings, and the services they offer their clients are also changing; therefore, getting exposure to that spectrum is important. Smaller firms offer young professionals more specific depth in task assignments. Given that there tend to be fewer specialists on staff, young professionals, in my experience, often build exposure to more areas of a project. They are often in the room during client information exchange and build experience in construction administration.

Practical Activity

Simply describe your internship experience to your class. What were your expectations? Were they met? Did you feel support from those at the firm? Identify the sponsoring firm or company. Then describe your activities there, who you met, and the "atmosphere" of the place. Would you work for that firm as a full-time employee should they ask? Give reasons why or why not. Your class will be interested in your experience and will want to compare it to their own internships. Invite comparisons and then, as a class, decide factors that make for "great," "good," "satisfactory," and "unsatisfactory" internships.

Review Questions

1. What are the functions of résumés, and what are their component parts?

2. What three forms of résumés are commonly used, and when might one be more preferable to use over others?

3. What is the purpose of a cover letter, and what are some basic types of cover letters?

4. Describe portfolios and their purposes. What do they usually contain?

5. Why should interior designers keep their portfolios current as their levels of experience and expertise increase?

6. Describe internships and why they are important to both students and the interior design firms sponsoring them.

7. How might you incorporate social media as part of your job search? What are the benefits or doing so?

8. What are the focus and needs concepts described in the chapter as they relate to interviews? Why are they important to remember?

9. According to sources in this chapter, what is one way to address salary concerns during the interview process? As well, what are several activities prospective employees should not do during an interview?

10. What might be the benefits of working in a small to mid-sized design firm instead of a large concern?

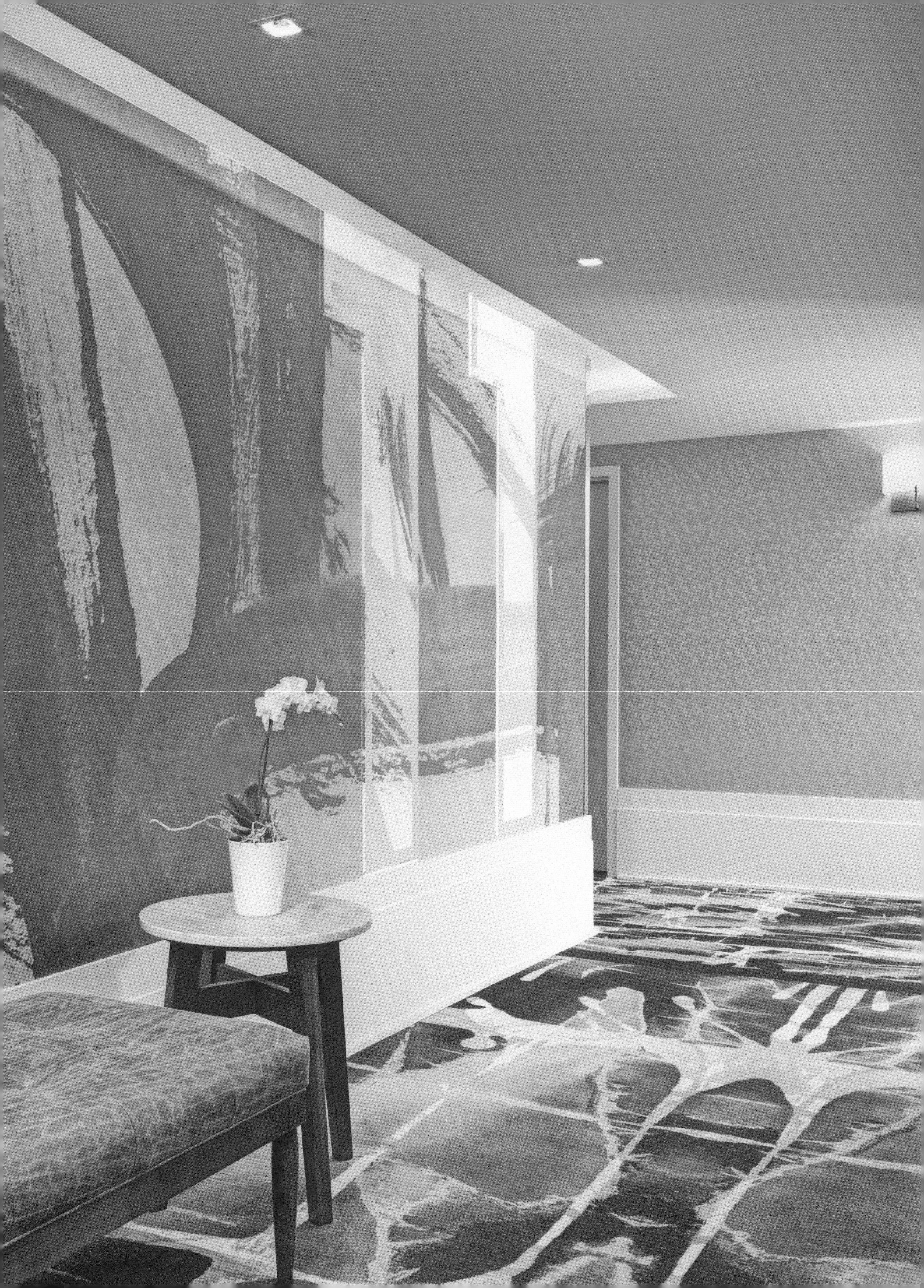

CHAPTER 15
PLANNING YOUR CAREER

MENTOR MEMO
I have the best job in the world. What job description can state that every day will be different and no two clients will ever be the same, making every day an adventure? I suspect that there are very few. For a professional interior designer, it is a job the wraps both beauty and function into one story. I warn you, this is a field that requires continuing education, which you will both hate and love, hopefully more of the latter. It is a marathon not a sprint, and you won't realize how much you have learned until you need to explain it to your peers and new designers working for you. Many designers choose to become product representatives, or talented educators. Both are great fields and are necessary to the design industry. In the event you choose to stay in the interior design field, often (but not always) a choice will need to be made: What portion of the design process do I excel at?

After reading this chapter, you will be able to

- Identify your personal interests and use them to focus your first career choices;
- Describe career options available to interior designers;
- Discuss the merits and challenges found in different work situations;
- Explain emerging practice areas and issues in interior design;
- Define the "Glocal" phenomenon and explain how it applies to interior designers and their work.

INTRODUCTION TO PLANNING YOUR CAREER

Who doesn't want to have the best job in the world? It is possible you, too, can come to believe you have obtained just that. To be sure, getting to that point will take time, careful planning, hard work, and, perhaps, a bit of luck. For now, you should have as much information as possible to consider perspectives to guide your decisions. You will find those very things here. Going forward, be inspired! With your knowledge of design principles and practices, you have many career directions. You may pursue interior design, or work

Interior designers seek to improve the quality of interior spaces throughout their careers.

in other areas with the knowledge you have. So, which career path might you choose first? How might you later transition your career as your experiences grow over time? This chapter surveys but some of the exciting possibilities to consider as you answer those questions, as you work your way toward your own best job. As part of this overview, you will find career insights shared by a practicing, accomplished interior designer. This is not the last but the very first of many chapters to come in your career.

CAREER EVALUATION: IDENTIFYING YOUR INTERESTS AND FOCUSING ON YOUR FIRST CAREER CHOICES

As you approach the world of work, you may wonder: "What's next?" Before identifying specific career options, step back, take time, and define what is important to you. When planning your initial career focus, many career advisers suggest doing such tasks as identifying your inspiration and defining what really interests you. Then, with those ideas in mind, they suggest applying what you know toward those motivations. So, if you are unsure about what to do regarding your career, try this idea: Step back from

Commercial interior designers conceive and realize spaces such as multiple hotel suites, each attractive to travelers and all profitable to businesses.

276 • PART 5 YOU AND YOUR CAREER

interior design altogether! Instead, think about those pastimes and activities you enjoy. Perhaps you like theater or shopping? Maybe traveling, experiencing the excitement found in places you visit, is your passion. Do you collect items on those trips? Then blog about them and how and where you acquired them? What sports are you interested in? Maybe your favorite pastime involves working with children?

The kinds of things you may like to do are endless. So, too, are the options available to you in interior design, based on those interests! After asking yourself such preliminary questions, explore how interior design, your new profession, can meld with your long-standing interests. What might you do as an interior designer to help others enjoy these activities? For example, how might you apply your knowledge of interior design to make public spaces such as theaters, shops, and sporting venues more attractive, functionally more efficient, even memorable in their own right? Similarly, how might you assist other collectors, to better address their needs for display, storage, and security of their item, through interior design? If you enjoy spending time with children, how might you apply the evidence-based programming skills you have acquired to better serve the needs of parents, schools, and childcare centers?

A passion for interior design interested you enough to study it; discovering and pursuing ways to apply that passion may be your key to career success. Career options exist. You just have to look for them. An overview of but a few of those options can help frame your initial career search. The following excerpt will help to put any career choice you might make into the larger context of the interior design profession and its practices as previously described throughout this text.

MENTOR MEMO

If the practice of interior design were a stool, there would be three legs to that stool. One would be pure design, the aesthetic delivery of the solution. The second would be business development and predesign services, which entails finding the client, building a relationship, and preparing them for the creative process through strategic planning or programming. And the third is delivery, which involves as much creativity and depth of knowledge as the other two but speaks to the execution and second part of the process. Ten years into my own career I chose the management and business development (BD) leg of the stool. And, though my career path had afforded me the opportunity to work in the other focuses, BD is where I seemed best suited. And, something I learned from my mentor, and the review process.

Simply because you choose the area to focus on, does not mean you are off the hook for the others. True designers are always thinking about securing the work and the tools needed to deliver it well. Regardless of the sector—healthcare, education, commercial, residential—every team or person tends to have strength in one of these areas. Just know that it takes all three legs of the stool to deliver a project and have it be successful.

INTERIOR DESIGN CAREER OPTIONS

From obvious to obscure, available career options may be described using the broad categories defining the interior design profession. Each area of practice comes with details to know, to interpret for yourself. By doing so, you will be better able to describe what these disciplines entail and whether they are right for you.

Bathroom and home spa planning is one highly specialized area that attracts many to interior design.

Residential Interior Design

Residential work is among the most talked about and publicized areas of the interior design profession. Think of the many magazines, television shows, and blogs related to this specialization and it is easy to see how extensive interest is in this area. As you have worked with this text, you have come to understand the disciple of **residential interior design** focuses on planning and executing safe, efficient, and attractive nonpublic spaces. These are usually dwellings of individual homeowners.

Within the ambit of residential interior design are many subspecialties such as kitchen, bath, and closet design; home theater and game room design; "aging in place" design; and design for residential spaces intended for artwork and collectable item presentation. Increasingly, interior designers who embrace and apply new technologies as part of their design intent are gaining recognition in this discipline. Would you know what to do, for example, if a prospective client asked you to synch the physical functions of their residence such as lights and climate controls to a "wearable"?

Other specialized areas of residential interior design include historic renovation and period-recreation design, residential lighting, media, and acoustic design, even private yacht and airplane interior design. Residential interior designers strive to establish spaces that reflect their clients' personalities, achievements, even aspirations, nearly becoming mind readers to their clients' unspoken desires. How do you feel about being entrusted not just to carry out not a project but to realize someone else's dream home?

Residential interior design work is cyclical. In other words, it "comes and goes Successful designers develop networks, or "pipelines" of prospective clients. By doing so, they are better able to have their next projects—and paychecks—lined up before and as current ones are completed. Establishing and maintaining such associations, relentlessly marketing their business, and making new contacts with interested (and financially qualified) clients all the time takes sustained energy, enduring patience, and, usually, sources of income such as a savings account when work is lacking. Would working under such conditions appeal to you?

Not only can residential work be variable, it can, as well, require unique interpersonal communication skills. Many clients may not fully know the profession and how interior designers work. Simply put, residential interior designers often must negotiate with prospective and actual clients about issues such as their own duties and fees as well as project expenses. Doing so can be a challenge. Social norms remain about discussing personal finances, including asking whether clients have the financial ability required to complete even the smallest projects. As you can imagine, these kinds of situations can be awkward if not handled well. For their part, designers may be at a disadvantage because they do not know actual project costs until they "cost it out" with vendors, providers, and others. Furthermore, clients may be successful business executives, entrepreneurs, and investors. As such, these individuals may be interested in receiving the benefits of designers' services at the "best" possible price—for them not the designer. This gives rise to an important question: Do you know your business as a residential interior designer well enough to raise blunt financial concerns to clients and understand when their business suggestions are not in the best financial interest of your business? One question sums up this issue. Who—you or the client—will pay for project merchandise? By allowing clients to do so, residential designers effectively take "off the table" one of the most historically remunerative methods by which they are compensated.

Throughout any money issues that may arise, residential interior designers may also be called upon to work within the realities of their clients' lives. In this fraught arena, designers must find professionally reasonable, fair, and, for them, financially profitable, resolutions in face of such myriad issues as births, "understandings," separations, divorces, and deaths. Would you be able to work under such conditions? Suppose a client of a current project introduces you to a new spouse, someone who fancies his or her skills in interior design and wants to "work with you" to complete the project. Would whether or not you would be willing to go forward under such a "partnership" depend on how paid up your account is with the client?

Successful residential interior designers can gain "rock star" status in their communities, even throughout the world. Creative talent, business acumen, and interpersonal adroitness, all coupled with keen communicative abilities are often cited as reasons for such renown. Do you think you have such skills?

Commercial or Contract Interior Design

Commercial, or **contract interior design,** is thought to be so named because projects in this discipline have been recognized and governed through formal "contracts" between interior designers, architecture and engineering firms, and business clients. Those clients may be corporations, both large and small, local and international in scale and include banks, law firms, hotels, retail stores, real estate developers, or, sometimes, very wealthy individuals.

Commercial interior design focuses on the establishment, modification, or otherwise enhancement of physical environments destined for use by large numbers of people. These spaces may be for nonpermanent, nonresidential use. In this respect, stores, schools, offices, theaters, restaurants, libraries, sports complexes, almost any interior the public experiences falls within this practice area. Locations with limited, controlled public access, including those with residential aspects, may also be included as with hotels, apartments, and even prisons.

To recap from previous chapters, commercial projects often begin when a design firm responds to an RFP, or request for proposal. These are, essentially, contests open to any and all participants. However, prospective clients often specify entrant qualifications, such as requiring past experience with projects similarly sized or budgeted to that proposed. From many possible contenders, there may be only a few design firms realistically positioned to respond. RFP documents often spell out highly detailed project requirements designers need to address and, to that end, require extensive project documentation. Thus, RFP-originated projects are challenging to address and require extensive use of firm resources just to make a submission, much less gain the project. To put this in this chapter's perspective, ask whether you would enjoy working on RFP documents, not knowing if you or your firm will obtain the project for which you may have worked so hard. Might your answer change after knowing most large firms have dedicated, salaried staff responsible for just such tasks?

This text has explored a great many business aspects of this specialty. The Mentor Memos have detailed experiential aspects of this kind of work as you have followed. From those recounts, you may have noted contract design work is highly detailed and disciplined. Contract interior designers place emphasis on project programming, evidence gathering, stakeholder input, and development of processes that integrate factual findings with ascertained goals, health and safety concerns, and, of course, engaging, interactive design. They are responsible for staying abreast of building and safety codes, "best practices" construction standards, and business conditions not just in their home countries, but wherever their projects are located. Would such challenges engage you?

Interior designers specializing in commercial work also are increasingly required to develop multidimensional relationships with other professionals. The design-build process, defined later, is one example of how commercial interior designers are now bringing projects to completion, especially international ones. This passage indicates commercial interior designers must be "team players", even when their role may not be clear—or made clear—to some clients. As noted in previous chapters, commercial interior designers quite frequently must work with licensed architects in order for projects to begin, to even be approved by local governments. Taken together, that fact and the following insight underscores a challenge commercial interior designers currently face: receiving recognition for their expertise and time to say nothing of the value they, as professionals, ultimately add to projects. That obstacle may well change over time through legal means, but it remains persistent at present. How would you feel about working with others under such conditions? What does this concept mean, practically? The following excerpt may help illustrate.

MENTOR MEMO

The prevalence of design build is also typical in international practice. Design-build suggests the designer and the contractor are working together and hired together as a team. The fees for design services are rolled into the complete cost of the project. We see more design-build in Asia and Malaysia than we do in North America. The P3 (Public-Private Partnerships) model, would not fall into this category. In DB, the design services are often given away at no cost. The professionals providing these services are paid by the contractor directly. The optics of this model are contradictory to establishing your credible value to a client and establishing value in the delivery model. This model seems to suit clients that are interested in very quick buildouts, and very tight budgets.

Retail and Wholesale Interior Design Professionals

Do you enjoy keeping up with the newest trends in interior design, the products incorporating the most innovative technologies? To borrow a phrase, do you "work well with others," such as other interior designers and those in construction professions. Do you also have a passion for detail? **Sales associates** in retail establishments and **vendor representatives (reps)** in trade-only showrooms often are degreed, accredited interior designers who enjoy sales. It makes sense that full-fledged professionals would be hired by these businesses. They have been instructed in the formalities of product specification, detailed end-user concerns, and building code compliance. With that background, associates and reps are able to assist consumers and other designers with their product knowledge and to specify, order, and install their companies' items. While both professions involve sales, there are subtle differences in how these kinds of establishments operate. How do you feel about working in sales as the principal way of earning a living?

Retail Sales Associates

Exciting career possibilities exist for interior designers in retail sales. Furniture and furnishings retailers selling merchandise directly to consumers frequently hire degreed, accredited interior designers. You are likely familiar with these establishments. They may be large, freestanding stores, or sections of department and specialty stores, each devoted to selling furniture, rugs, window treatments, accessories, and other decorative items.

Usually, retail stores offer opportunities to work on residential projects; however, designers may also take on small commercial projects such as individual offices. These stores can serve as platforms for designers, particularly those not long out of school. From the personal contacts they make working in retail stores, designers may be able to develop a client base and open their own studios. For example, designers may develop personal relationships with store customers over time, assisting first with initial purchases and then with then small projects, perhaps later being in charge of the interior design work for an entire house. This career offers potentially lucrative opportunities to designers able to develop a cadre of clients from whom they receive not just projects but referrals to yet more clients. In this way, they are able to build a record of successive sales and income over time.

Designers working in retail typically are paid a small hourly wage combined with commissions earned from the merchandise they sell. Some stores are strictly "straight commission," meaning associates earn nothing if they do not sell or earn only a small "draw" salary for their time. Both approaches can produce high earnings for designers who work out of established stores and have built a regular clientele base with an extensive referral network of new customers. However, retail sales may be less satisfactory for those without the financial ability to withstand periods where few or no sales occur. Benefits such as health or retirement plan participation vary depending on the size and location of the retailer—another factor to take into account when considering retail sales. The emphasis in retail businesses is on the sale of merchandise carried in or ordered through the store. Even though this arrangement offers opportunities to those with strong interpersonal and sales skills, retail work may not hold the interest of designers interested in more advanced interior design work. How about you? What do you think?

Retail, it should be noted, may prove limiting to even those designers with strong selling skills and established clienteles. Stores may limit the range of products available. It is not uncommon for stores to require designers working there to specify only items produced by the group of manufacturers already represented in the store. Thus, designers are limited to selling items "off the floor," that is, already on hand, or that can be ordered from such existing suppliers. This arrangement can be disadvantageous to clients, as they are shown only goods carried by the store, not those that might be better suited to the needs of their project.

As you are aware, designers provide more services than simply making merchandise available to clients. A logical question is whether retailers require designers to charge fees for such activities as producing schematics, even time spent in project management. Retailers, typically, do not make such demands. Rather, stores offset the expense of such activities (for which designers in other settings would have charged) against the revenue generated from the retail sales of merchandise. That markup could be equal to perhaps 50 or 100 percent of the wholesale cost of the merchandise. This means, simply, commissions earned by the designer from sales "include" whatever fee they might have earned performing design- and project-related tasks.

Vendor and Showroom Representatives

Careers in sales for interior designers are not limited to retail stores. Recall the showrooms you may have seen in trade marts, design centers, and other to-the-trade venues. Companies found in them include such business as Hermann-Miller, Knoll, and Steelcase. These **dealers** often hire degreed, accredited interior designers to work exclusively with their product line, or with those of a few manufacturers. Dealers in office furniture, in this example, have a staff of interior designers knowledgeable in issues such as space planning and capable of developing ways to use those manufacturers' products to meet the needs of users. A later section of this chapter explores issues that arise when showrooms and others do not hire educated, experienced, and accredited designers. Dealer showroom-based designers work with law and medical offices, among other clients, to plan office landscapes for efficient, safe, and attractive use. Designers working in dealer showrooms need to have knowledge of business practices such as the competitive bidding process and standards of building construction as well as state and local codes related to commercial buildings.

Designers employed by office furniture dealers are usually assigned to a team comprised of other designers. Together, this crew works on a series of projects by completing different tasks. Some team members may work on project issues such as space planning and schematic design preparation, whereas others focus on procurement of goods from the manufacturer by preparing and reviewing detailed specifications and purchase orders. Other staff designers may be responsible for calculating and administering bids the company submits to clients. These teams are usually called upon to present the dealer's design proposals once completed. As with any business, staff interior designers are called upon to prospect for new clients and develop referrals from existing ones.

Office furnishings dealers are not the only avenues for interior designers interested in working in commercial sales. In recent years, specialized dealers in a number of product lines have opened showrooms. Manufacturers of kitchen, bathroom, and closet components, often of very high quality and with correspondingly high retail prices, employ interior designers. These professionals often obtain specialized designations form professional groups such as the National Kitchen and Bath Association. As with their office furnishings counterparts, these designers usually work with only one, or perhaps a very few, product lines. Typically, they are knowledgeable about product details and how best to specify their installation.

Office furnishings dealers compensate staff designers by means of a salary and some benefits, such as participation in company-sponsored health and retirement plans. Designers may also receive a commission, or percentage of the sales price, of certain types of merchandise they sell, usually accessories or other selected items the dealer wishes to promote. Many entry-level designers seek out employment in dealer showrooms so they can gain experience while earning a predicable income.

There are several considerations to note about employment in dealer showrooms. The first may be the inherent limitations of the work. Designers often have little or no say about the clients or projects with whom they are required to work. In addition, designers must specify only those products or services provided by the dealer. These constraints may hinder designers wanting to select their own clients, projects, and products, as they would in private practice.

External economic factors play into the decision on the part of designers to work in dealer showrooms. During robust economies, greater demand for design services usually exists. Businesses and consumers feel more confident about spending to improve their establishments and homes; many opportunities exist for designers interested in working with dealers. In less prosperous time, conversely, less or no demand exists for such highly specialized products and for the dealers selling them. Then, showrooms significantly cut back staff numbers, even close their doors in certain locations. Designers without other professional avenues to pursue often find themselves out of work.

Academic Institutions

Did you have a special teacher, one who encouraged or even challenged you to pursue your interests to the best of your ability? If so, you know how important educators can be to others. Why not consider becoming such an influence to a new generation of students, working to prepare them to join the interior design profession? How might you pursue a career in interior design education? What career options are available?

The instructors you have encountered throughout your college-level interior design courses likely have both masters and Ph.D. (Doctorate) degrees. They find professional satisfaction in conducting research projects, writing, and promoting education. Should you consider an academic career, becoming a full professor of interior design, for example, you will likely follow their example. That means more years of education after obtaining your bachelor's degree. As you will find, colleges and universities require tenure track instructors (those seeking to advance through associate and assistant positions to full professor status) to have advanced degrees, published research papers in academic journals, and experience teaching. NCIDQ certification may be required, too, for instructors of studio, interior design practicum, courses. As well, schools often seek candidates proficient in obtaining grants, donations, and endowments to finance academic programs and courses. Academic instructors, thus, are called upon to know about "business development," just as those in design and architecture firms are.

To be sure, there are other avenues for interior designers interested in education. Opportunities exist to teach as nontenured faculty, referred to as adjuncts or lecturers.

Typically, schools offer these positions on a term-by-term basis, or as needed; they may not be permanent employment positions. Adjunct faculty members are compensated financially for their work, but they may not be eligible for full employment benefits afforded tenure-track faculty. The attractions of such positions are they allow interior designers the opportunity to share their knowledge as instructors, learn from their academic peers, and maintain their own design practices. If academia appeals to you, discuss with your professors how you might first work as an adjunct at your school and what is required to be a full professor.

Other Interior Design-Related Careers to Consider

This chapter has, so far, suggested some of the more obvious career paths and has sought to explain what they involve from a variety of perspectives. However, more career options exist besides those! Interior design skills are applicable to and necessary for a number of other industries. Have your thought about careers in the following industries, such as special event or convention planning? The follow chart may get you thinking about an exciting career, one you never even imagined.

THE MERITS AND CHALLENGES OF DIFFERENT WORK SITUATIONS

Do you want to go solo, to be your own boss and have control over a business you can truly call your own? On the other hand, do you see yourself as a corporate "player," someone who thrives in a structured working environment of other professionals? Solo or corporate? That theme has played throughout this chapter. What further considerations might there be about these different work environments, issues that haven't been addressed previously?

Many interior designers are self-employed and work from their own offices. Imagine the opportunities to go after the business—and only the business—that you want! Imagine, as well, having to complete projects, pay bills, maintain studio resources, and even answer phones (among other tasks), while trying to obtain new, profitable clients and have a personal or family life. Are you up for such a juggling act? If you truly are interested in having your own interior design business, why not ask someone who has done just that? How have they coped with issues such as the ones described here? What advice do they have for you? To be sure, challenges abound for those who work solo in interior design; however, many of those practitioners wouldn't have it any other way. Are you one of them?

Interior designers who work in trade showrooms as well as commercial interior designers work in highly structured settings. In these businesses and firms, they usually have formal job titles and are responsible for specific tasks. Career movement may be slow, as these designers may encounter a dilemma. For example, those working in showrooms, have no say about projects they work on; they may have as much experience as, or perhaps even more than, the designer of record, yet they receive no credit for their work, solutions they bring about, or problems they solve. They remain unknown. Associate interior designers in large firms may also toil on a succession of projects, doing the same kinds of tasks. Completing "spec" packs over and over and working on

BOX 15.1

CAREERS LIST

Many designers are self-employed or work in design or architectural firms. However, design skills are used in a number of industries. If you are thinking about a career in interior design, you may want to consider one of the following occupations:

Entertainment
Design staff (in-house) for
Amusement parks
Casinos
Movies
Television
Theaters/Auditoriums

Facilities Management
Facilities manager for
Assisted-living communities
Healthcare facilities
Industry
Office buildings
Museums
Parks
Public buildings and universities

Government and institutions
Design staff (in-house) for
Colleges, universities, and schools
Federal, state, and local government institutions (public buildings, schools, prisons)
Healthcare facilities (hospitals, clinics)
Medical furniture companies
Museum display designs
Hospitality industries (hotels, motels, restaurants, convention, and conference centers)
Senior housing
Special-needs housing

Manufacturers
Design staff (in-house) for
Carpet and floor coverings
Fabrics/textiles
Furniture
Lighting
Wall coverings

In-house interior design staff
Marketing staff
Product design staff
Sales representatives
Trade-show exhibit design staff
Education
Product design and development
Product/furniture design

Offices and Corporations
In-house design staff for corporations:
Office-design firms
Office-supply companies
Systems furniture dealerships
Real estate companies
Large developers with space-planning departments
Rehabilitation developers with in-house design departments
Freelance consultants for small firms
Staff space planner
Residences/residential developments
Children's spaces
Custom furniture design
Design to accommodate aging-in-place
Design for the physically challenged
Kitchen and bath design
Window treatment specialties

Retail
Colorists
Exhibit and display design firm staff
Home-fashion coordinator
Lighting design
Retail-store designers/space planners
Retail visual merchandising
Sales managers
Wholesale showroom designs

minute details, these designers usually do not oversee entire projects until they are well along in their careers. They are, in other words, responsible for necessary, tedious, but over time dead end work. They remain unknown as well. Such a dilemma is further compounded by the fact that to advance from firm associate to principal (one who is entitled to a share in the firm's profits and expenses) often requires designers to identify and obtain new clients for the firm. How can they go after new business and also service projects of those who already are principals of the design firm? Developing networks of new clients can be daunting under such circumstances. How might you find ways both to be a valued team member and at the same time to advance your career?

EMERGING ISSUES AND AREAS OF PRACTICE

Remaining up-to-date with the interior design industry might well be a specialty itself. Everything is constantly changing: New issues and new areas of practice chief are among them. This chapter concludes with an update from an internationally known contract interior designer about what to look out for as you begin and progress.

As you read about the issues explored next, think about how much you have to know, just to be aware of new developments and their importance.

Mentor Memo

Commoditization of the Interior Design Industry

Like any industry, the practice of interior design is continually evolving. Every firm offers a slightly different menu of services. Some are known for design, whereas others have a reputation for delivery and strategic planning, but the checklist of needs in order to obtain proper building permit and building life safety is fixed. The practice of interior design is also being practiced by real estate professionals offering project management or interior design services, furniture dealers providing space planning, and contractors providing everything prior to the build, at greatly reduced costs. This result of the commoditization of our industry is a plague that we fight daily. And, as a result, we need to work that much harder to educate the public why a qualified, licensed interior designer is the best choice when you are considering a new space, residential or commercial.

Increased Importance of Collaboration

It is likely you will collaborate with another practice during the course of your career. Learning to work with others, local or global, is essential. In my experience, being aware of your skills or your firm's skills is tricky because in doing so you are embracing your flaws as a practice. However, your clients will see this a wise and selfless, immediately establishing your credibility and clear intent to harness the most forward-thinking team that will produce the best end product for the client. It will not feel good initially to give work to another firm, but it will feel great when the clients come back to you tenfold.

Remaining Alert to Unethical Business Practices

Yes indeed! I found the wonderful stone from a foreign country that was the "only" solution for this project. This example takes place in the earlier parts of my career, and I simply did not know the right questions to ask and my primary concern was how it looked and whether the client approved it. Once presented, the client loved the product, and the contractor assisted me in vetting the realities of the twenty-week lead time to get the product into the country and to ship it. We monitored the large quantities of product, informed and photographed it as it was loaded. The entire project schedule was engineered to accommodate this incredible and rare product. Fast-forward twenty weeks. The entire project was waiting for the beautiful stone to arrive, but it never came. Why?

The supplier received a higher offer for the stone, which was already on the boat, and sold our order off the vessel. This unethical behavior was something that neither my client nor I was prepared for, but it does happen. Precautious should be taken to ensure the projects materials can be sourced and on site when needed. What questions should I have asked then that I know now? Take the time to fully research the available products. Finding an outstanding stone that only comes from Italy might be wonderful: however, ask some questions. Can it be shipped locally? How will it be transported? What is the unit of measure for the product? Will your local trades be able to install it, and how will be it warrantied? How much overage is shipped in the event of breakage? If a piece breaks once installed, will additional pieces need to be ordered to repair it?

How does the story end? The manufacturer scrambled to source a similar product and provided a credit to the client, for both the inconvenience and the reselection. Unfortunately, the damage had already been done.

THE GLOCAL PHENOMENON

Awareness of the world around you is critical for interior designers. They need to know not just what is going on where they are located but also what is happening in the larger world. There are many reasons for acquiring and sharpening this skill. For one, keeping abreast means becoming aware of new design trends and processes wherever they may

How you will be able to realize an interior such as this in a country foreign from your own underscores the Glocal phenomenon.

arise. In other words, it means keeping up with the interior design industry. The skill is also important as economic conditions ebb and flow. Some areas experience slower economic growth than others, whereas some regions "boom" with new opportunities. Thus, keeping up with business trends is critical for any designer's business to grow. Who knows where new clients and their projects may be found? How will you organize and complete such projects?

> **NOTES FROM THE FIELD**
>
> Going Global (also called *Glocal*) is something you should be aware of! For any interior designer, it is important to understand your client base and support structure is now global, not just local. The challenge for educators is wrapping their classes around the variations of international delivery and basic language barriers. Global + Local = Glocal. Regardless of the firm's size, specialty, or geographic location, the Web has connected us all. There are two sides to the global conversation; where your clients are located and where your products and support consultants reside. If your clients are abroad, consider the most basic questions. In what currency do I charge? How are taxes managed? What are my license restrictions? Can I deliver the entire project, or will I need to partner with a local architect? Can I charge for the travel, and how often will I need to be on site? In many countries, out-of-country interior designers are not permitted to complete construction documents or construction administration. These services must be completed by a locally managed LDI (local drawing institute). As global economies shift, we see out-of-country firms, marketing heavily to our local business communities with promises of new services and deliveries that will make their project special and unique. To a savvy client, "special and unique" can translate to "expensive and unbuildable." To the average client, this is a seductive offer. The regulatory institutions of the home country will have these requirements clearly outlined because, at the end of the project, you will need to apply for a permit, and only a licensed professional with a local certificate of practice can do so.

Practical Activity

Using the Notes from the Field as a guide, develop your own plan to address Glocal issues. To make this more applicable to you, assume you have obtained an interior design project, one you will oversee from your home country. The actual project, however, will take place in a faraway country. Outline steps to accomplish your project, based on the issues noted in this chapter.

Review Questions

1. Why is it important to identify your own personal interests as part of planning at least your initial career path? Give examples of your own interests and how they have shaped your interest in interior design and how you have pursued that interest so far.

2. Note just a few of the broad practice areas for interior designers. Give examples of those who have established themselves in these disciplines. In your estimation, how have they thrived in these areas?

3. Describe the "three legs" of interior design as explained in a Mentor Memo. Do you agree with this paradigm, or might you have a different understanding of the profession? If so, how does your take on it differ?

4. Describe some of the benefits of practicing interior design in a retail or wholesale selling environment. What might be deterrents for designers?

5. Why might working in residential interior design be—or not be—appealing, professionally, for some designers?

6. What kinds of career issues might designers working in large business settings like architecture and interior design firms anticipate?

7. Compare ways residential and contract interior design projects are obtained from information presented in this chapter.

8. Describe the education and credentials usually required for an academic career researching and teaching interior design.

9. What have been identified in the chapter as being emerging areas of practice and concern for interior designers?

10. Define the Glocal phenomenon, and suggest how it might impact you.

GLOSSARY

accept Agree to each and every term of an offer, making no change, and imposing no condition upon it.

acceptance Act of agreeing to an offer.

acknowledgment Document confirming an order and ensuring that a vendor correctly understands what exactly a purchaser has ordered.

active listening Paying close attention to someone's words to identify and evaluate the implications of what a person says.

actual damages Money awarded in a lawsuit that compensates an injured party for the actual amount of the financial loss the party incurred.

addendum Addition attached to a contract that covers changes made by a client after a contract is drafted but before it is signed.

advertising Methods of promotion that a designer or firm buys and pays for directly.

agency Relationship between an agent and a principal in which the agent represents the interests of the principal in a business relationship. See also *agent*; *principal*.

agent Party that acts for another party. See also *agency*; *principal*.

agreement Legally binding statement of what two or more parties promise to undertake.

agreement in restraint of trade Agreement in which one or more parties are restricted from engaging in certain competitive business activities. Such agreements violate antitrust laws.

amendment Written change to a contract to which all parties agree.

American Society of Interior Designers (ASID) Voluntary association that promulgates and enforces rules related to maintaining professional practices, such as ethics.

Americans with Disabilities Act (ADA) Law mandating that all new or renovated public and some private buildings be accessible to all individuals regardless of their physical abilities.

antitrust law Body of laws that curbs practices by monopolies designed to limit the ability of smaller, less powerful business entities to compete in the marketplace.

arbitrator Neutral third party who gathers information about the cause and nature of a dispute and decides on a resolution that is binding on all parties.

articles of incorporation Legal document that must be filed with the state when a corporation is formed.

balance sheet A financial accounting document used to show an entity's assets (property it owns or controls) and liabilities (obligations owed to others) at a specified, identifiable time.

behavioral interview Type of job interview in which the interviewer asks sophisticated questions based on behavioral traits the employer considers most appropriate for the particular position.

behavioral mapping Technique of collecting objective information about how a space is used by photographing it over a series of days and cataloging the range of emotions shown by people who are using the space.

bid Formal document in which a contractor proposes to complete a project at a stated cost.

bid bond Form of insurance issued by a third party that protects a client from loss if actual costs exceed estimated costs.

bid form See *tender*.

bilateral contract Contract that exists when one party makes a promise (usually a promise to pay sums of money) and, as a result of that first promise, another party promises to do something (or to not do something the party had a legal right to do) at some time.

binding agreement See *agreement*.

bodystorm Technique of collecting project information that involves first identifying different kinds of users or consumers and then acting out how they will interact in a space.

breach of contract Failure of a party to a contract to perform in the manner agreed to.

bribe Direct payment of some kind made to gain favorable treatment.

business entity Concern that exists to provide one or more services or products that is defined by its legal structure. Sole proprietorship, partnership, and corporation are types of business entities.

buy-in Client's assent to the final scope of service as described in the contract.

capacity Legal ability to enter into contracts.

case law See *common law*.

case study interview Type of job interview in which the interviewer describes possible job situations and asks questions about them to determine a job seeker's ability to solve business problems.

cash discount Price reduction given for paying the invoice within a certain amount of time.

chain of command Lines of authority within an organization.

change order Document authorizing changes that the client requests after a contract has been awarded and final documents have been signed.

close Point in the selling process when a prospect is asked directly to buy the product or service.

code of ethics Set of rules of professional conduct that members of a profession voluntarily agree to follow.

common law Legal principle that past decisions made by courts of law establish rules for making decisions about similar issues that may come up in the future.

common law of contracts See *contract law*.

comparative fault Degree to which a party to a lawsuit is at fault. Many states mandate that damages be apportioned based on comparative fault.

competitive bidding Process of inviting possible suppliers to submit bids on a project, comparing the bids, and selecting one supplier to perform the work.

complainant Person or organization that brings charges against another person or organization in administrative action.

complete performance Performance that satisfies every term agreed to in a contract.

confirmation of purchase Formal signed document confirming a client's agreement to purchase specific products and noting prices, quantities, and sufficient details to identify these products.

conflict of interest Situation in which someone has professional or personal loyalties, obligations, or financial interests that would make it difficult to act in an objective manner.

consideration Benefit one party to a contract gives to the other in exchange for a benefit received, as when one party pays a certain amount of money in exchange for the other party's performing a task.

consumer journey Technique of collecting project information that involves cataloging all the interactions a consumer or user has while in a space.

Continuing Education Unit (CEU) Unit of credit for completion of continuing education courses. In states that license or certify interior designers, laws establish the number of CEU practitioners must satisfy within specified time frames to remain in good standing.

contract Agreement made enforceable through legal action because certain requirements have been met.

contract administration phase Final stage of a project during which it is realized, bringing together all the products and services as specified and ordered by a designer and as approved by a client.

contract document Any of the papers that define a project, including drawings, plans, spec sheets, and schematic representations.

contract document phase Stage of a project during which appropriate documents are drawn up and purchase orders for the merchandise items are submitted to vendors.

contract interior design A term thought to have originated from this specialization's use of contracts and contractors. It generally refers to the practice of addressing accessibility, functional, and appearance issues related to spaces held open to the public or used for purposes other than an individual's dwelling.

contract law Body of laws that relates to legally enforceable agreements.

contributory negligence Negligence by an injured party in a lawsuit that was a factor in causing an injury.

conversational interview Informal type of job interview in which the interviewer invites the applicant to discuss various topics that may or may not seem to relate to the position.

corporation Legal entity that exists in its own right, apart from people who or organizations that own it, and continues after the owner(s) is (are) no longer engaged in it.

cost of sales All money spent by a business to produce sales income, including costs of labor, facilities, materials, supplies, transportation, and so forth.

counteroffer In contract negotiation, a proposal to add to or change the terms of an offer.

criminal conversion law Body of laws relating to exerting unauthorized use or control of someone else's property.

criminal law Body of laws that relates to preventing and punishing criminal acts. Actions involving violations of criminal law are brought by a governmental body.

critical listening See *active listening*.

custom contract Contract prepared especially for a particular project.

customer's own material (COM) A notation used when an interior designer specifies use of a textile product on an item different than those available through the item's maker.

dealer Wholesaler that sells the products of a number of manufacturers in a product category.

deceptive trade practice The making of any false or misleading statement by any seller of goods or services.

deliverables Documents, such as detailed construction drawings and related papers, concept boards, or any other form of media, that communicate a project's design intent to a client and to others.

design development phase Stage of a project during which a design is finalized and a designer prepares written specifications and cost estimates.

design intent Set of decisions a designer makes that seeks to address the aesthetic and functional issues a designer has identified for a project; design concept.

design study fee agreement Contract defining the services to be performed and the compensation for an introductory stage of a project.

direct labor expenses Total a company pays out to or for employees, including salary, benefits, and payroll taxes.

direct personnel expenses See *direct labor expenses*.

disclaimer Contract clause stating that a contractor assumes no responsibility for the actions of any service provider hired to work on a project.

discount Reduction in the suggested retail price, usually a percentage off. See also *cash discount*; *quantity discount*; *trade discount*.

discounting from retail Selling a product at a price lower than the retail price.

duress Use of threats to induce entry into a contractual relationship.

employee Person who works under an express or implied contract that gives an employer the right to control the details of work performance. An employee is entitled to benefits offered by the company as well as unemployment and worker's compensation insurance should employment end or on-the-job injury occur.

enforceability In contract law, condition of having the attributes needed to make an agreement enforceable.

estimate Statement giving an approximation of the anticipated cost of work to be done.

estoppel See *promissory estoppel*.

ethics See *code of ethics*.

expenses See *operating expenses*.

extreme user interviews Technique for collecting project information in which those who know very little or a great deal about a product or service, or about interior design in general, or a specific space, are asked to evaluate relevant experiences.

Federal Trade Commission (FTC) Regulatory agency created in 1914 with the power to investigate and prosecute possible violations of antitrust laws.

FOB (free on board) Shipping term that indicates the point at which responsibility for the cost of shipping shifts from a vendor to a purchaser. This designation is usually followed by the notation "factory" or by the buyer's destination to denote the point at which responsibility between a seller and buyer shifts.

force majeure Event or circumstance that is beyond the parties' ability to predict or control; acts of God.

Foundation for Interior Design Education and Research (FIDER) Organization responsible for reviewing and accrediting interior design educational programs.

fraudulent misrepresentation Act of deliberately giving incorrect or misleading information about the terms of a contract.

freight prepaid Arrangement in which the seller names the carrier and pays the freight costs.

general contractor Individual or organization that takes on the overall responsibility for constructions or modifications of physical structures and retains the labor of other service providers with specialized skills and knowledge about some aspect of the construction process.

general partner Partner in a business who shares fully in the management of a business and has full legal responsibility for the consequences of actions taken by the business.

general partnership Business owned by two or more people who share equally the risks, decision making, and profits, and who are equally liable for the consequences of actions taken by the business.

gross margin Difference in amount between net revenue and total cost of sales.

gross revenue All money paid to a business for the goods and services it sells.

human resources Managerial functions related to coordinating the activities of workers.

idle production capacity Costs associated with one's services that must be met whether one is working for a paying client.

income All money paid to a business for the goods and services it sells.

income statement A financial accounting document used to report all the revenues (income) and expenses (costs) of an entity for a specified, identifiable period.

independent contractor Worker who is hired by a company to produce a specific end product without close supervision and who is not entitled to company benefits or unemployment and worker's compensation insurance.

Individual Retirement Account (IRA) Type of retirement account that one can invest in up to a certain percent of one's earned income without paying taxes on either the amount deposited or the interest it earns until one withdraws it after retirement. Also known as a traditional IRA.

inferior performance Completion of a contract in a manner that greatly varies from, or is of a quality very different from, what was initially bargained for by the contracting parties.

instruction to bidders Document issued to all bidders on a project that contains information about the form bids should take.

interior decoration Vocation related to the furnishing and embellishment of a home.

Interior Design Educators Council (IDEC) A professional association comprised of those who teach interior design. There are different categories of membership available including professional, associate, affiliate, and graduate student depending on an educator's interest and accomplishment.

interior designer Service professional who is qualified by education, experience, and examination to enhance the function and quality of interior spaces (as defined by the National Council of Interior Design Qualification).

invitation to bid Notice soliciting bids from competing construction service providers.

invoice A claim for amounts of money owed, or a bill. An invoice may be issued both by manufacturers to interior designers and by designers to clients.

joint and severable liability Legally imposed arrangement in which the general partners in a business assume legal responsibility as a group and as individuals for the consequences of actions that are determined to have harmed others.

joint venture Partnership that exists for only so long as its members initially agreed it would continue or as long as a specific project takes to complete.

judicial committee Committee of a state board or national trade group formed to render decisions on ethics code violations and other related complaints.

kickback Money paid by a person or organization in exchange for having received some form of favorable treatment.

legality Condition of being valid for legal purposes.

letter of agreement Informal contract contained in the body of correspondence following an opening salutation.

libel Written statement that is false and is found to have injured another person's reputation and from which that person is found to have suffered some form of damage.

limited liability company (LLC) Form of business organization that combines the simplicity of a partnership with the protection against individual partners' assets offered by a corporation.

limited partner Backer who contributes funds to a business without making management decisions and whose liability is limited to the amount of money he or she invested in the business.

limited partnership Type of partnership in which some partners contribute funds and share in the profits but do not make management decisions.

line position Job that involves actually making a product or performing a service. In an organization chart, line positions are hierarchical, so one may move up the line to higher positions. See also *staff position*.

management Act of conducting, supervising, or controlling business affairs.

manufacturer's suggested retail price (MSRP) Price a maker asks, but cannot compel, the retailer to sell a product for.

market differentiation See *market segmentation*.

marketing Process of planning and executing the conception, pricing, promotion, and distribution of ideas, goods, and services to create exchanges that satisfy individual and organizational goals (as defined by the American Marketing Association).

marketing analysis Process of identifying information about the particular services a designer or design firm can provide and the specific group of consumers to whom these services might appeal.

marketing plan Statement describing marketing goals and the means by which they are to be achieved, including budgets and schedules.

market segmentation Process of matching specific services to potential users.

mechanic's lien (or mechanic and material man's lien) A legal impediment placed on real estate, which prevents sale to another owner until payment is tendered to a service provider who was not paid by the successive property owner.

mediator Neutral third party who gathers information about the cause and nature of a dispute and negotiates a resolution.

mission statement Short written description of the aims of an organization.

mistake Incorrect understanding of the terms of a contract.

mutual assent State of having all parties of a contract agree to accept the exact terms of a contract. See also *undue influence*.

mutuality State of having all parties of a contract agree to accept the exact terms of a contract.

National Council for Interior Design Qualification (NCIDQ) Organization that prepares and administers a commonly used qualifying examination to determine minimum competencies in interior design skills and knowledge.

negotiation Process of arriving at terms through dialogue and accommodation.

niche marketing See *market segmentation*.

nominal damages In a court action, relatively small award to the injured party, usually when any form of compensatory damages would be speculative or conjectural.

offer Contractual undertaking to do something that exists on the part of the parties when they are intent on entering into a binding agreement.

operating expenses Money paid out by a company in the course of doing business.

plaintiff Person or organization making legal charges against another person or organization.

portfolio Collection of representative examples of one's completed projects that functions as a visual synopsis of one's work and demonstrate one's creative and technical skills.

positioning See *market segmentation*.

principal (1) One of the people who has responsibility for the creative direction of a firm, interacting with important clients, and forming strategic plans concerning major firm activities; (2) party that engages and controls the work of an agent. See *agency*; *agreement*; *agent*.

privileged Not subject to disclosure in a court action without the consent of the parties between whom information was exchanged; applies to conversations a party to the action has with a doctor, lawyer, member of the clergy, or spouse.

product liability law Consumer protection legislation regarding products deemed to be defectively designed, manufactured, or marketed.

programming phase Stage of a project at which the designer ascertains information about goals a client has for a project and reasons for those goals.

promissory estoppel Doctrine that prevents someone from acting in a certain way because he or she relied on someone else's promise not to act in that way.

promotion In advertising, method used to bring a message on behalf of a product, service, or organization to potential customers or the general public.

proprietary information Confidential information about a company's products, business, products, and so forth.

psychological interview See *behavioral interview*.

publicity A free promotional tool used for getting the message before the market.

punch list Document created when a project is, or is almost, complete, listing errors in workmanship that need to be corrected.

quantity discount Price reduction offered based on the number of items ordered.

rep See *vendor representative*.

request for proposal (RFP) A written document issued by potential clients used to solicit interest in and suggestions from design practitioners about how they would address specific interior design needs, such as public spaces intended for large-scale use.

resale license Permit allowing a seller to pass on state and local sales taxes to a purchaser.

residential interior design The specialization of interior design practice that addresses functional and appearance concerns pertaining to nonpublic spaces used primarily for personal use and enjoyment.

restocking fee Fee, based on a percentage of the price, charged by a vendor for cancellations and returns.

résumé Document in which job seekers outline their education, employment history, skills, and career goals.

4Robinson-Patman Act Legislation containing a provision requiring that a merchant must charge all merchants the same price for a product.

Roth IRA Type of Individual Retirement Account into which one can invest any percentage of one's earned income without paying taxes on the interest it earns until one retires. Unlike a traditional

IRA, contributions are taxed in the year they are made, rather than when the money is withdrawn.

sales associate Trained interior designer employed by a supplier to assist customers in the showroom to merchandise and make purchases.

sales tax Tax based on, and usually a percentage of, the total price of a purchase.

schematic design phase Stage of managing an interior design project during which a designer develops an initial design intent, or concept, and prepares a preliminary budget and schedule for client review.

scope-of-service analysis Detailed written enumeration of the services a designer is hired to perform.

selling Act of presenting the attributes and benefits of goods or services to individuals or small groups with the aim of convincing a prospect to make a purchase.

selling price Amount at which a designer offers a product for sale to a client.

severability In contract law, state of contract being able to be divided into separate legal obligations so that if one clause is breached or found to be unenforceable, the remainder of the contract remains in effect.

shadowing Technique for gathering project information that involves following people as they interact in spaces.

Sherman Antitrust Act of 1890 Legislation aimed at curbing excessive commercial power by monopolies that interfere with smaller, less powerful businesses' abilities to compete in the marketplace.

slander Oral statement that is false and is found to have injured another person's reputation and from which that person is found to have suffered some form of damage.

sole proprietorship Business owned by one person that may operate in any commercially acceptable and viable manner an owner chooses.

specifications (specs) Document listing all details about the dimensions and nature of planned construction or modification of a physical structure and listing all materials that will be used.

staff position Job that provides support services to people in line positions. A person in a staff position usually reports to a person in a line position but is not part of the vertical hierarchy and does not supervise other employees. See also *line position*.

standard-form agreement Printed form with blanks that the parties fill in with the information requested.

standing Legal right to initiate a lawsuit because one is adequately affected by a matter in question, as when one is harmed or has suffered damage.

statement of cash flows A financial accounting document used to report the changes in amounts of cash available to a business through activities such as its operation, investment, and financing practices occurring within a specified, identifiable period.

statement of general conditions Document the client provides to bidders that includes information about the project such as the name of a client and the legal rights and responsibilities of the parties after the contract is awarded.

Self-Testing Exercises for Preprofessionals Program (STEP) A knowledge assessment and study skills workshop offered by local chapters of the ASID to prepare applicants for the NCIDQ exam.

storytelling Technique for gathering information for a project in which people are prompted to tell about their own experiences with using an item.

stress interview Type of job interview in which the interviewer uses a confrontational tone with the job seeker.

subcontractors Specialized service providers hired by a general contractor.

substantial completion Completion of a contract in a manner that differs, but not substantially, from what was initially bargained.

surety Third party, usually a specialized company or banking institution, that takes on the legal obligation to cover unbudgeted completion costs.

SWOT analysis Method of business decision making that assesses a problem or issue by identifying its strengths, weaknesses, opportunities, and threats.

target market Those individuals and groups to whom specific products or services might appeal.

tender Document submitted by a service provider stating the formal price for completing a project.

termination Expiration of a contract, either because the agreed-upon performance has been completed or the parties to the contract agree in writing to end it.

theft by check Criminal offense of passing a bank draft that is not inadequately covered by funds with the intent to deprive another of property.

360-degree feedback An approach to evaluation in which colleagues situated in the organizational scheme above, below, and laterally to a worker (as well as the worker) prepare written statements describing their perceptions about the quality of work produced by that individual.

tort law Branch of law covering civil wrong, as opposed to criminal, other than breaches of contract.

total gross revenue See *gross revenue*.

trade discount Reduction offered to design professionals.

undue influence Exercise of influence over a party to a contract that is powerful enough to supersede the exercise of that individual's own free will; duress.

unfocus group Technique for gathering project information similar to a focus group, but using a group made up of a wide variety of people.

unilateral contract Contract that exists when one party shows acceptance through his or her actions, rather than through verbal agreement.

unjust enrichment Acquisition of money or benefits that, in fairness, belong to someone else.

use tax Tax imposed in place of a sales tax on goods purchased from out of state or over the Internet.

valid Having legal weight; enforceable.

vendor An individual or entity offering others goods or services for sale or retention.

vendor representative Trained interior designer employed by a supplier to keep customers informed about products and services and to handle customer requests, problems, and so forth.

CREDITS

Chapter 1
Agnes Elisabeth Szucs/Getty Images/Flickr RF
Monty Rakusen's Studio/Getty Images/Cultura RF

Chapter 2
Hero Images/Getty Images
Cultura/ Lilly Bloom

Chapter 3
UIG via Getty Images—Architect; MCM Architecture
UIG via Getty Images—Architect; MCM Architecture

Chapter 4
UIG via Getty Images
mauro grigollo/iStock
sayhmogiStock
UIG via Getty Images
Matej Pribelsky/Getty Images

Chapter 5
Interior Design: Heidi Painchaud, Guy Painchaud, Bryan Chartier
Interior Design: Heidi Painchaud, Guy Painchaud, Bryan Chartier
Interior Design: Heidi Painchaud, Guy Painchaud, Bryan Chartier
Interior Design: Heidi Painchaud, Guy Painchaud, Bryan Chartier
Interior Design: Heidi Painchaud, Guy Painchaud, Bryan Chartier

Chapter 6
UIG via Getty Images
UIG via Getty Images

Chapter 7
Interior Design: Anthony Orasi Photography: Tony Hafkenscheid
Interior Design: Anthony Orasi Photography: Tony Hafkenscheid
Interior Design: Anthony Orasi Photography: Tony Hafkenscheid
Interior Design: Anthony Orasi Photography: Tony Hafkenscheid
interior Design: Anthony Orasi Photography: Tony Hafkenscheid
Interior Design: Anthony Orasi Photography: Tony Hafkenscheid

Chapter 8
Alija/Getty Images
UIG via Getty Images

Chapter 9
Chris Clor/Blend Images/Getty Images
Huber-Starke/Radius Images/Getty Images

Chapter 10
Tom Merton/Getty Images
Hero Images/Getty Images
Westend61/Getty Images
ShutterWorx/Getty Images

Chapter 11
Directors Guild of Canada/Directors Guild of Canada—Ontario Chapter Office 01: Reception
Directors Guild of Canada/Directors Guild of Canada—Ontario Chapter Office 02 Reception Seating
Directors Guild of Canada/Directors Guild of Canada—Ontario Chapter Office 03 Small meeting room
Directors Guild of Canada/Directors Guild of Canada—Ontario Chapter Office 04: Staff room

Chapter 12
UIG via Getty Images
Client: SilverBirch Hotels Interior Designer: Adele Rankin, Marina Plankeel Photographer: Brandon Barre; Photography courtesy of SilverBirch Hotels & Resorts
Client: SilverBirch Hotels Interior Designer: Adele Rankin, Marina Plankeel Photographer: Brandon Barre; Photography courtesy of SilverBirch Hotels & Resorts
Client: SilverBirch Hotels Interior Designer: Adele Rankin, Marina Plankeel Photographer: Brandon Barre; Photography courtesy of SilverBirch Hotels & Resorts
Client: SilverBirch Hotels Interior Designer: Adele Rankin, Marina Plankeel Photographer: Brandon Barre; Photography courtesy of SilverBirch Hotels & Resorts

Chapter 13
Client: Stratus, Cambridge Group of Clubs Interior Designer: Eduardo Mora Photographer: Brandon Barre
Client: Stratus, Cambridge Group of Clubs Interior Designer: Eduardo Mora Photographer: Brandon Barre
Client: Stratus, Cambridge Group of Clubs Interior Designer: Eduardo Mora Photographer: Brandon Barre
Client: Stratus, Cambridge Group of Clubs Interior Designer: Eduardo Mora Photographer: Brandon Barre
Client: Stratus, Cambridge Group of Clubs Interior Designer: Eduardo Mora Photographer: Brandon Barre
Client: Stratus, Cambridge Group of Clubs Interior Designer: Eduardo Mora Photographer: Brandon Barre

Chapter 14
Chris Ryan/Caiaimage/Getty Images
Innocenti/Cultura RF/Getty Images

Chapter 15
Client: Hotel Arts Interior Designer: Rachel Glazer. Photographer: Brandon Barre
Client: Hotel Arts Interior Designer: Rachel Glazer. Photographer: Brandon Barre
Client: Hotel Arts Interior Designer: Rachel Glazer. Photographer: Brandon Barre
Client: Hotel Arts Interior Designer: Rachel Glazer. Photographer: Brandon Barre

INDEX

A
Academic institutions, careers, 283–84
Acceptance, contract, 77, 203
Accountants, interior design practice, 104–5
Accounting, 6, 21
    accounts receivable, credit and interest, 176–77
    finance measurement, 93–94
Active listening, troubleshooting, 16–19
Addendum, 247, 291
Administration, finances, 90, 92–93
Admissibility, written records, 84–85
Advertising, 135
Agents, 74–76
Agreement, 291
    design study fee, 207, 292
    letter, 202–3
Amendment, contract, 206, 291
American Institute of Decorators (AID), 30, 37
American Institute of Interior Decorators, 30
American Marketing Association (AMA), 128, 133, 134
American National Standards Institute (ANSI), 192
American Society for Testing and Materials (ASTM), 192
American Society of Interior Designers (ASID), 12, 17, 33–34, 203, 221, 245, 271, 291
    code of ethics, 42, 44, 45, 48–49, 51, 52–54
    examples of code of ethics, 54–59
    formation, 31, 37
    publications, 86
Americans with Disabilities Act (ADA), 15, 79, 291
Analysis of scope of services. *See* Scope-of-service analysis
Architecture, prohibition against, 66
Articles of incorporation, 71, 291
Authenticity, 141

B
Balance sheet, 94
Balance sheets, 90
Bank loans, business funding, 98–99
Basis of design (BOD), 38
Behavioral interview, 269, 291
Behavioral mapping, 155, 291
Bentham, Jeremy, 43
Bid bond, 245, 291
Bids, 243
Bilateral contract, 77
Billing, 21, 177–78
Brand identity, 134, 142–43
Breach of contract, 77–78, 291
Bribes, 45, 162, 291
Brokerage services, 136
Budget, 18–19, 21
Budgets, marketing, 129, 131
Building codes, 79–80
Business. *See also* Management
    calculating expenses, 164–67
    calculating revenue, 163–64
    developmental stages of, 119–21
    federal law, 72–73
    financial need of, 163–67
    internal factors in development, 119–21
    services offered by, 121
Business funding, 96–104
    credit cards, 100–101
    gifts, 102–4
    loans from banks and financial institutions, 98–99
    personal savings, 101–2
    private sources, 96, 101–4
    public sources, 96, 98–101
    Small Business Administration (SBA) loan guarantees, 99–100
Business management. *See* Management
Buying and selling goods, 10

C
Career planning, 21, 123, 124, 275–76
    academic institutions, 283–84
    careers list, 285
    commercial or contract interior design, 279–80
    emerging issues, 287–88
    evaluation, 276–77
    glocal phenomenon, 287–88
    interior design options, 277–84
    merits and challenges of work situations, 284, 286
    residential interior design, 278–79
    retail and wholesale interior design professionals, 281
    retail sales associates, 281–82
    vendor and showroom representatives, 282–83
Case study interview, 269, 291
Cash discounts, 224, 291
Cash flow, 92, 100–101
Certified Managerial Accountants (CMAs), 104
Certified Public Accountants (CPAs), 104
Chain of command, 114
Change orders, 247, 292
Charging clients, 161–62
    accounts receivable, credit and interest, 176–77
    billing and collection procedures, 177
    billing scenarios, 177–78
    calculating expenses, 164–67
    calculating revenue, 163–64
    combination methods, 168, 173–74
    cost plus percentage markup, 172

Charging clients (*continued*)
    discounting of percentage off retail, 173
    financial need of business, 163–67
    methods, 167–68
    project's potential for profit, 175–76
    rate-based methods, 168, 169–71
    retail method, 171–72
    sale of merchandise-based methods, 168, 171–73
    square-foot method, 174
    strategy for, 162–63, 176
    value-based method, 174–75
Client relationship
    contracts and, 202–6, 210–11
    designer, 201, 234–35
    vendor, 234–35
Clients
    active listening to, 16–19
    communicating cost information, 231–33
    evaluating needs of, 149–50
    merchandise and vendors, 230–34
    shopping with, 234
    time issues, 233
Cloud technology, 141–42
Code of ethics. *See also* Ethics
    ASID (American Society of Interior Designers), 52–54
    enforcement of, 49–50
    examples of ASID, 54–59
    interpretation of, 48–49
Codman, Ogden, Jr., 29
Collaboration, 287
Combination methods, charging clients, 173–74
Commercial interior design, 279–80
Commoditization, interior design, 287
Comparative fault, 81, 292
Competition, interior design services, 133–34
Competitive bidding, 46, 292
    design projects, 192, 195, 232, 242, 282
    process, 244–47
Competitive landscape, 133
Complainant, 49–50, 292
Confirmation of purchase, 229, 292
Conflicts of interest, ethics, 45–48
Consideration, contract, 77, 204, 292
Construction Administration (CA), 26
Construction Documentation (CD), 26
Construction Specifications Institute (CSI), 193
Contract administration phase, 292
    associated tasks, 195
    interior design project, 14, 15–16, 184, 194–95

residential interior design, 244
standard-form agreement, 215
Contract document phase, 292
    associated tasks, 193–94
    documents related to, 193–94
    interior design project, 14, 15, 184
    residential interior design, 244
Contract interior design, 279–80, 292
Contracts, 76–78, 201
    acceptance, 77
    bilateral, 77
    breach of, 77–78
    client relationship and, 202–6
    custom contracts, 203
    forms of interior design, 202–3
    general requirements, 203–4
    interior design provisions, 205–6
    letter agreements, 202–3
    nominal damages, 78
    offer, 77
    practical realities, 210–11
    presentation and negotiation, 206–7
    request for proposal (RFP) process, 207, 294
    residential interior design, 207
    specific requirements, 204–5
    standard-form agreements, 203, 214–16, 295
    unilateral, 77
    validity of, 77
    working with clients and, 210–11, 212
    working with legal advisers and, 211
Contributory negligence, 81, 292
Conversational interview, 268, 292
Cooperative advertisement, 136
Corporation, 68, 71–72, 85, 292
Corporations, blending partnerships and, 72
Cost of sales, 164, 166–67, 292
Cost plus percentage markup, 172, 173
Council for Interior Design Accreditation (CIDA), 32–34
Cover letter, 256, 259, 260
Craftspeople, 240–41
Creative expectations, designers, 150–51
Credit, extending to customers, 93
Credit cards business funding, 100–101
Custom contracts, 203, 292

D

Damage control, 139
Dealers, 282–83
Deceptive trade practice laws, 82, 83–84, 292
Decisional managerial role, 112
Decision making
    consequences of business, 12

factors influencing management, 116–18
SWOT analysis, 10, 11–12
Decorator, 30
Design centers, 220
Design Development (DD), 26
Design development phase, 292
    associated tasks, 191
    documents related to, 191–93
    interior design project, 14, 15, 183–84
    residential interior design, 243
Designer, 30
    markups, 223–24
    relationships, 201, 234–35
Design intent, 292
    client image, 208–9
    project management, 183
Design study fee agreement, 207, 292
de Wolfe, Elsie, 26, 29
Direct labor expense, 164, 292
Direct personnel expense (DPE), 165, 167, 292
Disclaimer, 82, 206, 213, 292
Discounting of percentage off retail, 173
Discounts, vendor, 223–24, 292
Documents
    contract administration phase, 195
    contract document phase, 193–94
    design development phase, 191–93
    functions of, 185–86, 187
    programming phase, 188–89
    schematic design phase, 190
Draper, Dorothy, 29

E

Education, interior design, 22, 32
Effectiveness ratios, 95
Employee, 113
Employment interview
    interview formats, 268–69
    key issues, 271–72
    preparation for, 266, 268–72
    prohibited questions, 271–72
    questions, 269–71
    salary discussions, 271
    what to expect, 266, 268
Employment laws, management influence, 118–19
Engagement, 141
Engineering, prohibition against, 66
Entertainment, careers list, 285
Entrepreneurial profession, interior design as, 5–6, 8–9
Environmental poetics, 155
Ethics, 8, 41–42
    alertness to unethical business practice, 287–88

business context of, 45–48
confidential information, 20
conflicts of interest, 45–48
definition and understanding of, 43–44
enforcement of code, 49–50
interior design, 50
interpretation of code of, 48–49
management and human resources, 45
perspectives on, 42–43
stakeholder confidence, 46
use of company resources, 45–46
Evaluation
career, 276–77
client needs, 149–50
project, 152–53
service providers, 242–43
worker performance, 115
Exchange, 134
Expenses
calculating, 164–67
handling business, 92–93
External teams, interior design, 38
Extreme user interviews, 155, 293

F

Facilities management, careers list, 285
Federal law
business activity, 72–73
employee pay and benefits, 119
employment laws, 118–19
Feedback, 360-degree, 115, 295
Finances, 9. *See also* Business funding
administration, 90, 92–93
evaluation, 91, 94–96
large and small projects, 106
measurement, 90, 93–94
planning business, 89–90
Financial expectations, 151
Financial institution loans, business funding, 98–99
Fire-safety codes, 79–80
Fixed fee, 169–70, 173
Force majeure, 205–6, 293
Foundation for Interior Design Education and Research (FIDER), 31–32, 263, 293
Free on board (FOB), 225, 293
Freight prepaid, 225, 293
Furniture line, 221

G

General contractors, 240, 293
Generally Accepted Accounting Principles (GAAP), 104
General partnerships, 69–70
General sales tax (GST), 225

Gifts, business funding, 102–4
Globalization interior design, 67
Glocal phenomenon, 287–88
Government and institutions, careers list, 285
Green Building Certification Institute (GBCI), 35
Gross margin, 166–67, 223, 293
Gross revenue, 163–64, 166–67, 293

H

Highly leveraged, debt ratios, 95
Historical records, 169
Hourly rate
cost plus percentage markup with, 173
determining fees, 170–71
Human resources, ethics, 45

I

IDEO (design firm in Palo Alto, CA), 154–55
Idle production capacity, 134
Implied contract, 113, 122, 292
Inbound marketing, 141
Income statement, 94
Income statements, 90
Inconsistency, 134
Independent contractors, 113, 241, 243, 293
Industrial Revolution, impact on interior design, 27–28
Information
managerial role, 112
methods of gathering and assessing, 154–56
task of communicating, 115
Inseparability, 134
Interior design
accountants in practice, 104–5
advancing profession and career, 10–11
career options, 277–84
characteristics of profession, 5–6
CIDA accredited programs, 32–33
education, 32
engaging in authorized practice of, 65–67
as entrepreneurial profession, 5–6
external teams, 38
historical overview of, 26–32
internal teams, 38
laws and globalization of, 67
legally imposed prohibitions on, 66–67
National Council for Interior Design Qualification and NCIDQ exam, 33–35
opportunities at schools, 22
preparing profession for future, 37

professional practice skills, 4–5
prohibition against architecture and engineering, 66
as recognized profession, 5
tort law and standard of care, 80
working definition of professional practices, 6–7
Interior design business
commoditization of, 287
organization chart, 114
structure of, 114–15
Interior designers
Americans with Disabilities Act (ADA), 79
building and fire-safety codes, 79–80
contracts, 76–78
duties, 151–52
fixtures, furnishings and equipment, 80–84
laws related to, 73–84
licensing and registration of, 35–36
preparing for future, 36–37
protection of, 84–86
purchasing products for resale to clients, 78
residential, 197–98
tort law, 80–81
work on behalf of clients, 74–76
Interior design history, 26–32
changes in perspectives and names, 30–31
early origins, 27
factors influencing rise of, 29–30
impact of Industrial Revolution, 27–28
professional organizations, 30, 31–32
roles for women, 28–29
urbanization, 28
Interior design projects, procedures and processes, 13–16
Internal teams, interior design, 38
International Interior Design Association (IIDA), 33, 42, 203
Internship, 263–66
documentation and activities, 265–66
organizations sponsoring, 264–65
participation in, 263–64
student considerations about, 265
timesheet, 267
Internships, 22
Interpersonal, managerial role, 112
Interview. *See* Employment interview
Inventory, 134

J

Joint ventures, 71
Judicial committees, 50, 293

K
Kant, Immanuel, 43, 44
Kickback, 45, 47, 293

L
Law, 6, 8–9, 64
    admissibility of written records, 84–85
    agreements, 20
    Americans with Disabilities Act (ADA), 15, 79, 291
    building codes, 79–80
    contracts, 76–78
    corporate business form, 71–72
    deceptive trade practices, 82, 83–84, 292
    employment laws, 118–19
    engaging in authorized practice of interior design, 65–67
    fixtures, furnishings and equipment, 80–84
    knowing the right questions, 85–86
    legal definition of interior designer profession, 64
    participating in legally recognized business, 68–72
    partnerships, 69–71
    practice laws, 36
    product liability, 82
    recognizing federal, 72–73
    remedies, 12
    sales of goods, 10
    sole proprietorships, 68–69
    tort law and standard of care, 80
    Uniform Commercial Code (UCC), 78
    work of interior designers, 73–84
    work on behalf of clients, 74–76
LEED (Leadership in Energy and Environmental Design), 35, 249
Legal advisers, working with, 211
Legal capacity, contract, 204
Legal purpose, contract, 204
Leiserowitz, Nila R., 174
Letter agreements, 202–3
Licensing, interior designers, 35–36
Limitation of liability, 211, 213, 227
Limited liability company (LLC), 72, 211, 293
Limited partnerships, 71
Line positions, 114
Line workers, 110
Liquidity ratios, 95–96
List price, 223, 224
Loans, business funding, 98–99

M
Management, 111
    career plans, 123, 124
    communicating information, 115–16
    ethics, 45
    evaluating workers, 115–16
    factors influencing decisions, 116–18
    functions, 111–13
    future goals, 123
    influence of employment laws, 118–19
    interior design businesses, 109–11
    internal factors in business development, 119–21
    organization chart, 114
    personnel, 113–14
    policies and procedures, 122
    project team, 123
    structure of interior design business, 114–15
Management skills, 9, 20–21
Managers, functional roles of, 112–13
Manufacturers, careers list, 285
Manufacturers' suggested retail price (MSRP), 223, 224
Market differentiation, 131, 294
Marketing, 6, 9, 20
    advertising, 135
    analysis, 129
    basics of, 128–32
    brand building, 142–43
    brokerage services, 136
    competition for services, 133–34
    multichannel, 140–41
    niche, 131–32
    plans and budgets, 129, 131
    promoting your business, 127–28
    promotional methods, 134–40
    publicity, 139
    sales promotion, 135
    segmentation, 131–32
    selling, 137–39
    tech, 141–42
Marketing analysis, 129
Marketing budgets, 129, 131
Marketing plans, 129
Market segmentation, 131, 294
Markup from cost, 223–24
Mediation and arbitration agreements, contracts, 205
Merchandise
    availability of vendors and, 220–22
    cancellation, 229
    clients and vendors, 230–34
    damaged goods on delivery, 229–30
    forwarding, storage and installation, 226
    product delivery issues, 225–26
    return issues, 229
    tax issues for sales, 224–25
    terms and conditions of sale, 226, 227
Merchandise marts, 220
Mill, John Stuart, 43
Mission statements, 51
Moral imperative, 43
Moral principles, 43
Multichannel marketing, 140–41
Mutuality, contract, 204, 294

N
National Council for Interior Design Qualifications (NCIDQ), 5, 13, 32, 266, 294
    certification, 283
    exam, 33–35, 36
    interior design laws, 65
    mission of, 33
National Council on Qualification for the Lighting Professions (NCQLP), 35
National Kitchen and Bath Association (NKBA), 35
Negligence claims, 81–82, 292
Net income, 96, 166–67
Net neutrality, 142
Networking, 20
Niche marketing, 131–32
Nominal damages, nominal damages, 78, 294

O
Offer, contract, 77, 203
Offices and corporations, careers list, 285
Omnichannel marketing, 140
Operating expenses, 166–67, 294
Organization chart, 114
Outbound marketing, 141

P
Partnerships, 69–71
    blending corporations and, 72
    general, 69–71
    joint ventures, 71
    limited, 71
Permitting statute, 36
Personal savings, business funding, 101–2
Personal selling, 9, 135, 137–38
Personnel management, 110, 113
    employment laws, 118–19
Pitch, 136, 138, 148, 196
Plaintiffs, 49, 81, 294
Plato, 43
Portfolio, 262–63
Practice laws, 36
Principals, 74–76
Problem-solving strategies, scope-of-service analysis, 156–57
Product liability laws, 82, 294

Profession, interior design as, 5–6
Professional, 25–26
Professional conduct, ASID code of ethics, 52–54
Professionalism, project management, 182
Professional organizations, interior design, 30, 31–32
Professional practices
    applying skills, 19–22
    core skills defining, 8–11
    decision making, 10, 11–12
    developing formal definition for, 7–8
    developing skills, 12–13
    introduction to, 3–4
    troubleshooting strategies, 16–19
    working definition, 6–7
Professions, objectives of other, 6–7
Profit/Profitability, 10, 162
    project's potential, 175–76
    project management, 183
Profitability ratios, 96
Programming phase, 294
    associated tasks of, 186, 188
    documents related to, 188–89, 214
    interior design project, 14, 15, 183
    residential interior design, 244
Project discovery, 196
Project document ownership rights, contracts, 205
Project documents, functions of, 185–86, 187
Project management, 21, 182–84
    contract administration phase, 184, 194–95
    contract document phase, 184, 193–94
    design development phase, 183–84, 191–93
    design intent and, 183
    factors to consider, 196–98
    functions of project documents, 185–86, 187
    professionalism and, 182
    profitability and, 183
    programming phase, 183, 186, 188–90
    residential concerns, 197
    role of project manager, 184–85
    schematic design phase, 183, 190
    standard for agreement, 215
Project manager (PM), 38, 184–85
Project managers, 198–99
Project team management, 123
Promotional methods, 134–40
    advertising, 135
    brokerage services, 136
    publicity, 139
    sales promotion, 135
    selling, 137–39
Proprietary information, 46, 49, 294
Proprietary specifications, 192
Psychological interview, 269, 294
Publicity, 139

Q
Qualifying sales, 137
Quantity discounts, 224, 294

R
Rate-based methods, 168
    fixed fee, 169–70
    hourly rate, 170–71
Ratios, 91
    effectiveness, 95
    liquidity, 95–96
    profitability, 96
Recommendations, 243
Referrals, 138–39, 243
Registration, interior designers, 35–36
Remedies, consequences, 12
Request for proposal (RFP), 38, 58, 135, 149, 207, 294
Resale licenses, 224, 294
Residential interior design, 278–79
Residential interior designers, 197–98
Respect, 43
Restocking fees, 229, 294
Résumé, 256
    developing content of, 256–59
    format selection, 259
    getting you known, 261–62
Retail, careers list, 285
Retail method, 171–72
Retail sales associates, 281–82
Return on investment (ROI), 131
Revenue, 93, 163–64, 167
Reverse engineering, building a team, 38
Robinson-Patman Act, 73

S
Sale of merchandise-based methods
    charging clients, 168, 171–73
    cost plus percentage markup, 172
    discounting of percentage off retail, 173
    percentage of merchandise and product services, 173
    retail method, 171–72
Sales associates, 281
Sales promotion, 135, 136
Sales taxes, 224, 295
Savings, business funding, 101–2
Schematic design phase, 295
    associated tasks, 190
    documents related to, 190, 214
    interior design project, 14, 15, 183
Schematic Design (SD), 26
Scope-of-service analysis, 147, 148
    behavioral mapping, 155
    creative expectations, 150–51
    designer's duties, 151–52
    elements of, 150–51
    evaluating project needs, 152–53
    evaluation of client needs, 149–50
    extreme user interviews, 155
    financial expectations, 151
    gathering and assessing information, 154–56
    problem-solving strategies, 156–57
    project type and size, 153–54
    shadowing, 155
    storytelling, 155
    unfocus groups, 156
Self-certification, 36
Selling, 137–39
Service profession, objectives of, 7
Service providers, 239–40
    competitive bidding process, 244–47
    craftspeople, 240–41
    evaluation of, 242–43
    general contractors, 240, 293
    identification of, 241–42
    independent contractors, 241
    referrals, recommendations and bids, 243
    subcontractors, 240, 295
    troubleshooting, 248–50
    work strategies, 243–44
Services. See Scope-of-service analysis
Severability, 206, 295
Shadowing, 155, 295
Sherman Antitrust Act of 1890, 72–73
Showroom representatives, 282–83
Showrooms, 220–22
Sign off, 37, 76, 227, 232, 251
Sinclair, Upton, 29
Small Business Administration (SBA) loans, 99–100
Sole proprietorship, 71, 85, 295
    advantages and disadvantages, 68–69
    management, 110–11, 117
Square-foot method, charging client, 174
Staff members, 114
Stakeholder confidence, ethics and, 46
Standard-form agreements, 203, 214–16, 295
Standard of care, interior design, 80
Standing, 49, 295
Statement of cash flows, 90, 94
Storytelling, 155, 295
Strategic Planning Project, 94

Stress interview, 269, 295
Students in Free Enterprise (SIFE), 42
Subcontractors, 240, 295
Surety, 245, 295
SWOT (strengths, weaknesses, opportunities and threats) analysis, 10, 11–12

T

Target market, 131, 295
Taxes, merchandise sales, 224–25
Tech marketing, 141–42
Tender, 245, 295
Time frame, 18
Tort law, 80–81
Total gross revenue, 163–64, 293
Trade discounts, 224, 295
Trade sources, 21
Traditions, 51
Troubleshooting strategies, professional practice, 16–19

U

Unfocus groups, 156, 295
Uniform Commercial Code (UCC), 21, 78, 210, 225
Unilateral contract, 77
Unwritten rules, 51
Urbanization, interior design, 28
Use tax, 224, 295
Utilitarianism, 43

V

Value added tax (VAT), 225
Value-based method, charging client, 174–75
Values, 43, 51
Vendor representatives, 281
Vendors, 219
    anticipating and resolving problems, 226, 234
    availability, 220, 222
    client/designer relationship, 234, 235
    merchandise issues, 227, 230
    merchandise sales, 224, 225
    pricing policies, 223, 224
    product delivery, 225, 226
    representatives, 282–83

W

Walk-through, 195, 199, 250
Wharton, Edith, 29
Wheeler, Candice, 28–29
WiFi technology, 128, 141–42, 234
Women, role in society, 28–29
Word-of-mouth (WOM) marketing, 138–39, 242
Worker performance, evaluation, 115
Worker safety, 29, 30–31
Work exchange programs, 22
Work life, 255–56
    cover letter, 256, 259, 260
    employment interview, 266, 268–72
    internship participation, 263–66
    portfolio, 262–63
    résumé, 256–62
Written records, admissibility, 84–85